Localizing Transitional Justice

Interventions and Priorities After Mass Violence

**Edited by
Rosalind Shaw and Lars Waldorf, with Pierre Hazan**

Stanford University Press
Stanford, California

Stanford University Press
Stanford, California

© 2010 by the Board of Trustees of the Leland Stanford Junior University. All rights reserved.

No part of this book may be reproduced or transmitted in any form or by any means, electronic or mechanical, including photocopying and recording, or in any information storage or retrieval system without the prior written permission of Stanford University Press.

Printed in the United States of America on acid-free, archival-quality paper.

Library of Congress Cataloging-in-Publication Data

Localizing transitional justice : interventions and priorities after mass violence / edited by Rosalind Shaw and Lars Waldorf, with Pierre Hazan.

       p. cm. — (Stanford studies in human rights)

  Includes bibliographical references and index.

   ISBN 978-0-8047-6149-9 (cloth : alk. paper) — ISBN 978-0-8047-6150-5 (pbk. : alk. paper)

1. Transitional justice. 2. Human rights. 3. Crimes against humanity. I. Shaw, Rosalind. II. Waldorf, Lars. III. Hazan, Pierre. IV. Series: Stanford studies in human rights.

  JC571.L5868 2010

  340'.115—dc22

                                        2009052991

Typeset by Westchester Book Group in 10/14 Minion.

Localizing Transitional Justice

Stanford Studies in Human Rights

Contents

Preface

Ruti G. Teitel

WE ARE WITNESSING what I have elsewhere identified as a "global" and "normalized" phase of transitional justice, a proliferation of accountability mechanisms and processes at and across different levels—international, regional, domestic, and local (Teitel 2008). Yet it is often unclear what these developments actually mean, either theoretically or operationally, at the intersection of the international and the local. This challenge goes to the heart of this book. By focusing on issues of locality, this work puts in question prevailing assumptions and illuminates current controversies in the field through comparative and interdisciplinary research covering a wide ground.

This searching book sets out to get beyond generalizations about the global moment, to take a hard, close look at local realities and impacts on the ground, and to interrogate the state of current responses to conflict and repression. The contributors challenge the teleological assumptions of transitional justice, examining the concrete ways in which its mechanisms intersect with survivors' practices, standpoints, and priorities in specific places and times. They thereby refashion conventional understandings of "the local," "justice," and "transitions."

The range and depth of experience here are impressive. The various contributions probe across regions in far-ranging inquiries spanning Central and South America, Eastern Europe, the Middle East, Africa, and Southeast Asia, exploring complex forms of accountability. Through careful work on the ground, the contributors show persuasively that transitional justice developments have not moved along a linear and progressive trajectory but are instead reshaped through a diverse array of forums and interests, as well as through clashes among multiple rule-of-law values. In so doing, the contributions unsettle as they challenge the notion of so-called best practices of transitional justice that can be exported throughout.

A recurring theme throughout this scholarly inquiry is how to learn from local standpoints. If a global approach means we are somehow beyond the state and its democratization project, the place-based approach advocated by this book's editors returns us to survivors' experiences of the state and of the global processes that affect them—experiences that may generate other aims and priorities. Choosing between the local and the international has been said to involve the values of objectivity and fairness of a neutral judiciary as opposed to those of local discretion and accountability. But framing the dilemma this way can obscure the often profound disjuncture between survivors' priorities and the interests of international specialists. Moreover, who gets to decide?

As this book tacks between the ideals of transitional justice and the realities on the ground, it opens up an important evaluative space—one that is always guided by the central place of the victims of these mass crimes. Given the pervasive sense of threat and the ever-greater toll borne by civilians in contemporary conflict, this ought to be the guiding principle today. What is the impact of transitional justice measures on survivors? How can their well-being be reconciled with state building? By posing these fundamental questions, which are as much moral as legal and political, this book sheds light far beyond transitions.

RGT
New York City
May 2009

Acknowledgments

THIS BOOK HAS ITS origins in the discussions of six visiting fellows at Harvard University during the spring of 2005. At that time Pierre Hazan, Jamie O'Connell, and Habib Rahiab in Harvard Law School's Human Rights Program formed a transitional justice working group with Tiawan Gongloe, Fabienne Hara, and Rosalind Shaw at the Carr Center for Human Rights Policy. Zinaida Miller, then a JD student at Harvard Law School, also contributed to our exchanges of ideas. We are most grateful to Michael Ignatieff and Pierre Allan for their support of our endeavor, and to Jamie O'Connell as co-writer of funding applications. The following year, we brought additional scholars and practitioners together at the Rockefeller Foundation's Study and Conference Center in Bellagio, Italy. We wish to express our gratitude to the Rockefeller Foundation for providing such a supportive and beautiful environment in which to discuss some of the ideas presented here. We also wish to thank Tufts University's Jonathan M. Tisch College of Citizenship and Public Service for funding some of the participants' travel and accommodations as part of Rosalind Shaw's Tisch College Faculty Fellowship. This volume builds upon these two sets of discussions. We are especially grateful to Kate Wahl of Stanford University Press and Mark Goodale as series editor of Stanford Studies in Human Rights, both for their sustained interest in this project and for their expert guidance. We also express particular appreciation to the two anonymous reviewers for the Press, who gave us extraordinarily helpful feedback on an earlier version of the manuscript. Finally, we are indebted to all our contributors and to the original members of the transitional justice working group at Harvard. Although the only members of the working group represented in this volume are Pierre Hazan and Rosalind Shaw, all of you made its conception and development an inspiring experience.

Contributors

LAURA J. ARRIAZA is a JD candidate at the Washington College of Law at the American University. She was a 2008 Fulbright Fellow in Guatemala, conducting field research on reparations, and graduated from Tufts University with a Bachelor of Arts in 2005. She currently resides in Washington, D.C.

HILLEL COHEN is a research fellow at the Truman Institute for the Advancement of Peace at the Hebrew University of Jerusalem, where he also teaches history. His recent publications include *Good Arabs: The Israeli Security Agencies and the Israeli Arabs, 1948–1967* (2010) and *Army of Shadows: Palestinian Collaboration with Zionism 1917–1948* (2008).

RON DUDAI is a policy adviser at Amnesty International and is a visiting lecturer at the Centre for Applied Human Rights at the University of York (UK). Previously, he was a researcher at B'tselem, the leading human rights NGO working on the Israeli-Palestinian conflict. He conducted research for this volume when he was Chapman Visiting Fellow at the Institute of Commonwealth Studies at the University of London. In 2004, he was a Transitional Justice Fellow at the Institute for Justice in Reconciliation in South Africa, cosponsored by the International Center for Transitional Justice, and from 2004 to 2007 he was Research Fellow at the Programme in Law and Human Rights in the Middle East at the School of Oriental and African Studies at the University of London.

PATRICK FALVEY has worked with Burmese human rights groups in Thailand since 1998. He has initiated and managed projects on documentation of human rights violations, transitional justice trainings, and research among people affected by human rights violations in Burma. Working in a pre-transition setting, he explores the efficacy of applying a transitional justice framework to an ongoing conflict. Falvey holds a Master of Arts degree in applied anthropology from the American University.

SVERKER FINNSTRÖM is associate professor (docent) in cultural anthropology. Starting from 1997, Finnström has conducted recurrent fieldwork in Acholiland, northern Uganda, with a focus on young adults living in the immediate shadows of war. He divides his time between Stockholm University, where he teaches anthropology, and The Hugo Valentin Center of Uppsala University, where he is a researcher in political violence and genocide studies. Finnström is the author of *Living with Bad Surroundings: War, History, and Everyday Moments in Northern Uganda* (Duke University Press, 2008), for which he was honored with the 2009 Margaret Mead Award.

LAUREL E. FLETCHER is a clinical professor of law and director of the International Human Rights Law Clinic at the School of Law at the University of California, Berkeley. She utilizes an interdisciplinary, problem-based approach to human rights research, advocacy, and policy. Her current publications include *The Guantánamo Effect: Exposing the Consequences of U.S. Detention and Interrogation Practices* (2009), coauthored with Eric Stover. This book provides the findings of a two-year study of former detainees who were held in U.S. custody in Afghanistan and Guantánamo Bay, Cuba.

PIERRE HAZAN is a visiting professor at the Graduate Institute for International and Development Studies in Geneva, Switzerland. He worked in the UN Office of the High Commissioner for Human Rights (2008–9), including as a political advisor to the High Commissioner. Pierre Hazan has held a Jennings Randolph Senior Fellowship at the United States Institute of Peace in Washington, D.C. (2005–6) and a Fellowship at Harvard Law School (2004–5). For fifteen years, he was the UN Diplomatic Correspondent in Geneva for the French daily *Liberation* and with the Swiss *Le Temps*. His recent publications include *Judging War, Judging History: Behind Truth and Reconciliation* (2010), and *Justice in a Time of War* (2004). He also produced a number of TV documentaries on universal jurisdiction and on the International Criminal Tribunal for Rwanda.

ANN NEE is an associate at Cleary Gottlieb Steen & Hamilton LLP in New York City. She received a JD from Harvard Law School and an MALD from the Fletcher School of Law and Diplomacy, Tufts University.

MOSES CHRISPUS OKELLO holds a Master's in International Human Rights Law and a post-graduate diploma in Forced Migration Refugee Studies. He is currently head of the Research and Advocacy Department at the Refugee Law Project, within which he also coordinates the Beyond Juba Project (www.beyondjuba.org), a transitional justice project of the Refugee Law Project (RLP) and The Human Rights and Peace Centre (HURIPEC), all of the Faculty of Law, Makerere University. Moses' involvement with the African Transitional Justice Research Network (ATJRN) has seen him engage with organizations in Africa (in particular West, East, and Southern Africa) and beyond the continent. He has contributed book chapters, published in international peer reviewed journals, and is a member of the Editorial Board of the *International Journal of Transitional Justice*. His research interests include conflict analysis, forced migration, transitional justice, gender, and international human rights law more broadly.

PHUONG N. PHAM is director of research and visiting associate professor at the University of California's Human Rights Center and International and Area Studies, and adjunct associate professor at the Payson Center for International Development, Tulane University. A social epidemiologist, Pham works internationally to examine the consequences of war, disasters, mass violence and human rights violations, and the impact of reconstruction policies. She has recently completed work in Rwanda, Iraq, northern Uganda, Democratic Republic of Congo, Cambodia, and post-Katrina New Orleans. Pham also worked with schools of public health in Vietnam, Rwanda and DRC, supporting institutional, faculty, and curriculum development.

NAOMI ROHT-ARRIAZA is a professor of law at the University of California, Hastings College of the Law in San Francisco. She is the author of *Impunity and Human Rights in International Law and Practice* (1995) and *The Pinochet Effect: Transnational Justice in the Age of Human Rights* (2005), and co-editor of *Transitional Justice in the Twenty-First Century: Beyond Truth versus Justice* (2006) as well as numerous law review articles on transitional justice, international criminal accountability, universal jurisdiction, and reparations issues.

She has worked extensively in Latin America, participated as an expert witness in cases filed under the Alien Tort Statute, and has been a project adviser and participant for the International Center of Transitional Justice. She is a National Board Member of Human Rights Advocates, and a member of the legal advisory board of the Center for Justice and Accountability, where she advises on universal jurisdiction cases, especially the Guatemala Genocide case.

FIONA C. ROSS is an associate professor of social anthropology at the University of Cape Town in South Africa. She has published widely on the Truth and Reconciliation Commission in South Africa, including a monograph, *Bearing Witness: Women and the Truth and Reconciliation Commission in South Africa* (2003). Her latest book, *Raw Life, New Hope*, a study of everyday life in a shanty town on the outskirts of Cape Town was published in 2009.

ROSALIND SHAW is an associate professor of anthropology at Tufts University. Recent awards include a Jennings Randolph Senior Fellowship at the U.S. Institute of Peace, a MacArthur Foundation Research and Writing Grant, and a Fellowship at the Carr Center for Human Rights Policy at Harvard University. Her recent publications include "Memory Frictions: Localizing Truth and Reconciliation in Sierra Leone," *International Journal of Transitional Justice* (2007); "Displacing Violence: Making Pentecostal Memory in Postwar Sierra Leone," *Cultural Anthropology* (2007); and *Memories of the Slave Trade: Ritual and the Historical Imagination in Sierra Leone* (2002).

RUTI G. TEITEL is Ernst C. Stiefel Professor of Comparative Law at New York Law School. She was a Senior Fellow at the Orville H. Schell, Jr. Center for International Human Rights at Yale Law School, is a member of the Council on Foreign Relations, and a member of the Steering Committee of Human Rights Watch Europe/Central Asia. Her recent publications include the critically acclaimed book *Transitional Justice* (2000), as well as articles published in the *Yale Law Journal*, the *Harvard Law Review*, the *New York Times*, and *Legal Affairs*, and at findlaw.com.

KIMBERLY THEIDON is a medical anthropologist focusing on Latin America. Her research interests include critical theory applied to medicine, psychology, and anthropology, domestic, structural, and political violence, transitional justice, reconciliation, and the politics of postwar reparations. She is the author of *Entre Prójimos: El conflicto armado interno y la política de la reconciliación en el Perú* (2004) and *Intimate Enemies: Violence and Reconciliation in Peru* (Stanford University Press, forthcoming). She is currently involved in two research projects. She is completing research on "Transitional Subjects: The Disarmament, Demobilization, and Reintegration of Former Combatants in Colombia," in which she works with former combatants from the paramilitaries, the FARC, and the ELN. In Peru, she is conducting "El Dorado: Coca, Conflict and Control in the Apurímac and Ene River Valley," an ethnographically-grounded study of alternative development and forms of governmentality in the foremost coca growing region of Peru. Dr. Theidon is an associate professor of anthropology at Harvard University, and the director of Praxis Institute for Social Justice.

PETER UVIN is academic dean and Henry J. Leir Professor of International Humanitarian Studies at the Fletcher School. He has written extensively on the intersection of human rights, development, and conflict resolution and has been a frequent consultant to agencies working in Africa on these same issues. In 2006–7, he received a Guggenheim Fellowship. His recent publications include *Life After Violence: A People's History of Burundi* (2008), *Human Rights and Development* (2004), and *Aiding Violence: The Development Enterprise in Rwanda* (1998).

PATRICK VINCK is the director of the Initiative for Vulnerable Populations at the University of California, Berkeley's Human Rights Center, and adjunct associate professor at the Payson Center for International Development, Tulane University. Vinck holds a degree in agricultural engineering and a Ph.D. in International Development. His research lies as the nexus between war and complex emergencies, peace building, international development, public policy, and vulnerability analysis. He has developed and managed rural development projects in Africa, and, most recently, conducted research on conflicts and transition in the Central African Republic, Democratic Republic of Congo, and Uganda.

LARS WALDORF is a senior lecturer in the Centre for Applied Human Rights at the University of York (UK). He was a Fellow at the Human Rights Program at Harvard Law School after running Human Rights Watch's field office in

Rwanda (2002–4) and covering genocide trials at the United Nations International Criminal Tribunal for Rwanda (2001). He is writing a book on Rwanda's community genocide trials (*gacaca*) with support from the United States Institute of Peace. He previously taught at The New School and Harvard. Before becoming a human rights advocate, he litigated civil rights cases in the U.S. for nine years. His publications include several reports, articles, and book chapters on Rwanda and transitional justice.

HARVEY M. WEINSTEIN is Senior Research Fellow at the Human Rights Center of the University of California, Berkeley, and a clinical professor in the School of Public Health. He was associate director of the Human Rights Center from 1998 to 2005, where he directed the Forced Migration and Health Project from 1997 to 1999 and was co-principal investigator on three other projects. In 2005, he was involved in a study of human rights violations after the tsunami in five South Asian countries. He is co-editor of the *International Journal of Transitional Justice*. His recent publications include *My Neighbor, My Enemy: Justice and Community after Mass Atrocity* (2004), coedited with Eric Stover; and *Psychiatry and the CIA: Victims of Mind Control* (1990); as well as recent reports including "After the Tsunami: Human Rights in Vulnerable Populations" and "Iraqi Voices: Attitudes Towards Justice and Social Reconstruction."

Localizing Transitional Justice

PART I

Frames

Chapter 1

Introduction

Localizing Transitional Justice

Rosalind Shaw and Lars Waldorf

Rethinking the Paradigm of Transitional Justice

Since the turn of the millennium, the field of transitional justice has been increasingly challenged by the very people it is designed to serve: survivors of mass violence. Transitional justice has grown over the past twenty years into a normalized and globalized form of intervention following civil war and political repression (Teitel 2003). It embodies a liberal vision of history as progress (Hazan, this volume), a redemptive model in which the harms of the past may be repaired in order to produce a future characterized by the nonrecurrence of violence, the rule of law, and a culture of human rights. This vision is put into practice through a set of legal mechanisms and commemorative projects—war crimes prosecutions, truth commissions, purges of perpetrators, reparations, memorials—that is often conceived as a "toolkit" for use all over the world. But as the heated public controversy over the International Criminal Court's involvement in Uganda indicates, the current phase of transitional justice is frequently marked by disconnections between international legal norms and local priorities and practices. When national and international accountability mechanisms are engaged in specific places and times, they are often evaded, critiqued, reshaped, and driven in unexpected directions.

In this volume, we wish to problematize the local engagement of justice interventions and, in so doing, to rethink the orthodox transitional justice paradigm and the analyses, policies, and practices that it engenders. The contributors to this book promote this rethinking process by interrogating the teleological assumptions of transitional justice and by examining the concrete ways in which its mechanisms actually work.

The paradigm of transitional justice, we argue, is increasingly destabilized by its local applications. Because this is especially apparent when we focus on specific places and times, the contributors to this volume examine how transitional justice actually functions in those places and times and attend to local experience, priorities, and practices. If attention to locality shows us how foundational assumptions and practices of transitional justice break down, it can also show us new sets of possibilities. Too often, an engagement with "realities on the ground" signifies a focus on practical outcomes alone ("lessons learned," "best practices"), while the intellectual and normative frame of transitional justice floats above these in the realm of the transcendent. Here, though, we wish to disturb the dichotomy between the concrete and the conceptual, arguing that the very nature of transitional justice—its underlying teleology of evolution and progress, its dualistic moral vision, its dominant models of memory, speech, and personhood, and its privileging of criminal justice and civil/political rights over other forms—is exposed, challenged, disassembled, and reconfigured precisely in its local engagements (see Tsing 2004).

Recently, transitional justice has itself undergone a shift toward the local. Customary law and other forms of local justice currently receive unprecedented attention as complements to tribunals and truth commissions. And increasingly, transitional justice policymakers conduct surveys to consult people in areas of conflict and post-conflict about their priorities for transitional justice. But closer examination reveals a paradox. This latest phase of transitional justice is marked not only by a fascination with locality, but also by a return to Nuremberg's international norms against impunity and a UN prohibition against granting amnesties for war crimes. Although policymakers and scholars now routinely recognize the importance of adapting mechanisms of transitional justice to local circumstances, such adaptation tends to be conceptualized in ways that do not modify the foundational assumptions of transitional justice. Often, for example, local human rights NGOs are assumed to represent "the local voice," while interactions with ordinary civilians tend to be limited to top-down "outreach" or "sensitization" processes such as workshops and information sessions. And while survivors of violence are increasingly surveyed about their priorities for justice, there is not always agreement as to how surveys should be conducted, interpreted, and translated into practice. Survivors are in any case unlikely to get what they ask for if it contradicts international legal norms.

Kofi Annan's influential report to the United Nations Security Council on "The Rule of Law and Transitional Justice in Conflict and Post-Conflict Societies" provides a prominent instance of this paradox. Annan affirms that

> Success will depend on a number of critical factors, among them the need to ensure a common basis in international norms and standards and to mobilize the necessary resources for a sustainable investment in justice. We must learn as well to eschew one-size-fits-all formulas and the importation of foreign models, and, instead, base our support on national assessments, national participation and national needs and aspirations. (2004a:1)

Thus while Annan argues that models of transitional justice can and should be adapted to a specific context, these models must at the same time reflect transcendent values that cannot be modified. He also identifies "the context" in question as that of the nation-state. Here, then, is the conundrum. Increasingly, visible signs of "the local" are incorporated into transitional justice by adapting customary law processes and by involving local NGOs and local elites. Yet local experiences, needs, and priorities often remain subsumed within international legal norms and national political agendas.

In transitional justice discourse, the challenges of localization are sometimes cast in terms of a "clash" between "local (and implicitly 'traditional') culture" and "universal" justice norms. But just as anthropologists studying human rights have changed the terms of the intractable debate between cultural relativism and human rights by recasting ideas of "culture" and examining human rights practice and discourse in particular contexts (e.g., Cowan, Dembour, and Wilson 2001; Goodale 2006b; Merry 2006; Wilson 1997), we use a place-based approach to move us from the model of collision to one of engagement (albeit a frictional engagement: see Shaw 2007). Thus in this volume the contributors explore the complex, unpredictable, and unequal encounter among international norms, national agendas, and local practices and priorities through the operations of transitional justice in particular locations. This is far from being a purely academic exercise. By taking a deeper, more critical look at these operations in specific places and times; by examining the hierarchies, power relations, and heterogeneous interests that frame them; and by tracing how people respond to and sometimes transform them, we wish to lay a foundation for postviolence processes based on more responsive forms of place-based engagement and broader understandings of justice.

Reframing "the Local"

Yet what is "the local"? This is not merely an abstract question, since concepts of locality have direct consequences for the ways in which organizations, policymakers, and practitioners approach concrete locations. Recently, Mark Goodale (2006a) has challenged the conceptualization of "the local" in human rights discourse and most of the social sciences, criticizing the prevalent notion of a nested set of "levels" descending from the global to the regional, from the regional to the national, and from the national to the local. This language of "levels" obscures the fact that no location in the world exists in detachment from national and global processes. It would be hard to find places that, however remote from metropolitan centers, are not pervaded by circulations of ideas and images from human rights to hip-hop.

When we conceptualize "the local" as a level, we place it in a different frame and set it up to carry meanings of remoteness, marginality, and circumscribed contours (see Gupta and Ferguson 1997a:43). To borrow Appadurai's language, we render it as a form of spatial incarceration (1988:37). Through a levels-based definition, we depoliticize locality, constructing it as a residual category characterized both by separation (from "the national," "the international," and "the global") and by absence (of modernity). In place of these absences, we make "culture"—often presumed to be "naturally the property of a spatially localized people" (Gupta and Ferguson 1997b:3)—the most salient feature of "the local." The implications for transitional justice and human rights practice are significant. When we construct "the local" as a level, this predisposes us to marginalize the experiences, understandings, and priorities of people within this residual space. And since, according to this conceptualization, locality can provide no basis for knowledge beyond that of "culture" or "tradition," "local knowledge" becomes conflated with "tradition," while knowledge beyond "tradition" must come from outside.

Rather than approaching "the local" as a level, what if we view it as a standpoint based in a particular locality but not bounded by it? "The local" now becomes the shifted center from which the rest of the world is viewed. The reality with which we have to begin—and without which transitional justice cannot be legitimate or effective—is that of a nuanced understanding of what justice, redress, and social reconstruction look like from place-based standpoints.

As a first step, we need to ask how people affected by armed conflict and political repression experience the mechanisms designed to address their needs. Over the past ten years or so, scholars and practitioners have begun to explore this question through close methodological engagement in specific sites (e.g., Cobban 2007; Fletcher and Weinstein 2004; Kelsall 2005, 2006; Laplante and Theidon 2007; Ross 2003a; Shaw 2007; Stover 2005; Stover and Weinstein 2004; Wilson 2001). As the chapters in Part Two of this volume explore, the "counterviews" gained from local experiences of justice mechanisms often present a startling contrast to the formal goals of these mechanisms and, in many cases, force a reexamination of some fundamental premises of transitional justice.

As a second step, we need to place particular emphasis on survivors' priorities for postviolence reconstruction. This forms the focus of Weinstein, Fletcher, Vinck, and Pham's chapter in this volume. Asking "Whose priorities take priority?" they draw attention to the gap between the idealized goals and assumptions of transitional justice and the realities of life on the ground. They locate this gap in historical context, reviewing the discrepancies that have emerged at different genealogical phases of transitional justice and addressing the challenges these discrepancies pose—among which the authors give precedence to "our ability to question assumptions and to hear what the beneficiaries of justice believe to be important." This, in turn, prompts them to explore the methodological challenge of how to listen to local priorities, to which we turn later. From their comparison between the priorities of international justice and those of people affected by violence, Weinstein et al. conclude that "[m]any involved with international justice have lost sight of its goals in favor of developing and maintaining an international system of criminal law over and above what might be the needs and desires of the victims of abuse."

These struggles over justice and reconstruction now unfold on a terrain configured by the U.S.-led war on terror. Since September 11, 2001, this "war" has transformed international norms, reconfigured the power of states, intersected in paradoxical ways with transitional justice, and created new frictions with local priorities for dealing with the aftermath of violence. Pierre Hazan's contribution to this volume provides a crucial analytical frame by exploring the ways in which the war on terror is eroding the redemptive paradigm of transitional justice. The events of September 11 created a geostrategic rupture in which, he argues, the dominant discourse of global security is displacing the optimistic model of political evolution through transitional justice. These events also ushered in a new realpolitik: "in this neo-conservative vision," observes Hazan, "the alliance with repressive regimes is from now on interpreted as a strategic necessity in the name of the global war for the 'defense of freedom.'" If the paradigm of transitional justice has been destabilized from below, it is now, in key areas, crumbling from above. In places that are not considered particularly relevant to the war on terror—several of which are examined in the current volume—the international community still regards transitional justice as offering a useful toolkit for responding to specific instances of violence. But even here, argues Hazan, transitional justice is becoming decoupled from the encompassing vision of moral and political progress that prevailed "between the fall of the Berlin Wall and the fall of the twin towers in New York."

"Victims" and "Perpetrators": Rethinking Justice

Where this moral vision still obtain its most basic assumption is perhaps that of victims' rights to justice. This premise underlies a recurring feature that structures much transitional justice discourse and practice: the dichotomy between "victims" and "perpetrators." While this dichotomy characterizes many legal approaches, the postauthoritarian context in which transitional justice developed, with its legacy of large power imbalances between citizens as victims and repressive state agents as abductors, torturers, and murderers, may have reinforced it. But in intrastate conflicts originating in part from *structural* violence, this dichotomy tends to be less clear. Not only are such conflicts typically moral gray zones with blurred boundaries between "victims" and "perpetrators," but this Manichean division also has major—although unintended—consequences for people placed in either category.

One of these is a profound depoliticization: neither "victims" nor "perpetrators" are political actors. Writing about the International Criminal Court and its intervention in Uganda, Kamari Clarke (2007) views the ICC's universalizing jurisdictional claims over "victims" through the lens of Agamben's (1998) concept of "bare life." Such claims reduce people to mere existence "marked by a condition of pre-political absolute victimhood" that "exists in tension with the attempts to produce political beings found in the struggles of individuals from postcolonial African regions to implement their own forms of justice" (2007:137). In order to relocate people as political agents within international justice, she concludes, we need to "rethink the conditions within which we envisage justice in the first place" (2007:158).

Finnström, in this volume, examines how justice mechanisms have similarly depoliticized the other half of this binary: the perpetrators. In northern Uganda, the Lord's Resistance Army's (LRA) violence has been so horrendous that the ICC fails to confront the complex politics and history of the conflict in northern Uganda, including systemic abuses by the Ugandan state, and reduces the conflict to the evil or insane actions of LRA perpetrators. At the same time, however, Uganda's 1999 Amnesty Law and related initiatives of forgiveness by local leaders may also be viewed as mechanisms that depoliticize. Each, Finnström argues, is premised on a hierarchical relationship in which the rebels are reduced from political subjects to children or criminals. This is not to deny or diminish the abuses committed by the LRA, but to relocate these crimes—along with those of the government and army—in a political space. By excluding the rebels from the political realm, neither the "retributive" ICC nor the "restorative" amnesty will enable an understanding of the range of political, social, and economic injustice in northern Uganda that brought about and sustains this conflict. Instead, Finnström suggests, "both restorative and retributive justice, even amnesty laws, can become weapons of war rather than tools of peacemaking."

These depoliticizing representations, moreover, circumscribe the workings of justice mechanisms. Kimberly Theidon, in this volume, examines how Peru's Truth and Reconciliation Commission (TRC) produced a category of "innocent victims" that intersected in insidious ways with the Peruvian government's war against terrorism, with problematic consequences for human rights and national reconciliation today. Although the TRC's mandate was to explore the truth concerning Peru's civil war, the state's war on terrorism constrained the truth that could be told. Specifically, the main rebel group—the Sendero Luminoso (SL)—remained so demonized that those who had been part of it were denied the opportunity to testify before the Commission. Because of this exclusion, there was no opportunity to explore why so many people (mostly poor and nonwhite) had supported the SL, and to thereby address the structural causes of the violence. And because the image of the "terrorist" in the Peruvian state came to be layered upon the same conceptual space occupied by "the primitive," the stakes were especially high for those in Andean communities.

This stigmatization shaped the kinds of testimonies that the TRC received in rural areas, as Theidon shows. Building on the TRC's binary categories of "victims" and "perpetrators," communities developed their own standardized narratives of innocent victimhood. By repressing alternative histories, the discourse of "innocent victims" silenced an important source of the broader truth the TRC was investigating. And by creating "resentful silences," it also disabled another part of the TRC's mandate: national reconciliation. The TRC has not, as a result, been effective in mitigating the polarization and division that the state's war on terrorism created. Currently, legitimate claims for social justice and rights are dismissed as a "rekindling of the ashes of terrorism," while those accused of belonging to or sympathizing with the SL are denied rights altogether.

Finally, as scholars and policymakers seek to integrate transitional justice goals with programs of disarmament, demobilization, and reintegration (DDR) after armed conflicts, they also integrate the sharp moral dualism of these goals. In her chapter, Rosalind Shaw critiques approaches that divide survivors of armed conflict into "victims" entitled to reparations and "perpetrators" subject to accountability mechanisms that, it is assumed, will facilitate reintegration. This latter assumption draws apparent support from the international consensus that Sierra Leone's "experiment" with two concurrent transitional justice mechanisms—the TRC and the Special Court for Sierra Leone—was "successful." Shaw examines the politics of knowledge through which the alleged success of the Sierra Leone experiment became an accepted "fact," and traces the TRC and Special Court's local articulations both with Sierra Leone's DDR program and with informal reintegration practices. This transitional justice experiment intensified processes of exclusion produced by DDR—especially for young, lower-ranking ex-combatants whose marginalization had contributed to Sierra Leone's conflict in the first place. This intensified exclusion, Shaw argues, does not derive from an inherent incommensurability between transitional justice and DDR. Rather, it is rooted in narrow definitions of justice shaped by the "victim–perpetrator" dichotomy that do not adequately address forms of preconflict injustice. If understandings of "justice" were repoliticized and rehistoricized, she suggests, it would entirely transform what it means to link justice with reintegration.

Recasting Silences

If the above studies prompt a reevaluation of our definition of justice, those to which we now turn direct us to reconsider our assumptions concerning truth and memory. In the field of transitional justice, these are premised upon further assumptions about the proper work of speech and remembering, models of personhood, and understandings of damage, social repair, and redress. Such ideas are differently constituted through diverse histories and asymmetries of power and critically shape the local engagement of transitional justice. Ideas concerning the empowering, redemptive, and apotropaic powers of speaking and remembering, for example, were forged over the *longue durée* of western religious and psychological thought (Shaw 2007) and entered the transitional justice paradigm during the postauthoritarian period at the end of the Cold War, when truth telling and public remembering became critical weapons against the repressive violence of strong states (Neier 1999). But subsequently, during its current globalized phase (Teitel 2003), transitional justice is more usually applied after (and, increasingly, during) low-intensity intrastate conflicts in weak or collapsed states characterized by violence "among neighbors" (Theidon 2004). Those who have to live with their neighbors in contexts of chronic insecurity do not necessarily share the priorities, memory projects, and speech practices of transitional justice mechanisms that developed to address the aftermath of political repression in other places.

In many areas with a long history of successive layers of violence—slave trades, colonial rule, political subordination, state failure—people have often developed ideas and practices that foster some measure of protection. In Burundi, Rwanda, and Sierra Leone, for example, complex practices of secrecy, concealment, silence, ambiguity, dissimulation, and indirection have developed as strategies for living with the threat of death (e.g., Ferme 2001; Lame 2005; Shaw 2000, 2007).

Such protective mechanisms acquire particular salience in a repressive state. In this volume, Waldorf examines how cultural practices of secrecy that developed as defensive strategies for living under unpredictable rulers during Rwanda's past remain relevant to Rwanda's post-genocide politics. Whereas truth telling originated as a human-rights tool *against* state repression, truth telling in the modern *gacaca* courts under the current regime has become a coercive tool of the state. Since gacaca courts do not hear cases of war crimes committed by the current government, since participation is compulsory, and since those who testify are threatened and occasionally killed by those they accuse, the truth-seeking practices of gacaca form a site of particular fear, danger, and mistrust.

One's own community may also engender profound contradictions. In Fiona Ross's chapter we have a compelling analysis of silence as a protective mechanism for South African women. For those in charge of South Africa's TRC, women's silences about rape formed an obstacle to the Commission's goal of breaking the silence surrounding acts of violence under apartheid. Rather than speaking out about their own experiences—which, the TRC claimed, would help heal their wounds—women testified about the consequences of violence for their families and communities. Women thereby resisted the category of "rape victim" through which the TRC often sought to define them, seeking instead to rectify the broader social relationships and networks in which they lived. We have to look at these silences, Ross argues, in terms of how the violence of apartheid was folded into the structural violence of kinship relations. She views women's silences before the TRC through the lens of the recent rape trial of Jacob Zuma, the current president of South Africa, in order to examine the social costs and physical risks for women who talk about rape. Because in many cases of sexual violence the perpetrators come from the family or community (as in the Zuma trial), women who directly verbalize acts of rape violate the ideology both of the family and of the liberation struggle itself, thereby placing themselves in the role of betrayer—and in danger of social death and further physical abuse. Given these gendered risks of speaking, Ross concludes, those involved in transitional justice should reexamine the assumption that women in general and rape survivors in particular bear a special responsibility to talk about rape.

Ross's and Waldorf's chapters raise critical questions. What happens when repressive states enact transitional justice as victor's justice? How does transitional justice connect to established forms of structural violence, social asymmetries of power, the "gray zone" where perpetrators may also be victims, and processes of social reconstruction? If those involved in transitional justice respect protective silences, does this reinforce broader silences around violence? Paul van Zyl observed that silence may open the door for zealots and authoritarians to stir up resentments at a politically opportune moment, whereas the process of working with the past often narrows the capacity to use the past for repressive purposes. While he agreed that we need to be attentive to the desire for silence, and should not impose on people to "break the silence," he emphasized the need to find strategies to enable people to engage with the past—such as creating spaces that help people feel safe to speak (pers. comm., November 2, 2006).

Laura Arriaza and Naomi Roht-Arriaza's chapter in this volume attests to the importance of such safe spaces. They describe local initiatives in Guatemala called "houses of memory" that extend the documentary and commemorative work of truth commissions through oral history projects. Because these projects are built upon community participation, and because those who record testimonies are trusted, they have been able to document more in their respective localities than Guatemala's two national truth commissions. But safe spaces are not easy to create where the community is itself a site of potential or actual violence—especially given that attempts to protect witnesses in transitional justice mechanisms are notoriously underfunded.

Several of this volume's contributors, moreover, felt that, important as they are, safe space strategies still place emphasis on "getting victims to talk" (e.g., Ross, in this volume; Theidon 2007a). Since we cannot assume that breaking silence is always in the best interests of those who have been abused, and given the enormous insecurity in which survivors of violence often live, what are the ethics of inciting people to talk about things that we cannot repair? If, on the other hand, we respect their silences, is inaction the only alternative? Theidon (2007a) argues that the bulk of the responsibility to speak should be transferred from those whom speech most endangers to others such as perpetrators and bystanders. At a fundamental level, such silences highlight the need to address the structural features that make people vulnerable. And this, in turn, means looking beyond a single short-term "transition" and investing in the long term.

Silences deserve our attention for another reason: their diversity (see Ross, this volume). In the post-conflict situations that now form the most usual contexts for transitional justice, silence is not necessarily the product of the repressive political silencing with which it came to be associated in the post–Cold War phase of transitional justice (and still is in many strong states). For people in face-to-face relationships in conditions of unending insecurity, it may be truth telling that subverts the process of living together, while in some contexts survivors may shape silence into a modality of reintegration.

Thus Nee and Uvin (in this volume) found very little support in the Burundian communities in their study for either prosecutions or a truth commission. Many of their informants feared that a post-conflict justice or truth-telling mechanism could endanger the political transition that has at last brought the country some measure of peace and stability. Instead, their informants spontaneously expressed the wish for dialogue, and sometimes went on to describe the local, face-to-face mechanisms they desired, and that they hoped would foster interpersonal coexistence. These imagined processes, although based on dialogue, would bring their own silences: they were neither truth telling nor justice mechanisms as the latter are normally understood. But they drew upon a strong normative value of compromise and social repair that derives, Nee and Uvin argue, not from trust in others but from its absence. In this weak state, in a context of past and present vulnerability, life depends on the capacity to maintain and repair relationships.

The same is true of another weak state—Sierra Leone. In this volume, Shaw describes how, after a long history of violence in this region, people selectively integrated those ex-combatants who demonstrated through their enactment of key social values (humility, sobriety, work, and reciprocity)—but not through extensive truth telling about the past—that they could be members of a moral community in the present. When Sierra Leone's TRC was established, and when district hearings were held, participants sought to use these for their own purposes. During the closing reconciliation ceremonies, many ex-combatants made "apologies" that—while full of silences about specific acts of violence—nevertheless enacted moral norms critical to local processes of reintegration. Thus ex-combatants and the audience reconfigured what was intended to be a ritual of verbal accountability into a ritual of social morality that drew upon local techniques of selective reintegration. They thereby retooled it "from below" into an alternate mechanism that would facilitate coexistence.

This is not, however, to idealize either this redirected TRC ritual or the local practices on which it drew: both reconstituted the subordination of youth to senior elite men. But if we want to understand how transitional justice mechanisms are locally engaged, we have to acknowledge the risks of both silence *and* testimony in chronically insecure conditions. What is at stake when we ask people to talk? In contexts in which nobody can rely on the police or army (and certainly not the international community) to protect them from future violence, the maintenance of relationships—including those that are unequal and exploitative—through selective forms of speech and silence may provide the only form of security (however contradictory) to which people have access.

Customary Law and Local Justice Initiatives

To create a locally effective transitional justice, one obvious strategy is to employ local practices and institutions. How have such efforts fared so far? Since customary law is typically defined as a "local tradition," and since it also takes the familiar form of courts and prosecutions, it is often taken to be emblematic of "the local" and has become the focus of several efforts to incorporate it into post-conflict justice initiatives. Most post-conflict states of the global South have dualist legal systems: formal state law and informal customary law. Often incorrectly viewed as "indigenous" and static, customary law is not, in fact, a stable body of fixed rules, but rather a set of changing practices (Moore 1986:38–39 and 318–19; Rose 2002:191). Many people romanticize customary law as "indigenous," "harmonious," and "restorative" despite the efforts of anthropologists to reveal its colonial remodeling, imported influences, social control, elite manipulation, retributive dimensions, and "harmony ideology" (Chanock 1985; Moore 1986; Nader 1990; Rose 1992).

Customary law has proved highly flexible and adaptive, developing under missionary Christianity, the colonial state, postindependence nationalism, rural socialism, state failure, and war. For example, Menkhaus (2000) examined how "traditional conflict management" played an important role amidst armed conflict in northern Somalia in the early 1990s. Today, customary law flourishes in post-conflict rural Sierra Leone (Maru 2006:431). And South African chiefs continue to adjudicate customary law with the blessing of the 1994 constitution—even though traditional leaders and customary law had been widely discredited by grand apartheid's Bantustans (Kessel and Oomen 1997:574–75).

What accounts for this resilience? Customary law remains far more accessible (and sometimes more legitimate) for the rural poor than formal state law. Furthermore, customary law deals with issues of great concern to them: land and family. As Moore observed of Chagga law in northern Tanzania: "'customary law' remained a critical element in the lives of rural people on the mountain because it determined access to land, and because it framed the structure of family and lineage on which the whole system of social support depended" (1986:317).

Recently, there has been a surge of enthusiasm for adding customary law to the transitional justice "toolkit" (Brooks 2003; Cobban 2007; Huyse and Salter 2008; Zartman 2000). This is partly a reaction to the length and expense of internationalized criminal trials but is also inspired by a newfound pragmatism and a concern with local ownership. All of these impulses are evident in the UN Secretary General's 2004 report on transitional justice. There, Annan stated that "due regard must be given to indigenous and informal traditions for administering justice or settling disputes, to help them to continue their often vital role and to do so in conformity with both international standards and local tradition" (UN 2004a:18). Once again, though, he elided the tensions among international norms, national politics, and local needs, and conflated locality with "tradition."

After conflict, customary law offers several possible advantages. First, it has greater capacity (and sometimes greater legitimacy) than devastated or discredited formal justice systems. Second, it may be more responsive to local needs than either state or international justice mechanisms. Third, it can provide some limited accountability for the lower-level perpetrators and bystanders whose numbers challenge resource-strapped courts and truth commissions. Finally, it can provide some limited restitution for a wide range of victims—something that is rarely forthcoming from post-conflict states.

While customary law may be accessible, however, it may also help to reconstitute pre-conflict structures of exploitation. In Sierra Leone, for instance, chiefs have long been notorious for imposing arbitrary and excessive fines on young men. Not only do senior men in general and chiefs in particular monopolize land and wives, but because of the chiefs' control of customary law, young men also fear losing the product of their labor through fines (Archibald and Richards 2002:343–50; Richards 2005:578–79). Many young ex-combatants cited this lack of opportunity, and the unjust system of customary law that sustains it, as having given them an incentive to improve their situation by fighting with an armed group (ibid.).

When transitional justice policymakers sought to incorporate customary law, they initially viewed it as a way to complement and legitimize new, non-prosecutorial transitional justice mechanisms, such as the national truth commissions in Sierra Leone and East Timor. Thus Sierra Leone's TRC was authorized to "seek assistance from traditional and religious leaders to facilitate its public sessions and in resolving local conflicts arising from past violations or abuses or in support of healing and reconciliation" (TRC Act 2000, § 7[2]). This TRC did not, however, incorporate customary law as an accountability mechanism but created reconciliation rituals, presided over by chiefs and religious leaders, during the closing ceremonies of the district hearings outside the national capital. Although described as "traditional," these were, in fact, constructed rituals put together from familiar ritual elements such as prayers, invocations, libations, and the sharing and chewing of kola nuts. At the same time, the Commission eschewed local rituals of swearing, which, as Kelsall (2005:385) argues, may have limited its ability to induce confessions. As Shaw observes in this volume, these TRC reconciliation rituals were often effective in fostering the reintegration of (mostly high-ranking) ex-combatants. Yet the rituals also served to reaffirm young men's subordination to "big men," resentment over which had watered the roots of Sierra Leone's armed conflict in the first place.

In contrast, East Timor's Commission for Truth, Reception, and Reconciliation (CAVR) achieved a more extensive incorporation of customary law into its workings. Nearly three-quarters of its community reconciliation hearings involved adaptations of a local dispute resolution practice, *nahe biti boot*, named for the unfolding of a large woven mat (*biti boot*), where disputants and community notables would resolve differences (CAVR 2006, pt. 9, at 7, 27). Hearings often began with invocations and ended with reconciliation ceremonies that entailed chewing betel nut, sacrificing small animals, and celebratory feasting (CAVR 2006, pt. 9, at 18, 23–24; Judicial System Monitoring Programme 2004:11; Pigou 2003:64, 75). Local ritual leaders generally participated in the hearings and reconciliation ceremonies (Hohe and Nixon 2003:55). According to Elizabeth Drexler (2009), however, many survivors of the violence were dissatisfied. Given the external origins of the violence—the harsh Indonesian occupation that divided the Timorese, promoted the growth of local militias, and culminated in the brutal repression of 1999—no more than a very limited redress was possible through the confessions of local rank-and-file deponents at the hearings. Nevertheless, Drexler notes that these hearings were broadly effective as a vehicle for local reintegration.

While customary law was incorporated as an adjunct to East Timor's truth commission, in the past few years it has also been promoted as a transitional justice mechanism in its own right. In this volume, Waldorf and Finnström examine the two mechanisms that have attracted the most attention in this regard: gacaca courts in post-genocide Rwanda and reconciliation rituals in northern Uganda. Both cases reveal how local accountability mechanisms come under considerable pressure to mete out retributive justice and to serve the state's legitimating needs.

Post-genocide Rwanda has responded to mass violence with mass justice, creating 11,000 community courts (gacaca) to try hundreds of thousands of suspected *génocidaires*. As Waldorf observes, gacaca adds an innovative tool to the transitional justice toolkit. First, it is a homegrown response to mass violence, and one that explicitly contests the international community's preference for international criminal tribunals and national truth commissions. Second, gacaca represents the most ambitious adaptation (and scaling up) of customary law for transitional justice. At the same time, however, it reinforces the preference within the transitional justice paradigm for state-centered retributive justice and for individualized prosecutions.

Despite claims that gacaca represents "traditional" Rwandan justice, Waldorf argues that it is more accurately described as state-imposed "informalism." The Rwandan government transformed customary gacaca beyond recognition by converting local, ad hoc practices into formal, coercive state structures. Post-genocide gacaca consequently lacks legitimacy and popularity, so the state has to enforce participation. In the short term, at least, gacaca has failed to promote truth telling and reconciliation, while also promoting a dangerous form of collective guilt. Nonetheless, gacaca has managed to achieve some local-level restitution and some recovery of victims' remains. But overall, gacaca provides an object lesson in why it is essential to distinguish carefully between local initiatives produced bottom-up from communities and "customary" processes imposed top-down by states (Merry 2006).

In neighboring Uganda, local practices of accountability and reconciliation pose a profound challenge to the transitional justice paradigm. Just when it looked as though transitional justice had become universalized, normalized, and heterodox (Teitel 2003), the ICC's first arrest warrants for Lord's Resistance Army (LRA) leaders in northern Uganda resurrected the fierce debates and stark choices of the 1980s and 1990s: peace versus justice, amnesty versus impunity, retributive versus restorative justice. But whereas those earlier debates took place around national mechanisms, this time controversy erupted over local mechanisms: Acholi reconciliation ceremonies.

During the current conflict in northern Uganda, some Acholi have adapted such rituals as *nyono tong gweno* ("stepping on the egg") and *mato oput* ("drinking the bitter root") to cleanse, integrate, and reconcile former LRA combatants. Claims and counterclaims concerning the status of these practices have developed as part of a heated debate concerning the ICC's involvement in northern Uganda (Allen 2006, 2007; Baines 2007; Finnström, this volume; Harlacher et al. 2006). In 2003, Uganda's president referred the LRA's crimes in northern Uganda to the ICC. Although the ICC Prosecutor recognized "the need to respect the diversity of legal systems, traditions and cultures" (Office of the Prosecutor of the International Criminal Court 2003), he issued arrest warrants for the LRA leadership over objections from Acholi community leaders, who argued that warrants would prolong the twenty-year civil war and derail efforts to reintegrate ex-combatants. In response, the LRA leadership refused to end the war unless the ICC withdrew its arrest warrants, while the ICC Prosecutor insisted the LRA must be criminally punished either by the ICC or Ugandan courts. Meanwhile, the Ugandan government, upon learning that the ICC might probe crimes committed by government forces, has sought since late 2004 to withdraw its referral to the ICC and to use "internal reconciliation mechanisms" instead. Thus just as Rwanda's government has appropriated gacaca courts, the Ugandan government seeks to bend local practices to its own purposes.

The problem is really foundational. The ICC was always an uneasy and unstable compromise between international justice and state sovereignty. Under the doctrine of "complementarity," the ICC is supposed to be a court of last resort, stepping in only where states are "unwilling or unable" to prosecute. Yet, as Schabas (2007:175) observes, the relationship between international and national justice "is far from 'complementary'": "Rather, the two systems function in opposition and to some extent with hostility *vis-à-vis* each other." It is ironic that it took a local, nonretributive mechanism—something completely ignored by the ICC statute—to bring this latent hostility into open confrontation.

Caught somewhere in the middle are the people of northern Uganda, who deeply mistrust the government's motives, resent the ICC's high-handedness, and fear a resumption of LRA attacks (Finnström, this volume). Moreover, Finnström cautions, if only LRA combatants undergo mato oput, this would not address the crimes committed by the Ugandan government. Given the substantial political grievances of northern Uganda, Finnström emphasizes that "neither ritual action nor international claims to justice can replace political efforts at peacemaking"—which, sadly, have failed so far.

In addition, the equation of local justice with customary law deflects attention from other locally based practices of redress. If the problems of the post-genocide gacaca courts result in international disenchantment with customary law, the conflation of "the local" with "the customary" may thus have the effect of discrediting local practices altogether. In a place-based transitional justice, we need to explore a broader range of ideas, practices, and processes that people actually use—including those adapted from elsewhere and those that develop through synergies with actors beyond the immediate locale (e.g., Arriaza and Roht-Arriaza, this volume; Theidon 2007b). In some contexts of conflict and post-conflict, people use ritual and religious practice to work upon past and present violence as a means of "living with bad surroundings"

(Finnström 2008b)—and sometimes transforming them. In others, practices of redress and repair may not involve ritual, but rather draw upon the performance of everyday life as a means of remaking relationships (Nordstrom 1997; Theidon 2006b; Finnström, this volume; Shaw, this volume). Thus Nee and Uvin (this volume) describe how in most areas of Burundi, where personal survival depends upon a network of relationships, people found ways of restoring these relationships without any rituals or mechanisms: "people seemed just to return and to arrange themselves with their neighbors. They negotiate, talk it out, sometimes check with local authorities, usually find a compromise and move on." In other contexts, again, collaborative partnerships between external actors and local populations may act as catalysts for local initiatives through which people create the conditions for justice, coexistence, and a civil life (see Theidon 2007b:86–88).

Politics, Priorities, and Pragmatic Pluralism

In addition to exploring initiatives and everyday practices that people use on the ground, a place-based approach requires us to listen to survivors' priorities. But how do survivors' priorities intersect with those of international institutions and donors, and with the political interests of their own state? To highlight the gap between institutional and survivor priorities, and to illustrate how we can learn from survivors, Weinstein et al. (this volume) examine attitudes toward justice and reconciliation in six post-conflict countries. Quantitative surveys, they argue, enable us to recognize the heterogeneity of survivors by examining patterns of responses across a wide range of boundaries, and by investigating the significance of demographic factors, contrasting experiences of violence, and other crucial differences. Combining surveys with qualitative techniques such as interviews and focus groups that allow for richer responses, they reveal the inadequacy of a homogenized vision of "victims" by identifying multiple constituencies (such as those based on ethnic and sectarian identity) within each country: these constituencies heavily shape attitudes toward justice and reconciliation. These attitudes change over time, such that the "snapshot" image provided by a survey may represent only one point in an unfolding post-conflict trajectory. Finally, understandings of justice in all these countries and constituencies tend to be broader than those of the relevant national or international justice mechanisms, going beyond criminal prosecutions to encompass such dimensions as social justice and security.

Like Weinstein et al., Nee and Uvin frame their study of Burundians' attitudes toward post-conflict justice (this volume) by examining "whether prosecutions and truth commissions can be transferred wholesale from the political transitions where they developed to the community-based violence settings where they are now applied." They found that, rather than prosecutions that may put Burundi's fragile political stability at risk, and rather than a classic truth-telling mechanism that uncovers every detail of the violent past, most Burundians call for local mechanisms that promote dialogue in order to restore relationships. In addition, they identify minority constituencies with different concepts of and priorities for justice. Thus in a deeply divided community—a (Tutsi) IDP camp surrounded by (Hutu) *collines*—with a long history of attacks and mistrust, the authors found that ethnicity strongly shaped support for either prosecutions or a truth commission. In an ethnically integrated community with relatively low levels of poverty and malnutrition, in contrast, they found both a stronger sense of the future and a rejection of both prosecutions and a truth commission, in favor of local processes of dialogue. Nee and Uvin thereby reveal both the politicized nature of attitudes toward justice and—critically—the importance of both security and distributive justice in configuring post-conflict priorities.

As in Burundi, issues of security and of the politicization of justice have contributed to weak public support for gacaca courts in Rwanda (Waldorf, this volume). We have already discussed above the risks of gacaca's public truth telling, its exacerbation of ethnic tensions, and its implementation of victor's justice. Nevertheless, gacaca remained a priority for the Rwandan government. Waldorf traces how it was retooled over the years in response to changing government priorities: it was simplified to speed it up, radically revised to reduce the vast numbers of génocidaires in Rwanda's prisons, and rendered coercive to counter the widespread reluctance to participate. Because of the current fascination with "traditional" justice that fits the transitional justice paradigm, moreover, international donors and policymakers ignored or dismissed local responses to gacaca and continued to support it.

These conclusions from Burundi and Rwanda resonate strongly with the current debate over the ICC's intervention and local priorities in northern Uganda. Finnström argues that it is fundamentally misguided to regard Acholi, who have to live in a Primo Levian "gray zone" without clear distinctions between victims and perpetrators, as bearers of a single, linear strategy for coping with violence— *either* peace *or* accountability, *either* retributive *or* restorative justice, *either* modernity *or* "tradition."

On the basis of his ethnographic research among Acholi communities for over a decade, Finnström describes what we might term a pragmatic pluralism, in which people select, in different contexts and different historical moments, which of several strategies will best allow them to survive and to reconstruct their lives. "The much-debated issue about the restorative and retributive dimensions of justice," he argues, "is not really about any final either-or. Rather, in the moments of everyday life, it is a kind of acceptance of the complexities of the situation so that life can go on."

Layered, contextually variable responses of this kind—which are by no means restricted to northern Uganda (see Jackson 2005)—broaden our understanding beyond the "snapshot" views offered by surveys, and are all too often misread in terms of "confusion" or "contradiction." Pluralist responses to violence, in which the door to alternate possibilities is never closed, are especially clear when traced through participant observation across "the moments of everyday life" as contexts shift and new contingencies unfold.

Finnström identifies this pragmatic pluralism as fundamental to processes of coexistence in northern Uganda. Drawing upon John Borneman's thesis on reconciliation (2002), he conceptualizes these processes in minimalist terms as a departure from violence by sharing a present—but not necessarily agreeing on a past—that is nonrepetitive. To foster such a project, Finnström also follows Borneman in emphasizing the role of the "third party" and the cultivation of intersubjective "practices of listening." While Borneman suggests that the ICC might serve as such a third party, however, Finnström's informants claim that the ICC is not listening to them. Because of this, Finnström argues, the ICC is not subjecting itself to conditions that promote a nonrepetitive present and future.

Place-Based Practice: Recasting Transitions

How, though, might these processes of rethinking and engagement be translated into transitional justice practice? In the three final chapters of this volume, scholars and practitioners examine a variety of locally engaged initiatives in very different contexts of conflict or post-conflict that offer models for national and international justice. First, Laura Arriaza and Naomi Roht-Arriaza explore such initiatives for social reconstruction and transformation in Guatemala. During Guatemala's period of *la violencia,* experiences of violence varied so much in different parts of the country that it was difficult for national mechanisms to provide adequate, or even relevant, local responses. Locally based initiatives, the authors find, respond much better to this heterogeneity of experience. While there appears to be a strong discourse of "indigenous traditions" in these initiatives, their locality extends beyond claims of tradition and indigeneity to encompass ideas and techniques refashioned from external sources. They include oral history projects, community museums, community-sponsored psychosocial interventions, community-generated exhumations, and local mediation practices that create new spaces for truth telling, commemoration, dialogue, and justice. Generalizing from their Guatemala research, Arriaza and Roht-Arriaza argue against the co-opting and formalizing of such insider-driven initiatives by governments, international organizations, and transitional justice actors. Instead, they suggest that national and international initiatives study locally based practices in order to gain a better understanding of conditions on the ground, local priorities, and effective practices.

These suggestions move us away from standard approaches to localization in transitional justice that have largely been conceptualized as the formalization of customary law. By encouraging attention to ideas and practices that survivors of violence are actually using, to the ways in which they use them, and to what they mean to them, Arriaza and Roht-Arriaza seek to ground postconflict justice more firmly in local techniques and priorities for reconstruction. And by mapping out how national and international initiatives can learn from this grounding and collaborate with local initiatives, they begin to identify some of the practical applications of a place-based approach to transitional justice.

Second, Ron Dudai and Hillel Cohen explore a range of home-grown civil society initiatives in Israel–Palestine—a context in which the conflict has not ended, and no national or international transitional justice process is envisaged. All are initiatives through which participants engage with the past, whether as ex-combatants from both sides who talk about their past actions, bereaved Palestinians and Israelis who exchange their personal narratives of loss, schoolteachers who design joint Israeli–Palestinian textbooks, or activists who lead commemorative tours of destroyed Palestinian villages. These groups seek ways of communicating this knowledge in personal, embodied ways that are more likely to overcome denial.

Because these movements are broadly oppositional not only to official Israeli and Palestinian leaderships but also to dominant attitudes among their mainstream publics, they raise important questions about what it means to be "place-based." We have argued in this introduction both for an understanding of locality in terms of emplaced standpoints and for the need to listen to the experience and priorities of those affected by armed conflict or political repression. But how does this translate into contexts of ethnic or nationalist conflict—especially in combination with state violence and asymmetries of power—in which perceptions of exclusive victimhood and collective denial of the other's suffering characterize the mainstream? So charged are these perceptions that during and since the Oslo peace process, negotiators have agreed not to discuss past wrongs in order to allow discussions to move forward. Yet because the past remains such an inflammatory issue for Israeli and Palestinian publics, this official neglect has not been effective. Given this context, it is still crucial to begin, as do the groups in question, by acknowledging the standpoints and priorities of those who live with the violence. But as conflict-transformation initiatives these groups use equally emplaced forms of knowledge—experiential engagement with others' pasts and lived realities—in order to work upon those standpoints. This alternative knowledge, Dudai and Cohen conclude, helps to reconfigure mainstream discourse.

Finally, Patrick Falvey discusses locally engaged rights and transitional justice initiatives in a very different context of ongoing conflict and state violence: that of Burma. Falvey stresses that local actors—especially members of the various grassroots communities that have suffered under military repression—should be involved in justice policy decisions *before* Burma's transition. "The early involvement of local actors in defining [justice] goals," he writes, "may lead to the development of a transitional justice policy that is more effective in addressing the priorities and concerns of those people most affected by the violence." Waiting until the transition itself would, he points out, result in rapid, crisis-driven decisions by political elites to which local communities would have little or no access. Falvey examines the work of local human rights groups that work with local communities to learn their experiences and understandings of justice, document human rights violations, initiate truth-seeking and protest campaigns, and conduct transitional justice trainings with community leaders that culminate in simulations. These initiatives sometimes develop different justice emphases from those of international human rights groups, arising from their engagement with local experiences and grievances. One such emphasis concerns the structural violence of extensive economic hardships: these grievances exploded into the mass demonstrations of August 2007, following a sudden fuel price increase.

Given the heterogeneity of Burma, with both a democracy movement and several ethnic self-determination struggles, an emplaced approach is crucial. "Any transitional justice policy," Falvey emphasizes, "needs to take into account the diversity of Burma, the diversity of the suffering, but also the related variance in ideas about justice, peace, and reconciliation." If a transition is to be successful, Falvey argues, the diverse groups of people most affected by the violence should have a role in defining it; without such collaboration, renewed conflict may erupt. Thus through trainings and simulations, local organizations seek to convey an embodied knowledge of transitional justice to support local actors in shaping the terms of a transition.

The Guatemalan, Israeli–Palestinian, and Burmese initiatives discussed in this section place locally grounded research, alternative understandings of justice, local practices, and survivors' experiences at the center of their work. But they also take their local engagement to a different level. While many transitional justice initiatives now include outreach programs ("we'll tell you what we are doing"), and some, in addition, engage in consultation ("we'll ask you what you want"), these initiatives go further by building collaborative relationships, the aim of which is to enable people and communities affected by violence not only to express their standpoints but also to *participate* in decisions about justice and social reconstruction. In so doing, these programs not only take us beyond the paradigm of transitional justice but also create new forms of place-based practice.

Organization and Conclusions

In this volume, we seek to recast approaches to locality prevalent in transitional justice, moving from ideas of the local as a "level" to understandings in terms of place-based standpoints. We also wish to shift transitional justice debates beyond the impasse between those who argue for "local culture" and those who argue for "universal principles." Thus our contributors interrogate the teleological assumptions of transitional justice, examining the concrete ways in which its mechanisms intersect with survivors' practices, standpoints, and priorities in specific places and times, and thereby refashioning conventional understandings of "the local," "justice," and "transitions."

This book is divided into four parts. Part One offers intellectual frames for reconfiguring transitional justice and its local engagement. Part Two, "Local Engagements," concerns the ways in which people affected by armed conflict and political repression experience—and sometimes rework—the justice mechanisms designed to address their needs. The essays in Part Three, "Power,

Politics, and Priorities," critically explore disjunctures between the goals of transitional justice and survivors' approaches to postviolence reconstruction. Finally, the essays in Part Four, "Practicing Place-Based Justice," explore a range of initiatives that work through an emplaced engagement with survivors' experiences.

By making a critical, place-based examination of these mechanisms and practices on the ground, by exploring the power relations and heterogeneous interests that frame them, and by tracing how ordinary people respond to and sometimes transform them, our goals are both scholarly and oriented toward policy and practice. Thus the chapters of this book illustrate why, rather than formalizing and co-opting local forms of justice, national and international justice mechanisms should find other ways of grounding their interventions in local conditions, techniques, and priorities for reconstruction. They also demonstrate why methods for understanding the priorities of those who have survived mass violence should be designed in light of the knowledge that these priorities are often layered and complex and may change over time. This attention to the pluralistic, stratified character of local priorities leads us both to more diverse views of "justice" and to a rethinking of "transitional justice" as a succession of processes over the long term rather than a couple of years of "transition." Such processes, in turn, require the development of new forms of practice that move beyond consultation to forms of grassroots collaboration— which, of course, have their own contradictions (Hale 2008). In the current era of the "war on terror," it is even more urgent to develop these processes in conjunction with survivors, and to do so by moving beyond the standard dichotomy between "victims" and "perpetrators." We hope that this volume thereby lays a foundation for more locally responsive approaches to social reconstruction.

Chapter 2

Stay the Hand of Justice

Whose Priorities Take Priority?

Harvey M. Weinstein, Laurel E. Fletcher, Patrick Vinck, and Phuong N. Pham

There's bound to be a sense of tremendous sort of feeling of being cheated by the victims. But even more important, the Serbs who are beginning to realize that they were responsible for this, needed this verdict. They saw the television film of this massacre in Srebrenica, involving Serb soldiers, and a guilty verdict would, in my view, have made them face reality.

—*David Owen on the death of Slobodan Milosevic (Besheer 2006)*

It is not the first time we have had such incidents, even if these were horrible. It is not the first time that things were done and families came together. Often you gave a cow or a beer and families shared together, and the conflict was regulated in that way.

—*Elderly man interviewed in Rubengera, Rwanda, June 12, 2002*

The Challenge

The 2004 report of the Secretary-General of the United Nations on rule of law and transitional justice strikes to the heart of the major dilemma of transitional justice: "We must learn as well to eschew one-size-fits-all formulas and the importation of foreign models, and instead, base our support on national assessments, national participation and national needs and aspirations" (United Nations 2004a:1). Missing from this assessment is recognition of the dynamic interplay of international power and ambitions, and in particular the role of the United Nations in muddying the waters of accountability. This chapter focuses on two critical factors that should be considered in instituting transitional justice interventions: first, the interrelationship between international and local politics and the impact of domestic politics on the choice and implementation of any particular transitional justice mechanism; and second, the gap that may exist between international norms and expectations for justice and the attitudes, beliefs, and goals of the people whose lives were negatively affected by policies of the prior regime or the mass violence that may have erupted. In this section, we begin by reviewing how power and politics shape justice mechanisms and by examining the discrepancy between idealized goals and on-the-ground realities in recent implementations of transitional justice.

After more than a decade of contemporary international responses to criminal justice, the world community is still left with questions about the validity and utility of the mechanisms that we have initiated. Debates about domestic, international, and mixed tribunals (Chesterman 2002; Posner and Vermeule 2004; Roper and Barria 2005), the role of punishment and forgiveness (Aldana 2006), the value and limitations of amnesties (Sarkin and Daly 2004), the morality of truth commissions (Bhargava 2000), and the relationship of these concerns to the social reconstruction of societies are found in the literatures of several disciplines. While we recognize that international criminal law has evolved and created new standards of accountability, we raise questions in this chapter about beneficiaries, priorities, and the reactionary if not parochial nature of the human rights field, and propose a challenge to those who see transitional justice as the first and perhaps most important step in protecting the security of those whose lives are threatened by violence and terror. While we cast a critical eye on transitional justice in this chapter, we are aware that these processes do not occur in a vacuum: there may be conflicting political agendas; resources may be allocated to competing programs; expectations may be unrealistic, and coordination nonexistent. Ultimately, despite the evolution of what is entailed in transitional justice, considerable questions remain, and it is not clear whether, to what extent, or under what conditions transitional justice is capable of fulfilling its prophetic ambitions.

In his 2006 report titled "Indifference and Accountability: The United Nations and the Politics of International Justice in East Timor," David Cohen illustrates the vagaries and limitations of international criminal justice (2006:7). He describes a "lack of political will" to provide resources and support; "failure to establish clear ownership of the process between the UN and East Timor"; failure to meet basic international standards of operation; failure to address the needs of victims, witnesses, and communities; lack of competent judges; failure to provide a clear mandate for the prosecution; and, tellingly, a country left without an operating judiciary at the end of the process. The study findings reveal how East Timor was abandoned by the world community (Nevins 2005) and how international attempts at transitional justice are hampered by the real world of international politics and by unrealistic goals and expectations.

In February 2006, the Sierra Leone Working Group on Truth and Reconciliation released its preliminary study of the performance of Sierra Leone's Truth and Reconciliation Commission. While acknowledging that some progress had been made in operations, they noted: "It has been a deeply flawed and problematic process from its birth in 1999, when the peace agreement was signed" (Sierra Leone Working Group on Truth and Reconciliation 2006, Introduction). Two areas of great concern loomed large: first, many believed that the arrival of the Special Court "effectively relegated the TRC to 'second class status' in the hierarchy of accountability mechanisms and that donors increasingly deserted the TRC." Second, the report raised the question of whether the "official view" at the international level would deem the concurrent processes as a success and that the combined approach would be recommended as best practice. This was not the view of Sierra Leoneans, especially since many reported a lack of a "genuine partnership" with local civil society organizations.

The report surfaces the lack of attention paid by transitional justice mechanisms to those whose lives are directly affected by war, repression, and human rights violations. Its authors note: "It is particularly important that Sierra Leonean voices are heard at the international level, where criteria for assessing the successes and failures of the 'experiment' may be different from those locally and where different agendas may shape the conclusions reached. People have a right to know the truth about the Truth and Reconciliation Commission" (Sierra Leone Working Group on Truth and Reconciliation 2006:1.3).

Critiques of the Sierra Leone process have been echoed from outside as well. James Cockayne confronts the impacts of international politics and societal dynamics around the "under-resourcing, politicization[,] complex operational challenges . . . and . . . unrealistic expectations" that the Special Court for Sierra Leone faced (2005:674). However, the assumption made here is that criminal prosecutions are the essential first element of transition and that they bear a direct relationship to peace and stability. The challenges for transitional justice are more complex and must confront international and local politics, questions about reconciliation, and democracy (Cobban 2006:22–28). Complicating these concerns is the naïveté that underlies the imposition of specific models of justice in nonwestern societies.

Rosalind Shaw's 2005 report on the Sierra Leone Truth and Reconciliation Commission for the United States Institute of Peace raised different but related questions, the foundation of which lies in cultural practice. Shaw noted that "there was little popular support for bringing such a commission to Sierra Leone, since most people preferred a 'forgive and forget' approach" (2005:4). Further, she describes how, in this country, "social forgetting has been a cornerstone of techniques of reintegration and healing for child and adult ex-combatants. Speaking of the war in public often undermines these processes, and many believe it encourages violence" (2005:9). To many, this startling conclusion flies in the face of the now-popular juggernaut of truth telling—a confessional approach to confronting past events that presupposes that "revealing is healing" (Hamber 2001:4).[1] No one has yet demonstrated that this approach is relevant across cultures or nations.

And yet the idea of culturally relevant alternatives to transitional justice is fraught as well with controversy and risk. The Rwandan solution of utilizing a supposedly traditional mechanism of conflict resolution, the *gacaca* courts, has shown once again how politics and justice can become inextricably linked (Longman and Des Forges 2004a; Oomen 2005; Reyntjens 2004; Waldorf 2006). Barbara Oomen describes how the government of Rwanda has manipulated the international community with phrases like "transparency" and "good governance," while setting up a judicial process that prevents any examination of human rights violations committed by the regime itself (2005). Gacaca has led to scores of accused seeking safety outside the country, and the government imposed mandatory attendance at gacaca hearings as the empty promises of reconciliation became apparent. Oomen notes that "this particular form of justice has been made subservient to the government's political mission" (2005:905). Meanwhile, human rights organizations have been shuttered, and the government works hard to discredit any opposition.

Recently, the *Economist* lauded the capture of Liberian accused war criminal Charles Taylor and his transfer to The Hague (Anonymous 2006). As the President of Liberia grappled with the rebuilding of a country that was left in ruins, international pressure mounted on her to demand that Taylor be tried. Clearly, this posed a dilemma—where should he be tried? Would a trial in

Sierra Leone disrupt rebuilding plans? What priority should the costs of a trial assume among the widespread economic needs facing Liberia? The *Economist* notes that "the former Liberian president's trial may herald the end of impunity for Africa's 'big men,' traditionally regarded as too powerful to punish. It also marks a step forward for international justice" (Anonymous 2006). But what does "the end of impunity" mean in practice? And is the "step forward" the most critical step to take for Liberia?

We suggest that part of the problem in assessing the benefits of the approaches now subsumed under the term *transitional justice* lies in an expansion of these purported benefits. We need to calibrate our expectations. Many scholars and practitioners assume that transitional justice will lead to reconciliation and forgiveness, deter further abuses, combat impunity, promote social reconstruction, and alleviate the effects of trauma.[2] The expectations of the international community for trials should be limited to an agreement that retributive punishment is appropriate and sufficient in and of itself; that reconciliation processes may be of another order entirely, and that the relationship between justice and reconciliation remains unclear. While truth commissions, trials, vetting, memorials, and reparations may all play some as-yet-undefined role in the social reconstruction of societies, the contributions will vary depending on context and on the priorities assigned to them by those affected. The voices and opinions of those whose human rights have been abused must be heeded.

This poses a challenge to human rights organizations that have fought long and hard for judicial interventions. Yet, given the findings of those who study transitional justice, we suggest that it is time to open up the dialogue and to stop falling back on poorly crafted rationalizations for traditional (primarily western) conceptions of what is moral and right. The involvement of Africans, Asians, and people from other cultures and communities, including indigenous peoples, in dealing with these egregious abuses raises the possibility that we should revisit the transitional justice "toolkit" and reconsider the established paradigm.

Historical Perspective

Gary Jonathan Bass, in his 2000 book, *Stay the Hand of Vengeance: The Politics of War Crimes Tribunals,* introduces the text with a quote from Justice Robert Jackson's opening statement at the Nuremberg Trials: "That four great nations, flushed with victory and stung with injury, stay the hand of vengeance and voluntarily submit their captive enemies to the judgment of the law is one of the most significant tributes that Power has ever paid to Reason" (2000:147). However, as Ruti Teitel notes, the mechanisms for responding to violations of international humanitarian law have evolved considerably since the Nuremberg trials: "The genealogical perspective situates transitional justice in a political context, moving away from essentializing approaches and thereby illuminating the dynamic relationship between transitional justice and politics over time" (2003:94). Jack Snyder and Leslie Vinjamuri (2003–4), in evaluating the successes of international justice, suggest that the international community has achieved minimal success in the area of prevention. They conclude that "legalism, focusing on the universal enforcement of international humanitarian law and persuasion campaigns to spread benign human rights norms," has been minimally effective. They find "little support for the central empirical assumptions that underpin this approach. Trials do little to deter further violence and are not highly correlated with the consolidation of peaceful democracy" (2003–4:43).[3]

We are at a stalemate on how best to respond to atrocity crimes. Despite the increased recognition that trials are limited in their effects and may have untoward consequences, they still remain the privileged response of the international community—Iraq, Cambodia, and Uganda being the most recent examples. Tension has emerged around the indictment by the International Criminal Court (ICC) of five leaders of the Lord's Resistance Army in Uganda, while the government of Uganda and many of its people argue for peace negotiations and amnesty (International Center for Transitional Justice and U.C. Berkeley Human Rights Center 2005). The stakes are high and disagreement runs the risk of polarization. How do we value the cost of a tribunal? Do we abandon victims if we argue for a response that addresses the greater good of a community? How do we know what victims want? Is there such a category as "victims" or should we recognize the variability in the category? We place this inquiry in historical context, relating it to the "expectations gap" and the political challenges of transitional justice.

Origins of Transitional Justice

The concept of transitional justice is relatively new and still evolving. Since its debut in the late 1980s, as dictatorships fell in Latin America and the end of the Cold War brought independent states in eastern Europe, the concept has been used to refer to the challenges faced by new regimes as they put the past

behind them and transitioned from authoritarian or repressive rule to democracy. World events overtook this original idea of transitional justice as
civil wars and regional conflicts unleashed widespread bloodshed and human
rights violations on a mass scale. Nevertheless, transitional justice absorbed
these new developments and continued to be invoked as a necessary ingredi-
ent in any peace process. This suggests that the elasticity of the term may be
stretched beyond its usefulness. Addressing the harm of the past is a *process*
that may unfold over the course of years, if not decades, and the nature of the
response may take multiple forms.

One of the earliest and most influential developments in the field of transitional justice was the 1988 Aspen Institute conference titled "State Crimes:
Punishment or Pardon" to consider the "moral, political and jurisprudential
issues that arise when a government that has engaged in gross violations of
human rights is succeeded by a regime more inclined to respect those rights"
(Henkin 1995:184). The conference participants identified the primary fault
lines and factors that confronted new regimes brought into power after authoritarian or repressive rule: whether there is a moral duty for successor regimes to punish human rights violators under the former regime or whether
states should emphasize measures to foster national reconciliation; the nature
and extent of international legal obligations of successor states to prosecute
wrongdoers; what duties successor states had to investigate and publicize the
truth of the violations that took place under the prior regime; and the extent
of political discretion new regimes could exercise legitimately to address the
past, taking into account the political, social, and economic vulnerabilities
that threaten emerging democracies (Aspen Institute Papers 1988).

These dilemmas endured and proliferated with the fall of the Berlin Wall
in 1989 and commanded the attention of increasing numbers of diplomats,
scholars, and advocates. By the time Neil Kritz published his work on transitional justice in 1995, the term had unquestionably entered the lexicon of international law and relations. There was consensus that the past could not be
ignored. Rather, it must be addressed in an intentional manner, lest stability
be purchased on the cheap, grievances left festering, and violence simmering
just below the surface—arguments that are hypothetical in nature, since there
is no evidence to support these views. Kritz's book documents the rich debates
and proliferation of policy choices regarding transitional justice measures. In
the book, the decision to seek criminal sanctions continues to occupy center
stage. Whether to prosecute, whom to prosecute, legal barriers to prosecutions,

their political feasibility, alternatives to criminal sanctions, and how to respond to victims presented a thicket of questions with no clear answers. However, there was recognition that universal claims of human rights and the rule of law are often in tension with the exigencies demanded by the specific context of a particular transition.

Transitional Justice and Mass Violence

The conflicts in the Balkans and Rwanda in the early 1990s introduced a new dimension to transitional justice. Pursuit of accountability for the atrocities committed during these wars linked the cases of the former Yugoslavia and Rwanda conceptually to those of emerging democracies, a development that has changed the field. In 2000, the Ford Foundation spearheaded an effort to establish the first international organization devoted exclusively to supporting transitional justice. The mission statement of that group, the International Center for Transitional Justice, announced that the organization "works in societies emerging from *repressive rule or armed conflict,* as well as in established democracies where historical injustices or systemic abuse remain unresolved."[4] Broadening the conceptual framework of transitional justice strengthened the momentum of the field but also served to obscure possible distinctions between types of transitions.

Accountability for past abuses has remained the galvanizing principle behind transitional justice for many in the international community, and criminal sanctions continue to be the privileged option. Human rights advocates pressed the case for prosecutions of political leaders and military architects of repression and mass violence, arguing that international law permitted—if not demanded—an end to impunity, and that a legalized response strengthened the rule of law in societies emerging from repression. While debates around these issues continue, a moral and political consensus has emerged within the international community to prosecute serious violations of international criminal law. The institutional expression of this commitment began with the ad hoc criminal tribunals for the former Yugoslavia and Rwanda in 1993 and 1994, continued with support for internationalized courts for Sierra Leone and East Timor, and culminated with the establishment of the International Criminal Court in 2002. Since the discussions within the international community tended to be led by lawyers, it is not surprising that the focus has remained on retributive justice with underlying rationales based on moral justifications for the primacy of law. While this view relies upon principles of morality, legal theory, conceptions of democracy, and theology, there has been little room for consideration of broader or alternative approaches, especially those that might emerge out of different or non-western conceptions of justice.

Truth Commissions as an Alternative to Trials

Given the normative shift toward prosecutions, the simultaneous acknowledgment within the field of transitional justice that truth commissions are an acceptable—if not in some instances preferred—alternative to criminal sanctions has been particularly striking. South Africa's choice in 1995 to address the abuses of the apartheid regime through a truth commission became a watershed event in transitional justice. The South Africa Truth and Reconciliation Commission (TRC), with the authority to grant amnesty for political crimes if the perpetrator made a full disclosure of the events and to compensate victims, disrupted several paradigms of transitional justice. First, the South Africa case challenged conventional wisdom that amnesties necessarily buried the truth about the past. Second, subordinating prosecutions to a truth commission in which perpetrators had to testify publicly about their crimes and victims had the opportunity to confront wrongdoers tested the notion that truth commissions necessarily trade justice for truth. Finally, South African supporters of the TRC defended the commission as a preferred mechanism for transitional justice on the basis that it was consistent with cultural values (ubuntu) that prioritize social harmony and reconciliation over retribution. Thus the TRC constituted a natural extension of the restorative justice principles that framed the political agreement enabling a peaceful transition to majority rule.

Synthesis and Evolution of Transitional Justice

The influence of these two trends in transitional justice—international promotion of prosecutions and integration of local priorities and conditions—continues. The next wave of initiatives has been marked by hybrid or internationalized tribunals that integrate international law and judges into domestic adjudication of war crimes committed in the conflicts in Cambodia, East Timor, Kosovo, and Sierra Leone. Similarly, Rwanda's decision to adapt a "customary" dispute resolution process—gacaca—to pursue accountability expanded the transitional justice lexicon. East Timor also incorporated a customary dispute resolution mechanism into its efforts to respond to the wave of violence that accompanied the vote for independence. And in Sierra Leone, while controversial, the country witnessed the simultaneous operation of a truth commission and an internationalized court. Currently, transitional justice might be characterized as a menu of options for mechanisms—driven by principles of accountability—from which countries may pick and choose to craft a considered response to a period of widespread violence or repression. However, an important question is whether we remain too fixed in our perspective, and whether we have limited our array of options, prematurely becoming closed to other interventions that might be dramatically different.

An examination of transitional periods across countries points to the messy, incomplete, or continually contested nature of transitional justice (Fletcher and Weinstein, 2009). In some countries, implementation of alternatives to prosecutions does not resolve the demands by some for accountability. Decisions to amnesty perpetrators, even with a truth commission, as in Argentina or Guatemala,[5] do not staunch efforts to find justice in other venues. Or in the case of Cambodia, efforts to hold accountable the Khmer Rouge leadership for the genocide spanned decades after the group was forced from power. These extended periods of activity to implement justice raise questions about whether there are outer limits to what might reasonably be termed a period of transition and when such a transition ends.

It is time to reconsider whether the term *transitional justice* accurately captures the dynamic processes unfolding on the ground. There may be a discrete political episode during which the regime change takes place, yet the term *transition* denotes a temporary state in which movement occurs, transporting a country from the past (violence/repression) to the future (peace/democracy). However, progress toward social reconstruction may be halting, and marking the end of a "transition" by the first free elections is a poor metric to determine a lasting peace. Broadening the aims of transitional justice to support social reconstruction reveals some noteworthy limits of current approaches. Looking beyond the initial outburst of hope that often accompanies the end of a violent or repressive period, a review of how transitional justice interventions unfold over time in different political contexts and cultures raises a number of questions. Despite the emphasis on the importance of trials, what evidence is there that justice is more than a rhetorical talisman for social transformation? In fact, the focus on trials leads us to question whether the emergence of criminal accountability for mass atrocities has dislodged or obscured the importance of other processes and interventions needed to create an enduring platform for social stability after protracted, state-sponsored violence. How should we conceptualize the relationship between prosecutions and these other interventions? What consideration should we give to the timing or sequencing of these events? Has our rhetoric outstripped the evidence?

Finally, while some transitional justice policymakers reject the notion that "revealing is healing," many remain wedded to the idea that justice will alleviate the pain of traumatic experience. Yet, as Kirsten Campbell so eloquently reveals, "the trauma of law is that it cannot represent justice. The trauma of justice is its juridical impossibility. . . . [Justice] requires a fundamental change to the social order which made possible the originary trauma of crimes against humanity. In this sense, justice remains the event yet to come" (2001:6). While we would prefer the easy answer that trials and punishment will assuage the grief of trauma, the ideal of closure remains that—just an ideal.

The Ongoing Challenge

Over the past decade the eruption of identity-based conflicts has made apparent several critical dimensions of post-conflict reconstruction, with important application to the concept of transitional justice. First, conceptions of justice vary among individuals, communities and cultures; second, how communities respond to these violations may reflect mechanisms that differ considerably from western models of justice; third, timing is a critical factor. When is the appropriate time for which kind of intervention, recognizing that priorities change over the months and years after overt conflict has ended? Fourth, responses are context-bound and heavily influenced by the relevant political dimensions; and finally, while community consultation is a key component of determining the appropriate response, how does one best make that determination? We must ask whether and when local desires should trump international law, or indeed whether the universal application of international humanitarian law is paramount.

What Do We Know About Attitudes Toward Justice? Evidence from the Field

We must ask those rebuilding their societies after mass violence what they want. However, this is not a straightforward process. For example, whom do we ask? If we survey people in a certain village or town, will their answers be representative of all those who have been victimized? If we ask elites, politicians, journalists, or NGO officials, how will we be certain that their perspectives are not simply unique to their positions? These are critical concerns, as peace building and social reconstruction depend on the motivation of those affected to commit to working across former enemy lines and where issues of betrayal and trust are paramount. Most investigations have employed interview techniques to gather data. Yet these investigations are always open to the critique that the informants or the questions asked were biased in some specific manner. Interviews may illuminate aspects of the violence or responses to it, but they may be less helpful in delineating broad patterns of victimization or other impacts in a society. Our research team has incorporated several methods to examine the complexities of mass violence and the processes that have emerged to cope with the consequences of that violence. To the traditional interview, focus group, and ethnographic methods, we have added cross-sectional surveys.

Survey methodology allows us to do several things: first, to examine broad patterns of experiences, attitudes, and responses across geographic and socioeconomic boundaries; second, to look at the influence of demographic differences; third, to look at important associations of factors that may influence attitudes; and finally, to minimize biases that may distort our understanding of events by random selection of respondents. Surveys have limitations, including the quality and validity of the questions asked, and do not allow the respondent to explore, associate, and provide the richness that intensive interviews allow. However, as a human rights tool, surveys do much more than reflect popular opinion. They allow us to formulate a pattern of factors that may inhibit or promote social reconstruction. This broad perspective offers valid and representative information that can inform the peacebuilding processes.

Over the last decade, our population-based data raise questions about the goals of trials, the beneficiaries of trials, motivations for justice, and the ongoing tension between rich and poor countries. We focus specifically on the range of attitudes toward justice and types of judicial mechanisms, and what we can learn about how these attitudes may relate to post-conflict social reconstruction. We look across five different countries (Bosnia-Herzegovina, Croatia, Rwanda, Uganda, and Iraq) to see how attitudes reflect differences in culture, geography, war experience, and type of intervention. We examine four issues of importance to local communities—attitudes toward justice, attitudes toward reconciliation, the importance of identity groups, and the effects of trauma. In each case, we look at how local responses may differ from those put into place at the national or international level and thus promote tension between universal responses to international crimes and uniquely contextual responses.

Such tensions may have the untoward effect of heightening animosity among former protagonists and thus inhibit social reconstruction.

Attitudes Toward Justice

Our findings suggest that how people feel about judicial mechanisms is strongly influenced by experience of the violence, prior experiences with those on the other side, beliefs in retributive justice, access to accurate information, cultural beliefs and practices, and identity group membership.[6]

In Bosnia and Herzegovina, attitudes toward the International Criminal Tribunal for the Former Yugoslavia (ICTY) were related to identity group, war experience, postwar geography, and the ability of a group to acknowledge the deeds of its own war criminals. These influences changed over time as refugee returns occurred and the Office of the High Representative asserted control over the media reportage that promoted ethnic hatred. Our ethnographic studies revealed that justice is not always defined as "trials" or legal interventions. For some: "The greatest justice for me would be to let me live and die in peace there where I was born"; for others, "Punishing criminals would bring satisfaction." However, many were suspicious as to whether local courts had the capacity to provide justice that was untainted by political interference and corruption. We concluded that it was important to recognize that we could not make sweeping statements about what "victims" want; that view in itself diminishes the agency of those who have lost so much.

In Rwanda, we examined more closely the attitudes of Rwandans toward specific legal interventions—the International Criminal Tribunal for Rwanda (ICTR), domestic genocide trials, and gacaca (Pham, Weinstein, and Longman 2004; Stover and Weinstein 2004:206–25). As in the Balkans, our findings suggested that attitudes toward legal interventions are not straightforward but are influenced by social, demographic, and economic factors. Ninety-two percent of respondents supported the use of trials to punish the guilty, but they often espoused different goals, such as rebuilding trust or recognizing the suffering of survivors. At the time of the study, there was significantly greater support for gacaca than the other two forms of legal intervention. Another important dynamic was that the more educated were significantly less supportive of any of the approaches.

In Iraq, we examined attitudes toward transitional justice mechanisms three months after the U.S.-led invasion of the country. Primarily because of security issues and the difficulty in finding local partners, our study employed a qualitative methodology. In July and August 2003, we conducted interviews and focus groups with representatives from a broad spectrum of the Iraqi population. We polled 395 people through thirty-eight individual interviews and forty-nine focus groups in north, central, and southern Iraq. Respondents included members of all ethnic, religious, and political groups, victim groups, members of civil society organizations, and leaders of religious and political organizations.

Our research showed that for Iraqis, concepts of justice focused on what constituted a just society, the antithesis of the old order. There was common agreement that perpetrators should be held accountable through fair trials, transparent and Iraqi-based with international support. There was a profound distrust of United Nations involvement and great support for the United States to distance itself in favor of international input. While many believed strongly in retributive justice and even vengeance, Iraqis expressed a hierarchy of who should be tried and supported the death penalty for those found guilty. Many recognized and encouraged a process of memorialization, education, and other forms of recording historical memory, but there was little knowledge of truth commissions or more formal mechanisms of remembering the past.

In northern Uganda, controversy has marked discussions among local communities, the state, and the International Criminal Court. The focus of controversy is whether members and leaders of the Lord's Resistance Army should be held criminally accountable for the more than twenty years of abductions, displacement, mutilations, rapes, and killings. The crux of the question is peace (including the possibility of amnesties) versus criminal prosecutions. In December 2003, President Museveni of Uganda asked the ICC to take up the problem. At the same time, the government of Uganda has pursued a peace process mediated by the government of South Sudan that would involve amnesties in the search for a way to end the conflict (Shukla and Martin 2009).[7] The intervention of the International Criminal Court sparked controversy among civil society organizations in northern Uganda. There were conflicting reports about what the Acholi (the major population group) and others in the north wanted as an outcome and what process would best meet their priorities and contribute to peace. Some argued that traditional reintegration and reconciliation mechanisms involving ceremonies such as the *mato oput* and "bending of the spears" were best adapted to deal with perpetrators. Further, it was argued that the involvement of the ICC and the threat of prosecution and trials would jeopardize peace talks between the government of Uganda and the LRA.

We asked 2,550 northern Ugandans, "Is it important for you that persons responsible for abuses in northern Uganda are held accountable for their actions?" More than three-quarters of those surveyed responded "yes." We also asked what they would like to see happen to the LRA leaders who were responsible for the mass atrocities. More than one-half (66%) wanted punishment in the form of trials, imprisonment, and execution. To add to the complexity, 71 percent stated that they would accept amnesty if it were the only road to peace, but if there were peace, 54 percent would prefer peace with trials over peace with amnesty (46%). Surprisingly, Acholi respondents, generally considered the principal victims of the LRA, were more willing to accept amnesty than were the Lango and Teso (the response pattern between districts also confirmed this finding). Finally, when asked to define justice, only 31 percent defined justice as trials, and this varied across districts. In other districts, reconciliation was offered as a definition (in one district, 35% chose this option).[8]

Attitudes Toward Reconciliation

In epidemiological surveys, it is essential that terms be conceptually defined so that we are measuring valid indicators. A term like *reconciliation* is open to many definitions and interpretations, and the more specific we are, the clearer our understanding of this concept as an outcome. In Bosnia and Herzegovina, the "Readiness for Reconciliation" scale was defined by three variables—readiness to accept the presence of members of the "opposing" nationality in eight different situations, readiness to be reconciled with the conflicted nationalities, and readiness to accept interstate cooperation. In Rwanda, the "Openness to Reconciliation" scale consisted of eighteen questions that represented four factors—social justice, nonviolence, community, and interdependence.

In the Balkans, we learned that reconciliation is a multidetermined process heavily influenced by individual, interpersonal, and societal factors. Those who were not ethnocentric, nationalistic, or authoritarian were more likely to support reconciliation. Those who believed in the value of trials and the importance of the ICTY were also more likely to be open to reconciliation. Finally, those with positive prewar experiences across ethnic lines were more positively influenced toward reconciliation. In Rwanda attitudes toward reconciliation were not clear-cut. Trials in another country or at the ICTR were seen as least contributory to reconciliation, while there was more support for Rwandan trials and gacaca as making a significant or very significant contribution, 69 percent and 84 percent respectively. However, when we statistically analyzed the responses of the participants using our specific definition of reconciliation, we found little relationship between attitudes toward the various trials and openness to reconciliation.

In Iraq, shortly after the release of the country from dictatorship, rage and pain suffused the populace. Yet most had an understanding that revenge would only recapitulate the violence of the past. On the specific question of reconciliation, however, the results of our study were not definitive. Across different ethnic groups, participants understood reconciliation in terms of the concept of unity and trust. However, there were differences in how the groups applied the term, and so there was no agreement on the topic. Some believed that with the end of the Hussein era, unity now existed and that divisions had been promoted by the prior regime. Many felt that the history of injustice united all the Iraqi people; the Kurds saw it as opening the possibility of improving Kurdish–Arab relations. We found different interpretations of reconciliation that varied with geography, ethnicity, minority status, and focus on individual versus societal need. There was universal support for accountability, yet little relationship existed between legal justice and reconciliation.

The survey in Uganda also suggested that definitions of reconciliation are not straightforward and varied with geography and ethnicity. When asked, "What is reconciliation?" 52 percent associated the concept with "forgiveness," 62 percent in non-Acholi districts and 43 percent in Acholi districts. Twenty-four percent associated reconciliation with confession, but only 6 percent associated reconciliation with justice (however, 18 percent associated justice with reconciliation). Only 9 percent associated reconciliation with "traditional" ceremonies. The latter finding is inconsistent with those reported in other studies (Hovil and Quinn 2005; Baines 2007). These kinds of discrepancies can reflect such problems as wording of questions, variability in concepts (although the questions are pretested), and differences based on who is asking the questions. Such discrepancies can be minimized by utilizing multiple methods of inquiry.

Influence of Identity Group

The identity group to which one belongs influences attitudes toward any form of transitional justice. In each country studied, ethnic identity surfaces as a critical dimension that must be considered in social reconstruction. In Bosnia-Herzogovina, our findings suggested that attitudes toward the ICTY were viewed through a nationalist lens. The Bosniaks, acknowledged by the international community as the principal victims of the war, felt very positively about the ICTY; Serbs and Croats felt negatively because of their belief that members of their group were being singled out for prosecution. However, our studies indicated that over time (one to two years), following the initial survey, attitudes were changing in a positive direction in some groups and negatively in others. Attitudes toward a contested institution are bound to change as more information becomes available; they will also be influenced by the political climate, and the actions of the institution itself. Those who were less ethnocentric and nationalist were more likely to believe in reconciliation.

In Rwanda, our study found significant differences between Hutu and Tutsi on a variety of attitudes and beliefs. These differences were found in expectations of trials: for example, while a majority of Tutsi strongly agreed that trials should punish the guilty, a majority of Hutu merely agreed. On the other hand, Tutsi showed stronger support for reparations. Differences were found in attitudes toward the three types of trial possibilities—ICTR, Rwandan trials, and gacaca. For example, 37 percent of Hutu held positive views of the ICTR, and 14.3 percent negative, compared to 21.9 percent of Tutsi who held positive views, and 35.1 percent negative. We also found that a larger percentage of Hutu felt more strongly that members of the Rwandan Patriotic Front who committed crimes should be tried. A small difference was found between Hutu and Tutsi in their support for social justice (a factor in the reconciliation scale), with Tutsi being somewhat more supportive. But on the whole, openness to reconciliation was found in both groups, although it was modified by such factors as education and symptoms of exposure to trauma.

As the Iraq study employed a qualitative design, ethnic differences are not quantified. However, our data indicate that at the time of the study, each group shared attitudes born out of a common experience of human rights violations, and each group was aware of how those violations affected the other. Iraqis were united in their hatred of the Saddam Hussein regime. They pled common cause with their countrymen in their rage against the arbitrary nature of the violent regime: "Saddam did not succeed in killing the Iraqi person, but he succeeded in terrifying the Iraqi spirit." However, at the same time, each ethnic group focused on what specifically had been done to their people.

The Uganda study demonstrated that ethnicity, specifically Acholi versus non-Acholi identity, influenced attitudes toward trials, amnesty, peace, and the relationship between peace and justice. For example, those from non-Acholi districts were twice as likely to want "peace with trials and punishment" than "peace with amnesty." In Gulu, where the population is primarily Acholi, the majority of respondents believed that pursuing justice would threaten a peace process. Similarly, respondents from the Acholi districts were three times less likely to want trials than were respondents from non-Acholi districts. How much these differences emerge from cultural beliefs and values, from fatigue after a twenty-year history of horrendous violence, or from a lack of faith in a British-developed judicial system is unclear. However, these data do indicate that identity-group membership is a critical determinant in attitudes toward justice in northern Uganda.

Exposure to Trauma

In the Balkan countries we found no correlation between the level of traumatic experience and the desire for war crimes trials or with positive attitudes toward the ICTY. One respondent stated: "I have nothing out of this belated justice. . . . Things lost will not be returned to me, nor will this ease my suffering." Trauma experience was negatively associated with readiness for reconciliation if respondents had experienced negative prewar interactions with members of the opposing group. On the other hand, we also heard: "Punishing criminals would bring us satisfaction." These kinds of discrepancies demonstrate once again why multiple methodologies are useful. In this study, exposure to trauma was measured by a scale developed in Croatia weighted to account for severity of exposure, and while a validated instrument, it may not be capturing the dimensions of trauma effects that would influence attitudes toward justice. However, it also is possible that the qualitative responses do not accurately capture these relationships at a population level.

In Rwanda, the association of traumatic experience with attitudes toward trials was also unclear—the more the respondents had been exposed to traumatic events, the more negative they were to domestic trials, especially gacaca, and the more positive they were toward the ICTR. If respondents reported symptoms of post-traumatic stress disorder (PTSD; a proxy for emotional effects in our study), the more negative they were toward classical domestic trials. The experience of trauma appeared to influence attitudes toward trials, but not in any clear-cut manner. In addition, both exposure to trauma events and symptoms of traumatic experience, as determined by a scale that measures PTSD, demonstrated a relationship to openness to reconciliation. Greater trauma exposure lessened support for three of the reconciliation dimensions, and

PTSD lessened support on two of the factors. We conclude that while support existed to hold trials within Rwanda and even outside, this support was influenced by politics, war experience, the type of legal intervention proposed, lack of information, ethnicity, education, and traumatic exposure. Relationships were far from clear, and when looked at in relation to their contribution to reconciliation, the association was murky indeed.

We did not specifically examine trauma exposure in Iraq as we did in the Balkans, Rwanda, and Uganda. However, participants in the interviews and focus groups did volunteer much about the impact of the Hussein era on their lives. Thus a Shi'a woman told us, "Our life was full of lies and fear," and a Kurdish woman lamented, "We spent our lives crying tears of pain and suffering and we became really fed up or disappointed and we gave up." Our data indicated that the prevalence of trauma exposure had been extremely high and that these experiences led to widespread fear, cynicism, and mistrust. These attitudes manifested themselves in a strong desire for accountability from all groups, as well as distrust of the international community for their prior support of the Baathist regime. While they welcomed international support and resources for Iraqi trials, they felt strongly that the trials must be held in Iraq, with Iraqi judges.

The levels of exposure to trauma in northern Uganda were among the highest that have been formally reported. Respondents answered whether they had been exposed to eleven major violent events, such as abduction, killings, mutilation, and sexual violation. Some 40 percent reported that they had been abducted, 58 percent that they had witnessed a child abduction, and 45 percent that they had witnessed the death of a family member. The greater the exposure to trauma, the more the respondents wanted to have accountability and trials. The only exception to this relationship was that exposure to more trauma was associated with the belief that former enemies could live together. Further, those who had been exposed to at least one of the traumatic events were more likely to support amnesty. Finally, responses were modified by ethnicity.

What these studies show is the complexity of the relationships among justice, peace, and reconciliation. Attitudes were modified by ethnicity, geography, education, and exposure to traumatic events. The data offer further evidence for the importance of considering a range of solutions and for understanding not only the nature of the conflict but also the characteristics of the populations affected by the violence.

Discussion

Each of these countries was examined at a particular point in time, and the events that led up to the "transitional period" were quite different. In the Balkan countries, an internationally supported peace agreement set out a political mechanism to assure peace and stability; in Rwanda, a victorious army assumed power in 1994; in Iraq, we interviewed our respondents three months after an international invasion had ended decades of human rights abuses; and in Uganda, the survey was carried out in the midst of ongoing atrocities. There are distinct similarities and differences among the countries that we studied. In all, one's identity group strongly influences attitudes toward trials, as does local politics. Lack of information about legal structures and alternatives influences attitudes in Rwanda, Iraq, and Uganda. In these countries, the legal institutions suffer from a profound lack of confidence in their fairness and capability to administer justice.

Time is an important dimension—as we saw in the Balkans, attitudes toward trials, the ICTY, and the former enemy changed over time. In Iraq, at the time of the survey, there appeared to be a commitment to a unified country—a belief that clearly has changed in the intervening time. In Rwanda, the initial and overwhelming enthusiasm for gacaca has been tempered by its one-sided approach to justice. In all of these settings, the involvement of the international community is viewed with ambivalence. Definitions of justice vary by country, although retributive justice appears to be very important to some groups in all. How, when, and by whom it is meted out remains an open question. While in the Balkans there was no clear relationship between trauma experience and desire for trials, there were some associations in Rwanda, particularly to the type of trial. In Uganda, there is a relationship between exposure to trauma and desire for trials, but this is not clear-cut: the Acholi most supported amnesty.

Finally, local politics—the legacy of the Dayton Accord, the RPF victory and government in Rwanda, the U.S.-led invasion in Iraq, the relationship between President Museveni's government and the people of northern Uganda—profoundly shape the responses of identity groups to whatever form of transitional justice is proposed. And these attitudes are influenced, in turn, by cultural practices and historical experience. These data illustrate the futility of simplistic responses to mass violence. Each country and culture must be considered separately, and interventions must be developed that make sense for the populations of concern.

Closing the Gap: Transformative Justice for Survivors of Human Rights Violations

In this chapter we question the established rhetoric about transitional justice. We raise these issues to highlight their importance and to emphasize the need for further study, discussion, and theory. If we do not attend to these challenges and see them as opportunities, the efforts of the international community to respond to the needs of post-conflict societies may be seriously undermined. We end by summarizing seven important challenges faced by the field of transitional justice.

First, we cannot assume that legal justice is desired or the highest priority in all countries after periods of repression or violence. Culture and history may lead to different definitions of justice and to different paths for achieving it; justice can be defined broadly, and retributive justice is only one part of that definition. Second, we find that attitudes toward legal justice are influenced by trust in the preexisting legal institutions and the political dynamics in the country. Third, the primacy of western legal systems and thinking over that of other forms of legal intervention must be examined. Fourth, international justice that is isolated from the development of a competent domestic judicial system sabotages an important dimension of building a democratic society. Fifth, we must broaden our conceptions about victims and their needs. There is no unitary concept of victimhood—there are many types of victims, and they may not think in the same way about the meaning of justice; the equation of justice with some ethereal conception of psychological catharsis must be challenged. Sixth, our analysis suggests that many involved with international justice have lost sight of its goals in favor of developing and maintaining an international system of criminal law over and above what might be the needs and desires of the victims of abuse. Positive effects that might emerge may be undermined by UN policymakers and bureaucratic procedures, insensitive and inexperienced lawyers, and systems that are out of touch with events on the frontlines. Finally, we must stop the equation of justice with reconciliation and acknowledge that many steps may be taken to rebuild societies. At this point, we do not know which are most critical or even if there is any universal program to implement.

Our studies in the Balkans, Rwanda, Iraq, and Uganda reveal that priorities for post-conflict justice vary with identity group, type of violence and human rights abuses, country, culture, and time. If transitional justice is indeed to become transformative, then the "toolkit" that has become the menu of transitional justice options must be expanded and evolve into interventions that reflect a broadened view of responses to human rights violations. Dilemmas abound—what do we do with perpetrators for whom trials may be put off to another time? What about those for whom trials are the most important next step? How do we judge the moral choice—trials for individual victims versus the greater good of a peaceful society? Is there "no peace without justice" or "no justice without peace"? We suggest that the lessons of the last twenty years have put us in a better position to reframe the questions and to explore new options. The ultimate challenge will be our ability to test assumptions and hear what the beneficiaries of justice believe to be important.

Chapter 3

Transitional Justice After September 11

A New Rapport with Evil

Pierre Hazan

Michel Foucault (2001) emphasizes that the methods of producing truth are contingent on the epochs in which they are devised. Transitional justice (TJ), in that it is a system for regulating violence, is no exception: it is the product of its time, of an ideological vision and a philosophy of history that the attacks on September 11, 2001, and the Bush administration's subsequent "war on terror" have shattered. In the following lines, I will analyze transitional justice's rapport with violence and history to better decode the effects of the break that was September 11 on local conflicts, in particular in Uganda, Sudan, Lebanon, Afghanistan, and Morocco. To sum up what I will demonstrate later, the so-called war on terror has used TJ mechanisms, when they fitted strategic goals, independently of the local priorities of the populations affected by the violence. The axioms of TJ, which were supposed to contribute to the rule of law, foster a human rights culture, promote national reconciliation, heal trauma, and bring closure, were too often misused.

Transitional justice mechanisms are the products of a complex set of variables determined by a dialectical process between local and international factors. The establishment of the South African Truth and Reconciliation Commission (TRC) and the creation of the International Tribunal for Former Yugoslavia (ICTY) would have been unthinkable during the Cold War. South Africa was one of the many places of confrontation between East and West, preventing any peaceful transition during the Cold War. Likewise, the Soviet Union would have vetoed the establishment of any international criminal tribunal in its sphere of influence during the bipolar era. By the same token, the ICC Rome Statute would have been difficult to envisage after 9/11. The international campaign, which launched hundreds if not thousands of NGOs from the South and the North and mobilized the support of the media and public opinion, weakened after the attacks against the twin towers and the subsequent "war on terror." Indeed, transitional justice is the product of a specific time in history.

Transitional justice stems from a paradigm of transition developed by a few American political scientists (O'Donnell and Schmitter 1986) in the mid-1980s. The Reagan administration had made the paradigm of transition its own by celebrating "the worldwide democratic revolution" then unfolding. The concept of transition rapidly entered into the interpretation of the new international reality. It sought to take account of the multiple and heterogeneous processes by which, practically simultaneously, states as different as Mauritania, Mongolia, and El Salvador were experiencing political liberalization and some hundred countries seemed to be "in transition" toward democracy. The collapse of communist regimes symbolized by the fall of the Berlin Wall established the paradigm of transition and marks the triumph of political and economic liberalism. Thomas Carothers (2002) has demonstrated how the transition paradigm became the prism through which to understand the political changes occurring in some one hundred countries, which had, most of the time, little in common. The speech titled "Toward a New World Order" by President George H. W. Bush to a joint session of the U.S. Congress on September 11, 1990, not only consecrates the geopolitical rupture that is the end of the Cold War but also marks the fact that in the analysis of international relations, "the congenital evangelism of liberalism gets the upper hand on the negative anthropology of realism," in the words of Ariel Colonomos (2005). This optimism was found at the heart of the new system of thought about the idea of political and moral progress of societies. It was on a par with the development of multilateralism, the rising power of NGOs, and the short-lived renewal of the United Nations. It was in this specific context that the concept of transitional justice was born, at the beginning of the 1990s. It drew a new rapport of society with evil at the same time that it articulated a new rapport between politics and morality. In practice, transitional justice was soon established as a new discipline taught in universities, feeding on experiences of democratic transition conducted in Latin America, South Africa, and central and eastern Europe. These processes of transition also translate into the values of the new world order, when the United States was at the height of its power.

Under the auspices of President H. W. Bush and the Pentagon, a new representation of war appeared during the first Gulf War in 1991: that of a "clean war," described in terms borrowed from medicine ("surgical strikes"), with the development of new arms of precision. In fact, the West would see few images of the 200,000 Iraqis killed during that war. The American authorities at that time exported the idea of a war that is aseptic, technological, abstract, quasi-virtual. This image of a clean war carried the myth of management of warfare as if taken from administrative science. The Clinton administration, entering in 1993, soon adopted the doctrine of "zero dead," a myth of war as painless, at least for the United States. In the realm of fantasy, there is even the idea that war—by definition, the unleashing of violence—can be, from now on, managed without human cost, at least for the "civilized" nation. This idea of conflict and post-conflict management proved central to the development of transitional justice. It established, in fact, the idea that mass crimes could similarly be managed by a "toolbox" so as to reconcile divided societies.[1] This approach fit into the strategic reflection of the Democratic administration, which intended to lean essentially on nonmilitary means. The political analyst Joseph Nye (2004) calls this strategy "soft power," that is, the capacity of the United States, "the Benevolent Hegemon," to influence other states by the seduction and attraction of the American model, rather than by the brutal imposition of its own order. The moral imperative—the rhetoric of human rights and humanitarian action—was promoted in the new U.S. strategic doctrine:

> Promoting democracy does more than foster our ideals. It advances our interests because we know that the larger the pool of democracies, the better off we, and the entire community of nations, will be. Democracies create free markets that offer economic opportunity, make for more reliable trading partners and are far less likely to wage war on one another. (The White House 1996)

The Clinton administration was not always consistent in applying its doctrine. Let us recall its staunch opposition at the UN Security Council in order to prevent a military intervention aiming at stopping the genocide in Rwanda.[2] Nevertheless, it was in the perspective of its strategic doctrine that the Clinton administration developed new forms of the regulation of violence that would become the dominant features of transitional justice.

First, there was what we might call the judicialization of international relations. The charge of crimes against humanity was used for the first time during the Nuremberg Trials. It postulated already, in the name of common humanity, the limitless character of justice. But the political context of the Cold War blocked the development of international criminal law. It was only after the end of the Cold War that crimes against humanity attained a central place in international relations. It became doubly synchronous with the new geopolitical environment. First, crimes against humanity, by the revulsion they provoke, legitimized the construction of a globalized world and participated, by this fact, in the elaboration of a global judicial order. It is only through American political, financial, and logistic support that the international tribunals of ex-Yugoslavia and Rwanda would develop in the 1990s (as well as the hybrid tribunals of Sierra Leone and Cambodia in this millennium).

This judicialization criminalized the enemy and placed the United States on the side of "good." Crimes against humanity participated in setting new political and judicial boundaries between "civilization" and "barbarity," for the term *crime against humanity* served in the ideological construction of the new post–Cold War enemy. The Cold War functioned according to common rules (nuclear dissuasion, the red telephone). The enemy was recognized as a rational adversary with whom one could do business (the ABM treaty, for example). The metaphor of chess reflected the East–West confrontation, as well as the rules common to both players. In the post–Cold War world, the enemy was no longer the adversary of old. He had become a delinquent, as shown in the introduction of a new category of state, "the rogue state," whose chiefs are considered to be dangerous criminals, blood-thirsty warlords, and predators like Charles Taylor, deserving only punishment. This transformation of the adversary into a criminal permitted, in the name of protecting humanity, intervention beyond state boundaries. This is the essential component of transitional justice, which by means of indictments participates in the construction of a new world order. It was this new ideological environment, based on an alleged new morality of international politics, that contributed to the development of specific TJ mechanisms in Latin America, in central and eastern Europe, and in South Africa. But the rising appeal of transitional justice was not simply the result of a top-down effect of the values and of the new geostrategic map. The local experiments of TJ gave a concrete and innovative substance to the rather abstract concept of transition.

Second, there developed what we might call the diplomacy of repentance: the moral dimension of U.S. foreign policy played a strategic role in establishing its *soft power*. It participated in the construction of a Manichean representation of history, which is no longer seen in terms of a power struggle, but in categories of "Good versus Evil." This moralism also translates into the possibility of redemption through the expression of repentance. In fact, President Clinton was the head of state who apologized the most for policies carried out by his or her country. He apologized for the abandonment of the Tutsi people during the genocide of 1994, for the support of Latin American dictatorships, for the deportation and enslavement of millions of Africans, and for the racist experiments at Tuskegee, during which hundreds of African Americans infected with syphilis were deliberately left without treatment. Following President Clinton, a long list of heads of state and government, in turn, apologized for the crimes of history, to the point that the Nigerian writer and 1986 Nobel Prize winner Wole Soyinka (1999) wrote that "the world seems seized by a frenzy of excuses." Nations saw fit to issue apologies to peoples and countries they had wronged (see Gibney, Howard-Hassmann, Coicaud, and Steiner 2008). Indeed, in the 2001 World Conference Against Racism, the Durban Declaration and Program of Action adopted by consensus by the UN Member States, recommended to issue apologies "with a view to closing those dark chapters in history."[3]

Third, there were reparations for historical crimes. President Clinton committed his administration at the highest level (Secretary of State Madeleine Albright, Under-Secretary Stuart Eizenstat, and former president of the Federal Reserve Bank Paul Volcker) to forcing a settlement between the Jewish American NGOs (in particular, the World Jewish Congress [WJC]) and the Swiss banks concerned with the dormant accounts of Jews assassinated by the Nazis over a half-century earlier. Clinton's support of the WJC was notable in the organization of an unprecedented international conference (The Washington Conference on Holocaust-era assets hosted by the State Department in December 1998 and attended by forty-three governments), where the question of compensation was raised for acts that occurred fifty years before. Negotiations with the Swiss banks were settled with a financial agreement of US$1.25 billion dollars awarded to the survivors and their families. But above all, this compensation process contributed to the emergence of language, values, and norms that would unleash a torrent of claims from other groups persecuted in history.

Through a number of mechanisms, transitional justice bears a promise of reconciliation for people that war has divided or who have been harshly oppressed. Transitional justice, in essence, says that mass crimes constitute a blood debt that one part of society owes another. This blood debt must be paid to break the cycle of vengeance and violence.[4] The debt, by the act of recognition that it creates, builds a bridge between the past and the future. It constitutes this time of transition that, through recognition, leads to the establishment of a state of law, democracy, and, in the end, the guarantee of nonrepetition of the terrible acts that have occurred. In other words, by the political and juridical recognition of crime and by eventual financial compensation, the blood debt is paid. The damages of history are thus collectable. In a vocabulary of bookkeeping, transitional justice thus promises the settling of accounts. It refuses the inevitability of the irreparable, the irreconcilable in history. A product of political liberalism, transitional justice hammers out a new relationship of society with evil: it claims to answer both to the crimes of the past and to the violence of the present; it intends to participate in the healing of society and the reestablishment of a state of law and democracy. It claims, also, to redress history by moralizing it, repairing it through trials, and by commemoration and memorial commissions. There is hubris in transitional justice, reflected in the extraordinary optimism that—in spite of the Rwandan genocide in 1994 and the crimes committed in Bosnia (1992–95)—prevails between the fall of the Berlin Wall and the fall of the twin towers in New York, inspired by the theses of Francis Fukuyama concerning the end of history.

To describe society's new relationship with evil, the French philosopher Jacques Derrida (1999), has forged the neologism of *mondialatinisation*, that is, a cultural Christianization of the world according to the forms of the Roman Catholic Church, especially the idea of sin and repentance. But even more than mondialatinisation, the "ameriglobalization" of the world must be acknowledged. For the Clinton administration has played a decisive role in the development of transitional justice. The contribution of Nelson Mandela and the experience of the South African TRC, the role of Vaclav Havel in the Czech Republic, or the Chilean and Argentinean experiences in Latin America should in no way be minimized. Let us emphasize, however, one point: these processes, whether they concerned the end of communism, apartheid, or military dictatorships, all fit into an ideological vision in keeping with the establishment of a pluralistic democracy and a state of law as well as the neoliberal globalization conducted by the United States. This last point requires a revocation of the place of the state in society and international relationships. In other words, transitional justice marks both the passage toward democracy of certain states and a new organization of the world under American leadership.

In this context of neoliberal globalization, transitional justice plays an essential role in limiting state power. It undermines the foundation of national sovereignty. How? By developing a juridical vision that breaks with the traditional approach of law linked until now to state territory and to a particular time fixed by prescription for all crimes, including crimes against humanity and war crimes. The Westphalian world is characterized by closure—geographic, with the existence of borders, and temporal, with the statute of limitations, including for the most abominable crimes. The German philosopher of law Carl Schmitt holds, besides, that the localization of law in a concrete order is a condition indispensable to its realization. Transitional justice breaks with this organization of the world. It is, by definition, post-Westphalian: the imprescriptibility of crimes against humanity and the development of international and transnational criminal justice open—at least in theory—toward an unlimited world.

What Changed on September 11?

Transitional justice is based, as we have seen, on a liberal philosophy of history. The war against terror clears away this vision of history's natural progression toward democracy. The emphasis on security, brought by the necessity to wage a war "unlike any other we have seen" (Bush 2001), puts an end to the eschatological dimension of transitional justice. The concept of transition—the definition of which was always problematic—no longer appears to be an explanatory political category. Multilateralism has given way to the unilateralism of the Bush administration, marked by military intervention in Iraq, fed by a civil war that has provoked the death of hundreds of thousands of Iraqi civilians and over three thousand American soldiers.

The so-called war on terror also marks the defeat of *soft power* and the return of *hard power*. Democracy must sometimes be exported through force of arms, is the essence of the message of the neoconservatives. With September 11, the security paradigm takes charge and brings with it an erosion of standards of international humanitarian law. This undermines the foundation of transitional justice, for TJ functions according to the rituals of purification based on trial, whether in its real form (national, international, or transnational justice), or in its metaphorical form stripped of any penal sanction (truth commissions). The war against terror puts into question the centrality of law, even if law is used on a regular basis to demonize the adversary. For example, the trial of Saddam Hussein, which scarcely fit the criteria of a "fair trial," as

Human Rights Watch (2006) pointed out, had "serious administrative, procedural and substantive legal defects," such as "regular failure to disclose key
evidence . . . ; lapses of judicial demeanor that undermined the apparent impartiality of the presiding judge . . .".[5]

Violence now appears as an essential agent in the protection of "civilization." The obsession with security promoted by the Bush White House reinterpreted as "laxist" the ban on torture and the Geneva Conventions, the base
of humanitarian law. The radical opposition of George W. Bush to the ICC
underlined the return to an intransigent conception of sovereignty.

What made the Bush administration exceptional was the radicalism of its
unilateralism coated in moralism, what Pierre Hassner (2002) called "Wilson-
ism in boots." But as Michael Ignatieff (2005) explores in *American Exceptionalism*, neoconservative ideology, although extreme, has roots in the American
political culture:

> For most Americans human rights are American values writ large, the export
> version of its own Bill of Rights.
>
> But if human rights are American values writ large, then, paradoxically,
> Americans have nothing to learn from international human rights. In the
> messianic American moral project, America teaches the meaning of liberty to
> the world; it does not learn from others. Messianism does help to explain the
> paradox of exceptional multilateralism. Indeed, it suggests that American ex-
> ceptionalism is not so paradoxical after all: since 1945, the United States has
> explicitly sought to fulfill its messianic mission at the lowest possible cost to its
> national interest and with the lowest possible impingement upon its own do-
> mestic rights system. (2005:14)

The Bush administration was more extreme in doing that. The ICC example is
emblematic: the Clinton administration signed the ICC treaty, but with no
intention to ratify it. The Bush administration un-signed the ICC treaty and
tried—with counterproductive effects—to sanction whose who did, except its
NATO allies.

The controversy over the ICC that pitted the Bush administration against
Europeans illustrates two radically different concepts of the relation between
law and politics. The ICC incarnates the subordination of politics to the universal reign of reason. The new court is founded on the conviction that "soft
power" and the law in particular can domesticate the violence of conflicts and

thus regulate international tensions. The Bush administration considered this pure illusion. In a provocative article illustrating the latter administration's approach, the neoconservative Robert Kagan jeers at the "Nervous Nellies" of Europe who, in contrast to the Americans, have deserted the battlefield. Kagan (2002) crystallizes this dialectic between soft and hard power with a telling metaphor: Europeans, he says, come from the feminine planet of Venus, while Americans are from the virile world of Mars.

Still in this neoconservative vision, the alliance with repressive regimes is from now on interpreted as a strategic necessity in the name of the global war for the "defense of freedom." Realpolitik has, of course, always forced alliances with nondemocratic regimes. Famously, but with relative success, in the 1980s, the U.S. ambassador to the UN, Jeanne Kirkpatrick, delineated the difference between authoritarian regimes (i.e., a code word for military dictatorships in Latin America), which the United States should support, and totalitarian regimes (i.e., communist regimes), which the United States should oppose. Between the Cold War and the war on terror, the moral justification to forge alliances with repressive regimes has changed. Contrary to the war on terror, the enemy was seen as rational during the bipolar era, and it was hence possible to make "deals" (illustrated by the US–USSR ABM treaty and the period of détente) perceived as impossible with the jihadists.

After September 11, the struggle against impunity, the core element of transitional justice is put into question. It is seen according to the return on investment it might produce, measured in short-term military or political gains. Of course, strategic legalism existed prior to 9/11. But, as Stanley Hoffmann (in Ignatieff 2005) observes, whereas the lesson of past realists (Niebuhr, Morgenthau, Kennan, even Kissinger) had been the kind of discerning prudence and moderation Thucydides had praised, the new voices are exceptional in their paean to American might; many of the more traditional realists, in academia and in government, are worried by the excesses of the present ones, so much closer to Alcibiades than to Pericles.

After 9/11, the narrower definition of national interest, the return to hard power, and the marginalization of humanitarian law engineered by the Bush administration created a new international environment. The whole concept of transition was shattered. The fact that the United States, the only superpower of the time, under the Bush administration decided to emancipate from some of the constraints of international humanitarian law—that ironically the

United States since 1945 enshrined in networks in regional and international organizations—profoundly affected TJ mechanisms in many countries, such as Uganda, Sudan, Lebanon, Afghanistan, and Morocco.

Localized Justice and the War on Terror

The conflict between the Museveni government and the LRA in Uganda is emblematic of the war on terror's impact. The expectations of the populations in northern Uganda affected by the war, especially given the fact that the Ugandan armed forces were also responsible for crimes against Acholi civilians, were discarded by the Ugandan government, the United States, and the ICC. Three months after 9/11, the Bush administration put the Ugandan rebel movement, the Lord's Resistance Army (LRA), on its list of terrorist organizations.[6] There is no doubt that the LRA was the author of horrific mass crimes. But the vast majority of them had been committed long before 9/11, at a time when the LRA was not classified as "terrorist" by the U.S. government. This decision, aimed at criminalizing the LRA with the Bush administration's new catchall concept of the war on terror, paved the way to the first indictments ever made by the ICC (against LRA leaders). The fact that the indictments did not materialize in any arrests was of secondary importance, as the objective was mostly political: in criminalizing the LRA, the U.S. government wanted to strengthen its ally, the Museveni government, and to target the Islamic Sudanese government. The Bashir government in Sudan was on the State Department's list of countries supporting terrorist groups, including the LRA. Bashir was also seen as overwhelmingly responsible for the crimes committed against the Darfurians. In fact, the Bush administration, as Stephen Kostas (in Totten and Markusen 2006) points out, was a prisoner of internal contradictions: with the mass crimes happening in Darfur, the Bush administration did not want to experience "another Rwanda," which had hurt President Clinton a few years earlier. It wanted also to demonstrate that it could speak on human rights issues, at a time when its legitimacy was being jeopardized by the treatment of detainees in Guantanamo and Abu Ghraib. But at the same time, President Bush did not want to send American troops to stop mass crimes.[7] That is why, despite the radical ideological hostility of the Bush administration toward the ICC, the latter intervened—with American support—to indict a Sudanese minister and possibly the Sudanese president and others for mass crimes committed in Darfur.[8] In other words, one of the instruments of TJ—the ICC—in the context of Uganda and Sudan dovetailed with the internal constraints of the

Bush administration and with the objectives of the war on terror, with the result that the combination of the ICC intervention, the deployment of African peacekeepers, and outside pressures was able to limit but not to end the massive human rights violations in Darfur.

Indeed, in divided societies, where the direction of transition is still unclear (transition to a new conflict or to a less volatile peace?), the encompassing TJ vision of moral and political progress is disconnected from the selective use of TJ mechanisms. The Hariri tribunal in Lebanon provides a striking example of a TJ instrument used to affect the regional balance of power. The United States and France were the key architects of UN Security Council Resolution 1757 of May 2007, which established the principle of a "hybrid" tribunal destined to judge for the first time the perpetrators of the "terrorist attacks" that killed former Prime Minister Rafiq Hariri and other prominent Lebanese personalities in 2005. The aim of this "antiterrorist" tribunal was political: the struggle against impunity was seen as instrumental in order to target the Syrian regime and to limit its interference in Lebanon. Paris and Washington perceived the Assad regime as being the mastermind of these murders, and more generally as hostile to French and U.S. interests. But no country—including France and the United States—has ever denounced the amnesty laws that granted impunity to the Lebanese warlords responsible for some horrendous massacres committed during the civil war (1975–91), which claimed 200,000 lives, warlords who (at least a number of them) are still active politically today. This selectivity in the struggle against impunity increased the already existing polarization of Lebanese society, both camps reading the hybrid tribunal in purely political terms, either to deplore it or to show satisfaction regarding the use of a legal weapon on Syria, regardless of such supposed virtues of TJ as promoting national reconciliation.

Afghanistan is another example par excellence of how the TJ toolkit could be used or discarded according to the strategic objectives of various governments, independently of the desire of the population. Neither the authorities nor the UN (which is profoundly implicated)—nor even more so, the United States, which has deployed thousands of soldiers and is the foremost political supporter of President Karzaï—have opened the slightest inquiry against the perpetrators of war crimes and crimes against humanity. In fact, since the late 1970s Afghanistan has experienced a continuous state of civil war punctuated by foreign occupations in the forms of the 1979 Soviet invasion and the 2001 U.S.-led invasion that toppled the Taliban government. Warlords from all sides committed gross human rights violations, such as mass bombardments of villages, arbitrary detentions, summary executions of prisoners, torture, rape of women and children, forced disappearances, and massacres. Despite this grim history, the United States and, subsequently, the UN, have even been active agents in the process of co-opting the warlords to political power in the idea that this alliance would allow them to hit the Taliban. Until the 2009 elections, there was no significant pressure on the Kabul government from the United States to sideline warlords, war criminals and human rights abusers who hold positions of authority in the central or local government or in the security forces. In January 2005, the UN even buried a report that it had itself ordered, a report accusing Afghan parliamentarians of being responsible for massacre and torture (Walsh 2006). This 220-page report prepared by the UN High Commissioner for Human Rights detailed atrocities committed by communists, mujahadeen, Soviet, and Taliban fighters, over twenty-three years of conflict. It named leading Afghan politicians and officials accused of orchestrating massacres, torture, mass rape, and other war crimes. In its report presented in 2004 to the UN General Assembly, Cherif Bassiouni, the UN's independent expert on Afghanistan, writes: "Afghan people find it particularly disturbing to see the leaders of such groups (warlords and local commanders) who are known to have committed gross violations of fundamental human rights, war crimes and crimes against humanity, benefit from impunity, and even become part of what is deemed the legitimate government" (Bassiouni 2004:14). The sole consequence of this report was the termination of the mandate of the UN independent expert Cherif Bassiouni under pressure from the Bush administration, according to him.

The Afghan Independent Human Rights Commission (AIHRC 2005) also judges that the policy of impunity has contributed not to consolidating but to weakening the government and to handicapping the future of the country. "We are of the view," it states, "that a total lack of accountability, and an approach that allows anyone into positions in power, without examination of their tendencies to commit atrocities, is a threat to Afghanistan's long-term potential to create a peaceful and stable environment for its citizens" (AIHRC:43). This policy of impunity has proven to be counterproductive as much in military terms as in political and constitutes a dangerous precedent for violations of rules of international humanitarian law.[9] Despite the presence since the end of 2001 of tens of thousands of NATO soldiers and the mobilization of the Afghan army, the Kabul government hardly controls the country. Thousands of civilians have perished, and more continue to die.

This is not to say that the struggle against impunity—one of the main assumptions of TJ theory—targeting the warlords would have been a magic wand immediately solving all the security problems of Afghanistan and building a democracy in the short term. But it is difficult to imagine that it would have produced worse results than the actual situation. This is also the analysis of the Afghan Independent Human Rights Commission. Its report, "A Call for Justice" (2005:17), was based on a national consultation that surveyed the preferences of 6,000 Afghans living in thirty-two out of the thirty-four provinces, as well as refugees living in Pakistan and Iran. It claims that the vast majority of the population (76 percent) wanted the warlords to answer to their crimes in the near future, thinking it would increase security. As is rightly pointed out in this volume by Harvey Weinstein et al, surveys made in a war environment raise difficult methodological questions. But empirical evidence demonstrates that a significant part of the Afghan population saw impunity as endangering their environment and their lives. Their motivation to support the idea of prosecuting warlords was pragmatic: accountability for past and present crimes was seen as the best survival strategy. The local priorities of the people affected by the violence and the national and international actors were decoupled.

It is striking to note that the Ugandan and Afghan cases illustrate how the war on terror has affected localized TJ in a radically different way, either by soliciting or by discarding it. In both cases, security objectives—locally defined as overriding priorities—were not met. It is also striking to note that the populations directly affected by the conflict had expectations that were never taken into account. And their preferences—although it must be stressed that none of these communities or societies have a monolithic view on amnesty or prosecution—were determined by pragmatic choices about daily survival, not by the promises of transitional justice.

Morocco: The Truth Commission and the "War on Terror"

The context of the war on terror also affected the process of Morocco's TRC. It colored the process of its creation, its mandate, its functioning, its conclusions, its perception by public opinion, and its impact. In fact, the credibility of this truth commission never stopped being affected by the context, at once national and international, of the war on terror. The Commission began operations when Morocco had become one of the principal battlefields in the war against terror after the Casablanca bombings of May 16, 2002, which killed forty-five people, and the Madrid bombing perpetrated by Moroccan citizens in March 2003, which killed two hundred persons and injured a thousand more. According to U.S. Major General Jonathan S. Gration (2006), Director of Strategy, Policy, and Assessments for the US European Command (EUCOM), Morocco and all of North Africa "is a strategic region in the war against terrorism. We consider it to be a regional threat whose shock waves can affect the stability of Europe and Africa."[10] Some top Moroccan officials in the Interior Ministry wanted to use the TRC "to fight terrorism," conducting the war on two fronts: the "hard war," the repressive dismantling of cells, and the "soft war," which consists of bringing the population over to our side. The TRC was one of the elements of this "soft war." In this perspective, the TRC was part of a larger operation to win the trust of the people, thereby shrinking the core of "terrorist" sympathizers. In practice, however, the use of the TRC in the antiterrorist "soft war" led to considerable difficulties, including contradictions between the security rationale and the democratic agenda. The government preferred to reassure the agents of repression engaged in dismantling Salafist networks. The monarchy guaranteed them not only impunity, but also the possibility of refusing to collaborate with the TRC, a prerogative that they employed widely. For the Palace, the Commission's objective of "truth" was not allowed to destabilize the security apparatus in such a "sensitive" period. The limitations imposed on the TRC's mandate weakened the Commission's effectiveness and, ultimately, the credibility of its work.[11]

In Morocco, the idea of establishing a truth and reconciliation commission emerged initially from a wide array of NGOs gathered around the "Forum for Truth and Justice" for human rights violations committed over decades, in particular under Hassan II, father of the current king, Mohammed VI. This bottom-up demand on the regime got an unexpected answer. The king (with the support of some human rights defenders) created a TRC by royal decree, without any form of parliamentary or political consultation, to investigate human rights violations committed since the independence of the country in 1956 to 1999.[12] This bottom-up demand transformed into a top-down process—according to Article 23 of the constitution, the king is of divine nature—had profound and lasting consequences for the TRC.

The fact that the political parties and the society were sidelined created suspicion of the TRC, although half of the commissioners were former political prisoners and the Commission was headed by one of them. The mandate of the TRC was also constrained by the war on terror. The most obvious limitation was the impunity given to former torturers. During the public hearings, their names could not be disclosed: this was a precondition for the victims to testify (see Hazan 2006, 2007). From the viewpoint of the Palace, the apparatus of state security was seen as essential to ensure the stability of the regime and should not be weakened by direct accusations.

Victims were divided on the value of the TRC. Some of them were anxious to testify, others were opposed to this body. The first group felt that the monarchy was acknowledging their suffering. The second group deemed that the TRC was a whitewashing exercise by the Palace. This dual perspective reflected the division in the local human rights community, and beyond it, of the whole society. In fact, perceptions of the Moroccan TRC varied greatly, depending on a wide spectrum of political, ideological, social, geographical, generational, and moral factors. In some communities, such as Figuig, close to the Algerian border, the public hearing of the TRC mobilized the local population, which seemed—in the absence of a study—in large part to feel vindicated by this acknowledgment of the wrongs of the past that hurt this community so much. On the other hand, the TRC was unable to hold a public hearing in Layoune due to the current low-level conflict over the sovereignty in Western Sahara. The pro-independentist Sarawhis were hostile to a TRC created by a monarchy they did not recognize as theirs—neither did they recognize its claim that Western Sahara was an integral part of Morocco. In other regions, most Islamists were critical of a TRC that was investigating human rights violations of the past, but not human rights violations committed by the state apparatus in the context of the war on terror.

How can such a society subscribe to a democratization process, of which the TRC is the symbol, if, in the name of the war against terror, the security forces carry out mass arrests (over three thousand Islamists were arrested after the attacks on Casablanca) marked by abuse and sometimes serious blunders? One of the commissioners, Abdelhay Moudden, noted, "People tell us: how can you investigate the past when, even if they are not comparable to the past, human rights abuses continue and are even encouraged by our American allies?" (see Hazan 2007:177). In practice, the security rationale of the war on terror proves to be not compatible with a concern for transparency and accountability for earlier human rights violations, even if the Moroccan TRC did achieve some positive results. Indeed, the TRC managed to give legitimacy to the word of victims of the decades of repression. It identified hundreds of bodies of the "disappeared." It paid reparations to individual victims and communities that had been victims of the repression. And it proposed reforms that, if put in place, would transform Morocco into a constitutional monarchy.

The Moroccan case is thus paradigmatic of the effects of the war on terror on transitional justice. The TRC was able to break some new ground, but its ambition, its perception, and ultimately its credibility, has been affected by the international environment.

Conclusion

The political failure of "Bushism," in the wars waged today in Iraq and Afghanistan as well as in its methods of intervention, is no doubt historically dated, as confirmed by the first decisions taken by President Obama to close Guantanamo in the near future, to shut the remaining CIA network of secret prisons around the world, to ban abusive interrogation techniques, and to apply the Geneva Conventions.

As a result of the Bush era and the post-9/11 international environment, transitional justice no longer represents the hope for change and global democracy that it did in the 1990s. After the Berlin Wall crumbled, western democracies appeared to be a triumphant political model. Today, this is no longer the case. American hyperpower is now contested, and not only by Al-Qaida. Capitalist but autocratic powers such as China and Russia are emerging; so are India, Brazil, and other countries. The European Union, in theory a standardbearer of the values of human rights and international justice, remains a political midget. This geostrategic remapping is affecting the values and norms of transitional justice.

The writer and concentration camp survivor Jean Améry reminds us that law seeks to operate a moral inversion of time. This is also the ambition of transitional justice. In elaborating a new narrative system, in inviting participation in the writing of a new account of justice, transitional justice invites society to seize the crime that has occurred in order to renew itself. Does this ambition remain justified given the new international environment? It does. Transitional justice cannot be reduced to strategic legalism. It remains relevant in many contexts. Even if it is no longer the expression of a new world order, it represents useful methods for managing violence in specific conflicts. But these mechanisms of justice are useful only as long as the local populations feel ownership. Too often, unfortunately, the short-term political and strategic interests of big powers, which often coincide with the views of governments in conflict zones, override local priorities and discard the question of ownership of a political process. The war on terror gravely accentuated this trend. Too many times, transitional justice has been used to complement hard military power, while both ignoring the priorities of populations affected by the violence and perverting the mechanisms allegedly used to serve their interests.

PART II

Local Engagements

Chapter 4

An Acknowledged Failure

Women, Voice, Violence, and the South African Truth and Reconciliation Commission

Fiona C. Ross

Grandmother pleads to be heard. I have not spoken, she cries. I ask only for a humble silence in which I can be heard. You have said that a woman cannot speak.... Can a woman not speak the word that oppresses her heart, grows heavy on her tongue, heavy, pulling her to the ground? I do not speak and my word has grown roots on my tongue filling my mouth. Will my word grow into a tree while I water it every day with silence?

—*Yvonne Vera*, Under the Tongue

In many ways, women's experiences in the political conflicts of the past are not evident in these summaries.... We have not been able to do justice to them. This remains unfinished business.

—*Report vol. 7:7*

The fruits of our liberation have not reached many of our women.

—President Thabo Mbeki, Women's Day speech, August 9, 2006

The more I look at my life as a woman, the more I take the stance of a startled anthropologist.

—*Susan Griffin*, Made from This Earth

Since the inception of democracy in 1994, South Africa has made considerable progress in securing women's rights. The Gender Commission, constitutionally established, acts as a watchdog over policy; women's organizations scrutinize annual budgets to ensure gender equity; gendered affirmative action and equal opportunity processes have been established. Yet, notwithstanding the fact that one-third of parliamentarians and some 40 percent of Cabinet members are women, gender inequality and violence against women have been identified as major hindrances to true democracy in South Africa (Mbeki 2006; PCAS 2006). South African media routinely describe violence against women, particularly rape, as being of epidemic proportions.[1] I offer some data on rape here to give a sense of scale, fully aware of the paucity of figures in the face of violence.

Helen Moffett states that "South Africa has higher levels of rape of women and children than anywhere else in the world not at war or embroiled in civil conflict" (2006: 129);[2] at least one in three women will be raped during her lifetime. Most rapes are committed by people known to the victims: trust and betrayal are woven together in the act of violence. At the time of the hearings of South Africa's Truth and Reconciliation Commission, Rape Crisis reported that a woman was raped every thirty-six seconds (cited in Shifman, Madlala-Routledge, and Smith 1997). Approximately 51,500 cases of rape were reported to the police in the period 1995–96 and almost 52,000 in 1997–98 (Rape Crisis 2006).[3] Rates of rape have not decreased since then: according to official police statistics, 55,000 cases of rape were reported in South Africa in 2004–5 (SAPS 2005). Rape Crisis (2006) reports that every day 147 women are raped in South Africa. It is estimated that only one in nine rape victims ever reports the crime, and of these cases, only 7 percent are successfully prosecuted (OneinNine.org.za 2006). Approximately 40 percent of reported rapes in the late 1990s were committed against children under the age of eighteen (Statistics South Africa 2000:2), usually by people close to them, including family members and teachers.

The trial of South Africa's Deputy President (now President) Jacob Zuma on charges of rape in 2006 focused public attention on sexual violence and women's rights in South Africa in a way that the acclaimed Truth and Reconciliation Commission did not. Despite its rhetoric of "the whole truth" and "national healing," the Commission's human rights violations committee, which collected statements and held public hearings between 1996 and 1998, found it very difficult to access statements about sexual violence. Only 500 of approximately 33,000 cases of human rights violations concerned sexual violence, and only 40 percent of statements where a deponent's gender is given concerned women (Report 1998 vol. 4:295). The Commission recognized that it had been unsuccessful in relation to women's experiences of violence. The Zuma trial, on the other hand, unleashed considerable public discussion about gendered violence, particularly the stakes of speaking about rape. Here, I explore some of the complexities of silence and speech in relation to sexual violence and questions of justice. Drawing on Zuma's trial, the Commission's work, and Yvonne Vera's novel *Under the Tongue*, I consider their implications for projects that aim to liberate through giving voice to experience.

Late in 2005, almost ten years after the Truth and Reconciliation Commission was signed into law, a young woman accused Jacob Zuma, then Deputy-President of South Africa, Deputy-President of the ANC, leader of the Moral Regeneration Movement, and Chancellor of the University of Zululand, of rape. It was a high-profile case: Zuma was anticipated to be South Africa's next president. The complainant is legally entitled not to be named: identified in the press as Khwezi, she was frequently referred to as "the accuser"; a misnomer that says much about local perceptions of what the trial was actually about. Zuma was a close family friend, known to her since her childhood in exile. He was so close that she regularly confided in him, sought his advice, and called him *umalume* (uncle).[4] During the trial, she presented him as a father figure. Categories are confused: friend, father figure, uncle, deputy-president, potential lover, rapist, accused. Friend, daughter figure, niece, activist, potential lover, victim, complainant.

The trial was controversial. The appellant was accused of seeking to sabotage Zuma's political career. She was subject to public opprobrium. Her lengthy cross-examination, described by Presiding Judge Willem Van der Merwe as "thorough" and "fair" (2006:38), was felt by many critics to be cruel and humiliating. In a controversial legal decision, the judge allowed her sexual and psychiatric past to be made public.[5] Zuma was not asked to testify similarly about his past. At Khwezi's request, her legal counsel did not object to questions posed during cross-examination, explaining that she wanted to get it over as quickly as possible. Many women describe their response to rape the same way. It's horrifying to suspect that the experience of testifying might echo some of the structure of the event in question, and yet this is what women report time and again.[6]

During the trial, age-old stereotypes of women were brought into play: she was presented as a harlot, a crazy woman who cries rape, a saboteur of an innocent man's career. Her representation by the defense came close to character assassination: she was portrayed as temptress, slut, devious, hysterical, mad, irrational, inconsistent. The public outcry that greeted her claims of having been raped several times was appalling. She was accused of being a serial accuser, of inviting sex and then calling it rape, of entrapment. Her statement that she had been violated as a child in the ANC camps in exile was greeted by some sections of the public with disbelief, despite regular media reports of child rape.[7] The trial generated enormous public reaction. The media carried daily updates, expert opinion, letters, open radio debates. Supporters on both sides—men and women—ringed the court where the hearing was held. Police were called in to control the crowds. Some of Zuma's supporters carried placards that said, "Kill the bitch."

The trial made it clear that South Africa has made progress in making it possible to speak of sexual violence.[8] As Khwezi noted, "In our mothers' time, they could not just tell about rape. In a case like this, they would have just been quiet. They would not have told. It was just not an option. Who would they have told and what would have been the response?" (Cavanagh and Mabele 2006). Yet it also reveals how dangerous it is to speak of rape: for all the optimism inherent in her evaluation, Khwezi's own situation was and remains precarious. She had found it very difficult to continue with the trial; she was defined and judged by others throughout; she was angered and hurt by the ways in which her life was interpreted by the defense, the media, public opinion, and in the court's judgment. Her home was burgled twice; she received death threats; during and after the trial she was part of a witness protection program. Fearing for her safety, she left South Africa after the trial. She has taken a new identity in another country. We are unlikely to hear from her again. In asserting her voice, her body disappeared. It is as though her life has ended. For her there is indeed an undoing of the world in the aftermath of violence, a literal leave-taking from the familiar, and a symbolic death. Zuma, acquitted in May 2006, has been restored to his former political positions and, despite another court case,[9] has become President of the Republic.

While there are considerable differences between a trial and a truth commission, common to both are the difficulties of finding a language in which to speak of violence. Ten years prior to the Zuma trial, the South African Commission's Human Rights Violations hearings had made use of a "storytelling" methodology (Tutu 1996:7; Report 1998) in which "victims" were encouraged to narrate their experiences of violation. It anticipated that the act of speech would serve two functions: firstly, to restore to "victims" their "civil and human dignity," as the Act that brought the Commission into being describes it; and secondly, to assist in restoring a "proper" chronology, in which the past would not haunt the present or shadow the future. As one participant at a Commission-related workshop in 1996 put it, the Commission was to be "the full-stop at the end of apartheid."

Women's testimonies before the Commission were generally broader in scope than men's: they were more likely than men to describe the effects of violence on family and community life, and, according to Mark Sanders (2007), to make demands on custom. They were also more likely to testify to the reverberations of suffering through generations and through time. But, much to the Commission's alarm, and despite encouragement, women gave scant account of their own suffering or experiences of violence, least of all of sexual violation (see Goldblatt and Meintjes 1997; Ross 2003a; and Report 1998).[10] This was after the Commission, concerned that it was not gathering 'the whole truth' of women's experiences, instituted several mechanisms to ensure that women testified about their own experiences of harm, including reminding deponents to address their own hurts and hosting special 'Women's hearings' (see Report 1998 vol. 4, ch. 10; Ross 2003a). The Commission's model of truth was such that it assumed that women bore a special responsibility for talking about sexual violence. It expected that women could and should testify about it, and that they would do so under certain conditions, notably the provision of a 'safe space' within which to speak.

Volume 4, chapter 10 of the Commission's (1998) Report deals with 'women,' and volume 5 offers a set of findings about women's experiences. No similar findings are offered for men. The Commission found that

> The state was responsible for the severe ill treatment of women in custody in the form of harassment and the deliberate withholding of medical attention, food and water.
>
> Women were abused by the security forces in ways which specifically exploited their vulnerabilities as women, for example rape or the threat of rape and other forms of sexual abuse, threats against family and children, removal of children from their care, false stories about illness and/or death of family members and children, and humiliation and abuse around biological functions such as menstruation and childbirth.
>
> Women in exile, particularly those in camps, were subjected to various forms of sexual abuse and harassment, including rape. (Report 1998 vol. 5:256)

While important, the finding is problematic. It naturalizes violence in gendered terms, implying that the violence described is applicable only to women, whereas many men experienced similar abuses. It makes no mention of the ways structures of masculine power shape and reinforce social and material inequalities that endure.[11] It also does not discuss the fact that sexual violence was and remains widespread and is not confined merely to detention or camps but was and remains part of the social fabric of daily life for many.

Volume 7 of the Report acknowledges that the Commission failed in relation to women's experiences of violence, especially sexual violence:

> In many ways, women's experiences in the political conflicts of the past are not evident in these summaries. Males dominate as victims within the narrow mandate of violations examined by the Commission—killings, torture, abduction, and severe ill treatment. . . .
>
> Violations involving sexual torture are also inadequately documented in these summaries. Despite the fact that rape formed part of the fabric of political conflict in the East Rand townships and in the bloody battles in KwaZulu Natal during the early nineties, it was infrequently reported in HRV statements to the Commission. (Report 2004 vol. 7:7)

The Commission did not offer the kind of gendered perspective on violence that might have contributed to an understanding of the causes of gender violence, its patterning under apartheid, or the silences that so often accompany it. It acknowledged that women's "personal truths" could not easily be verified and that the process of social truth telling was fraught with complexities of gender, but it does not explain why its process, particularly the internationally lauded public human rights violations hearings, were so opaque to women's experiences of harm.

The Commission consistently underestimated two features of violence. Firstly, some forms of violence articulated with and were exacerbated by apartheid but have longer histories. Sexual violence is one such.[12] The Commission's temporal ambit (1960–94) precluded adequate assessment of the *longue durée* of certain forms of violence, such as sexual violence. As a result, it was unable to contextualize sexual violence within historical patterns of gendered relations or to identify the specific configurations of that relationship under apartheid.[13] The consequence was that it was unable to locate individual narratives of harm within historical accounts of patriarchies' changing forms. Understanding harm in terms of gross violations of human rights, the Commission misidentifies oppression as individual injury. Women experienced the violences of colonialism, capitalism, and apartheid and their aftermaths differently from men, but when they spoke in forms that the Commission was not legally enabled to hear, it assumed that women had not spoken, had not offered of their experience, had failed as witnesses, or had not been as affected by apartheid's violence as had men. A closer focus on the effects of colonialism and apartheid on everyday life might have offered a more credible account, one that identifies differential gender implications and outcomes and frames these in such a way that masculine experience is not offered as the norm against which women are measured. Doing so would enable a careful tracing of the systemic violence of apartheid that inscribed itself in different ways on men and women, old and young, black and white, and on the kinds of relationships and opportunities that they were able to forge from the prevailing conditions of possibility. Rather than a simple numeric accounting of gross violations of human rights and a broad description of apartheid, we would then have an historically informed assessment of gender relations over time, a record of the ways that sexual violence is embedded in changing economic and political relationships and regimes. In other words, the Commission might have offered a gender theory about apartheid violence that would have given grounds for ongoing debate and discussion and effective implementation of social and economic transformation.

Secondly, the Commission underestimated the dangers to women of testifying in public. Drawing from a model that holds that speech is cathartic and that persons are autonomous individuals with the capacity to choose freely how to engage in institutional processes, it read the absence of women's testimony of direct harm as silence caused by reticence, propriety, or lack of education about rights. It was therefore unable to deal with silences or gaps that emerged in its own historical record, even as it noted them. The remainder of the chapter deals with these aspects.

Speaking of Harm

In the discussion that follows, I take as given the positive effects of speaking about violence for those who receive adequate support. Yet, as we have seen from the Zuma trial, it is not an easy matter to speak of sexual violence, and the stakes are higher than the Commission and courts admit. One of the risks lies in the risk of fixing identities. While it has taken considerable effort by gender activists and trauma experts to make the power of rape and its traumatic effects known and to call for support and care, rape is anticipated to be the most significant feature of a life, and those who experience it are often defined thereafter entirely in its terms—the victim or survivor. There is a tendency in current discourses to assume that rape and sexual violence are limitless experiences, that there is no life (or no life worthy of being called lived) beyond them (see Sunder Rajan 1993; Mulla 2005). Most writing about rape, including the Commission's Report, treats victims as though frozen in time at the event of violence, as though they cannot move beyond it. The event of rape is presented as an ending that inaugurates a new persona. It is a reductive model that assumes a direct congruence between a particular aspect of one's experience and one's identity. The effect is to dehistoricize violence and to reify the subject.

I have explored one example of this in detail elsewhere (see Ross 2003a: 77–102; Ross 2005); here I offer a summary to illustrate. Yvonne Khutwane testified before the human rights violations hearings in Worcester in 1996. Involved in anti-apartheid activism from the 1960s, she had been arrested by the police in 1985 and held in detention, where she was assaulted and sexually abused. She fell ill with meningitis while in detention, but medical treatment was withheld for a long time before she was treated. She was released on bail, and eventually charges were dropped. Meanwhile, in her community, rumor circulated that she had betrayed others while in detention. Relationships with her political peers and community members soured, culminating in an arson attack on her home. She asked the Commission to investigate the reason for the attack, her degradation, and the reason that she had been ostracized. She later told me that she had not intended to speak of sexual violation at the hearings but was relieved that she had, and had initially received much support from her friends and neighbors for her disclosure.

Despite the fact that she asked for an investigation into communal relations, the Commission focused on the event of sexual violation as the defining feature of her testimony, and media reports on the hearings retain that framing. She was repositioned as a victim of sexual abuse, a framing that has remained constant in most of the representations of her testimony (see Ross 2003a:89–93), including in the Commission's summary of her case (Report 2004 vol. 7:204), despite the fact that she has been successful in remaining in her community since the trial in 1987, has managed to repair many relationships damaged at the time, and is an active member of her political organization, working alongside some of those who had earlier accused her of betrayal, and even running (unsuccessfully) for office in local elections.

Another example will suffice to make my point. Zanele Zingxondo testified in Beaufort West. As a young woman, she had been involved in anti-apartheid activism. At the age of nineteen, she was arrested on suspicion of having been involved in a "necklacing" murder. While in detention she was subjected to violent abuse, including sexual torture, and was threatened with rape. She told the Commission that her mother had died never truly believing her innocence, and asked for an investigation that would clear her name. The Commission's focus during the hearings was on sexual torture, and in its 1998 Report (vol. 2:192; vol. 3:446), extracts of her testimony describing sexual violence are cited. There is no discussion of the broader aspects of her case in the summary offered in volume 7 (2004:897), and no finding regarding her involvement or otherwise in the murder.

In both the case studies I've offered here, while the women described events of sexual abuse at the hands of security personnel (i.e., people outside their immediate community),[14] both requested the Commission to address issues related to their lives in community; to clear their names, to give them the grounds to reestablish legitimacy in familial, communal, or local political relationships. In other words, both were concerned with how to live their lives in the aftermath of various events of violence.

Such concerns may become still more pressing when the event of violence is perpetrated by members of one's community. For example, two young women testifying before the Commission's hearings in KwaZulu-Natal (October 1996) reported on having been raped by neighbors who were members of opposition political organizations. The Commission reports

> In two of the three rape cases heard (at this hearing), the women had never spoken about their experiences before. In one of these instances, a woman was gang-raped by some ANC youths over a period of a month and conceived a child. She reported that one of the men who raped her began visiting her home regularly and claimed parenthood of the child, which she was finding very difficult. (Report 1998 vol. 1:419)

Here, violence is afforded legitimacy by kinship's claims. A child conceived in violence becomes the grounds through which a patrilineal order is legitimated, and the violence of the act of conception—and of the claims made on its basis—is occluded. The young woman concerned must quite literally live with the past—both in the form of her child and the presence and persistence of the man who claims paternity. Her complaint reveals that the value of a woman and that of a child are weighed differently; in accord with local custom, the father has rights to incorporate the child into a patrilineal kinship order, but at the cost of the emotional experiences and wishes of the child's mother. While the case is doubtless more complex than presented in the Report, the point remains: kinship is allowed to exert a claim that absorbs violence into the social and the everyday. It transforms the problem to be solved from one of rape to one of paternity; from one of violence to one of legitimacy; from an illegitimate act to a socially legitimate outcome valorized by patrilineal custom and patriarchal ideal.

These findings should give us some pause in relation to contemporary emphases on vernacular forms of "restorative justice." For example, during the Zuma rape trial, the defense gave evidence that after the event in question, traditional marriage negotiations had been initiated, thus implying that sexual relations had been consensual. Khwezi's supporters saw this as an attempt to legitimate rape through appeals to tradition. Similarly, two women with whom I have worked describe being forcibly abducted and held against their wills in locked rooms, without food, until they went through with what they described as "traditional" marriage ritual abduction procedures. Both were clearly disoriented and deeply distressed by the events, even in their narration many years later. Here, socially sanctioned relations mask coercion and violence.

Part of what is at stake is the question of how to live with others in the present. Sexual violence may undermine trust in the social institutions of everyday life. Each case described here is concerned with questions of trust and betrayal and the ways that these shape the possibilities of everyday life. Yvonne Khutwane describes the betrayal in an (admittedly corrupt) state institution's failure to protect her; the betrayal of which her comrades accused her; the betrayal by what she felt to be her political community and the consequent attack on her home. Zanele Zingxondo speaks similarly of prison and of the ways in which her mother's fears betrayed the ideal relationship between mother and child. There is too the betrayal of death: her mother died before the distrust between them could be resolved, leaving behind unfinished business that she alone must bear, and which the Commission did not ameliorate. In effect, notwithstanding her call on the Commission, her case does not rest before the dead. Khwezi describes betrayal by a respected figure; the attempt to transform the event into a sanctioned form speaks to the ways that culture might betray one. The women describing how their comrades or political foes raped them are commenting on the fragility of neighborliness and local codes of dignity and respect. Their bodies become the ongoing sites of contestation over power and meaning: a feature common to rape in all war situations, and a feature that many feminists argue underpins nationalism.

Trust and Betrayal

Given this layering of betrayal, speaking of violence calls for trust of various kinds: trust in the capacity to attend to suffering, in institutions anticipated to assist, in social relations and potential support networks, in the discretion of another. It is clear that trust is easily betrayed or undermined. It cannot be taken for granted. Words are not received into a vacuum; language is shared and is molded by existing forms of power that shift over time. The power that shapes social worlds is not always easily put into words, particularly where women are held responsible for the actions of others. When it is, the result implicates many of the taken-for-granted structures of everyday life and the ways that language folds into ongoing relationships.

This is a difficulty that novelist Yvonne Vera grapples with in her book *Under the Tongue,* the most evocative and delicate account of violence, voice, and silence I have ever read. The protagonist, a young woman named Zhizha, wrestles with the fact of a father's intimate violence, which has initiated her into the puzzle of language's limitations in the face of suffering, and thence into silences common to womanhood. *Under the Tongue* is set during the Chimurenga, Zimbabwe's War of Liberation, and is centrally concerned with voice, its erosion, and with the need to restore language to life in the aftermath of (intimate) violence. Zhizha's mother has joined the freedom fighters, an act that receives no sanction from her family or community. She has left Zhizha to live with her grandparents and father. Sexually abused by her father, Zhizha must learn to speak the betrayal that lies like a stone under her tongue. It is compounded by the silence her family maintains about her mother's whereabouts, her activities, and even her name. Zhizha is surrounded by that which has not been said, which may not be named. Through her grandmother, an ally, she learns of the layering of silence in the face of the violence, sometimes indefinable, that shapes women's lives.

In an evocative passage Zhizha's grandmother compares women to trees. Unlike trees, which have many branches with which to carry the experience they cannot utter, people have tongues. And yet she wonders, "Perhaps it is better to have many arms to carry your pain and no tongue with which to speak it" (1996:52). The quandary of what to do with experience here takes form: to speak it, and in so doing to share it, or to carry it, silent and alone? In contexts of violence, speech may be dangerous, especially when what could be spoken would be a description of masculine violence that undermines familial propriety and the myth of masculine care on which certain versions of the family—and, one might add, the nation—are constructed. (This is apparent too in Khwezi's accusation against her 'malume, then Deputy President of the ruling party and of the Republic.) Indeed, Zhizha's grandmother comments that some talk is so dangerous that "only the departed can speak our sorrow and survive" (p. 42): it is only through the voices of the dead that experience can be given expression and thence a home in language.[15] But she also asks: "Why must we be silent? . . . We have tongues with which to dream." Zhizha knows that "the best words are those that are shared and embraced, those that give birth to other words more fruitful than themselves, stronger than themselves" (p. 16). And, right at the end of the novel, she notes, "A word does not rot unless it is carried in the mouth too long, under the tongue."

Central to the novel is the problem of language in the face of suffering and remaking the world after violence. "A word is like a wound that has dried," says Zhizha's grandmother (p. 53). "Dried," note, not "healed." Zhizha's story offers the paradox: language is insufficient to experience, and yet certain words may offer new beginnings. The problem is to find the forms that can acknowledge experience and that hold potential for the future. Naming experience would undermine the world as Zhizha and others know it. The horror of her experience is that her father's power takes its form not only through the conventions of patrilineal societies and the ways that these are shaped in support of patriarchal power, but also through betrayal of an intimate kind. There is a quadrupling of power here: that of men over women, of elders over youth, of fathers over families, and of violence sexually enacted. If Zhizha describes her father's violence, she undermines the principles of patriarchy and a particular social form premised on it, yet by not speaking, terror remains rooted in her life, and a particular form of masculine power remains embedded as the principle on which social life is formed. This is precisely the quandary that faced Khwezi and the women who might have testified before the Commission. To name the betrayal is to pull at the foundations of power. This is why feminists have long espoused finding a voice and speaking of experience. But the ease of this rhetoric belies the complexities of the process and the moral decision making that is involved in "speaking out"—aspects that are only too clear in the work of the Truth Commission and the events of the Zuma trial.

In contexts in which women are often blamed for the harm they experience, especially when that harm is sexual, it ought not be surprising that many would prefer not to speak, or find themselves unable to do so, particularly when doing so incriminates not just another individual, but a set of cultural assumptions and the social forms that they shape. It takes courage both to speak of harms done and to be silent in their face and aftermath. Part of the stakes of talking about rape is the undoing of familiarity. It is not just specific relationships—between oneself and a rapist—that are implicated. To speak about rape is to speak about larger systems of power that are at the base of the world one inhabits.

The stakes of naming sexual violence are greater than simply acknowledging one's singular experience of harm: sexual violence is always about power and betrayal. It implicates more than just individuals. Its horrifying irony is that it often forces the sufferer into the position of betrayal too.

At the opening of the Commission's Women's Hearings on July 28, 1997 in Johannesburg, Thenjiwe Mtintso, head of the Gender Commission, former Commander of uMkhonto weSizwe, the ANC's armed wing, commented on this directly, saying,

> When today they [testifiers] make their sobs, they must know there's a flood of tears from those who did not even dare to come here today . . . because we are not yet ready to make those outward sighs of pain. As they try to free themselves today of the burden, they must know that they are freeing some of us who are not yet ready, Chairperson. I speak as one of those . . . I could not sleep last night, because I sat with myself, I sat with my conscience. I sat with the refusal to open those wounds. (cited in Ross 2003a:24)

Speaking about not-speaking, Mtintso struggles with the implications of testimony. By speaking, she would betray her comrades and the values of the struggle; by keeping silent, she would be refusing solidarity with other women. Either way, her decision implicated others, structures of power, relationships, and values. It is clear that conscience and morality are at stake and that one may be caught between conflicting desires—to free oneself of a burden, to refuse to open wounds; to reveal, to conceal. Her comment hints at the complexities of silence and the costs of being called to speak of personal experience. And her comment that other women speak for those who are unable draws our attention to the weight of responsibility.

When Dangerous Words Are Uttered

The Commission assumed that catharsis of some kind followed on speech, that speaking directly of sufferings sustained in the past might offer healing. It also anticipated that breaking silences would end repression and inaugurate freedom—personal, social, and political. This is an important cultural model, shaped largely by the principles of psychotherapy. It is not necessarily a universal or transhistorical model and does not take account of the diversity of ways in which experience is articulated or otherwise made known and addressed.[16] Human rights and feminist calls to speak directly demand that a language of "less hurt"—a linguistic form that protects individuals from experience—is translated into an often cruel realist discourse anticipated to heal. For example, human rights workers involved in collecting statements for the Commission on Historical Clarification in Guatemala told me with frustration that they frequently had to reformulate the opaque speech of peasant women who reported the deaths of kin by saying, "He went away," or their own experiences of sexual violence as "I was hurt" into the coarser objectivist discourse of legal language: "He was abducted/ murdered/ disappeared"; "He raped me." In each instance, two acts of translation are performed: one that locates a locus of blame, and the other that distills tentativeness into certainty.

There are dangers to what I call "straight-talk." Circumlocution enables people to say what might otherwise be too dangerous to say. Its negative effect is to protect the perpetrator and blame the victim. Straight-talk directly exposes the power relations in violence, but at the cost of uncertainty—a person who has disappeared may yet reappear; one who has been murdered will not. It may be that in speaking elliptically, women protect themselves from the finality that straight talk creates.

Let me give another example, this one drawn from the South African instance. A complaint about the Commission's human rights violations hearings offered by people I interviewed early in its process was that in insisting that suffering be explicitly articulated, the proceedings were undignified and rendered sufferers vulnerable to the bare assessments of others. The comment is predicated on an understanding that language encodes ideal patterns of respect and avoidance that are central premises of social life in Southern Africa.

For speakers of Nguni and Sotho languages, this takes linguistic form in *ukuhlonipha,* which calls for delicacy and circumspection in speech and behavior. Its codes are status-, age-, and gender-specific; different modes of address are used depending on audience and relationship (Kunene 1958; Finlayson 1984). Matters of sex and violence are, in customary ideal, encoded in metaphor and elliptical speech—alluded to, rather than named directly. Utilizing a direct language of suffering sometimes contravened these ideals, leaving sufferers denuded of the shelter that less-direct but widely understood forms of expression might offer. And, as the Commission's translators made clear (Krog 1998), when people did use these forms of speech, it was often difficult for them to remold them into bare speech.

The assumption that truth is neutral belies the complex processes of interpretation and entextualization that go on in real life (Ross 2003a and b; Gready 2003). Notwithstanding evidence that demonstrates very clearly that women's safety cannot be secured when certain kinds of experience are made public (I am thinking here particularly of the horrifying violence sometimes visited on women who publicly disclose their HIV-positive status), there is still a normative assumption that silence is intrinsically damaging, and speech healing. But the disclosure of painful experience is difficult, not least because it opens one to the assessment of others. And, as feminists have long known, and as the events that unfolded during the Zuma rape trial illustrated, there is far more to being heard than simply speaking.

For young women in particular the costs of public speech may be high. Very few young women gave statements to the Commission or testified about their experiences of violence.[17] None of the ten young women with whom I worked closely between 1996 and 1999 (see Ross 2003a) spoke publicly, and those few who did make statements to the Commission did so with some reluctance, usually after prompting by senior women in the community or by their families. The women were afraid that their deeply hurtful experiences might become public and thereby expose them to judgment and censure. A few young women who did testify elsewhere told me that they had been humiliated to speak of "intimate" matters publicly.

Finding a voice in which to speak and a linguistic form that might do justice to experience is thus not simple. The matter is compounded by the fact that people inhabit multiple speech communities and that speech acts offered in one site may circulate in a variety of sites where they carry different cadences and are subject to diverse interpretations over time. There is as yet little examination of the social lives of testimonies and the consequences of their circulation for women who speak outside of conventional or normative modes. As Khwezi commented after Zuma had been found not guilty of rape, "It was weird to read about yourself and your life and these processes as understood and written by others" (Cavanagh and Mabele 2006). The Commission assumed that the public space of human rights violations was neutral and that the interpretations offered in the hearings would necessarily and naturally be the same as those that circulated elsewhere. It also assumed that the weight and value given to experience couched in terms of human rights in that setting would be sufficient to secure the narrative and interpretive framework outside of the hearings. Courts frequently operate with the same expectation: that words offered in that context will be given similar interpretations and values outside of it. In fact, accounts that exonerate or explain experience in one context may undermine it in another, as different interpretations are brought to bear. Some women were shocked to realize the weight of convention that worked against them outside that setting and that obviated the invitation. Some found unexpected support and relief in testifying or in hearing the testimony of others that reflected their experience. For others, testifying publicly—whether before the Commission or a court—may precipitate an annihilation of the world or a dismembering of the self rather than a cathartic experience, even if the law offers (limited) redress. This was glaringly obvious in the Zuma rape trial, where Khwezi's sexual identity, her HIV-positive status, and the claim that she had been raped several times (including once as a small child in exile) were subject to widespread disbelief, both by the defense and large sectors of the general public.[18] The fact that Khwezi no longer resides in South Africa reveals that it is naïve to assume that speaking truth necessarily indemnifies one from negative consequences: the consequences may be life-threatening.

My work on testimonies offered before the Commission (Ross 2003a and b) shows that testimonies were reinterpreted in the light of local knowledge and gendered codes of conduct. Some people who testified before the Commission's human rights violations hearings found it disturbing that their testimonies were widely circulated in the mass media (see Ross 2003b). Reinterpretations were often less than generous and were sometimes cruel, especially for women whose activities stood outside the registers of local conventions of girlish or womanly propriety. Thus young women who had been actively involved in political resistance to the state, or who had borne children out of wedlock, or who had been detained, raped, or tortured were particularly vulnerable to accusations of impropriety; and, unless they were widely acknowledged to have been leaders in the struggle against apartheid, they tended not to speak of their own activities in the past lest it invite negative assessments. They had learned from prior experience that gender stereotypes often hold more weight than actual relationships and events. For example, one man, a trusted comrade of women I worked with, asked me why I was working with women when their roles in struggle had been minimal and limited to being convenient lovers—this despite the fact that the same women to whom he referred had been instrumental in establishing a variety of organizations that opposed apartheid, creating links with underground liberation movements, and keeping secret from the police and even their families the whereabouts of the men in question. The women with whom I worked did not—and do not—reveal secrets, either about their activities in struggle or about inequitable gender relations between comrades at the time. Although it is rumored that some among them had been raped, none has ever acknowledged this. Some withstood severe physical torture and solitary confinement without betraying their comrades. They trusted one another with intimate knowledge and did not betray that trust. Yet still the stereotype endures. Given the weight and power of general forms of gendered stereotyping explicit in his comment and reinforced in the events of the Zuma trial, it is not surprising that people may prefer to keep silent about painful experience.

Silence

While contemporary belief generally holds that silence is damaging, the historian Theodore Zeldin notes that silence was valued above speech in many peasant societies. He quotes a Finnish proverb: "One word is enough to make a lot of trouble" (1998:32); and he notes that "there are many reasons for not speaking, above all the fear of making a fool of oneself" (ibid.), and, I would add, the fear of upsetting the status quo, rendering oneself vulnerable to accusation or to unsympathetic assessment. The conundrum is of course that silence may offer legitimacy to violence. Those who wish to expose their experiences of sexual violation stand uncomfortably between these two positions. Many women do not speak out because they are afraid: of retribution, further violence, judgment, pulling at power's foundations, rendering their worlds uninhabitable. Some are silent out of a kind of perverse hope: that the event was an aberration, not to be repeated, unique. This silence is a product of the way that violence individualizes: social patterns of disregard for women and historical patterns of violence against women are obscured in the immediacy of damage inflicted on the body. (Indeed, it is partly because the Commission focused on *events* of violence, rather than on historical processes, that its findings on causes of violence are so limited.)

There is a temporal dimension to the expression and reception of harsh experience; it may take time for events to settle in such a way that they can be narrated. Alan Feldman notes in his study of violence in Northern Ireland, "The event is not what happens. The event is that which can be narrated" (1991:14).[19] Silence may point to the limitations of particular discursive forms; some things simply cannot be articulated within the sanctioned languages and social spaces currently available to experience. It may take time for changing discursive possibilities to sediment in such a way that they become accepted. In the absence of such, certain kinds of experience slip from the record or seep into silence.

This poses challenges to transitional justice processes predicated on the disclosure of experience. Priscilla Hayner warns that Commissions need to pay attention to addressing women's experiences, lest they "remain largely shrouded in silence and hidden from the history books" (2001:79). Michel-Rolph Trouillot argues that "silence enters the process of historical production at four crucial moments: the moment of fact creation (the making of *sources*), the moment of fact assembly (the making of *archives*), the moment of fact retrieval (the making of *narratives*), and the moment of retrospective significance (the making of *history* in the final instance)" (1995:26, emphasis original). The silencing of women's experiences at each of these stages is apparent in the Commission's work: in the use of a definition of suffering (gross violations of human rights) that prioritizes the forms of violence men experience and undervalues the systemic and gendered dimensions of oppression inherent in apartheid; in the elision of women's experiences from the assemblage of materials that comprise the Commission's Report; in the ways in which women testified and the analyses of testimonies in the Report, and in the "truth" to which it has given rise, in which women are represented as an appendage of largely male experience.

Writing of silences in literature, feminist scholar Tillie Olsen (1980:6–21 and 142–51) distinguishes between natural and unnatural silences. Natural silences are "that necessary time for renewal, lying fallow, gestation, in the natural cycle of creation"; "a receptive waiting" (p. 14). These kinds of silence are fecund, unlike unnatural silences—"the unnatural thwarting of that which struggles to come into being, but cannot" (p. 6). Olsen identifies varieties of silence within the latter: those of the marginal and marginalized, those imposed by censorship or by political activism, absences that register as silences, premature silencers that, to paraphrase her, ravage and obliterate the capacity for speech (p. 149), and silences that arise because experience is not recognized (p. 10).

Each of these forms of silence has a counterpart in the Commission's work. Women's experiences were marginalized by the emphasis on gross violations of human rights, the kinds of language and the spaces within which testimonies could be offered. They are set off from men's experiences, offered as separate. One might argue that the paucity of contemporary forms to recognize and acknowledge diverse experience constitutes a form of symbolic violence that curtails creativity and freedom—Olsen's premature silencers. For example, the emphasis on spectacular events of violence—abduction, torture, killing, and severe ill-treatment—forecloses an understanding of the subtleties of oppression and the diverse ways in which apartheid affected different categories of people. An emphasis on individual gross violations of human rights generates a biased accounting of the past that holds experiences that were mainly masculine to be the norm, prematurely silencing the expression of women's experiences.

This operates also as a kind of censorship or filtering device that admits only some kinds of experience as valid, while discounting others. For example, the Commission's account of violence in Zwelethemba, the small town in which I worked between 1996 and 1999, offers a litany of male death and damage, to the exclusion of women's activities, the harms they suffered, and the ways in which people tried to create meaningful lives for themselves and others. The Report on the area (1998 vol. 3:427–29) clearly holds the state responsible for much of the violence experienced in Zwelethemba in the 1980s. The account is largely concerned with male death: only one woman is included in the events, and that because during the incident her brother-in-law was killed. Many of the women with whom I worked in Zwelethemba had participated in struggle activities and were present, some injured, during the events described in the Report (see Ross 2003a:77–161). Many had been involved as activists in the struggle against apartheid and oppression since the 1950s. Young people were involved in protest against Afrikaans as a medium of instruction since 1976, and protests against Bantu education were sustained in the area. Yet none of this is included in the Report. There is scant account of the brutality of a range of different police, military, and paramilitary interventions. By 1985, most of the senior leadership of local struggle activities—trade unionists, members of the United Democratic Front, underground ANC operatives—had been jailed. The mantle of leadership fell on the youth. Pamela Reynolds (2005) has documented the extraordinary scale of that responsibility and the seriousness with which the young people of the time accepted it and its consequences, many of which were devastating for the individuals concerned and their kin, and the effects of which continue to reverberate through everyday activities. The Commission's Report does not describe the tensions that existed between residents of Zwelethemba or the betrayals of some by others, the effects of which endure into the present and shape everyday interpersonal relations (see Reynolds 2005; Ross and Reynolds 2004). There is no record of the bravery of the young or the complex work of making and remaking everyday life that is so often undertaken by women. We are offered only an account of gross violations of human rights, with no consideration of the broader social context or understanding of the relations between men and women, young and old.

Women's experiences register an absence in the historical record that the Commission created—in part, I have argued elsewhere (Ross 2003a), because insufficient attention is paid to the subtle content of women's speech that describes the undoing of everyday life that apartheid wrought, the hardships of creating and maintaining social relationships in fraught conditions, and the ways in which grief and social repair are folded into everyday activities. And I have already shown how women testifiers were faced with the prospect of betraying either their cause or a population in deciding whether to testify: cast into a position of self-censorship, they faced the prospect of betrayal at many levels.

Silence is complex. It may be a response to fear, a wish not to attract (further) violence, a physiological response to danger. These aspects of silence complicate simplistic understandings of responses to sexual violence both at the time of an event of violence and in its aftermath. For example, Khwezi stated that she did not scream when Zuma approached her or during intercourse. The defense made much of this, arguing that her silence was evidence of consent and that therefore there was no rape. There was no acknowledgment of the context and the ways in which propriety—deeply ingrained social conventions—might have shaped her responses. Faced with the nakedness of a man one respects, one may avert the gaze and still the voice. Faced with the threat of violent incursion, one's body may freeze. That one's voice and body are not responsive to one's will in such circumstances is well documented. It is not just to call this kind of silence "consent." The point was made by Merle Friedman, a psychologist called to witness for the complainant, who noted that "freeze, flight, fight, fright, faint provides a more complete description of the human acute stress response sequence than current descriptions" (cited in Maughan, Gordin, and Gifford 2006:1). And even in cross-examination we have a strange inversion of the legal processes that attend to other crimes: the complainant rather than the defendant is forced to defend herself and her actions.[20] Here, the event takes second place, is (temporarily) silenced in the focus on the complainant, her sexual past, and her physical responses.

Where particular experiences are considered to be defiling or polluting, as violence, incarceration, and death often are,[21] silence may be a means to protect the self and others, holding experience at bay or within so that its harm cannot ramify outward. In such cases, stillness may be an act of bravery, not of cowardice or of an inability to confront experience. Sometimes the voice flees from experience. At several human rights violations hearings, witnesses simply wept or were unable to complete their testimonies. Sometimes they were able to recover sufficiently to continue testifying; at other times their stumbling demanded careful attention. Silence may also point to the ways in which some experience is discounted or diminished. It may be a refusal to speak in terms that do not do justice to the self. And, as is evident in Vera's sympathetic account of Zhizha's coming to voice in *Under the Tongue,* it is not always possible to speak directly or easily of certain kinds of violence—to do so would be to render the remaining world so unstable as to be uninhabitable, both for oneself and for others who are equally vulnerable. We do not yet know what the individual costs of such silence may be, but we can anticipate that they are great indeed.

Veena Das (2000, 2007) has shown that much of the way that women rebuild social worlds in the aftermath of violence rests on determined efforts not to speak, not to subject others to the horror of one's experience or to render them responsible for one's well-being. Silence here is a courageous act, one that sets aside personal well-being in the interests of the greater community. Yet, as Lester Olsen (1997:65) notes, "Silence may be more decorous than a scream, but silence is unlikely to secure necessary support, assistance and care from concerned communities, or to bring about social or political change."

There is, then, as Das notes, an ethical charge: to attend to the suffering of others, even when, especially when, this cannot be articulated. Silence calls for empathic engagement and an assessment of the subtleties of the unspoken in everyday life. In other words, what appears to be silence or absence may actually indicate a failure of recognition and of empathy, an institutional incapacity to attend to suffering.

Listening and Attentiveness

One consequence of women's silences is that they are often read as individual moral failures rather than as institutional failures. In other words, "women" are considered to be the problem, rather than the institutions and processes that do not admit different experiences, that protect power from direct speech, or that do not admit the complexity of speech and silence as acts that have bearings and consequences in social worlds.

An early submission on gender to the Commission (Goldblatt and Meintjes 1997) proposed that the Commission create "safe spaces" in which women might speak of violence. My work suggests that while important, such spaces are unlikely to be sufficient to the task of revealing harm. The unfolding of words, silence, and experience in the sites I've selected points to the ways in which certain kinds of violence are folded into everyday life. They indicate the enormous difficulty of shaping everyday language to admit certain kinds of experience, and the recalcitrance of attentiveness in the face of power, pain, and betrayal. They hint at the complexity of finding voice, articulating experience, and transforming existing gender relations. It is here, at the intersection of words and silence, that attentiveness is called forth.

Das argues that failure to recognize an affirmation of pain is to participate in and perpetuate violence (1996:88). This suggests a responsibility to recognize silence: ideally, it calls for(th) an ethical obligation. Too often, however, hearing is shaped by preconceived ideas about the other, and silence may precipitate a turning away, a refusal of the gesture of listening attentively. Das notes that this is not a failing of the intellect, but one of the spirit (1996:88).

The argument I've put forward here challenges conventional understandings of transitional justice and of ordinary legal procedures. I hope to have shown that a hospitable model of justice cannot rest on documentation of gross violations of human rights alone. It needs to take account of historical continuities in violence and suffering, the complexities of language in relation to pain, and the different ways in which our understandings of the intersections of violence, silence, and voice affect knowledge production and its uses. It needs to insist on a relation among justice, attentiveness, and responsibility. It needs also to be aware of the implicit violence of failures of attention and responsibility, erasures of experience, and infelicities of spirit.

Chapter 5

Histories of Innocence

Postwar Stories in Peru

Kimberly Theidon

On November 1, 2006, Peruvian president Alan García announced he would be proposing a new law that would include the death penalty as one sanction for terrorism. He argued, "We are not going to allow Shining Path to return and paint their slogans on the walls of our universities. Once this law is approved, anyone who commits the serious crime of terrorism will find themselves facing a firing squad. A war forewarned does not kill people."

As one might imagine, García's comments sparked intense debate in Peru, a country in which a series of democratically elected governments waged a twenty-year war against terrorism. President García himself presided over one of those previous administrations, from 1985 to 1990, and he would subsequently be named as one of the political leaders alleged to have abdicated democratic authority in an effort to finish terrorism by whatever means necessary.

In its 2003 Final Report, the Peruvian Truth and Reconciliation Commission determined that the country's twenty-year war on terror resulted in the greatest loss of human life and resources in all of Peru's history as a republic. However, listening to President García three years after the TRC completed its work, I did not hear *nunca más*; rather, his words provoked a disturbing sense of déjà vu.

In this chapter I want to reflect upon certain legacies of Peru's war on terror—and to consider some of the legacies of the Truth and Reconciliation Commission that was established to investigate that bloody period of violence, to determine responsibility for human rights violations, and to make recommendations that would promote "sustainable peace and national reconciliation." I am motivated by three main concerns: What are the consequences of Peru's war on terror, and how did these consequences inform both the truth the TRC was able to tell and the "communal memory projects" people have forged in former Shining Path strongholds? How does the "logic of innocence" affect individuals, collectives, and political life following the internal armed conflict? Finally, I consider the contentious politics of victimhood and reparations in post–truth commission Peru.

An Uncivil Democracy

Many are called but few are chosen.... We must know how to die fully conscious of what we are doing because, in fact, we are going to die.

—Shining Path militant, diary entry from March 1985[1]

From 1980 to 1992, an internal war raged between the guerrilla group Sendero Luminoso, the *rondas campesinas* (armed peasant patrols), and the Peruvian armed forces. Founded by Abimael Gúzman, the Communist Party of Peru-Shining Path (Sendero Luminoso) began its campaign to overthrow the Peruvian state in 1980 in an attack on the Andean village of Chuschi. This band of revolutionaries positioned themselves as the vanguard in a revolution to guide the nation toward an imminent communist utopia (Degregori 1990; Stern 1998). Drawing upon Maoist theories of guerrilla warfare, they planned a top-down revolution in which the cadres of Sendero Luminoso would mobilize the peasantry, surround the cities, and strangle the urbanized coast into submission. However, the relentless march toward the future was doubly interrupted: the initial governmental response was a brutal counterinsurgency war in which "Andean peasant" became conflated with "terrorist," and many peasants themselves rebelled *against* the revolution (Starn 1995).

In response, the Peruvian government declared a far-reaching state of emergency and sent the military to control SL's terrorist violence with brutal counterinsurgency strategies resulting in massive and indiscriminate violence against the rural Quechua-speaking and Ashaninka populations (Manrique 1989; Peruvian Truth and Reconciliation Commission [hereafter, TRC] 2003; Theidon 2004). In addition to army troops and special counterinsurgency forces (*Sinchis*), numerous paramilitary groups secretly carried out the government's antiterrorist campaign at the margin of the law (TRC 2003; Laplante 2007b). Rural communities did not passively remain "between two fires"; rather, some communities sided with Shining Path, while others formed government-supported self-defense committees (*rondas campesinas*). The violence escalated dramatically and lethally.

While each new administration sought to control the terrorist threat, authoritarian leader Alberto Fujimori's (1990–2000) draconian measures not only appeared to defeat terrorism but also subjected the population to violent—albeit more selective—repression. In 1992, Fujimori enacted a series of executive antiterrorist decrees as part of his National Emergency and Reconstruction government. These laws led to massive detentions and the routine use of torture. The many defects in the legislative design of the antiterrorist legislation provoked a vociferous national and international outcry due to the grave violation of fundamental individual rights (Laplante 2007c). Stripping away due process protections, these laws permitted arbitrary arrest, excommunicado interrogation, denial of habeas corpus, conditions that permitted mistreatment and torture to elicit coerced confessions, "faceless" (masked) judges, military trials, and limited or no opportunity for an adequate defense. Convictions were often based solely on police assertions, coerced confessions, or the uncorroborated testimony of detainees "naming names" in hopes of a reduced sentence (Instituto de Defensa Legal 1995:52–68; Laplante 2006). An estimated 20,000 people were jailed during this period on not much more than a rumor, a grudge, or a declaration given by a torture victim in hopes the pain would stop. Long after the arrest of Abimael Guzmán and the military defeat of SL in 1992, the specter of terrorism was used to justify authoritarian measures, leading one of Peru's foremost public intellectuals to note that Fujimori won the war—it was the *postwar that defeated him* (Degregori 2006).[2]

Peru's political transition was abrupt and prompted more by elite and middle-class concerns with corruption than with human rights violations (Theidon 2004). As thousands of "Vladivideos" surfaced—the name referring to the head of Peru's Internal Intelligence Unit, Vladimiro Montesinos—the rampant corruption of Fujimori's administration became undeniable. In video after video, Montesinos was seen paying bribes to elected officials, and to members of the entertainment, financial, and business communities. Fujimori fled the country in November 2000, seeking refuge in Japan. A transitional government was subsequently appointed under the direction of Valentín Paniagua, who seized the opportunity to address the human and institutional damage caused by the internal armed conflict by forming the Truth and Reconciliation Commission in July 2001. Established by executive decree, the TRC's mandate included "the clarification of the process, acts and responsibilities" of terrorist violence and human rights violations, such as forced disappearance, torture and grave lesions, assassinations, and kidnapping, among others.[3]

The TRC labored for two years, holding thirteen public audiences, collecting testimonies, reviewing studies, consulting experts, and reading CIA documents, among other "truth-gathering" methods. Unlike other truth commissions, Peru's investigations included the identification of criminal responsibility, since the Inter-American Court of Human Rights had annulled Fujimori's 1995 amnesty laws (Laplante 2007a,c). The brunt of its work relied on 16,917 testimonies, collected primarily from victims (Theidon 2003a). The Peruvian TRC also proposed the Program of Integral Reparations (PIR), one of the most comprehensive reparations programs to date (Guillerot and Magarell 2006; Laplante and Theidon 2007). The PIR was designed to reaffirm the dignity of victims, offering hope for the future despite the loss of loved ones or the disruption of life projects, and explicitly linked the PIR to the goals of sustainable peace and the promotion of national reconciliation.

It was on August 28, 2003, that the commissioners of the Peruvian TRC submitted their Final Report to President Alejandro Toledo and the nation. Peru thus joined the growing list of countries that have implemented truth commissions as a means of transitioning from a period of armed conflict and authoritarian rule toward the founding of a procedural democracy.

However, while joining a growing trend, Peru also presents a series of exceptions. Peru was a triumphant state: there were no negotiations with the guerrillas of Shining Path, because the leadership was largely incarcerated and the movement militarily defeated. Thus the TRC was not a component of a peace process between opponents locked in a stalemate.

Additionally, the findings of the commission are striking. Of the deaths reported to the TRC, 54 percent were attributable to non-state actors, in particular to the guerrillas of Sendero Luminoso. Without minimizing the brutality of the armed forces, this figure points to a high level of civilian participation in the killing. However, while most Shining Path leaders are in jail, many community-level militants are not, having been either released from prison or never incarcerated. They live on the margins, shunned by a society in which the subject of "subversion" remains taboo. Despite the country's massive truth-seeking effort, there is scant political or discursive space in Peru to explore *why* so many people joined SL and remained sympathetic to the movement even under military repression.

Indeed, Shining Path remains monolithically demonized in Peru, in contrast to other Latin American countries in which insurgent or guerrilla movements were perceived by many people to be fighting for social justice—and at times eventually assumed legitimate political roles. Among the factors that explain this difference is the context in which SL began its armed struggle: Peru was not ruled by a military dictatorship, but rather by a democratically elected civilian government. Additionally, although the original ideological discourse appealed to principles of social justice and equality, Shining Path militants became increasingly authoritarian and lethally violent, unmatched by any other armed leftist group in Latin America.

However, I insist on disaggregating the category "terrorist" to reveal the vast variation in motivations, actions, and intent. The image of the "terrorist" is a key figure that organizes political discourse and action in our contemporary world. Yet, beyond the abstract image of the terrorist—that free-floating signifier—what is the work of this figure in particular historical and political contexts? In the Peruvian case, this is an ethnically saturated category.

Over the years I have participated in many social protests in Ayacucho, and one could trace recent history in part through the changing slogans and banners people have carried as they marched around that quintessentially public space, the central plaza of Huamanga. In 2001, as the truth commission was gearing up, a group of men and women of diverse ages entered the plaza beneath a carefully hand-lettered sign: "*Señor Vargas Llosa, no hay salvajes aquí*" (Mr. Vargas Llosa, there are no savages here). The protesters were referring to an earlier government commission sent to Ayacucho, presided over by the Peruvian novelist Mario Vargas Llosa.

The "Savage Slot"

It was January 1983, early in the course of Peru's internal war, when eight journalists from Lima's leading newspapers headed out for the highland village of Huaychao, located in the department of Ayacucho. The men had arrived from Lima to investigate rumors that the "Indians" had been killing the Senderistas. In 1983 the war in the interior still had an enigmatic quality for many residents of Lima, due to the profound cleavages that characterize Peru. Indeed, in part because the war was still a mystery to many urban Peruvians, the journalists fashioned their trip as an expedition in search of the "truth."

They spent the night in the city of Huamanga before heading out at dawn for the lengthy trip to Huaychao. Their route took them through Uchuraccay, where the journalists arrived in the village unannounced, accompanied by a Quechua-speaking guide. Although the sequence of events still prompts feverish debate, the photos taken by one of the journalists as he and his friends were dying established one thing: the villagers surrounded the journalists and began killing them with rocks and machetes, convinced they were under attack. The bodies were then buried in shallow graves in the ravine that runs the length of the village.

At the national level, the events at Uchuraccay marked the initiation of the war in the highlands, and thus the journalists' deaths became an intensely debated national theme. Although Sendero Luminoso had initiated their armed struggle three years earlier, and the armed forces had been sent to Ayacucho a month prior to the killings to begin the counterinsurgency campaign, until Uchuraccay the violence had not captured significant national attention. However, the photos that were subsequently developed from the camera that had been buried with journalist Willy Retto would be placed on the cover of every major Peruvian publication, constructing a "mediatic spectacle of political violence" (Peralta 2000) that would become one of the emblematic national memories of the war.

In the aftermath of the killings, President Fernando Belaúnde established an investigatory commission to determine what had happened and why. Headed by the novelist Mario Vargas Llosa, the commission was composed of three anthropologists, a psychoanalyst, a jurist, and two linguists who were sent to study Peru's "ethnic other" and the circumstances of the journalists' deaths. The three anthropologists were well-known and respected members of the academic community, and were included on the basis that anthropologists specialized in the study of "indigenous communities." And so the Commission members accepted their charge and headed via helicopter to Uchuraccay, where they spent one morning investigating the killings as background for their final report.

In their report, the *Informe de la Comisión Investigadora de los Sucesos de Uchuraccay*, the authors offered a "hierarchy of causes" (truths?) that revolved around two key explanatory factors: the primitiveness of the highlanders, who allegedly lived as they had since the time of the conquest, and the intrinsically violent nature of the "Indians" (Vargas Llosa et al. 1983). Drawing upon a substantial body of literature emphasizing the "endemic violence of the Andes" and "*la rabia Andina*" (Andean rage), the members of the commission attributed the killings to the pervasive "culture of violence" that allegedly characterizes these villagers. In the widely circulated *Informe,* the Commission suggested that one could not really blame the villagers—they were just doing what came *naturally.* The image of the intrinsically violent ethnic "other" is a remarkably resilient archetype in the dramatis personae of war.

In underscoring the role of cultural incommensurability as the real culprit, the authors stated that the deaths of the eight journalists provided the most conclusive evidence that even after four hundred years of contact between European culture and Andean culture, it had still not been possible to develop a true dialogue (Vargas Llosa et al. 1983:77). They grounded their findings in the assertion that two irreconcilable worlds coexist in Peru: modern/ civilized/coastal Peru, with Lima as its center, and the traditional/savage/ archaic Peru, mapped onto the highland communities, particularly Ayacucho. Somehow, in a perverse twist on Murra's concept of *pisos ecológicos* (ecological niches), civilization had never found a way to scale the steep mountain slopes of Peru's interior (Murra 1975).

Indeed, in a subsequent interview with the journal *Caretas,* Vargas Llosa elaborated on the notion of "the two Perus" consisting of "men who participate in the 20th century and men such as these villagers of Uchuraccay who live in the 19th century, or perhaps even the 18th. The enormous distance that exists between the two Perus is what lies behind this tragedy." As such, these highland villages were akin to museum exhibits, frozen in time and placed outside of history, resulting in an "Andean world that is so backward and so violent" (Vargas Llosa 1983).

Thus the TRC was not the first commission to arrive from Lima seeking the "truth" about violent events, and the Ayacuchanos assembled in the plaza in 2001 were serving notice: there would be no "savage slot" this time around. Yes, there would be a reworking of the social imaginary; unfortunately, the "savage" would cede to the "terrorist."

Los Rezagos del Terrorismo: The Ashes of Terrorism

In Peru's 2006 presidential elections, the same poor and marginalized population that embraced SL's revolutionary discourse massively supported the extreme populist Ollanta Humala and his nationalistic rhetoric. These elections alarmed the powerful urban elites, provoking weeks of anxious commentary in a country still divided along racial and class lines. Despite avoiding the "close call" of Humala's near victory, 2007 was a tumultuous year in Peru due to nationwide social protests involving thousands of rural Peruvians demanding to share in the benefits of Peru's growing economy. However, President Alan García consistently denounced the protesters as being pro-SL terrorists, in a blatant attempt to delegitimize the protesters' grievances. Thus even though Peru appears as a "success case" in recent texts on counterterrorism strategies (Heiberg, O'Leary, and Tirman 2007; Richardson 2006), the manner in which the government defeated SL has not resulted in "closing the books" on recent history (Elster 2004). Rather, one legacy of the Peruvian war on terror is a polarized and divided society in which demands for social justice—the expression of legitimate political claims—are frequently denounced as the "rekindling of the ashes of terrorism" (Del Pino and Theidon 2000). In a political strategy familiar from other Latin American contexts, García has followed Fujimori in justifying repressive tactics as part of "national security" and "defense of La Patria" against terrorists, playing the "fear card" designed to ensure the public condones potential "excesses and errors" (Feitlowitz 1999; Robben 2007).

The examples are abundant, but I limit myself to just one. In 2006, university students in Ayacucho took to the streets to protest an increase in university fees. For years the national media, when covering these protests, had produced images that made the events I routinely participated in unrecognizable to me. On the cover of the newspapers, selected images would sensationalize the protests, focusing on a few riled-up young people who remained isolated from the majority of the protesters. These young, brown, Ayacuchano faces would be splashed on the front pages, implicitly—and at times explicitly— suggesting the "ashes of terrorism" were rekindling. Thus when students marched into the central plaza in 2006, they carried a banner prominently unfurled above their heads: "We are university students, not terrorists." They were attempting to control the circulation of their images, fully aware of how they might be manipulated in the ongoing polarization of public debate in Peru. Despite its laudable efforts to provide a public forum for those whose voices had been historically excluded, the TRC perpetuated certain silences.

Commissioning Truth, Constructing Silences

Truth commissions emphasize the "recovery" and "telling" of truth in response to regimes in which state actors maintained control through enforced silence and the denial of violent repression (Cohen 2001; Hayner 2001). These commissions have become part of a global trend for demanding the truth in societies emerging from violent conflict or authoritarian rule (Kelsall 2005:362).

In the earliest truth commissions, the primary perpetrator of violence and terror was the state, which contributed to constructing the binary identities of "victim" and "perpetrator." Framed by this binary, truth commissions tend to replace the adversarial character of criminal proceedings with a "victim-centered" approach emphasizing empathic listening to private and public testimonies that catalogue atrocities inflicted on "innocent victims" (Hayner 2001; Minow 1998; Theidon 2007a). A collective narrative emerges that proves systematic violations of human rights and tends to foreground suffering rather than protagonism, thereby forging a sense of "traumatic citizenship" as a leveling device (Theidon, Sept. 2003). Truth commissions develop victim typologies: these victim categories establish discursive space and subject positions from which people speak. Testimonies of perpetrators usually figure into the truth-seeking process when confessions are exchanged for amnesties, such as in South Africa and various Southern Cone countries (Feitlowitz 1999; Wilson 2001).

This truth seeking usually occurs within sensitive political contexts and amidst polarized positions and group identities. In the Peruvian case, one particularly tense moment during the TRC occurred when one of the commissioners, Sofia Macher, referred to Shining Path as a political party. The media seized upon this statement, excoriating the TRC for being sympathetic to terrorists. The controversy was so vitriolic that the president of the TRC, Salomón Lerner, was summoned before a congressional committee on July 15, 2002, to defend the use of the term *political party* in reference to SL. Dr. Lerner presented a list of dictionary definitions of *political* and *party*, attempting to explain why SL could be defined this way without implying an "apology for terrorism" (Lerner 2002).

In such polarized contexts, truth commissions are structurally inclined to overlook the gray zone in which categories of perpetrator and victim blur (Levi 1995). Indeed, truth commissions tend to construct a popular discourse that presents two distinct homogeneous groups, imagined as mutually exclusive: victims and perpetrators (Borer 2003). Within the Latin American context, the "between two fires" approach has been the regional appropriation of this dichotomy.[4] However, in constructing people as victims, these commissions may silence other relationships people have with their pasts (Theidon 2007a). Additionally, the messiness of war frequently blurs the dichotomy. Let me trace some of that "messiness" in former Shining Path strongholds in the department of Ayacucho.

Histories of Innocence

We went to Lima to demand our rights, but nobody paid any attention. For campesinos there is no justice. If you demand your rights, they say you're a *terruco* [terrorist] from Cayara.

—*Anonymous*

As I mentioned earlier, in the polarized debates about Sendero Luminoso in Peru, it is controversial to even suggest that Sendero was a political party. This polarization in turn informs the debates about human rights. In sum, only the innocent have rights in Peru.[5] That is, any sympathy that one may have had for Sendero disqualifies the person from being the subject of rights.[6] This game has been extremely useful to the armed forces, to the Apristas, and to members of the conservative Catholic church: implying that a person or group had something to do with Sendero has been a strategy used to justify the use of violence against them, both in the past and in the present.[7]

This dichotomy between the guilty and the innocent has also shaped how people in former Shining Path strongholds press their claim and elaborate collective memory projects. Over the past five years, I have conducted qualitative research with four communities that were Shining Path support bases.[8] I was interested in understanding what had motivated people to join or sympathize with SL, how they now view their participation, and how they interact within these communities as well as with the state. Although the literature on transitional justice has focused almost exclusively on the international and national spheres, transitional justice is not the monopoly of international tribunals or of states: communities also mobilize the ritual and symbolic elements of these transitional processes to deal with the deep cleavages left—or accentuated—by civil conflicts. In short, I wanted to enter the gray zone in hopes that if I stayed there long enough, I might begin to understand the complicated and contradictory logics that exist when introducing a politics of scale into our analysis of transitional justice.

Within the context of the truth commission, communal authorities set about developing their own "memory projects." In every community with which I have worked, there were assemblies held to discuss what would be said to the TRC's mobile teams when they arrived to take testimonies. There was an effort to close the narrative ranks, prompted by the many secrets people keep about a lengthy, fratricidal conflict as well as the expectations a commission generates. I attended numerous assemblies in which authorities reminded everyone what they had decided to talk about—which deaths would be discussed and which ones silenced in the interest of yielding a collective history of innocence.

As part of their work, truth commissions construct typologies of victims—and of perpetrators. These categories inform the memory projects that people and communities develop. There is much emphasis on the politics of memory, and on memory as a cultural form. I want also to consider the economics of memory: among the conditions of possibility for the elaboration of "collective truths" are changing economic circumstances and motivations. Commissions generate expectations. It did not matter how many times people were told they would not necessarily receive reparations for giving their testimony: giving one's testimony was in part instrumental, and it would be ingenuous to think otherwise. Memories were narrated with new possibilities and aspirations in mind. While giving testimony can be prompted by various factors, the hope of some economic relief was a very important incentive—and innocent victimhood was the narrative strategy.

Let me provide an example that allows us to tease out several of the issues with which we are concerned. The truth commission conducted focus groups—in addition to taking individual testimonies—as part of their work on regional histories (*estudios en profundidad*). In June 2002, the TRC team held a focus group in one former Shining Path support base with which I have worked. The transcript from the focus group provides us with an opportunity to situate truths within the dynamics of winners and losers, and to appreciate the historicity of memory.

The transcript of the focus group is fairly lengthy, so I will briefly summarize the main themes addressed. I will not name the community, but it was located in the central-south of Ayacucho and had been one of Sendero's important support bases.[9] The groups were recorded and subsequently transcribed; I quote from the written transcriptions in the present tense to preserve people's statements.

The meeting begins with the two facilitators introducing themselves; each of them are subsequently addressed as "Señor Comisión de la Verdad" or "Señores de la Verdad." To start the conversation, one of them asks, "How was it here when your paisanos lived—before there was so much death?"

One of the men replies: "Here we were, peaceful, without fights—without hating each other. During fiestas we drank, we ate. When someone died we visited them. When someone called, we answered. Then all of this [SL] appeared. We've been innocent. They [the soldiers] cut our throats because we were innocent."

The other men join in with details about when "Sendero arrived," talking animatedly about one of the teachers who was a local *cabecilla* (SL leader). A series of killings are detailed, followed yet again by the insistence "All of these things they did to us, to innocent people." Another man adds, "The children trembled with fear. So did the women."

What follows in the transcript is the first attempt to quiet one of the women who tries to speak. The men admonish her: "You shouldn't talk unless you know [the story] really well, or we'll vary the information. This machine [tape recorder] will tell everything just the way it is in Lima." She falls silent.[10]

There is more discussion about their innocence, and then the talk turns to a local massacre. Another woman tries to speak; she is also told to be quiet.

In describing the army massacre, one of the men notes: "We decided the men should escape. They hated the men—we didn't think they'd do anything to the women."

They were wrong in that assessment, and what follows is a description of how the soldiers began raping and killing the women. The details of the massacre are gruesome, and the actions of the soldiers despicable. Once again, a woman tries to speak up and the men tell her to be quiet. The men return to the theme of innocence, this time insisting, "Our pueblo was innocent."

The lengthy transcripts of the focus group are striking for many reasons. These communities were considered "red zones," and, given the outcome of the armed conflict, this history still confers a certain stigma. Of course, some sectors continue to justify the actions of Shining Path, arguing that the political violence was the result of the marginalization and poverty that the Peruvian state was not and continues to be incapable of resolving. But for many people, there is a sense of guilt for the destruction they associate with their ties to Sendero Luminoso.

Additionally, pressing demands on innocent victims plays with the dualism that informs the logic of law and these commissions charged with historical clarification. In the assemblies held in this community prior to the arrival of the TRC, it was decided that people should talk only about those who died at the hands of the soldiers. As explained to me, the concern was twofold: when authorities convened the assemblies and began forging their memory projects, they told people that widows and orphans were groups of interest to the commission. As the president of this community told me, "One of the orphans stood up and said he was ready to tell the commission about his father's death. 'I'll tell them how Antonio Sullqa and Clemente Gamboa killed him—how they slit his throat . . .' Well, there were Antonio and Clemente standing right there across from him! We knew we couldn't talk about it like that, or everyone would be killing each other again." Thus, the communal authorities decided that only certain deaths would be talked about with the TRC—those that occurred at the hands of the armed forces. Additionally, they were concerned that if people began talking about killings *within* the community, it would be taken as proof of Sendero's presence and their sympathies during the war. Thus, the memory project focused on "innocent victims," and the women were consistently told to be quiet for fear they would "vary the information."

If indeed it is socially acceptable to demonize Sendero Luminoso, there is much less discursive space to talk about why people supported SL. There is a Faustian bargain here: the campesinos of the central-south can exercise protagonism today if they retrospectively adopt the role of passive victims during the internal armed conflict. The less they portray themselves as protagonists then, the more persuasive their demands on the state are today. Thus most people in these communities attempt to construct their life histories at a sizable distance from any sympathy whatsoever with Sendero.

On several occasions, someone pulled aside a member of my research team to assure them that everyone else was exaggerating their losses during the violence: "Oh, look at how he plays the victim—but that's not how it was! He was one of those *puriqkuna* [SL militants, literally "those who walk," referring to the constant movement of the guerrillas]. And now he wants to say he was a victim! Me? Yes, I really was a victim—but he wasn't." People compete for a higher rank on the hierarchy of victimhood. This "innocence" is based on a logic that has guided the discourse of human rights in Peru: the subject of rights is the subject without moral taint—the innocent subject.

This prompts me to consider Mahmood Mamdani's work on the Rwandan genocide, in which civilian participation in the killing was massive. He juxtaposes "victor's justice" with "survivor's justice," advocating for the latter as a means of combining the logic of reconciliation with the logic of justice:

> To transcend the previous oppositional terms is to forge a new community of survivors of civil war, [the survivors being] those who continue to be blessed with life following war. The concept of the "survivor" seeks to transcend the bipolar notions of victims and perpetrators. (2001:272)

According to Mamdani, the price of victor's justice is very high (ibid.). The victor must be permanently vigilant for fear that the winner's booty be snatched away. The winners live fearing the next cycle of violence, when those they violently suppressed rise up in revenge. Consequently, the price of victor's justice is either a continuation of civil war or a permanent divorce. When the enemies have been intimate, permanent divorce is not really an alternative. Thus, the work of justice and the work of coexistence are intertwined and both require a reorganization of power and resources. Within this reorganization, it is necessary to formulate multiple subject positions that do not freeze people in the past.

Additionally, the contentious politics of victimhood was further magnified by Peru's July 2005 Reparations Law and how the law defines *victim*. In circumvention of international human rights law and the principle of nondiscrimination, Article 4 of the Reparations Law states that "members of subversive organizations are not considered victims and thus not beneficiaries of the programs enumerated in this law."[11] To be a "good victim" now requires disavowing political protagonism in the past.

I believe the discourse of innocence paralyzes the process of reconciliation in Peru. In these former Shining Path strongholds, I asked people how they viewed the Peruvian state and the possibility of reconciliation. In Cayara, where the military committed a massacre on May 14, 1988, on the grounds that the villagers were SL militants, one of the communal authorities explained why his is a *pueblo resentido* (a resentful town):

> If there are people [military] who have participated and are alive, the TRC should sanction them, according to the law. Maybe not punish the soldiers, because they were under orders. It's more that they should punish the intellectual authors like General Valdivia and Dr. Alan García, because he came here with such arrogance and called us "terrucos." At least, as former president of our country, he should explain all of this. To achieve reconciliation between the state and us, there would need to be an agreement between the two, and it would have to be after the sanction we were talking about. Reconciliation means, for me it means, that both sides reconcile, to live in peace and tranquility, and that there is justice. That is reconciliation.

Striking was his demand that the "intellectual authors" be punished, citing the general who oversaw the massacre as well as former and current President García. This conversation occurred in March 2003 and was echoed by many other members of the community, who assured me that when García arrived following the massacre, "he called us all terrucos—he called our dead family members terrucos and said they deserved to die. He even said our pigs were terrucos!"[12]

During the subsequent 2006 presidential campaign, many people in this community (and another that had suffered a military massacre in 1985) told my research team how worried they were: "If García is elected again—oh, he must be angry that we denounced the massacre to the human rights people. This time, he'll make certain they kill us all, so that no one is left alive to tell." While these fears may seem extreme, the fear was palpable. Importantly, that such worries were deemed credible provides powerful insight into how these Peruvians view their government.

In addition to these concerns, the logic of innocence has other corrosive effects. This logic does not permit the construction of a more just society, because if only the "innocent" have rights, then there will certainly be those who feel entitled to do whatever they want with the guilty. The TRC's Final Report leaves little doubt regarding the deadly consequences of that approach. As long as there is no discursive space to talk about why so many people joined Sendero and, in some cases, remained sympathizers even under military repression—as long as there is no discursive space not subject to the Faustian bargain—there will be a repressed history of struggle that continues to generate bitterness in these "pueblos resentidos" of the central-south.

National Reconciliation? Reconciling What and with Whom?

There is no reconciliation possible with the assassins of Shining Path.

—Alan García, Correo, August 14, 2003

With Shining Path there can be no pact, no political solution and no form of reconciliation.

—Congresswoman and former presidential candidate Lourdes Flores Nano, La República, August 10, 2003

Reconciliation is multidimensional: the individual with himself or herself, members of a community with one another, between communities or states, between the individual and his or her gods, and between civil society sectors and the state. I would like now to briefly consider the final dimension, emphasizing the need to distinguish between vertical and horizontal reconciliation (Theidon 2004). Elsewhere I have discussed the micropolitics of reconciliation practiced in communities in northern Ayacucho, noting that locally based processes of administering both retributive and restorative justice have been remarkably successful in terms of reincorporating *arrepentidos* and in breaking the cycle of revenge (Theidon 2006b). However, to date, the armed representatives of the state have been neither punished nor forgiven. That responsibility—legally and morally—lies with the state.

When I visited Ayacucho in November 2001, the TRC was just beginning its work. I asked people how they felt about the armed forces and the abuses they had committed in their communities. Many people were still afraid to speak openly about civil–military relations and their conflictive, abusive trajectories. However, those who did comment expressed a common refrain: "So, *los doctores* from Lima think they can come here and tell us to reconcile? If the soldiers want to reconcile with us, then let them come here and apologize and repent for what they did." A few women also added, "And let the generals spend at least a few months in prison so they understand what it means to suffer." We see an emphasis on apology, on the administration of justice, and on dialogue. These are important steps in the reconstruction of coexistence—what villagers mean when they refer to reconciliation.

In his analysis of the South African TRC, Wilson criticizes the ways in which the concept of reconciliation was deployed in a top-down direction, leaving scant space to speak about the sentiments of retribution or vengeance that characterized popular conceptions of justice. The gap between national and local processes was notable: the South African Truth and Reconciliation Commission did not develop mechanisms for translating their vision of "national reconciliation" to the townships. Rather, Wilson argues that political and religious elites appropriated the term *reconciliation* as a metanarrative for reconstructing the nation-state and their own hegemony following the apartheid regime (Wilson 2001).

In Peru, the national–local gap has also been a problem—but in reverse. In the weeks leading up to the presentation of the TRC's Final Report, members of the *criollo* political elite lined up to distance themselves from the very idea of reconciliation. Their declarations were multiple and adamant: "There is no reconciliation possible with the assassins of Shining Path,"[13] and "With Shining Path there can be no pact, no political solution and no form of reconciliation."[14]

Even former president Valentín Paniagua, the man who led the country during the transitional government and signed the executive decree establishing the truth commission, insisted he had created the Truth Commission there—with no "R" and nothing more.[15] Adding their voice to the cacophony were members of the armed forces, representatives of the conservative wing of the Catholic Church, and certain businessmen who were committed to the restricted circulation of the Final Report and its recommendations regarding themes such as accountability and reparations.

When I listened to Alan García's testimony—and the subsequent declarations of other political officials—I found myself wondering just who constituted "*El Perú*" that would neither forgive, nor forget, nor enter into dialogue. What a distanced and indulgent position to take! I choose the words *distant* and *indulgent* because the economic and political elites who live in the enclave communities of Lima's wealthiest neighborhoods do not live with the daily legacies of a fratricidal conflict. They do not interact with neighbors who forged different—and frequently lethal—alliances during the war. Nor did they live with the midnight military raids, during which soldiers hauled off the men and lined up to rape the women. Listening to former President García, we are reminded that when members of the criollo political elite imagine the community that constitutes "*El Perú*," no Quechua-speaking campesino appears in the portrait.

I recall the debates during the interim government. The middle- and upper-class residents of Lima were more concerned with the corruption charges against the various administrations of the 1980s and 1990s than they were with the charges of human rights violations. The issue of corruption affected people of their same socioeconomic status, while the great majority of the dead and disappeared would never have crossed the thresholds of their homes, except perhaps to clean them. How easy to say "never" to reconciliation with the "assassins of Shining Path," and what an enormous lack of vision on the part of those elected officials who should provide leadership during this transitional process. "El Perú" that the political and economic elites invoke has yet to enter into dialogue with those sectors of the population that bore the brunt of the internal armed conflict. The TRC cited the ethnic discrimination that influenced the course of the internal armed conflict in Peru, and that discrimination continues to inform notions of who and what is to be reconciled. "El Perú" has a responsibility to consider the brutality exercised by many

Peruvians, some in the name of defending the state and others in the name of overthrowing it.

It is useful to reflect upon the gap between the discourse of certain political leaders regarding the theme of reconciliation and the micropolitics of reconciliation practiced in the communities with which I have worked. The gap invites us to consider the extent to which "democratic transitions" and processes of "national reconciliation" may be little more than the reconfiguration of elites' pacts of domination or governability, unless these national processes are articulated with social reconstruction locally. In the top-down version of "national reconciliation," there is little change in the demographics of the interlocutors or in the structure of the exclusionary logics of the nation-state. Thus while the "savage slot" may recede, the ethnically saturated category of the terrorist will continue to be a useful tool to stifle dissent.

Conclusion

In this chapter I have offered a place-based analysis of the complexities involved when introducing a politics of scale into our study of transitional justice and post-conflict reconstruction. To date, most studies of transitional justice have focused on the transnational or national dimensions; however, the ethnographic study of local engagements with global institutions—be they truth commissions or the figure of the "terrorist"—reveals their contradictory logics and unintended consequences.

In Peru, the Commission's Final Report played an important role in bringing former President Alberto Fujimori to trial for corruption and human rights violations. This is a stunning accomplishment a mere five years after the TRC completed its work. However, the Final Report also established certain narrative terms of engagement, and subject positions that are a prerequisite for access to redress and reparations. In tying the right to redress to an individual's "innocence," the Peruvian state distorts the content and practice of citizenship. The right to voice dissent and to peacefully place demands upon the state are rights that should belong to all Peruvians, not just those who are forced to erase their past in the hopes of securing their future.

In conclusion, many have suggested that history is written by the victors, and certainly the capacity to elaborate and impose histories with hegemonic pretensions in a postwar context reflects power relations between the victors and the vanquished. However, the losers also write their histories, albeit in the silences, in the margins, and in the rancor that characterizes postwar social worlds. My research in Peru compels me to question the victim-centered approach of truth commissions, and the resentful silences this may inadvertently create. Truth commissions—and other technologies of truth—must recognize political protagonism even while condemning the forms it may take. That recognition may be crucial to serving both the needs of history and those of justice.

Chapter 6

Linking Justice with Reintegration?
Ex-Combatants and the Sierra Leone Experiment
Rosalind Shaw

"DDR, TRC: All the Same Thing!"

Turning off the main highway that cuts through northern Sierra Leone, a pot-holed road lined with burned-out houses takes you to Lunsar. A booming iron-mining town in the 1930s, Lunsar began its decline when the mines closed in 1976. In the Marampa Hills nearby, monkeys play on huge pieces of rusting mine equipment that loom out of the mist. When you reach Lunsar's town center, a "Mobil" sign swings atop a closed gas station with its pumps ripped out, the sign's plastic colors startling against the layer of laterite dust that covers everything else. Because of its strategic location on the highway, the town was taken and retaken in a series of battles between the Revolutionary United Front (RUF) rebels and the national army during Sierra Leone's eleven-year civil war (1991–2002). In early 1999, the RUF drove out the army and occupied Lunsar for two years. During this time, according to an ex-RUF commander who had formed part of the occupation, one or two people were killed nearly every day, and looting was endemic. Although the mines had closed long before the occupation, the RUF went up into the hills and broke up what remained of the ruined machinery, assisted by residents who were angry at the town's long neglect by the government. Thus the direct violence of armed conflict was layered upon decades of the quiet violence of socioeconomic marginalization, which has continued unabated since the war ended in 2002.

By the time I conducted fieldwork in Lunsar in June 2003, Sierra Leone's National Committee for Disarmament, Demobilization, and Reintegration (NCDDR) was on its way to disarming an eventual 72,490 combatants from all armed groups (NCDDR 2004). Those who had gone through the first two stages of the Disarmament, Demobilization, and Reintegration (DDR) program were entitled to reintegration stipends of $150 and to six months of skills training, education, or agricultural programs. But many of Lunsar's noncombatants, unable to replace what they had lost during the war, were angry about these benefits. As I interviewed residents about the Truth and Reconciliation Commission (TRC) that was holding public hearings in other parts of the country at that time, many civilians spontaneously brought up DDR. While some felt that the DDR packages were crucial in providing ex-combatants with alternative livelihoods, others viewed them as an inequity. "DDR, TRC: All the same thing!" exclaimed one civilian. "Our wounds cannot be healed when we see the perpetrators being compensated and we get nothing!"

This perception that DDR and the TRC—completely separate entities—were "all the same thing" made sense from the standpoint of those struggling to reconstruct their lives. Both DDR and the TRC were large national postwar reconstruction operations funded by the international community; both shared (to different degrees) the goal of reintegrating ex-combatants; and both—despite the TRC's victim-oriented mandate—often appeared remote from survivors' concerns. This skepticism grew out of the bitter experience of living in a failing state that was perceived as having abandoned not just Lunsar, but most of "upcountry" Sierra Leone (Reno 1995; Richards 1996).

I locate this chapter in Sierra Leone's socioeconomic abjection in order to explore the intersection of transitional justice with DDR in contexts of enduring structural violence. This intersection became a site of multiple contradictions during Sierra Leone's transitional justice "experiment" with the concurrent operation of a truth commission and international criminal prosecutions—both of which also coincided with the final two years of national DDR and with local reintegration practices. These contradictions had deeply exclusionary consequences for ex-combatant youth, whose marginalization had contributed to Sierra Leone's civil war in the first place. While, as I explore below, DDR and post-conflict justice cannot be considered independent processes, efforts to integrate them tend to draw upon narrow definitions of justice that fail to engage with what "justice" and "reintegration" mean to all war-affected groups—including ex-combatants—in post-conflict settings shaped by pre-conflict injustice.

Linking Justice with Reintegration?

If some Sierra Leonean survivors felt that DDR and the TRC were "all the same thing," some international policymakers worry about the disjunctures between them. While those engaged in transitional justice take a "victim-centered" approach and prioritize justice, those engaged in DDR programs focus on combatants and prioritize security. Complaints in Sierra Leone and elsewhere about the unequal treatment of ex-combatants and noncombatants exemplify a recurring contradiction: while those who commit human rights abuses often receive DDR resources, most victims do not receive reparations—and if they do, these are typically delayed and inadequate.

Meanwhile, scholars and policymakers concerned with DDR recognize the need to rethink this process for other reasons. Standard DDR programs typically adopt a security-based approach that Knight and Özerdem (2004) characterize as "guns, camps, and cash," emphasizing the collection of weapons and the cantonment of former combatants. Relatively little emphasis is placed on the process of social reintegration, which has proved to be the "Achilles heel" of DDR (Meek and Malan 2004:12; see also Faltas 2005; Theidon 2007b). Several studies recognize that reintegration depends not only on ex-combatants themselves, but also, and crucially, on their relationship with their host communities (Coulter 2009; Faltas 2005; Humphreys and Weinstein 2005; Peters 2007; Richards et al. 2003; Theidon 2007b; Utas 2005a).

Some scholars and policymakers seek to address this neglect through transitional justice. Two major international policy conferences—the Stockholm Initiative on Disarmament, Demobilization, and Reintegration (SIDDR) in 2005 and the Second International Conference on Disarmament, Demobilization, Reintegration and Stability in Africa in 2007—have recommended that reintegration be linked with justice (SIDDR 2005; DDR and Stability in Africa 2007). Meanwhile, the International Center for Transitional Justice (ICTJ) is developing a framework for DDR programs designed to contribute both to transitional justice goals and to effective reintegration (Duthie 2005; ICTJ 2008b). One version of this linkage has been put into practice—with very mixed results—through the Justice and Peace Law in Colombia (e.g., Diaz 2007).

So far, those who seek to incorporate transitional-justice goals into DDR programs emphasize two forms of justice: reparatory material support for "victims" and legal accountability for "perpetrators" (Duthie 2005; ICTJ 2008b; SIDDR 2005). The first arises in part from survivors' critiques of DDR in several post-conflict states, as we have seen for Sierra Leone. But the second argument—that accountability for perpetrators through justice mechanisms will promote reintegration—appears to be based on transitional justice axioms rather than on circumstances on the ground. In the fullest expression of this argument, the SIDDR report states that "policies that by means of criminal prosecutions, truth-telling procedures or vetting offer receiving communities assurances that those that they are expected to welcome back are not responsible of serious crimes can only improve the chances that returning ex-combatants will indeed be reintegrated" (2005 p. 30, para. 56). This recurring claim about the relationship between truth telling, justice, and reintegration is not backed up by research on the outcomes of transitional justice in particular places and times, however (e.g., Cobban 2007; Fletcher and Weinstein 2002; Stover and Weinstein 2004; Waldorf 2006; and the chapters in this volume). If the "guns, camps, and cash" approach to DDR is replaced by axiomatic transitional justice assumptions, this simply exchanges one standard toolkit for another.

Together, these two ways of linking justice and reintegration replicate the "victim–perpetrator" dichotomy that structures transitional justice norms (see Theidon, this volume). Dividing survivors of armed conflict into "victims" entitled to reparations and "perpetrators" subject to "criminal prosecutions, truth-telling procedures or vetting" fails to adequately confront the moral "gray zone" of civil wars such as Sierra Leone's, as I discuss in the next section. It also obscures the fact that "injustice" in such contexts consists not only of human rights violations committed during the war, but also the abuses and structural violence that helped precipitate the war in the first place. Louise Arbour, former UN High Commissioner for Human Rights, has recently called for an expansion of transitional justice goals to address such long-term injustice. "Transitional justice," she argues, "must reach to, but also beyond the crimes . . . committed during the conflict . . . , into the human rights violations that pre-existed the conflict and . . . contributed to it. When making that search, it is likely that one would expose a great number of violations of economic, social and cultural . . . rights" (2006:3–4). Such an approach promises both to reshape transitional justice and to transform what it means to link justice with reintegration.

In the next section, I return to Sierra Leone to trace why such reshaping is necessary.

Experiencing DDR in Sierra Leone

We the youths own this country. But the government says we are not senior. But how can you be senior when there's no work? Because there's no work, youths go out to steal.

—*RUF ex-combatant, Lunsar, June 2003*

For a while, DDR stipends provided a focus for desperate noncombatants' feelings of injustice after Sierra Leone's civil war ended. But this resentment faded when DDR ended in January 2004. By the time I returned in July 2004, I heard no more such complaints. What endured was the long-term abjection that affects noncombatants and ex-combatants alike: Lunsar represents just one of the innumerable faces of Sierra Leone's downward trajectory. During twenty-four years of depredations by the ruling All People's Congress regime, from 1968 to 1992, the state was plundered while the majority of its population sank into deepening impoverishment (Reno 1995). As the state receded further, with a collapsing political economy and a series of institutional failures in the 1980s, the foundations were laid for Sierra Leone's civil war (Richards 1996).

This erosion of the state created a particular crisis for youth, who constitute the nation's majority: nearly 70 percent of Sierra Leoneans are under thirty (Leahy 2007:90). As the young ex-combatant put it in the quote that opens this section, youths "own" Sierra Leone. But this is true only numerically: youth unemployment—currently at a massive 60 percent (Sommers 2007b)—has been high for decades, the educational system dysfunctional, and the contrast with opportunities enjoyed by politicians' own children galling. Rural youth also face an exclusionary social hierarchy, in which senior men in elite lineages control land and use customary law to impose arbitrary fines and labor levies on young men (e.g., Richards 2005a; Sommers 2007b). For these and other reasons, the frustrations of socially excluded youth are linked to West Africa's armed conflicts (Peters 2007:37; Peters and Richards 1998; Richards 1996; Sommers 2007b; Utas 2005a). According to Sierra Leone's TRC Report, marginal youth formed the vast majority of combatants in the RUF, the CDF, and the expanded Sierra Leone Army (Truth and Reconciliation Commission, Sierra Leone 2005:2[2], p. 95, para. 455). While a large proportion of these young combatants were forcibly conscripted, some joined voluntarily (Peters and Richards 1998). Fighters from both categories sought to use their weapons to reverse their socioeconomic marginalization (Peters and Richards 1998; Richards 2005a; Utas 2005a).

After the war, moreover, the circumstances that gave rise to it remain in place. Sierra Leone is regularly ranked last or second-to-last in the UN's Human Development Index, and political corruption continues unabated. While several reports link youth frustrations with these conditions to the potential for future violence (e.g., Truth and Reconciliation Commission, Sierra Leone 2005:2[2], p. 95, para. 459), Sommers turns this link around to emphasize a different point: "given the conditions that most young people face," he argues, they are "extraordinarily peaceful" (2007b:13).

Its own claims of success notwithstanding (NCDDR 2004), Sierra Leone's DDR program was not effective in enabling tens of thousands of combatants to surmount the challenges of reintegration. Large numbers of people from armed groups—perhaps the majority (Peters 2007; Richards et al. 2003)—were excluded from registration, and therefore from DDR reintegration packages. First, in order to register, combatants were required to bring an automatic weapon: this discriminated against the Civil Defense Forces (CDF), since most of its fighters used knives, cutlasses, and shotguns (Richards et al. 2003). Second, during disarmament, commanders redistributed weapons to their own allies and relatives in order to channel DDR resources for their own advantage (Hoffman 2005; Peters 2007; Richards et al. 2003). Third, while many women and minors were armed combatants, many others were domestic workers, "bush wives," porters, and messengers who—lacking a weapon—were also excluded from DDR (Coulter 2009; McKay and Mazurana 2004). In addition, many women and girls who could have brought a weapon avoided registration because the formal identity of "ex-combatant" could undermine reintegration into their communities (Coulter 2009). Fourth, as I discuss below, fear of the Special Court and the TRC compounded ex-combatants' concerns about registration for DDR. And as Richards et al. (2003) observe, the lowest ranks were the most likely to be excluded.

For those ex-combatants who registered for DDR, additional challenges arose. Most ex-combatants chose a vocational skills training package, administered over six months, which rarely provided the basis for an independent livelihood (Coulter 2009; Richards et al. 2003:14). The same vocational skills were, in any case, offered throughout the country, flooding the market with an oversupply of (inadequately trained) carpenters, masons, electricians, mechanics, tailors, hairdressers, soapmakers, and batik cloth dyers (Coulter 2009; Peters 2007; see Utas 2005a:150 for Liberia). Unable to compete with established craftspeople, those ex-combatants who received tools as part of their DDR package often ended up selling them. Others again had no tools to sell, as DDR tools and stipends often failed to arrive. Complaints about the incomplete delivery of DDR packages extended countrywide (Peters 2007; Richards et al. 2003; Humphreys and Weinstein 2004:30–32). Amidst these complaints, and in the face of frequent allegations of corruption in the NCDDR and its implementing partners, the NCDDR dismissed a report it had commissioned when its authors investigated and supported some of these grievances (Richards et al. 2003; Peters 2007).

Some ex-combatants, it must be said, are pleased with their DDR packages, and have used them to establish new livelihoods (Humphreys and Weinstein 2004). Others have been successful in finding alternative livelihoods, either through apprenticeships or by entering new occupational groups such as motorbike taxi renters' associations (Richards et al. 2003). Yet many others unable to take these routes entered virtual servitude by working as diamond diggers in the east (ibid.). Others remained in the towns of their demobilization, struggling to live on occasional menial jobs. Young women from combatant groups—most of whom did not go through DDR and therefore received no packages—were often, in addition, abandoned with young children. Female ex-combatants thus had a limited set of choices, often engaging in prostitution, becoming long-term "girlfriends" in exchange for material support, or entering into exploitative marriages (Coulter 2009; McKay and Mazurana 2004; Richards et al. 2003; Peters 2007; Utas 2005b).

Livelihood issues also shaped whether ex-combatants could return home. Female ex-combatants—especially those with children—often confounded norms of ideal female behavior (Coulter 2009). Their reintegration into their families was improved, however, if they were able to establish a livelihood (ibid.). Male ex-combatant youth had to negotiate a different set of gendered social norms: they are usually expected to bring home resources of some kind, both as emblems of success and as expressions of support for their families. Although many families were concerned about the "rebel behavior" their children might bring home, these fears were often ameliorated if their children acted with appropriate moral responsibility toward their families. But without the means to acquire such resources, young male ex-combatants were reluctant to go home (Richards et al. 2003). Utas, writing of ex-combatant youth in Liberia, characterizes "reintegration" under circumstances such as these as, in fact, a form of remarginalization (2005a).

But not all Sierra Leonean ex-combatants were similarly remarginalized. Among the RUF in particular, many of those at the top of the hierarchy were offered more attractive DDR packages. Thus "computer training," note

Richards et al., "is aimed at an RUF 'elite,' tailoring and carpentry attracts the bush fighters with lower educational levels" (2003:16; see Peters 2007:42). In addition, some RUF commanders negotiating the disarmament of their units were granted projects in agricultural development and human rights—a privileged sector in this NGO-ized country. While such projects often enabled former members of the RUF elite to become prominent and productive civilians, they form a stark contrast to the outcomes of DDR for most lower-rank ex-combatants.

This remarginalization of ex-combatants and the structural violence that helped catalyze Sierra Leone's conflict highlight the relevance of Louise Arbour's call for an expanded understanding of justice.[1] Young Sierra Leoneans are keenly aware of the institutional structures and hierarchies that perpetuate their marginalization, and they express concerns about justice in the broader sense that Arbour details. Before the war ended, a series of chiefdom consultations organized in 1999–2000 precipitated what Archibald and Richards (2002) call a "popular debate about war and justice": young people wanted to discuss political corruption, unjust applications of customary law, and the exploitation of their labor. Aspects of this debate that concern urban youth were further developed in the TRC.[2] But instead of an articulation of justice and DDR that would properly address their exclusion, ex-combatants were subject to a justice experiment that exacerbated it.

Experimental Justice

> During the time of the disarmament many were afraid to go and register. They said that the pictures they take are not only for DDR and that the A, B, C, and D on the ID card stand for A is for Pademba Road [prison], B is for the Special Court, C is for the TRC and only D is for the disarmament. Everything—your name and picture—will be in the computer.
>
> —Female ex-RUF combatant, quoted in Peters 2007:47

When Sierra Leone's TRC and the Special Court for Sierra Leone both began their operations in 2002, it was the first time that a truth commission would operate concurrently with international criminal prosecutions. This precedent had its origins in changing international norms. Three years earlier, the 1999 Lome Peace Accord had given all combatants a blanket amnesty in an attempt to end the civil war. This, however, went against the grain of an international shift toward retributive justice: in protest, UN Special Representative

Francis Okello famously appended a handwritten caveat to the Lome Accord stating that the UN would not recognize amnesty for "crimes of genocide, crimes against humanity, war crimes and other serious violations of human rights and international law" (Human Rights Watch, May 19, 2000). While the Lome Accord recommended the establishment of a TRC to establish restorative justice, the Sierra Leone government subsequently asked for an international criminal tribunal to prosecute the RUF and ex-AFRC. In August 2000, the UN approved the Special Court for Sierra Leone—the first hybrid international court—to be jointly administered by the UN and the government of Sierra Leone, throwing the amnesty open to challenge.

Up to that point, many of those who studied and designed truth commissions believed that unless perpetrators were offered amnesty, they would be unwilling to testify before a truth commission (e.g., Rotberg and Thompson 2000). But Sierra Leone became "a laboratory in which to examine how the two bodies, special 'institutionalized' courts and truth commissions, relate to each other" (Schabas 2003:1065). Many policymakers hoped that the Sierra Leone experiment would help close the door to future trade-offs between truth and justice (defined, invariably, as criminal justice). Beyond this disturbing image of Sierra Leoneans as experimental subjects and those who ran the Special Court and TRC as white-coated scientists lay the even more troubling implication—sometimes made explicit by expatriates in Freetown—that Sierra Leone was less important in itself than as a model for other countries (Daniel Hoffman, pers. comm., February 20, 2004).

Central to this experiment were the attitudes of ex-combatants, whose testimony would be crucial to both the TRC and the Special Court. Thus before the TRC and Special Court became active, a Sierra Leonean NGO, the Post-Conflict Reintegration Initiative for Development and Empowerment (PRIDE), conducted a study of 176 ex-combatants. On the basis of questionnaires and focus groups, the authors concluded that despite anxieties about information sharing between the TRC and the Special Court, "ex-combatants are willing and eager to participate in the TRC because they believe the TRC will facilitate reintegration into their former communities" (2002:5). But this was a cautious optimism, which the authors qualified by warning, "there will probably be less willingness to cooperate with the Special Court than this report indicates" (ibid., 17). They also raised questions about some of the responses. Although 72 percent of the ex-combatants they surveyed had heard of the TRC, only 54 percent claimed to understand it; nevertheless, a full 79 percent expressed support for it (ibid., p. 36)! Concerning their results in Kailahun, an RUF stronghold, the authors commented, "expressions of concern from focus groups lead us to believe that many of the respondents were not being honest in their response" (ibid., p. 29). Finally, the authors noted, "One former RUF said that he thought persons may be expressing support for the Special Court in the hope that the Special Court may consider this in mitigation or divert attention away from investigating them," adding "the data must be read in the light of this reservation" (ibid., Annex 2, p. 38).

When the TRC began to collect statements in late 2002, it became clear that PRIDE's reservations were better predictors of ex-combatant participation than the study results themselves. Ex-combatant fears that the TRC was a "feeder court" for the Special Court were not soothed by the initial address of the TRC headquarters in Pademba Road, where Freetown's notorious prison is located. When the TRC headquarters were later moved to the Brookfields area of Freetown, close to the Special Court, rumors developed of an underground tunnel connecting the two (Kelsall 2005:381). According to one of the statement takers in Port Loko District, the site of the first TRC district hearings, angry and frightened ex-combatants in two towns drove the statement-taking team away, in one incident pelting their vehicle with rocks. "Do you think we don't know the Special Court sent you?" ex-combatants shouted before threatening to smash their windshield. Subsequently, these statement takers felt safer when they covered up the TRC logo on their vehicle and left their printed TRC T-shirts and caps at home.

As the TRC hearings moved from district to district in mid-2003, it was enough to be white and interested in talking to ex-combatants for my presence to arouse profound fear. In Lunsar, ex-combatants warned each other about me, saying, "If you talk to her, you will hear your name on Radio UN-AMSIL!" This referred to the practice of announcing the Special Court's indictments on the radio station run by the United Nations Assistance Mission for Sierra Leone. In the village of Mapetifu,[3] which I describe in the next section, the family of one ex-combatant denied that he lived there when I arrived. "The white woman works for the TRC!" someone exclaimed inside the house. Shortly afterward, the ex-combatant recognized me and came out himself to invite me in. Researchers working in other parts of the country at that time had similar experiences. When Richards et al. sought to talk to ex-combatants in the Bandafie, Kono District, "[t]he leader said he would arrange a meeting for the following day, but nobody was waiting when we returned, and no one in the vicinity was prepared to talk. As we were preparing to leave a large group of children started to chant 'TRC, TRC'" (2003:23). Further north, Chris Coulter, conducting PhD research on female ex-combatants, likewise writes: "My own research in Koinadugu in 2003/04 was affected by rumours of the TRC and the Special Court, and it took me quite some time to convince my informants that I had nothing to do with either" (2006:273).

During the TRC district hearings, ex-combatants often left town or laid low. In Port Loko District, TRC statement takers found only two ex-combatants willing to give statements, and neither was willing to testify at the district hearings. Ex-combatant participation in the hearings I attended in Bombali, Kambia, Moyamba, and Tonkolili Districts was either very low or was increased only by substantial behind-the-scenes persuasion. As a result of considerable effort by both TRC staff and the NGO PRIDE, and as, over time, no Special Court indictments were issued for ex-combatants who had testified before the TRC, ex-combatant participation increased (TRC Final Report 2005, vol. 2, p. 449, para. 59). But the damage had been done: the TRC's Final Report concludes that "[t]he Commission's ability to create a forum of exchange between victims and perpetrators was retarded by the presence of the Special Court" (2005, vol. 2, p. 111, para. 592). And by then, ex-combatant fears of the Special Court had affected more than just the TRC.

With national and international spotlights on the two transitional justice mechanisms, little attention was paid to their intersection with DDR and other initiatives for ex-combatants. In different parts of the country, ex-combatants conflated not just the Special Court and the TRC, but both of these mechanisms with DDR, which deterred many of them from registering for disarmament. As in the quote from the female RUF ex-combatant that opens this section, the NCDDR was widely believed to share the information from the photograph ID cards it issued with Sierra Leone's two transitional justice mechanisms, as well as with Pademba Road Prison (see also Richards et al. 2003:23). Coulter, working in Koinadugu District with female ex-combatants and former "bush wives," was told of even more serious concerns: "having one's picture taken for demobilization, to ensure correct distribution of benefits, was believed to lead to incarceration and possible execution by the TRC and the Special Court" (2006:274). Such fears also deterred ex-combatants from attending skills training programs. According to a senior staff member in the

Port Loko office of the UK Department for International Development (DFID), ex-combatant attendance for DDR skills training workshops with the DFID plummeted from over a hundred to around thirty during the TRC's Port Loko District Hearings in April 2003 (see also Coulter 2006:274 for Koinadugu District). The concurrent TRC and Special Court, then, cast a pall that intensified processes of exclusion already present in DDR.

Some of those involved in the TRC attributed these fears of information sharing between the two mechanisms to "confusion" (e.g., TRC Final Report 2005, vol. 2, p. 111, para. 591), and to ex-combatant "illiteracy" and "irrationality." Commissioner William Schabas, for example, argued that "confusion" between the TRC and the Special Court was natural: "most European law students have trouble explaining the distinctions between the European Court of Human Rights and the European Court of Justice. Who can really expect uneducated, illiterate peasants in the countryside of Sierra Leone to do better?" (2003:1064–65). To interpret ex-combatant fears as signs of "confusion" or "rural illiteracy" is not only to consign ex-combatants to the ranks of the irrational (and implicitly primitivized), but also to miss a crucial dimension of the meaning of these fears. Images of the TRC as the "child of the Special Court," of an underground tunnel connecting them, and of the DDR ID card that indexes a secret information flow among the NCDDR, the TRC, the Special Court, and Pademba Road Prison may be regarded not simply as factual statements but as *moral commentaries* on these mechanisms and institutions. What counted here was not merely the dissemination and clarity of official information about the relationships among them (which were, in fact, woefully inadequate), but rather "the underneath of things" (Ferme 2001)—the hidden reality inferred beneath public appearances in a state that ex-combatants had every reason to distrust.

For there were, inevitably, informal exchanges of information between the TRC and the Special Court. As Kelsall comments, "it was common to see representatives from the Court and the TRC lunching together in Freetown" (2005:381). According to some of those working with the TRC, a senior individual in the Commission was wont to declare that if he came across evidence useful to the Special Court, he would pass it on to the Special Court "under the table," because "justice is justice." At the end of the TRC's extended mandate in 2004, the Special Court hired former TRC employees, who not only were able to draw upon knowledge about ex-combatants they had gained while with the TRC but were also, according to a former senior TRC staff member, allegedly used as witnesses for the prosecution in the Court. Were ex-combatants, then, really as "irrational" and "confused" as they were said to be about information sharing?

When I returned from my 2003 field research on the TRC, I was surprised to read that the Sierra Leone experiment was broadly considered a success. "As the TRC hearings progressed during mid-2003," wrote former TRC commissioner William Schabas, "many perpetrators came forward to tell their stories to the Commission and, in some cases, to ask pardon or forgiveness of the victims. They did not appear at all concerned about the threat of prosecution by the Special Court" (2003:1051). Schabas concludes that the relationship between the TRC and the Special Court is "more synergistic than many might have thought" (2003:1065) and looks forward to the Sierra Leonean "laboratory" providing a future model for a "genuinely complementary approach, by which international prosecution co-exists with alternative accountability mechanisms" (2003:1066). Likewise, the former Chief Prosecutor of the Special Court, David Crane, asserts: "The Sierra Leone model is the right model. A plus B equals C. Truth plus justice equals sustainable peace" (Nichols 2005).

As Crane's formulaic statement implies, assumptions brought to Sierra Leone appear to have been recycled as conclusions, while neither the realities of the TRC's awkward journey across Sierra Leone nor the standpoints of "illiterate peasants" were allowed to intrude. These conclusions, in turn, have now become part of the taken-for-granted "facts" of transitional justice. "It is now generally recognized," states former UN Secretary-General Kofi Annan in his influential 2004 report on the rule of law and transitional justice, "that truth commissions can positively complement criminal tribunals, as the examples of Argentina, Peru, Timor-Leste and Sierra Leone suggest" (United Nations 2004a: para. 26, p. 9).

Reintegration from Below

If Sierra Leone's transitional justice mechanisms intensified the processes of exclusion produced by formal DDR, the TRC was itself reshaped in an unanticipated way by informal reintegration practices that had developed in many local communities. Attention to such practices, I argue, shows us how both host communities and ex-combatants seek to reconstitute civic trust by establishing the moral and social obligations on which this trust depends.[4] In this section, I explore some of these strategies in northern Sierra Leone and contrast them to those of truth commissions.

After the war, Ahmadu (a pseudonym), an ex-AFRC combatant, settled in the large village of Mapetifu (also a pseudonym) in Port Loko District and worked as a mason on a nearby construction project run by an international NGO. A small, slender man in his thirties, Ahmadu is a son of Kambia District to the northeast, where his wife and three children still lived. In 1998, he told me, he had been digging diamonds near the eastern town of Koidu, when he fled into the bush with his friends to avoid attack by the AFRC. But at 4:30 a.m., AFRC troops arrived and captured them: "They asked us, 'To join us or to cut [amputate] your hand, which one do you want?' We said, 'We will go with you.'" Ahmadu listed a succession of towns to which he was forced to travel over the next few months, portering headloads ("We carried their bundles, their wives' things") before his group was disarmed: "They called for a cease-fire, 20 July, 1999. We moved from Makeni to Kabala. Then UN-AMSIL arrived in Kabala. The UN gave disarmament tags to all those who had disarmed."

Ahmadu's narrative had many silences: conspicuously absent was any mention of violence beyond the original abduction. "Did the AFRC train you?" I asked. "No." "Did they give you a gun?" "No." Since bringing a weapon was the usual requirement for disarmament, it is unlikely that he would have been able to go through DDR without one. But Ahmadu did not know me well and was concerned about a different set of requirements: those that would help maintain the trust of his hosts and his employer. Like Ahmadu, many ex-combatants narrated highly condensed accounts that emphasized the time of their capture, their compulsion to join a combatant group under the threat of death or amputation, their forced labor, and eventually their departure through escape or (in Ahmadu's case) demobilization. Such postwar narratives have become formulaic and standardized. Coulter terms these accounts "NGO narratives" (2006:21–25, 48), since the ways in which war-affected people speak of violence have been structured by the need to present themselves as "victims" to humanitarian organizations (ibid., 55; see also Utas 2005b). This is not to suggest that these parts of their stories are necessarily untrue. Although an undetermined number of combatants joined voluntarily (Peters and Richards 1998), thousands were indeed captured, conscripted, and used for forced labor. But Sierra Leone's civil war, like most armed conflicts, was a "gray zone" with blurred boundaries between "victims" and "perpetrators": many abductees committed abuses themselves. During postwar reconstruction, however, both international humanitarian discourse and practices of local reintegration required a reinscription of clear boundaries. Ex-combatants who wished to settle needed to locate themselves as "victims."

Through narratives like Ahmadu's, ex-combatants construct a moral personhood affirming that their "hearts" (Temne *ta-buth*) or inner dispositions are not the "warm" or "angry" hearts of fighters. They were not acting "for themselves," as many expressed it: their agency was subsumed by their commanders. These narratives are not only a learned product of humanitarian discourses of victimhood, however. They also draw upon long-standing local models of personhood, power, and agency, in which "big people's" (in this case, commanders') power is manifest in their capacity for extension, for acting through the vehicle of their subordinates (Ferme 2001). The condition of the heart signaled by such narratives of subsumed agency is crucial for processes of social integration and coexistence. In Sierra Leone Krio and Temne (the dominant languages in Mapetifu), the English term *reconciliation* becomes "cool/settled heart" (Krio *kol at*; Temne *ka-buth ke-thofel*). When the heart (the center of feelings, thoughts, and intentions), is "cool," it is not angry ("warm") or resentful. It does not cause one to "think too much" about painful memories. Most people expressed the achievement of a "cool heart" in terms of a process of "forgetting," saying (for example) "I try to forget the war." A "cool heart" is, then, a necessary condition for proper social relationships with others and forms the basis for life in a community. By emphasizing his abduction and the coerced manner in which he joined the AFRC, Ahmadu affirmed that he was a moral person with a cool heart who represented no threat to the community.

After demobilization, Ahmadu learned masonry in a six-month skills-training program as part of his DDR package. In 2001 he found a job with an NGO and was brought to a village near Mapetifu to build a school. When that project was completed, he sought permission to settle in Mapetifu: "I met the people who own this town. . . . I told them, 'I am a stranger here. Now, [his NGO] has brought us here to work, to build houses. Please help me to find a place to sleep.' They said, 'Fine, we are glad.' They gave me the place." Here Ahmadu describes an arrangement that has a long ancestry in Sierra Leone: the landlord–stranger relationship. He gave a small amount—Le1,000 (approximately fifty U.S. cents at the time)—to his landlord every week when he received his pay, and he provided labor when his landlord needed it.

In Mapetifu, the "people who own the town"—the headman and other senior men—did not ask about Ahmadu's wartime actions and experiences. "They told me the rules of the town," he told me: "No cursing, no stealing, no using your neighbor's woman. When anyone offends you, lodge a complaint— don't fight. That's it." His integration into a landlord–stranger relationship was based on moral behavior in the community, especially his "humble" acceptance of civilian authority. "He [Ahmadu] is not a scattered man," Mapetifu's headman told me. "He is so humble. First, he came to us and explained his situation. So after exploring this, we accepted him. Above all, we accepted him because of his good behavior." To be "humble" was to manifest a contrast to the behavior of combatants during the war, whose weapons gave them power over civilians. At the same time, Ahmadu's humility meant his deference to local authority structures based on the dominance of senior elite men. "Humility" thus references both ex-combatants' respect for civilians and their reintegration into pre-conflict structures of inequality and marginalization.

Some adult ex-combatants did, however, tell brief, condensed narratives when they sought to settle or resettle in Mapetifu, usually focusing on their abduction and forced labor. The headman was aware of the formulaic nature of these accounts but accepted them anyway. He told me:

> Some, they explain all their ordeals. How they carried heavy loads. I ask them, "Did you join voluntarily, or were you seized?" ["Do you ask them about bad things they've done?" I asked.] No, and they don't tell me about this. All of them said they had been abducted. They say, "I was captured." Some, they explain, "We have escaped from the rebels." Some say, "We thank God to find ourselves here." And they beg for mercy. . . . We normally watch them for one or two weeks to see if they have really come to stay. Maybe their group is waiting in the bush. We watch for their character. ["What do you watch for?"] One of the things we watch for is whether he will smoke *ka-thai* (cannabis). We watch whether they drug themselves, whether they drink a lot, for these things inflame them. Even when they go from one part of the village to another, we watch them.

The headman thus cued the petitioners to position themselves either as combatants who acted "for themselves" or as victims whose agency was subsumed by others. Once they chose the latter, however, he showed no interest in questioning these stories or in probing their silences. Allowing the past's moral "grayness" to remain quietly layered beneath a surface reality of victimhood, the headman discouraged civilians in the town from asking about ex-combatants' pasts. Instead, he and other senior men took pains to observe, over a period of time, whether the ex-combatants' present behavior in the community confirmed the "cool" hearts that their stories suggested. Although the headman asked ex-combatants to explain how they became combatants, then, the making of moral relationships in the present took precedence over verbal accounts of the past. In order to begin again, civilians and ex-combatants collaborated in a remaking of moral subjectivities that contained the past. This remaking was based on a "truth" somewhat different from that pursued in truth commissions such as Sierra Leone's TRC.

Truth and Redemption in the Bombali District Hearings

Toward the end of the TRC's Bombali District Hearings on May 30, 2003, the commissioners introduced the closing ceremony in the town hall in Makeni, capital of the Northern Province. On the stage, in front of two Sierra Leonean flags, sat four figures of civilian authority: the Paramount Chief of Bombali Seborah Chiefdom, the Senior District Officer for Bombali District, the Chairman of the Makeni Christian Council, and the regional Chief Imam. This was the setting in which three former high-ranking RUF commanders would undergo a reconciliation ceremony.

Like Lunsar, Makeni and its surrounding towns had undergone over two years of occupation when the RUF and their former AFRC allies established Makeni as their headquarters in late 1998. When the TRC's Bombali District hearings came to town, it was, as in many other towns, the object of widespread ex-combatant fear: only three out of the seventeen people who testified were ex-combatants. All three were of high rank, since most ex-combatants felt it was not their place to speak. Like other district hearings, the Bombali hearings consisted overwhelmingly of truth telling, in which people, categorized as "victims," "witnesses," and "perpetrators" narrated their memories of violence. As in the other district hearings I observed, the three ex-combatants who testified gave formulaic narratives describing the internal organization and politics of the RUF, the ideology of the RUF, the RUF's strict laws against harming civilians, and how well the civilians in their power were treated; detailed accounts of troop movements, attacks, retreats, ambushes, their own promotions, and success within the movement; and often their encounters with the RUF leadership. No ex-combatant in these or any of the hearings I attended acknowledged any personal responsibility for specific acts of violence (cf. Payne 2008).

After five grueling days, the concluding reconciliation ceremony was typically a brief event, dubbed "drive-by reconciliation" by one observer, and conducted just before the exhausted TRC staff and commissioners headed back to Freetown. Central to these events were public apologies given by the ex-combatants, followed by their blessing by civilian authorities. In the closing ceremony of the Bombali hearings, none of the three senior ex-combatants acknowledged any specific personal wrongdoing, but the first two were clearly moved by the event. The first, Abdulai, fell to his knees before the audience and declared (in Sierra Leone Krio), emotion in his voice:

> I mean to say, what I have done, for the rest of my life, from '94 until this point, I believe it was a bad thing. . . . But if you, my family, don't leave me, God will not leave me. . . . If you forgive me, if you bless me, then God will put a blessing on my work, God will forgive me. But if you don't forgive me, if you don't bless me, the ending of my work, I will become zero, [until] the ending of my life. ["It's true!" audience members around me whispered.] So please, I beg you, for what I have done, I kneel down, I beg pardon for what I have done.

He moved to the table at which sat the four civilian leaders. When he dropped to his knees again and bowed his head, they laid their hands on him as a sign of blessing. The audience responded with approval.

The second ex-combatant, Mohamed, was a former RUF military police investigator. His words were even more equivocal, but he too fell to his knees and appeared to be genuinely affected by his participation in the ceremony:

> [T]his is war. War is trouble. War is destruction. I am here to apologize to the community of Makeni and environs. I was an officeholder, but I belonged to a group that did these crimes. People, please forgive me for what we have done. So I apologize. But please remember that I forgive. Let my brothers come and give testimony and get that everlasting blessing.

He knelt before the four leaders, was blessed, and again received an approving response.

The third ex-combatant, Ibrahim, notorious for his brutal treatment of civilians, had not been aware of the reconciliation ceremony until he heard it on the radio. He swaggered up to the town hall stage in shorts, a white T-shirt, a red baseball cap, and fashionable sunglasses—a legacy of a wartime eye injury. Remaining on his feet, he addressed the hall thus:

> I am trying to make you understand that it was war. War enters into a country because of God. I am asking everyone to forgive and forget. What happened will never happen again. If I have done anything wrong to people here in Sierra

Leone, they should forgive and forget. We should open a new page. What happened will not happen any more.

Turning to the four leaders at the table behind him, he remained standing, gave them a perfunctory bow, and shook the hand of each in turn. The audience exploded in angry teeth sucking.

Reconciliation Through Truth?

If truth commissions are performances, what was performed in these apologies and blessings? According to liberal understandings of transition, an apology involves a statement of individual responsibility and contrition based on truth (e.g., Minow 1998:117). Neither truth telling nor individual responsibility figured in these three ex-combatants' statements, however. Ibrahim Dube failed to acknowledge any offense at all, shifting moral responsibility onto God and even those he had harmed. Abdulai acknowledged accountability in vague and abstract terms, while Mohamed rationalized RUF atrocities as inevitable consequences of war and implied that his own forgiveness of others should be reciprocated by civilians. Neither of these avowals corresponds to the ideal-type apology specified in transitional justice literature, namely, an explicit verbal acknowledgment of specific wrongdoing with no attempt at rationalization. "To apologize," writes Tavuchis, "is to declare voluntarily that one has *no* excuse, defense, justification, or explanation for an action (or inaction)" (1991:17).

But as Kelsall (2005) argues for the Tonkolili District Hearings, these brief reconciliation ceremonies had an efficacy that cannot, given the equivocal content of the apologies and testimonies, be attributed to the power of truth telling. Abdulai's and Mohamed's "apologies" were popularly accepted. Their performance of truth as the recounting of specific actions was less significant than their embodied performance of the "truth" of moral subjectivities, the display of a change in the speakers' hearts. Unlike Ibrahim, who continued to act like a big man, Abdulai and Mohamed no longer behaved like commanders. "I am an ordinary soldier who says, 'Yes Sir,'" declared Abdulai, who had been incorporated into the new Sierra Leone army as a lowly private.

This performance of moral transformation was confirmed by blessings. Abdulai addressed the audience as "my family" and told them that only their blessing could open the way to God's blessings for him. Mohamed likewise encouraged his fellow ex-combatants to "come and give testimony and get that everlasting blessing." For Abdulai and Mohamed to "beg" the (civilian) audience in the TRC for forgiveness and blessing was an expression of their humility, their indebtedness, to those over whom they had once presided through force. This was underscored by their physical postures and gestures of subordination, kneeling in front of the audience and the representatives of civilian authority. Abdulai, moreover, referred to the audience as his "family," evoking both what children owe their families and acknowledging the parents' power to confer or withhold the blessings that determine their children's future.

Abdulai, Mohamed, and the audience thus drove the TRC's reconciliation ceremony along a different path from that envisaged in liberal models of transition. The "apologies" and blessings marked a transformation in Abdulai and Mohamed as moral subjects that had little to do with accountability for the past. It was not through their display of verbally discursive truth but through their embodied demonstration of "cool hearts," their changed basis for social relationships, that the audience accepted Abdulai's and Mohamed's less-than-explicit "apologies."

But in so doing, Abdulai and Mohamed also dramatized the reassertion of age and status hierarchies. Just as ex-combatants in Mapetifu were expected to display humility toward senior men from elite lineages, the TRC reconciliation ceremony ritualized ex-combatants' submission to chiefs, district officers, and religious leaders. And as in Mapetifu, this effectively meant reintegration into the very structures of power and exclusion that contributed to the war in the first place.

A year later, Abdulai was still in the army. After his public testimony and "apology," he gained celebrity as a poster child for the TRC. Television coverage of the Bombali District Hearings repeatedly showed him kneeling in a gesture of deference, "begging" the audience with his right arm extended in supplication. He currently appears in that position on the home page of the TRC website, in the middle of the top gallery (TRC 2005). Mohamed became the personal assistant of the Vice-Chairman of Makeni's City Council. He already knew the Vice-Chairman through his DDR skills training in a computer school, but Mohamed's TRC apology impressed the Vice-Chairman so much that he offered him the job. Ibrahim, however, fled Makeni soon after the TRC, fearful of being sent to the Special Court amidst negative responses to his "apology" from both civilians and TRC commissioners.

Conclusions

By making the TRC an object of fear for ex-combatants, the Sierra Leone experiment intensified what Richards et al. (2003) call the "DDR hierarchy." In the district hearings I attended, the TRC's reconciliation ceremonies facilitated the reintegration of most ex-combatants who testified. But as in DDR, in which educated elites received the most attractive reintegration packages, the ex-combatants who testified before the TRC were mostly of high rank. And just as the most marginalized were excluded from DDR registration altogether, lower-status ex-combatants avoided both the TRC and DDR, because of fears of information sharing with the Special Court. Given that these fears had such negative consequences for the structurally weakest ex-combatants, the integration of DDR and transitional justice should be approached with great caution.

Sierra Leone's experience thus directs us—as Louise Arbour (2006) urges—to think beyond narrow concepts of justice that derive from criminal law. Given Sierra Leone's decades of political corruption, economic free-fall, massive unemployment, successions of institutional failure, extractive rural institutions, and social exclusions of youth, it is not enough to address only the violations committed during armed conflict itself—important though these are. If justice mechanisms are to work in synergy with processes of reintegration to create civic trust, then they must extend beyond crimes of war to encompass social and economic justice in contexts of enduring structural violence.

These Sierra Leonean intersections also demonstrate that war-affected communities have their own expectations for (re)integration—expectations that DDR programs and transitional justice mechanisms need to discover. Communities put these expectations into practice through their own reintegration practices, which may reveal emphases different from those of verbal responses to attitude surveys. In Mapetifu and other communities in which I conducted research in northern Sierra Leone, ex-combatants were evaluated primarily in terms of their present enactment of social morality. Instead of pursuing a verbal exhumation of the past, their civilian hosts emphasized everyday actions that manifest social norms of humility, hard work, and sobriety.

In accordance with these expectations, ex-combatants and civilians redirected the conclusion of the TRC's Bombali District Hearings "from below." They transformed a context of discursive truth telling into an embodied performance of humility and regret (albeit generalized), thereby achieving their own articulation of transitional justice and reintegration. Yet while they reworked the "apologies" before the TRC from truth-telling performances to enactments of social morality, they were not able to rework the symbolic re-constitution of pre-conflict hierarchies in the same ceremony.

These kinds of contradictions, in which the practices used to address one form of injustice inadvertently strengthen another, will undoubtedly become more visible if we move beyond narrow definitions of justice. Yet when we consider the profound disconnection to local realities behind the international consensus that Sierra Leone's justice experiment "worked," simply being able to recognize and address such contradictions in the local engagement of justice and reintegration would be a measure of success. In postwar contexts shaped by prewar injustice, we need to link the processes of rethinking *both* DDR and transitional justice. And this, in turn, will mean finding better ways of integrating the standpoints of those who live with conflict and its aftermath—whether as combatants or noncombatants—into the discussion.

PART III

Power, Politics, and Priorities

Chapter 7

Reconciliation Grown Bitter?

War, Retribution, and Ritual Action in Northern Uganda

Sverker Finnström

Interventions, Priorities, and War in Uganda

In 1986, after five years of war in central Uganda, Yoweri Museveni's National Resistance Movement/Army (NRM/A) guerrillas captured state power. Ever since, war in northern Uganda has rolled back and forth, like the changes from rainy season to dry season and back to rainy season, with Joseph Kony's Lord's Resistance Army/Movement (LRA/M, LRA) and other groups fighting Museveni's government.

The LRA/M's human rights abuse record is horrendous. Among other things, they have abducted tens of thousands of minors, and by the turn of the millennium, they had made themselves world-infamous for their war crimes and crimes against humanity. In 2003, the Ugandan government requested the International Criminal Court (ICC) to prosecute the LRA/M rebels. The ICC accepted the request as one of its first cases. In fact, it was Luis Moreno-Ocampo, chief prosecutor of the court, who invited Museveni to file a case with the ICC (see, e.g., Clark 2008). Perhaps all parties involved thought Uganda to be an easy and black-and-white case, thus a good start for the newly established court.

This was, however, not to be the case. In late 2005 the ICC's arrest warrants of five LRA/M leaders became public, and the ICC immediately came under debate in northern Uganda, as had happened to already ongoing restorative and reconciliatory efforts, including encouragement to the rebels to give up fighting and instead surrender (see, e.g., Allen 2006, 2007; Branch 2007; Refugee Law Project 2005a; see also Weinstein et al., this volume). In this chapter I will connect these discussions to an intimately related debate on a blanket amnesty offered to the rebels in 2000. At that time, to many Ugandans' disappointment, LRA/M leaders refused to surrender under the amnesty law and were critical of local initiatives of reconciliation.

This chapter shows that the rebels' dismissal was not that surprising. In order to be able to disentangle important aspects of the various amnesty, justice, and reconciliatory interventions in the midst of war, my discussion revolves around anthropologist John Borneman's description of reconciliation as "an appreciation of the intersubjectivity of the present" and a social project, "not in terms of permanent peace or harmony, but as a project of *departure from violence*" (2002:286, 282). To reconcile, he proposes, is "to render no longer opposed." My understanding of reconciliation, thus, is not a final understanding of a fixed concept. Rather, the term must be contextualized if a futile either-or discussion is to be avoided of *either* restorative *or* retributive justice, the first alleged to be local, and the second universal. Borneman's discussion will help contextualize my argument. He argues that reconciliation does not necessarily mean that there needs to be consensus about the past or the future, but it does mean "sharing a present, a present that is nonrepetitive." To facilitate this, he "focuses on the role of the 'third party' and argues for cultivating 'practices of listening' after a violent conflict" (2002:282, 281). He mentions international courts as such potential third parties, but I will argue that ICC intervention in Uganda has not functioned as a third party in this sense. There have been abundant and rather militant statements from the court's chief prosecutor and his associates proving the opposite. I will, however, maintain that any justice project must be essentially open-ended, about repeated social activity and coexistence but not necessarily about ideas shared and meanings fixed.

In the effort to critically assess fixed, hard-line wartime arguments, my chapter proceeds in three stages. I begin with a sketch of some measures taken by the Ugandan government to end the war. I then look at the international involvement from two standpoints, the war on terror and the ICC effort to bring rebel leaders to dock. Second, I proceed to discuss two forms of ritualized reconciliation among the Acholi living in the immediate war zone, the debated *mato oput* ("to drink the bitter root") and the not-so-well-known *gomo tong* ("to bend the spears") rituals. Finally, in bringing these different layers together in a discussion of ritual action, I show that retributive justice, amnesty laws, and reconciliation are sources of hope, but more, of contest and confusion, and of feelings of inequality, even bitterness. For example, those LRA/M commanders who agreed to come out under the amnesty from 2000 have *surrendered to* rather than *reconciled with* the government and the surrounding society. Some enjoy their time in the same posh bars and hotels in Gulu town, northern Uganda, where you will find western staff of various humanitarian organizations, Ugandan high-ranking militaries, and even investigators from the ICC itself.

Such a geopolitical global order is not innocent. Rather, in this context both restorative and retributive justice, even amnesty laws, can become weapons of war rather than tools of peacemaking. For example, when the ICC entered the Ugandan stage, there was no genuine and consistent will to find a *political* and *national* solution to the conflict in northern Uganda—neither within the country nor beyond. On the contrary, the ICC intervention soon became part and parcel of an ongoing conflict. Not least, the Ugandan government was able to capitalize upon the ICC intervention.

Ugandan Debates: Amnesty, Anti-Terrorism, and Retribution

In 1999, in an effort to end war in the country, the Ugandan parliament passed a blanket amnesty (see, e.g., Allen 2006, 2007; Refugee Law Project 2005b). President Museveni, the army's commander-in-chief, immediately stated that he did not believe in it, and he delayed beyond the thirty days stipulated by the Ugandan constitution before he signed the law.

Even so, the amnesty law has had some significance. Many rebels in western Uganda, notably in the Allied Democratic Front (ADF) with bases in Congo, and the West Bank Nile Front (WNBF), based in northwestern Uganda, did eventually accept surrender under the amnesty. But initially, few senior LRA/M rebels surrendered, and the Ugandan army later claimed that over a thousand ADF rebels rearmed and regrouped in Congo (*Daily Monitor* [Uganda's independent daily], July 1, 2005).

The mixed response to the amnesty law must be seen through a global lens. Both the ADF and the LRA/M (but not the WNBF) were included on the U.S. government's list of terrorist groups in the aftermath of the September 11 attacks. The Ugandan president welcomed the rhetoric of "no dialogue" and the global war on terror, claiming that his enemies in arms are "al-Qaeda trainees" (as quoted in *Daily Monitor*, March 6, 2003). The Ugandan government even had an antiterrorist law of their own. When the Ugandan government thus backed the U.S.-led invasion of Iraq in 2003, the army had already launched its "Operation Iron Fist" military campaigns to flush out the LRA/M from its bases in Sudan. The campaigns were carried out on Sudanese territory with the approval of the government in Khartoum and with U.S. support, increasing the pressure on the LRA/M. Also, in the wake of the Iron Fist, arrests without warrants or a basis in civil law and an increased number of treason charges created fear and mistrust in the amnesty. The Ugandan army "arrested scores of civilians, with little evidence, on suspicion of rebel collaboration; some of the detainees are supporters of the unarmed political opposition" (Human Rights Watch, July 14, 2003:5).

When the ICC got involved on the ground, the Ugandan government claimed that its call for international justice should leave out possible war crimes committed by its own army. "Our position is if they [the ICC investigators] come across any allegations against government officials, they should let them be tried by the government," as the army spokesperson said (in *Daily Monitor*, August 16, 2004; see also Branch 2007:183, 188). An increasing number of Ugandan commentators and academics, however, have asked why the ICC decided not to proceed with its investigations of the Ugandan army's arbitrary killings and rape of civilians, torture, forced labor at gunpoint, or the forced displacement of millions of people to squalid camps, all potential crimes against humanity (e.g., Apuuli 2006; Otunnu 2006). Throughout the war, as well as in recent years, the "undisciplined" Ugandan army "has committed crimes against civilians with near total impunity" (Human Rights Watch, May 2005:2). The ICC responded to these requests by claiming that "the alleged crimes perpetrated by the Ugandan government were not grave enough to reach the threshold" (ICC representative quoted in Allen 2006:193; see also Branch 2007:188). To be accepted for trial, then, the suspected crimes must meet the court's "gravity threshold."

The gravity of war expands in time and space in ways that the ICC does not acknowledge. By international diplomatic consensus, when the ICC was created its mandate excluded crimes committed before 2002. Yet it was Museveni's military takeover back in 1986 that brought war to northern Uganda. Under his rule, thousands of suspected rebels were taken into detention, and torture and maltreatment became the order of the day in Acholiland. Amnesty International concluded that "there has been a consistent pattern of extrajudicial executions by soldiers since the NRM[/A of Museveni] came to power" (1992:29–30; see also Oywa 1995; Pirouet 1991). Since war reached the north in the mid-1980s, many Acholi have found it impossible to escape the past as expressed in the national memory. In southern Uganda, it is commonly held that the Acholi in the army during Milton Obote's second government (1980–85) and Tito Okello's (1985–86) government were particularly responsible for the atrocities committed in the counterinsurgency campaigns against Museveni's guerillas in the so-called Luwero Triangle, central Uganda, not least because of the fact that Okello was an Acholi (see, e.g., Mutibwa 1992: 157). My informants of course questioned the idea of the Acholi as collectively to be blamed for most of the violence in Uganda. During my fieldwork, for example, I encountered some young men, frustrated by the collective blame put upon the Acholi, who painstakingly collected data and statistics to challenge the image of the Acholi as violent and militaristic. One of them concluded that "the Luwero Triangle is used by the government to discredit the Acholi, internationally, nationally, and locally." Another young man more directly blamed Museveni for the many killings. "We Acholi are blamed for the deaths in Luwero," he said. "But it was Museveni's decision to start a bush war in Luwero that killed the people of Luwero."

And the legacy of violence has continued. Many of my informants in Acholiland claimed that a situation worse than that of the Amin era developed after Museveni's takeover. Others did not explicitly support the uprising, but according to a standard version I often encountered, there was no other way of surviving than to join the insurgency groups in one way or another (Finnström 2008b; see also Branch 2005; Brett 1995).

With this violent history in mind, it makes little sense for many Ugandans that the ICC does not have any mandate to investigate crimes committed before 2002. In addition, the ICC's clandestine approach on the ground, including its initial failure to communicate publicly its role and mandate to ordinary people, fueled the feeling among many Ugandans that it is working on behalf of the Ugandan government (see, e.g., Branch 2007:188; Clark 2008). Another complicating matter is that Uganda's strongest ally in its war on terror, the United States, does not acknowledge the ICC, as is the case with some other permanent members of the UN Security Council as well.

The complex political reality expands even more. Just after his military takeover in 1986, Museveni launched a national truth commission to account for the human rights violations in Uganda since independence in 1962, but he barred this commission from subsequently investigating any crimes committed after his takeover (Quinn 2004:413). The years from 1986 to 2002 remain outside the parameters of accountability. These are only a few dimensions of the complicated realpolitik of war and peace, with its selective impunity.

To end impunity is an enormous project, and to limit it in time and scope will foster suspicion. Yet there is also the problem with history that does not really have any end, but rather only endless layers, and even more so in the context of an ongoing conflict with no closure. "Ending impunity should not be confused with simply finding people guilty," writes Eltringham with reference to post-genocide Rwanda. "Rather, it entails a consistent and coherent effort to respond to *all* allegations of human rights abuses in a dogmatic, tenacious and transparent way" (2004:146). Even if such a project sounds infinite, Eltringham's call for a wider justice in the effort not to bracket off an arbitrary period of time pinpoints the ICC's dilemma in seeking only a partial justice that may play into the hands of those in (state) power. In a parallel development, some LRA/M commanders have bought themselves out by surrendering to the government under the amnesty; many Ugandans regard these, rather than the rebel high command itself, as "the worst killers" (Refugee Law Project 2005a:47). And over the years many former rebels and other human rights violators have joined the present government and its security apparatus, thus being granted immunity and even rewarded and promoted in military rank, something that has infused the present government with a "culture of impunity" (Obote-Odora 2005:3; cf. Eltringham 2004:ch. 5).

Bitter War: A Repetitive Present?

These developments make it difficult to continue ignoring the local emplacement of global processes. One problem in Uganda, as indicated, is that the ICC entered the stage when there was no after-the-conflict yet. And the many years of violence in northern Uganda, especially on behalf of the rebels, is just too horrendous and spectacular for most observers. This makes it difficult to see the complex politics of war behind the scenes, today and well before the coming of the ICC. The bracketing off shuns deep-seated political complexities. A simplified picture is drawn, making the situation somewhat parallel to what Wilson reports in his study of the South African reconciliation process: "An in-depth understanding of the social conditions . . . of wrongdoing is bypassed in favor of the moral category of 'evil' which resolves the problem of meaning" (2001:54). The story very much ends there, Wilson adds. In Uganda it is the media, international human rights organizations, and the Ugandan government that have had the upper hand in defining the discourse on meaning, while the LRA/M has become the moral category of evil, often reduced to its leader Joseph Kony (see Finnström 2008a).

Of course the LRA/M have made themselves coauthors in the process. Yet, with the framing of an apolitical crisis in northern Uganda, with only one guilty party, efforts to talk or even to reconcile with the rebels throughout the years have been dismissed as having little if any bearing on the ground. Allen (2007; see also 2005:85–86; 2006:165) on his side suggests that efforts of reconciliation are the result of an urban elite fantasy, created and promoted by Christian organizations, churchpeople, and clan leaders.

Here, I want to suggest a complementary interpretation. The potential of everyday *social* interaction, I hold, does not really demand any overall *cultural* consensus (Fernandez 1965). Before I present my ethnographic examples to develop this argument, I need to return to my use of the concept "reconciliation." In criticizing Borneman's thesis on reconciliation, Sampson (2003) suggests replacing the romantic ideas of reconciliation and dialogue—which he sees as essentially western ideas—with a more moderate version of coexistence. Sampson's argument is that the dialogue we often want to see in reconciliatory practices seldom involves any genuine dialogue. For some of my readers, the term *reconciliation* may have Christian connotations. But what if we turn to a specific ethnography, a lived reality, and its meanings and practices? Then we are back at Borneman's idea of reconciliation as "an appreciation of the intersubjectivity of the present" more than anything else (2002:86). In other words, my focus is on *meanings in use* rather than any fixity of concepts, in English or vernacular. In the context of war-torn Acholiland, to which I now will turn, ritual practices such as mato oput and gomo tong have been described in English as reconciliation, while another Acholi meaning in use, *culo kwo*, has been understood as revenge.

Rituals of Revenge or Compensation in Acholiland?

Gingyera-Pinycwa has suggested that the Acholi tradition of culo kwo is "retribution or the wreaking of vengeance" and a "serious source for continued insecurity." The tradition explains "much of the killing, maiming, and burning of villages" (1992:47, n. 52). Here, the violence is held to be specific to the Acholi.

In Acholi, *culo* is "to pay" or "to give," while *kwo* here is "an unreconciled killing," which creates enmity. The concept indicates the importance of giving compensation for a person who has been killed. This is part of the Acholi insti-tution of settling patrilineal clan feuds, in which the clan of a killed person ought to be compensated by the offending clan (Girling 1960:66–67). When I inquired, informants initially translated the concept as "revenge." However, in conver-sations it soon became clear to me that culo kwo is part of a larger context. Requests for apology, reunion, and reconciliation are central elements.

The actual ritual to redress the wrongs of a killing between clans involves many people and takes a full day. But the ritual is preceded by weeks, months, or even years of negotiations and investigations. The history of the case is out-lined, its context carefully delineated, evidence brought forward, compensa-tion decided upon. Compensation or "blood-wealth" (see, e.g., Evans-Pritchard 1940:121, 152–64; Hutchinson 1996:122–46), according to tradition to be pro-vided in cattle, will help a chosen young man from the offended clan to meet the bridewealth expenses and marry. This will eventually bring new children to the clan, it is hoped. As is the case with any birth, children born from such blood-turned-into-bridewealth unions embody the blessings from the ances-tors, thus a final proof of the successful reconciliation on the wider societal level of living and dead, of the past and the future.

The ritual is called mato oput, "to drink the bitter root." Culo kwo, repay-ing a life, elders told me, can be understood only in the context of mato oput, which I here want to describe in wide terms as the restoration of social rela-tionships. A blend of truth telling, accountability, compensation, and recon-ciliation, rather than revenge or blood vengeance, is the institutionalized Acholi way of handling disputes, homicides, and unnatural deaths. Ladit Ar-weny, an elderly friend, told me the following:

> A major and essential function of traditional chiefs was to act as arbitrators and reconcilers when disputes occur in order to restore peace and maintain harmonious relations between families, clans, and even tribes. That is the ma-jor role of a chief. Should he fail to do that, he is removed. The role of a chief is to maintain peace, nothing else. And killing will not make the compensation. [If] you kill a person, you compensate, you reconcile—by paying heavily, of course, but not death for death. (Gulu, January 1998)

The understanding of most of my Acholi informants, above exemplified with the words of an elderly man, is thus an alternative to Gingyera-Pinycwa's (1992:36–37), who searches for a cultural cause when it comes to the military violence in northern Uganda. Gingyera-Pinycwa proposes that ultimately culo kwo is a cause of the extreme violence that has taken place in Acholiland. This discrepancy in explanatory models highlights the point of studies that concentrate on consequences of the conflict rather than only looking for pseudo-ethnographic reasons for it. "Many who write about so-called violence-prone areas or a culture of violence, often assume that powerful social scripts of vengeance or even hatred get mechanically translated into social action," write Das and Kleinman (2000:11), as if the agency of the perpetrator is inherently determined by his or her culture.

To Drink the Bitter Root

Ritual action illustrates how the past is evoked in the effort to imagine and build a future. In 1988, a young Acholi man tried to rape a pregnant girl. The two belonged to different clans. The incident ended most unfortunately, when the girl fell badly and her head hit a rock. She miscarried and eventually died. Legal justice was done, and the young man was imprisoned. He did his time, was released, and later died for other reasons. His clan, however, still suffered as a result of his deed. "A homicide does not concern only the man who has committed it, but his close agnatic kinsmen also," as Evans-Pritchard noted for the Nuer in Sudan (1940:154; see also Hutchinson 1996:122–27). Bad omens like death and misfortune affect the offender's clan, also over generations. Acholi say that a barrier of bad atmosphere (*ojebu*) develops between the two clans, because intermarriage, trade, and joint parties between the involved clans are no longer possible, and the clans cannot socialize or share food or drink.

Yet such social barriers can be dissolved. The rapist's father decided to seek reconciliation. Bad developments, misfortune in the clan, and social pressure made him conclude that the matter needed to be resolved existentially as well. Court justice was clearly not enough if the cosmological imbalance and the social unrest were to be overcome. And perhaps his son's premature death was not just a coincidence? The man admitted his son's wrongdoing, and compensation was decided upon. Mato oput was conducted in early 1998. After ten years, then, the clans were reconciled. People, spirits, and ancestors alike were satisfied and thus calmed when the social barrier was ritually removed, as the merry atmosphere during the ritual indeed attested. In 1999, I had the opportunity to participate in this kind of ritual once again. This time the compensation was low, because the killing, caused by a car accident, had not been intentional.

In 2000, I again participated in the ritual. This time the play of two small boys, both only three years old, had ended unfortunately, when one boy hurt the other while they were playing with a stick. One boy injured his finger and eventually developed blood poisoning, only to die later. This was again not regarded as a naturally caused death, but rather, to quote Parkin (1985:7), a "bad death" that ought to be retracted ritually, even reconciled. The surviving boy was present during the ritual but did not drink the mixture of the bitter root because of his young age. The fathers of the boys drank the mixture instead. During the ritual, the elders in charge of the whole thing suggested that a boy is "responsible enough to drink *oput*" when he has started picking up an interest in girls. In Acholi terminology, despite "*being* [full] human beings" (sing.: *bedo dano*), children have not yet fully "*become* [moral and social] persons" (sing.: *odoko dano*). They are thus not held fully responsible for their acts (see also Pido 2000). The Acholi say that someone becomes a person (odoko dano) when he or she is able to take advice from elders and contributes to household maintenance, perhaps bringing water or food to visitors, which is done from the age of around ten (see also p'Bitek 1986:27). Yet in a deeper sense it refers to when young people become mature enough to have children of their own. It also refers to when they are old enough, as the discourse on child rebels as victims rather than perpetrators also suggests, to be held morally responsible for their acts, when their cultural agency is complete. In this context, children as survivors are more likely to be emphasized than their role as perpetrators. According to Ladit Arweny, the elderly man, "I think these children in the bush are out of culture now. In fact, they don't know what they are doing. They just don't know."

The above ethnographic examples are all from cases of single deaths, in which perpetrator and victim could be identified beyond any doubt, and where the offending party initiated reconciliation. As such, they are not really war-related. Indeed, I never came across any mato oput carried out in the course of coping with so-called battle-related deaths. Yet these (and other) rituals have been presented as the blueprint for the solution of the violent war, which thereby deepened the either-or debate between restorative and retributive measures (see, e.g, Pain 1997; Liu Institute, Gulu District NGO Forum, and Ker Kwaro Acholi 2005; cf. Allen 2007). My perspective is more moderate, and it refuses this dichotomy. Although the conflict obviously needs a political and national solution, my examples still say something about people's everyday concerns as they seek directionality in life and prepare themselves for a future in peace and social coexistence (see also Baines 2007:110). They do so because the great majority of bad deaths occur in any case in the shadows of war and displacement rather than in actual fighting (Finnström 2008b:12–13, 133, 200, 204). It must furthermore be noted that similar rituals have been performed between larger as well as smaller groups, even between ethnic groups, but then without individual bloodwealth compensation of the mato oput ritual. It is called the bending of the spears (*gomo tong*). Spears from each party involved are bent and made useless, and then passed on to the former enemy as a proof that fighting can never again be allowed between the two groups, as was done between the Payira and the Koch chiefdoms in their mutual effort to cope with increased colonial domination in the nineteenth century.

This has also happened more recently. During the Amin years, 1971–79, Acholi people were especially targeted by Amin's state violence. After Amin's fall, Acholi soldiers in the new army took their revenge on people living in the West Nile region, Amin's home area. Finally, however, elders of both sides decided that enough was enough. Tito Okello, the Acholi general who ousted Milton Obote in 1985, was instrumental in the retraction of violence, although critics have dismissed this as an unholy alliance with pro-Amin groups (e.g., Mutibwa 1992:171–75). Revenge was turned into reconciliation when the gomo tong ritual was performed. Ladit Arweny, one of the participants, in 1998 provided me with his written record of the case:

> Acholi traditional Chiefs and Elders initiated reconciliation with the people of West Nile, and peaceful reconciliation was performed on 11 February 1986 in Palero some twenty-six miles north of Gulu in Acholiland. From that time there would be no war or fighting between Acholi and Madi, Kakwa, Lugbara, or Alur of West Nile. (See also Gersony 1997:75; Leopold 2005:153–54.)

The ritual is not about remembering and assessing every detail of a long and violent conflict. Rather, it is about finding a consensual understanding about what the conflict essentially was about, and how to now coexist. After the bending of the spears in 1986, many West Nilers who left Acholiland after Amin's fall from power have returned peacefully, and elders do their best to guard the reconciliation accord sealed in ritual action.

Here, on the level of the everyday, is a hope for a peaceful Uganda. For example, Allen (1988–89) has suggested that the Acholi and the neighboring Madi, despite their different languages, have many concepts in common, and they sometimes share the social world. Many Acholi in the border region speak

Madi, and vice versa. To Allen's surprise, even in the early 1980s, when ethnic tension was high in the aftermath of Idi Amin's fall from power, Acholi intruders would leave Madi ancestral shrines in the villages untouched. Allen's Madi informants were less surprised, however, than Allen. "Ah well," a Madi man replied to the queries of the anthropologist, "it is because we are really the same people" (Allen 1988–89:54).

Interaction and social exchanges can remain frequent despite the fact that war tends to impose ethnic categorizations and cultural divisions on everyday realities. Far from being dislocated in a past that no longer exists, ritual action has always continued to be situated socially. Ritual action is a way of addressing present concerns. And we need to understand these ritual contexts to better understand the complexities of war and peace. During peace talks in 1993–94, for example, influential rebels refused to drink even the bottled sodas that the Ugandan army offered. Food provided for the rebels was accepted only if it was brought as living cattle, not meat, and the rebels then prepared the meals themselves. When an agreement was finally reached—if only to fail later—the two parties did celebrate together, but the rebels went to town to buy their own crates of sodas, while the army brought theirs. Sharing food and drink, rebels insisted, had to wait for later. Here too, the social barrier was evident, even performed, and it still is, as one rebel representative to the peace talks held in Juba, South Sudan, told me in 2007. Throughout the years, senior rebels have also been afraid of being poisoned, and the LRA/M leader has repeatedly raised the issue of some high-ranking rebels who had accepted an amnesty in the 1980s only to die in ambiguous circumstances, some while imprisoned on treason charges despite the amnesty: bad deaths indeed.

It is an anthropological truism that ritual action shifts in meaning and appearance over time. More, it is in the context of war and outside interventions that many Acholi seek societal hope in ritual action, exemplifying the existential effort to cope with a difficult situation, ultimately in order to be able to govern it and orient in everyday life. Sometimes rituals are transformed by state coercion or, as Allen (2007) delineates for the case of mato oput, by donor pressure. Yet most often they have been out of sight of formal legal structures, in both colonial and postcolonial times. As James writes for the Uduk people in Sudan, "When things go wrong in their own communities, they make their own judgements and sometimes they take their own action, and only rarely refer the matter to the constituted authorities" (1988:93). The legal power of the state apparatus and various juridical systems, James's informants concluded from experience, is unpredictably and arbitrarily exercised. Allen, in defending the ICC intervention in Uganda, however, dismisses local variants of ritual action as being recent inventions without popular support. The Acholi do not have any unique restorative justice system, he argues, almost as if it was a question of either-or. "People in northern Uganda require the same kinds of conventional legal mechanisms as everyone else living in modern states," he instead argues (2005:85; see also 2006:168). Like "decent people everywhere else," he adds, "they require a functioning state to make the best of their lives" (2008:52), while any "local justice approach socially infantilises the whole of the North" (2007:160).

Elsewhere I argue that one central reason for the long and bitter war is the very *absence* of a democratically functioning state, something that has unleashed the violence of the state's counterinsurgency campaigns (Finnström 2009). Branch too adds an important nuance to the debate:

> the legal processes carried out by the ICC are not "conventional" and do not correspond to the "modern state." Indeed, ICC interventions reject and suppress conventional, modern state-based legal mechanisms in favor of tenuous global mechanisms, thus bringing into question the very foundation of the modern state—namely, the concept of sovereignty. (2007:192)

In other words, ICC intervention is as "conventional" as any ritual action. Even more, ICC intervention is a human-made practice among other contextual practices, regardless of whether these practices are categorized as modern or traditional. Ultimately, it is not even about tradition against modernity, the first allegedly premodern, obsolete, and naive, and the second liable and a source of accountability, because it is exactly such categorizations that are irrelevant and obsolete. They are irrelevant because they do not tell us what people do with their beliefs in life situations and everyday struggles, and obsolete because they mask the very power relations that make global ambitions precede over local particularities.

To dismiss everyday ritual action by saying that the Acholi do not have any unique justice system is therefore misdirected in that it implicitly dichotomizes such ritual action against international justice interventions, compares them as essentially closed and fixed systems, and finally weighs them against each other, concluding that only the state and outside intervention are "functioning" and "decent" (or, from the opposite standpoint, vice versa). More, any reconciliatory effort is dismissed as an elitist and recent invention. The dichotomized debate is misdirected, because human action is always human-made and always changing, in Acholiland as well as in The Hague, where the ICC is located. Here many Ugandans are, and have always been, realists and pragmatic pluralists (see, e.g., Finnström 2008b:6–7, 208). In 1970 and long before the academic debate on the essence of modernity versus tradition, or the West versus the rest, Taban lo Liyong, a Sudanese poet raised in northern Uganda, wrote, "To live, our traditions have to be topical; to be topical they must be used as part and parcel of our contemporary contentions and controversies" (Liyong 1970:x). So traditions change, they always have, and in that sense they do not differ from expressions of modernity. Rather, with the help of all kinds of human-made interventions, people seek to cope with various problems, including those produced by the Ugandan government's failure to bring peace to the country. Ritual action in northern Uganda is one example of this, the creation of the ICC another. They both reflect the contemporary dynamics of globalization.

Nevertheless, neither ritual action nor international claims to justice can replace political efforts at peacemaking. In the Ugandan case, any reconciliation can come only after a successful peace negotiation. It is in this light that we must understand the skepticism not only among senior rebels, but also among young noncombatant adults, about the much-talked-of restorative justice and the amnesty law that preceded, and in part were nullified by, the ICC intervention.

Whose Justice?

Anyone who wants it in his or her heart can drink the bitter root and reconcile, I was sometimes told during fieldwork, even though the present war, as elders said, is very different from "wars of the past" (Finnström 2006). With time, the rebels can thus be reintegrated into society despite the violent deeds they are responsible for in Acholiland. They must if peace is to come, many argued. But to be allowed to go through reconciliatory rituals, elderly informants especially insisted, the offender needs to present the mediators with convincing evidence for the killing. Obviously, today this is not easily achieved. The more the conflict expands in space and over time, the more difficult to settle, as Evans-Pritchard (1940:157) once wrote for the Nuer in Sudan. In the heat of the battle, how can the source of the deadly bullet possibly be traced? Who laid the landmine? What caused all those bad deaths during wartime displacement? With time, perhaps, such questions will find answers in ritual action. As the Nuer have coped with their contemporary war experiences and innovatively transformed many of their rituals since the 1930s and the days of Evans-Pritchard (Hutchinson 1996:142–57), so many Acholi work to adjust some of their rituals to be able to deal existentially with contemporary dilemmas and controversies, as well as those related to the war (see, e.g., Behrend 1999:45, 106). But perhaps most importantly, according to many of my interlocutors, not only the rebels but the representatives of the Ugandan government and the president also ought to admit to killings, atrocities, looting, havoc, and destruction committed by the army in northern Uganda ever since 1986, if any path toward genuine peace is to be opened. The root causes of this war must be given proper address.

The ICC's idea of a "gravity threshold" is an example of how this appeal has been sidestepped. Instead, the ICC is now part of the realpolitik of war. When the semiautonomous government of Southern Sudan, with Riek Machar as chief facilitator, invited the rebels and the Ugandan government to new peace talks in July 2006, this was the best opportunity in many years, not least because of the fact that the South Sudanese leadership and Machar navigated carefully the diplomacy of the region's realities, at least initially. When Machar met the rebel leader for the first time, he intentionally addressed him as his brother, thus assuming the most basic rule in any successful peace talk—facilitating a feeling of equality between the parties. Talks commenced, and despite the Ugandan government's initial skepticism, the parties signed a historical cessation of hostilities agreement in August 2006, which later was turned into a permanent cease-fire. The ICC chief prosecutor, Luis Moreno-Ocampo, dismissed the peace initiative by asserting that the rebels were only buying time to regroup. In arguing this, and doing so from a privileged position in The Hague, he personified the ICC's unwillingness to cultivate the practices to pause and listen. "Well," a South Sudanese blogger and political analyst noted with frustration as Moreno-Ocampo's words rather than those of the government of Southern Sudan hit the world news, "these are words of a politician, not of an impartial international judge. And when so important a figure gets that close to local politics, justice flies out of the window" (Akec 2006). The government of Southern Sudan, on their side, had worked for a long time behind the scenes to gain rebel confidence. Important root causes were tabled during the talks, but with the rebel leadership's refusal to sign a final agreement because of the ICC indictments, and the subsequent bombings of rebel camps and resumed fighting in late 2008, the shaky dialogue, and a lot of hope with it, was lost.

Before these very developments, however, even those of my informants who saw the rebel leaders' violent conduct as a primary obstacle to peace were willing to welcome them back home, for rather pragmatic reasons. "People just want peace, full stop," as my friend Otim p'Ojok justified his position in the early days of the ICC intervention. His stand exemplifies the Primo Levian "gray zone" that he and his friends live with, a kind of historical and lived memory that preserves "traces of two quite different strategies of coping with violence—vengeance and forgiveness—and so leave open, at all times, the possibility of choosing how one will react to evil" (Jackson 2005:367). From such a gray zone, the much-debated issue about the restorative and retributive dimensions of justice is not really about any final either-or. Rather, in the moments of life, it is a kind of acceptance of the complexities of the situation so that life can go on (Jackson 2005:368). The majority of people, to speak with Jackson's analysis of Sierra Leone, are perhaps too powerless to cultivate feelings of retaliation. "They were simply realists, acutely aware of what they could and could not do," Jackson (2004:69) writes of his informants.

For Jackson, it is an existential "issue of power and powerlessness." For the ICC, the claim to power is as simple as it is firm: LRA/M leader Joseph Kony will be arrested at all costs, as claimed by the court's registrar (in *Daily Monitor*, May 30, 2008). For Joseph Kony himself, the claim to power takes a more violent twist. In various statements he questions the ICC intervention, and he has even claimed that he would rather die fighting than surrender to the ICC. The second-in-command, Okot Odhiambo, in early 2009 and after sustaining a serious bullet wound in the renewed fighting, allegedly hinted that he wanted to lay down arms with his group of fighters, but only if the ICC indictment against him were lifted. His plans to surrender eventually turned out to be a hoax, but indeed, the destiny of defected rebels will play a central role not only for any moves by other rebels fighting now and in the future, but also for any peace/war process as such and how that will connect to Uganda's political past.

Reconciliation Grown Bitter?

In the effort to end the war, local politicians as well as cultural and religious leaders have lobbied for the amnesty law and frequently asked the rebels to surrender, "to come out from the bush," claiming that the war is "useless." They have even asked the local population to follow their example to forgive the rebels for "all the bad things they have done." In this rhetoric, they have frequently labeled the LRA/M rebels as "our children in the bush." The children are encouraged to flee from the rebels, and on radio broadcasts, they have been informed that they will be well received. Rebel commanders too are encouraged to surrender. Even if it has good intentions, such rhetoric suggests an imposed fixity of meaning, a claim to cultural consensus from the powerful, even a kind of set manual for ritual action, as Allen's (e.g., 2007) critical analysis shows. But more importantly, in the rhetoric about the rebels as "children in the bush," the opponent is regarded as a minor who needs proper guidance. It also limits any future reconciliation to an Acholi affair only, between Acholi parents at home and their children in the bush. It localizes a national, even regional, conflict. As a young man commented concerning the mass installation of clan chiefs as peace promoters, facilitated by international NGOs, it is "a means to transfer the responsibility to the elders, about something that they don't know. . . . [It is the government's] use of elders to carry the blame, for what they don't know. Poor, poor elders. It's a great mistake. The elders are accepting a responsibility they cannot carry."

Consequently, when the amnesty law was finally endorsed by the Ugandan president in early 2000, senior LRA/M rebels were frustrated by the one-sided request for their surrender. They argued on their part that they are fighting not for the Acholi, but for all Ugandans. In arguing for this, I propose, the rebels opposed the Ugandan government's reinforcement of a hierarchical structure in the process of war and peace. In such a hierarchical structure, the political, cultural, and religious leaders indirectly promote themselves as the *superior* party to the conflict, the ones to forgive the *inferior* party. The latter are the rebels, or "the children in the bush," or even the "terrorists," "hyenas," and "bandits." As such, they are objectified as criminals and children only. They are effectively denied any political subjectivity, and the proposed reconciliation denies the intersubjectivity of the present that Borneman sees as central if the violent past is not to repeat itself.

Koch and colleagues (1977) have described reconciliation in the Fijian context, where one party must surrender, remain silent during the reconciliation ritual, and accept a lower status. Such a ritual of reconciliation "serves to reinforce hierarchical structures," adds Hagborg (2001:15), "because the superior forgives the inferior." The LRA/M commanders will not easily accept the lower status in such a hierarchy. As they stated in a letter, distributed in northern Uganda soon after the rebels' intrusion from their bases in Sudan in late 1999:

You who advocate mato oput [interclan reconciliation] or gomo tong [inter-chiefdom or even interethnic reconciliation] with Museveni know quite well that Museveni, who came to his leadership position through the barrel [of a gun], has never admitted that he has committed crimes against Ugandans. He has never apologized. . . . It was Museveni who first attacked us. His army. . . . was the first to kill us, to destroy our homesteads, including foodstuffs, rus-tling cattle, goats, sheep and even children. . . . Why should the religious lead-ers and cultural chiefs mislead the people, but not be honest and speak the truth to the people they administer? Mato oput and gomo tong ceremonies should not be taken as joking matters. . . . People . . . are ignorant when they say that Acholi should pardon us [LRA/M]. We are not fighting Acholi but Museveni's government and all his supporters. If there is any apology at all, it should be for the Acholi and all Ugandans to demand from Museveni and his cronies. This can be possible only when they confess their mistakes publicly. (Undated LRA/M letter distributed to the public, late December 1999, trans-lated from the Acholi original)

I heard the same argument repeated when interviewing LRA/M represen-tatives in 2007. And it was not really the ICC as such the rebels opposed, they told me, but the court's bias in investigating only one side of the conflict (see also Branch 2007:188–89). Similarly, the main problem with ICC interven-tion, according to most of my noncombatant informants, is not that Kony or Odhiambo are wanted for the crimes they have committed, but rather the court's bias. Having suffered in the shadows of war for so many years, victimized by both rebels and government forces, the ICC's mandate and principle of grav-ity, and its one-sided focus on a few selected rebel leaders, make little sense to my Ugandan friends. As was the case with James's (1988) Uduk informants, my informants held the outside intervention to be unpredictably and arbi-trarily exercised.

So That Life Can Go On

The coin has, as always, two sides. Accordingly, reconciliation also has two sides, most informants in Acholiland argued. So even if restorative and recon-ciliatory rituals cannot be equaled with international justice, the latter should perhaps pause for a moment to join the former and other practices of listen-ing. Only then may Uganda depart from its legacy of violence to instead enter a genuine political process of negotiation and national rebuilding. In the

interclan mato oput rituals that I have attended, there was no structural inequality between the parties. Rather the contrary—the ritual performance mani-
fests equality. Members of both the offending and offended parties consumed
the bitter root, always on neutral ground in the uncultivated bush, symboli-
cally selected on the path between two homesteads. They were always occasions
of great feasting and happy feelings, everyone sharing food and drink. Therefore, I suggest, in northern Uganda reconciliation cannot be hierarchical in the
sense that one party forgives the other only. Rather, all parties involved, also
those from the international community, must step out and genuinely admit
their respective wrongdoings if they are to be able to promote reconciliation.
Indeed, my informants held, this is necessary if peace is ever to come. In the
opinion of a male senior sixth-form student, whom I met just after the amnesty
law had been enacted:

> The rebels cannot accept anything as long as they are denied equality. The
> more ignored they are; the more determined [to fight] they will be. Mato oput
> comes in only at a later stage when equality is established. There can be no
> mato oput as long as there is inequality between the fighting parties. (Febru-
> ary 2000)

Reconciliation, my informants constantly remarked, can only be the final step
in any conflict settlement, which again illustrates Borneman's general thesis that
reconciliation comes only after conflicts (see also Refugee Law Project 2005a).
For this to happen in any profound way, as Ricoeur notes, there must be a mutual "recognition of the other as . . . equal in terms of rights and duties" (2000:6).

Here it is not really any illusive *cultural consensus* that people seek, I argue. Nor is it for researchers to delineate any essence of Acholi ways of life. It
is not even about delineating ritual detail to determine these as authentic,
thus allegedly "traditional," with ritual meaning forever set in time and space,
nor about dismissing them as only recently invented or inauthentic. Rather, as
Fernandez (1965:912) reminds us in a classic article, when we approach and
try to understand ritual activity, we need to be "aware of the range of cultural
ambiguities involved in social interaction." In ritual action people join hands
for a number of objectives rather than following a single predefined purpose.
It is about hope and a basic *social consensus,* where, as Fernandez's informants
said, "people understand each other" (1965:904). Fernandez builds on Ed-
mund Leach, another anthropological icon, and the latter's claim about the
essential vagueness of all ritual statements. "The remarkable integrative effect

of ritual," Fernandez writes, "rests in the fact that it can bring together in repeated activity persons who have quite a variant interpretation of the meaning of that activity." He concludes that if "coexistence is guaranteed socially,
coherence need not be sought culturally" (Fernandez 1965:912). The flexibility
of ritual action promotes the acceptance of the necessity for social interaction and everyday coexistence. Following its static principles and restricted
by its mandate, international retributive justice does not really tune in to this
flexibility of ever-changing meanings and local social realities. Still the talk
on the ground about reconciliation must be seen as an ambition to achieve
through ritual means a condition of social solidarity—or one-heartedness, as
Fernandez's informants put it. Kony and his colleagues can be part of this
ambition, but only if they want it in their hearts, I often heard informants
claim.

Let me give a final example of the acceptance of the necessity for social
interaction, or, in Fernandez's terms, social solidarity. To reconcile individual
cases in the local community may take time. In early 2000 a young man called
Otti asked some elders to facilitate the settlement of a homicide committed by
his late father. A fight between the father and another man in the 1950s had
ended with Otti's father spearing his rival to death. Charged with manslaughter, Otti's father was imprisoned by the colonial authorities. Legal justice was
done. Some forty years later, Otti was planning to marry, but his fiancée come
from the clan of his late father's victim. The fight that led to a bad death in the
1950s—that is, long before the father was married and Otti was born—now
had to be settled before any marital union could be blessed. Together with
some young men from the opposite side, an increasingly impatient Otti staged
a mock ambush that forced the negotiating elders to abandon their never-
ending discussions on the level of compensation, to instead reach quick social
consensus on how and when to perform the ritual. Soon thereafter I joined
Otti and the clans as they came together in ritual action.

This and my other mato oput stories tell us that most Acholi regard accountability as something much more profound than only legal justice done
in courts, and existentially so, but not necessarily that they disregard formal
trials as such. Such rituals are in no way any blueprint in the solution to the
war; still, as my cases illustrate, any future reconciliation, on any societal level,
must include inquiries into the complexity of the local social realities and
their particular histories. Local reconciliation cannot therefore be substituted
with or equaled to formal jurisdiction such as Uganda's amnesty law. Accord-

ing to the law, the rebels must report to the nearest government, police, or army authorities, renounce and abandon involvement in the war, and, finally, surrender all their weapons before amnesty can be granted (Republic of Uganda 2000). This the rebels will not easily do. They have claimed, "We are not going to lay down our arms as long as Museveni is still in Uganda as president, because the only language he understands is that of the barrel of the gun. We are not going to be intimidated or baited into compromise through Amnesty Law, because we have.a clear agenda for fighting Museveni" (undated LRA/M letter, distributed in late December 1999, translated from the Acholi original).

As illustrated by the rebels' claim, ever since independence in 1962, the political environment in Uganda has become increasingly polarized. Unless the political issues at stake are seriously addressed on the national level, amnesty laws and cultural practices of reconciliation on the local level may function, intentionally or unintentionally, as weapons of war and mistrust rather than as tools of genuine peacemaking. It would be "an act of wilful romantic naïveté," as Wilson (2001:11) shows in the case of South Africa, to conclude that African discourses on reconciliation alone are capable of bringing peace to social settings suffering from long-term armed conflicts or extreme political oppression, even more so if they are imposed by one party in the midst of ongoing conflict.

I am equally unsure whether the retributive justice of the ICC can end impunity in Uganda, because it will not necessarily facilitate a political understanding of the structural, historical, and even global conditions that caused and sustained the war. The ICC has basically proven unwilling to facilitate any genuine practice of listening. At the bottom of all this is the question of social injustices, regional unbalances, and political accountability on a wider and much more everyday scale in Ugandan society—freedom of movement and access to ancestral land, redistribution of national wealth, and everyday security and health. This, if anything, is what the functioning modern state is about. As Norbert Mao, a politician from northern Uganda, put it, "You cannot have justice if you don't have peace. You cannot talk about reconciliation when the structures which encourage violence have not been changed" (*Daily Monitor*, December 5, 2006; see also Branch 2007:193).

Putting down my pen here, in early 2009, I leave the analysis open by way of mentioning another Acholi ritual activity that can perhaps be more useful to start with, the *keto ajaa* ceremony ("to cut off the grass straw"), in which the opposing parties basically agree to disagree, not reconciling but cutting off the bitter debate in order to be able to proceed. It is an acceptance of the necessity for social interaction, to return to Fernandez (1965), and an agreement to orient action toward one another. Ritual action mediates lived paradoxes, and social life can be sustained. It is essentially about *habitus*, or those dispositions of "a present past that tends to perpetuate itself into the future" (Bourdieu 1990:54). As a young man in northern Uganda described the amnesty law while he offered me some tea to drink, "Say that I invite you for tea, and you happen to destroy my favorite cup. Then I say *jalo*—anyway, it is okay, nothing to do. But I didn't forgive you." To accept the situation so that life can go on.

Chapter 8

Silence and Dialogue

Burundians' Alternatives to Transitional Justice

Ann Nee and Peter Uvin

In the past fifteen years, the reach and expectations of transitional justice have expanded remarkably. Transitional justice has moved "from the exception to the norm" to "all transitional justice, all the time" (Teitel 2003:71). The core of the transitional justice paradigm is rooted in values promoting punishment of individuals who have engaged in criminal behavior, based on full information, formal procedures, and legal reasoning. More recently, truth commissions—although less strong in fulfilling the ideal of justice—have also come to hold a prized position (Hayner 2001; Kritz 1995; Minow 1998). The model of deterrence through punishment and reconciliation through truth telling is now seen as a near-universal ideal, transcending specific abuses, conflicts, or cultures. This assumption deserves closer examination. Whether the orthodox transitional justice model of prosecutions and truth commissions can be transplanted from the political transitions where it developed (e.g., South Africa, El Salvador) to the community-based-violence settings where they are now applied (e.g., Burundi) is unclear.

This chapter presents the results of two research studies in postwar Burundi. One is a qualitative study of perceptions of justice and reconciliation conducted in two communes in July and August of 2006.[1] The focus of that study was to solicit opinions about justice by ordinary community members, rather than NGO or justice professionals. The study involved thirty-five individuals living in a deeply divided commune, Ruhororo, in the north of the country, and eighteen individuals living in Nyanza Lac in the south of the country, where there were high refugee return rates and lower ethnic tensions after the war.[2] This study is augmented by results of a study done in those same two communes (Seventy-eight interviews in Ruhororo and seventy-four in Nyanza-Lac). This study consisted of open-ended interviews about people's sense of the future after twelve years of war. Its focus was not on transitional justice and reconciliation per se, but to the extent those subjects came up in the conversations, we draw on them too.

Our conclusions are by necessity provisional. At the time we did this research, we were among the first researchers to do fieldwork in Burundi in more than a decade. Our numbers are small, and our geographical coverage limited. In addition, justice is a difficult subject, being simultaneously very personal and highly political. Burundians express themselves in circumspect and often contradictory manners about such subjects; it takes a lot of context to situate what they tell us. Nonetheless, we believe the trends identified here are real. A significant source of confirmation is the open-ended research project that ran over a nine-month period and included one more rural commune (Busiga, also in the north—sixty-six interviews) and the capital, Bujumbura (172 interviews): the results of this research confirm what we describe here (Uvin 2008). Nonetheless, more research on this important subject is obviously welcome.

Burundians display four attitudes simultaneously when talking about transitional justice. First and most widespread is desire for silence. This silence is justified by arguments both practical and normative; it is intimately linked to the ways Burundians survive under very tough social and economic conditions. Second, there is a demand for punitive justice. These demands are frequently applied only to the other ethnic group; they seem to occur mainly among people who for various reasons are more politicized. Third, quite some people declare an interest in engaging in community-based dialogues of a conflict resolution nature—dialogues that acknowledge joint suffering and help to restore social relations but do not dig into the causes of the war or make individual judgments of guilt. Fourth, under certain circumstances, for individuals, such dialogues can even lead to genuine interpersonal reconciliation and forgiveness. Finally, the traditional mediation institution of bashingantahe remains a reference point, although the capacity and legitimacy of specific people associated with this institution vary widely.

Historical and Political Background

National Context

Burundi has just come out of twelve years of brutal civil war, which started in October 1993 when Melchior Ndadaye, the country's first democratically elected Hutu president, was killed in a coup d'état after exactly one hundred days in office. The coup itself formally failed a few days later, after an international outcry bolstered by freezes of aid. Yet the dynamics it set in motion remained: a constitutional crisis that was to last for years, ethnic and political violence throughout the country, and further confirmation for both sides that the other was not to be trusted.

The 1993 elections had been the end of almost three decades of Tutsi military rule (Lemarchand 1996; Reyntjens 2000). During that time, dissent was ruthlessly crushed. The main instance of this occurred in 1972, when almost all educated Hutu of any level were murdered by the (mono-ethnically Tutsi) army and hundreds of thousands more fled the country. The nature of the events of 1972 went largely unremarked by the international community. There were no calls for transitional justice, neither inside nor outside of Burundi. (Ndikumasabo and Vandeginste [2007:113–15] and Vandeginste [2007:6] well describe the impunity and miscarriages of justice that have prevailed during those decades.[3])

Immediately after the October 1993 coup, pogroms began against ordinary Tutsi in many parts of the country; thousands were killed. The army responded violently, killing many thousands in reprisal. People of both ethnicities fled their homes. The political process was deadlocked. Hutu rebel groups emerged, split, and launched attacks from Tanzania and the Congo. Tutsi youth gangs terrorized the capital: Bujumbura became ethnically cleansed, at an immense human toll. It is estimated that during those awful years, around 300,000 people were killed, over 500,000 fled abroad, and another 800,000 were displaced internally.

Under enormous international pressure, and with Tanzanian and then South African facilitation, the Arusha Peace and Reconciliation Agreement was eventually signed, on August 28, 2000. This negotiated settlement resulted from a mutually hurting stalemate in the battlefield. Fighting went on for years more, though, calming only after the signing of the Pretoria Protocol on Political, Defense, and Security Power-Sharing in October 2003 by the largest Hutu rebel movement, the CNDD/FDD (National Council for the Defense of Democracy—Forces for the Defense of Democracy), and the Burundian army. Even after that, the oldest rebel group, the FNL (National Liberation Forces in Burundi), did not begin to lay down arms until May 2008.

By mid-2006, when we did our research, a new, elected government had been in power for almost a year. The elections had gone peacefully, with the support of the international community, and were won by the CNDD/FDD. About half of all refugees had repatriated, and more than half of the IDPs had returned home as well.

Transitional Justice in Burundi

No one has ever been convicted in Burundi for ethno-political mass murder (Reyntjens 1995:7; Mubirigi 2007). By the time of the Arusha Agreement, however, the international normative enterprise of transitional justice had come into being, and under international pressure the Agreement included provisions for the usual mechanisms (Vandeginste 2007:9; Schweiger 2006). Article 6 of Protocol I requires the transitional government to request that the UN Security Council establish an "International Judicial Commission of Inquiry on genocide, war crimes and other crimes against humanity" responsible for investigating, classifying, and determining responsibility for such crimes from independence until the date of the signature of the peace agreement. This is to be followed by the "establishment by the United Nations Security Council of an international criminal tribunal to try and punish those responsible."

With respect to reconciliation, article 8 provides for the establishment, for two years, of a National Truth and Reconciliation Commission (NTRC) that would be mandated to investigate all "serious acts of violence" (excepting genocide, crimes against humanity, and war crimes) between independence and the signing of the peace accord; classify the crimes; and establish the identities of perpetrators and victims. It would also be asked to give recommendations to promote "reconciliation and forgiveness," indemnify or restore property, or grant amnesty. Finally, the NTRC would be "responsible for clarifying the entire history of Burundi, going as far back as possible in order to inform Burundians about their past. The purpose of this clarification exercise shall be to rewrite Burundi's history so that all Burundians can interpret it in the same way."

Progress on implementation of these measures has been close to nonexistent (Vandeginste 2007; Ndikumasabo and Vandeginste 2007). Legislation enacting the NTRC was passed in December 2004, but the commission has yet to be established. Following an investigation by the UN in 2005, a mixed National Truth and Reconciliation Commission (comprising three international and two national members) and a Special Chamber for War Crimes sited within the Burundian court system were proposed (Goldmann 2006:143; Schweiger 2006: 663). In May 2007, the UN and the government of Burundi reaffirmed their support for this plan but also indicated that they will not proceed without a lengthy "conversation" with all Burundians in order to gauge their desires regarding transitional justice, and to inform them of the mechanisms adopted. In early 2009, this is where things still stand—and many see this as simply a way of further delaying, if not avoiding, justice.

In 2006, 4,330 political prisoners (including many CNDD/FDD members) were released by the Commission on Political Prisoners. The recommendation for release was predicated on concerns about false accusations and a lack of due process for those imprisoned during the war, but there was no individualized review of cases prior to release. Those opposed to this decision—mainly Tutsi parties and sympathizers, but also some human rights organizations—decried it as the liberation of people who had committed serious war crimes, while many Hutu considered it an overdue liberation of unjustly and politically imprisoned freedom fighters (Ndikumasabo and Vandeginste 2007:116).

In the meantime, national and international human rights organizations continue to document occasional disappearances, murders, and torture; frequent instances of miscarriage of justice and widespread corruption in the justice sector; and an almost total nonexecution of judgments. While Burundi is a far freer state than it used to be, it does not remotely know—and has never known—rule of law in its modern form (Ndikumasabo and Vandeginste 2007; RCN 2006: 16 ff; OAG 2007).

Communal Profiles

Most of the data used for this research come from two communes, Ruhororo and Nyanza Lac. They were both highly affected by the war, with mass displacement and destruction. Yet they also represent rather different social dynamics, with Ruhororo far more internally divided than Nyanza Lac. The continued presence of many thousands of Tutsi living in a giant IDP camp in the center of Ruhororo stands as the most visible sign of its division.

Ruhororo   Hundreds of Tutsi died in pogroms immediately after the 1993 coup in Ruhororo (pop. approx. 55,000); thousands of Tutsi fled to displacement camps. For most of the war, it had the single largest camp of internally displaced people, with more than 20,000 persons. Numbers have fallen since 2003, but when we worked there, more than 8,000 IDPs still lived there, many for thirteen years.

Ruhororo saw violence throughout the war. At frequent intervals, IDPs and the military (all Tutsi) organized raids and attacks on the surrounding *collines* (hills—the way all Burundians designate rural spaces). This caused many of those still living in the hills to face periodic short-term displacement into the surrounding fields and forests; others fled to Tanzania. Ruhororo was also on the path the CNDD/FDD rebels took from their rear bases in Tanzania to their headquarters in the forest of Kibira. Over the years, then, Hutu rebels frequently attacked the IDP populations.

In 1998–99, local administrators in Ruhororo began concerted action to reduce the level of conflict. Several respondents described the efforts of a particular communal administrator who held meetings separately with IDPs and with groups in the collines in order to dissuade attacks and counterattacks. Gradually these had an effect, and along with the signing of the Arusha agreement, IDPs began to be able to return to their collines during the daytime to farm their fields, returning to the camp in the evening. Some eventually moved back full-time, but many others still have not, even after the peaceful elections. Our study focused on two places: the large IDP site in the center of town (exclusively Tutsi), and the surrounding rural collines (overwhelmingly Hutu).

Nyanza Lac   There were few anti-Tutsi pogroms in Nyanza Lac (pop. between 100,000 and 150,000) in 1993. Many Hutu did join the rebel movements, though. The town borders the biggest and oldest refugee camps in Tanzania and soon became the theater of brutal confrontations between the military and the rebels, with civilians of both ethnicities the victims. As a result of the fighting, from 1995 onward, most people living in the area were forced to flee, either to Tanzania or to IDP camps (which were, contrary to the North, of mixed ethnicity). The region became largely depopulated during the late 1990s.

After the signing of the ceasefire agreement in 2003, everyone rapidly left the IDP camps with little apparent compulsion; by the time of our research, there were no such camps left here. In explanation, some pointed to the terrible conditions in the camps due to the lack of NGOs in the region after several aid workers were killed. Others pointed to the lack of a genuine ethnic dimension to the displacement, so that once security was reestablished, return followed. Another explanation may lie in the fact that population density, poverty, and malnutrition are lower here than in much of the rest of the country. Indeed, this town has many markets, trade routes, and agricultural commercialization opportunities. It was also the foremost repatriation destination in Burundi, with thousands of returned refugees. We did our research in three different parts of town; there were few differences between them.

Study Results

Prosecution and Truth-Telling

The most striking insight resulting from both studies is that the majority of Burundians do not desire prosecutions and, to a lesser extent, truth-telling mechanisms. In our justice-focused survey, we asked people about the desirability of prosecutions and truth-telling mechanisms: the majority of respondents answered that they prefer that one or both of the mechanisms not be established. The sole exception was in the IDP camp in Ruhororo, one of the most polarized and divisive places in the country, where a majority of the inhabitants did support prosecutions.[4] The larger, non-justice-focused research confirms this result (including in the capital): we did not ask specific questions about justice mechanisms but simply invited them to talk about the past and the future, the state and the community they live in, and less than a handful spontaneously expressed a desire for transitional justice.

In short, the majority of people expressed sentiments in favor of "forgetting," akin to a general pardon, rather than prosecution. Many argued that because such large numbers of people of all ethnic groups committed crimes, nearly "the entire population" would be in jeopardy of prosecution if any were pursued.

> We must pardon everyone because if not, it will be like we will have to punish all the population. We must pardon everyone because all ethnic groups did bad acts. (thirty-eight-year-old female, Nyanza Lac)

If I look in the two groups, there have been errors everywhere, it is better to forget. If we try to look for criminals, we will find almost everyone is a criminal. (twenty-three-year-old female, Hutu, Ruhororo)

Other respondents argued that a pardon is better because it would enable the country to look toward constructing a future instead of dwelling on the past.

An amnesty is the best solution for Burundi to try to begin a new life, a new page in the history of our country. (thirty-eight-year-old woman, Nyanza Lac)

For those who committed crimes, we must educate them [not prosecute them]. We must show them that what they did is not good. Then they will change and become more like us and can help to rebuild the country. (forty-four-year-old female, Ruhororo IDP camp)

If we continue to punish those who committed crimes in the past during the crisis, no one will feel at ease. For example, years could pass, and sometimes, even if you are innocent, people could accuse you of using lies. To alleviate things, it must be done, we must pardon them. (thirty-five-year-old civil servant, Hutu, Ruhororo)

Still others emphasized that prosecutions and truth telling could not undo what had happened. They often repeated the same image: the dead won't come back, so what would be the point?

You can have lost your belongings and your family, but what will you gain if you stay angry? You are not going to see again the people you lost." (forty-eight-year-old male, returned IDP, Ruhororo)

My family—my wife and my six children—was killed. I know who did it. I sometimes meet them in the street: they greet me and I greet them. I have forgiven them: they can never bring back my family, so it is the best thing to do. It is best to forget and to get on with life. (forty-two-year-old ex-combatant, CNDD, Nyanza Lac)

The situation in Ruhororo, however, differed in the attitudes expressed elsewhere toward prosecution and truth telling. Here, the majority Hutu position (when asked to express an opinion) supported truth telling and opposed prosecutions, whereas the Tutsi position overwhelmingly supported prosecutions and opposed truth telling. This clearly relates to how these groups politically interpret the civil war. Many Tutsi define themselves as the victims of genocidal attacks. This is a fear many have grown up with; the events of 1993 and their continued displacement are the daily proof of the reality of that. They tend to want punishment for the perpetrators. Many Hutu, on the other hand, see the last twelve years as a fight for equal rights, a necessary attack against a decades-old system of social exclusion of which they were the victims. They largely expressed a preference for a truth commission to talk about the past.

Another factor explaining this difference between Hutu and Tutsi answers is the perception of the ethnic nature of the justice system. Hutu are suspicious of prosecutions because most of those imprisoned during the war were Hutu from the hills, and because the legal system in Burundi historically has been (and still primarily is) composed of Tutsi (OAG 2007:36; Schweiger 2006:659). In short, then, what justice means—and the approach to justice selected—is a highly politicized matter in a deeply divided community like Ruhororo.

This degree of politicization is not common to all Burundians. For starters, even in Ruhororo, there were exceptions to the dominant position—we quoted some above. Second, everywhere else in our research, most respondents, Hutu and Tutsi, declared they prefer to forget. At the same time, we believe that this politicization of justice lurks just below the surface everywhere: in situations where political or social antagonism mounts or where people are forced to choose (as in our justice survey), many revert to an ethnically based interpretation of justice. One confirmation of this can be found in the fact that among the political and intellectual class in Bujumbura, for example, radically divergent and biased positions on justice are far more common.

What we describe here is similar to the concept of "mythico-histories" Malkki (1995) described as prevailing in refugee camps in Tanzania, where a dominant discourse of Hutu purity and suffering pervaded all people's identities. Surprisingly, refugees living in a nearby city (outside of camps) presented a far more general "Burundian" identity, if not an outright Tanzanian one. Marc Sommers (1997a), in reviewing her book, argued that political control might account for this variation: in camps, radical political leaders are able to enforce a party rhetoric of grievance, whereas in the city this is much less easy. Above, we argued, similar to Malkki, that the more radical interpretation of justice we encountered in Ruhororo was the result of the conditions of life there—the longstanding violence, collective trauma, and torn social relations—but we cannot discard Sommers' interpretation: more research is needed. Both Hutu and Tutsi reflect these mythico-histories, and, when politicized, it leads them to highly partisan positions on the transitional justice debate. At the same time, under non-politicized conditions, they both prefer silence and forgetting. Why?

Why Talking About the Past Is Undesirable

A major reason invoked by people who preferred not to talk about the past was that doing so would lead to increased conflict.

> If we wrote everything that happened, that would be bad, because these acts must not be remembered. I find that if we return to go over all the past, there will be people who would be angry because we will remind them again of the unhappiness they have lived. If you need reconciliation, that means to forget all that happened. (forty-year-old woman, Nyanza Lac)

> We must not talk about the crisis because we understand that these times are over, and because of fear that it might start again. (fifty-four-year-old male, elected mushingantahe, Tutsi, IDP camp, Ruhororo)

Those who currently speak publicly—as opposed to among friends—about the crisis are seen as the ones who continue to hold onto the idea of pursuing violence. Thus talking has a negative contextual association with threats to continuing security.

> Those who talk about the past are those who still feel rancor. They talk about the past to show that they have not forgiven the others and that they still have this rancor. (twenty-three-year old-female, Hutu, Ruhororo)

Our conversations revealed many more reasons why the majority of Burundians prefer neither prosecution nor truth telling, but forgetting, moving on, and amnesty on the societal level. First, Burundi is a society where formal justice in a full, blind, equal-for-all version has not existed for decades. People have no belief that any judicial solution proposed to them will actually work as promised. One could therefore argue that their responses do not prove that Burundians do not prefer western-style transitional justice: it may be that they really would desire the full transitional justice menu if they believed they had a fair shot of actually getting it, but that they are cynical that it will ever come about.

For me, if I met someone who did something bad to me, if we had a justice system, I could bring this person before the tribunal and the law would know how to punish this person. But there is no justice system here to study the question of punishment. (seventy-year-old woman, returned 1972 refugee, Hutu, Nyanza Lac)

As someone who is one of the common people, I do not know how to respond to the question of whether people should be prosecuted. When I try to comprehend that, until now, the case of the assassination of the president [Ndadaye] has remained unsolved, like it has been thrown away, how can I imagine, if the killer of a president is not prosecuted, that the case of a simple peasant who was killed will be prosecuted? (seventy-year-old male, traditional mushingantahe, returned 1993 refugee, Nyanza Lac)

The effect of a historical absence of modern rule of law (the precolonial system was indeed a form of rule of law, albeit different from the one underlying both the modern state and the international transitional justice enterprise [Weilenmann 2005]) or of the sort of legal tradition that underlies the transitional justice agenda is felt in deeper, more socially anchored ways as well. In a context where rule of law and faith in any institution of justice are absent, people have developed other time-tested strategies for survival that strongly caution against placing faith in formal justice mechanisms. Many of these strategies are predicated on silence, on letting go, on forgetting—by the widow who now finds a measure of stability in the house of a man who killed her family; by the young woman who, by never talking about her rape, can find a husband; by the men who, by not bringing up the past, manage to work side by side in a cooperative. Ordinary Burundians are by necessity highly pragmatic—it is only the well-off or those living abroad who can afford principle.

Second, Burundians have a fine understanding of how the violence of the civil war spread among them. In our conversations, people frequently hinted at the fact that a lot of the violence was committed out of fear. Both in the city and in the countryside, waves of insecurity rolled over the population, wiping out all normality. Many people ended up being both victims and perpetrators in this climate of fear (see also Uvin 2008, ch. 8). They may have committed horrendous acts, which do not represent who they normally are or aspire to be. Many came to regret these acts later. People naturally have a hard time confronting or talking about this, and trials, with their exactness, public nature, limited scope, and single-minded focus on culpability, may simply not be the best tools for resolving what happened in people's lives during these awful years of insecurity and fear.

Related to this, some of those who favored pardons conveyed their view that the war was a time that was wholly outside of cognizable human experience. The incomprehensibility of the acts committed went to prove that the people who committed them were not themselves and could thus not be held entirely to account for their actions. Others also used this idea as a reason why they would personally forgive those who had harmed them during the war. Under this belief, amnesty for crimes committed during the crisis would not necessarily lead to further cycles of violence, because the exceptionalism of the crisis permitted a line to be drawn between crimes committed before and after the peace.

> As for people in armed groups, all the people in this time were animated by a satanic spirit. They have had time to change their behavior. (thirty-five-year-old woman, Nyanza Lac)

> For these people who continue to want vengeance, they also do not have peace. We must not prosecute them, but we should engage these people to try to re-educate them. It is like they are not part of society anymore, they just dream of doing bad things. We must educate them to change their behavior. (fifty-nine-year-old woman, returned 1972 refugee, Nyanza Lac)

Third, Burundians everywhere consider "the politicians" to be responsible for the war (this mirrors the scholarly consensus; e.g., Daley 2006; Lemarchand 1996); they talk about being manipulated by politicians who came in the night, of gangs of criminals being paid by politicians to fan the flames of violence, of unreliable politicians in Bujumbura cynically using the masses in their fight for personal benefits. This sense that the politicians are to blame is one of the most widespread opinions about the war and it is shared by Hutu and Tutsi—a possible basis on which to erect a scaffolding for reconciliation (Kadende-Kaiser and Kaiser 1997:47–48). Some people who favor prosecutions consequently argue that the politicians should be the first, or even the only ones, to be prosecuted. These responses correspond with the transitional justice principle of prosecuting those "most responsible" for crimes and may provide an indication that limited prosecutions in the proposed special chamber for Burundi might have some popular backing.

Most of these people who committed crimes were misled by politicians. They only executed what politicians said to do. We must forgive them and not prosecute them, because it was not their fault but that of the politicians. (forty-six-year-old male, returned IDP, Ruhororo)

The common people are the pillars of the politicians, they support the politicians in their bad works. If they don't have bad politicians, then the people won't do it again. Most people have only executed the orders of the politicians, like innocents. If we prosecute and punish the leaders, then the others should be pardoned. (sixty-seven-year-old male, traditional mushingantahe, Tutsi, IDP camp, Ruhororo)

A fourth reason given by people who opposed prosecutions and truth telling is a fear of endangering the transition. In all places where we did research, people repeated that the prosecution of politicians should be subordinate to the objective of maintaining security and peace.

Peace is necessary for simple country people—to cultivate, to eat, to have security. If the politicians are not prosecuted but there is peace, then I don't understand why people insist on punishing the politicians. (forty-six-year-old male, returned IDP, Tutsi, Ruhororo)

Burundians—both Hutu and Tutsi—are pleased with the transition: it brought them peace and a potential for development; for Hutu, it also created a more representative and stable system of government than anything they had known since independence. Full accountability of the key people involved in crimes could very conceivably undermine the transition. People high in the current elected government, the army, and the parliament, as well as still-powerful outsiders, could have to face trial. Their resistance could very well destroy the transition and reignite civil war. People clearly value security far higher than justice. It may be that this position will change after enough years of peace and democratic governance—only the future will tell.

Fifth, and different from the more practical or instrumental arguments presented so far, many of our interviewees seemed to display a normative preference in favor of silence. They treated the desire to talk about the past almost as a weakness. People talk about the past, the argument goes, because they cannot help it, because they cannot stop themselves, because they cannot forget. It would be better if they could avoid doing so. We will come back to the deep cultural basis of this attitude later.

We talk about the past when we get together, when we drink. We do not talk about why it started but of the sorrows we suffered. If possible, we must be silent, we should not speak on the subject of the crisis. Why should we continue talking about it when talking about it is not important? (fifty-five-year-old male, Nyanza Lac)

For me, I don't think it is good to talk about the past. But you cannot forget the periods of sorrow in your life. You can't forget those years. I don't know what to do if you have memories of bad things in your heart. But if you do talk, you need to only talk about what happened to you and that you don't want it to happen again. (twenty-one-year-old man, Nyanza Lac)

It is not good to talk about this, because there were lots of losses and we must not remind people of all that happened. We must forget everything that happened to start another life. If people came and said we should get together and tell our stories, I don't think it would be good. (thirty-nine-year-old female, Nyanza Lac)

The last, and very important, reason why most Burundians do not prefer the available transitional justice menu is that they overwhelmingly think of themselves as having moved beyond ethnicity and division. In our broader research, we asked people how *entente* was in their lives. The word is hard to translate in English: it refers to notions of getting along, living without friction—cohabitation or coexistence may be the best approximation (Chayes and Minow 2003).

In these conversations, the overwhelming majority of people everywhere in Burundi were very positive about the state of entente in their neighborhoods or collines. Whether in rural or in urban areas, poor or rich, almost everyone we spoke with made a similar argument when asked about entente; namely, "entente is good here, for we all live the same problems."[5] Note that what we are describing is not that ethnic identity has become less important or the mythico-histories less divergent, but rather that the salience of ethnic difference in daily life has become less. It is a redefinition not of ethnic identity, but rather of the daily social importance of that identity that has taken place.

Once again, the only place where a different situation prevailed is the IDP camp in Ruhororo, where a significant number of people (about 40 percent) said that entente was not good. This limited exceptionalism in the IDP camp was not a reflection of a broader Tutsi reflex. We interviewed many Tutsi throughout the country, and it is only in the Ruhororo IDP camp that a sizable proportion of interviewees differed from the general position. This suggests, once again, that much of what we heard in the IDP camp in Ruhororo is a reflection of isolation and trauma. The people who live there live separated—a well-defined island of Tutsi in what many of them still perceive as a hostile sea of Hutu. The people living in the IDP camp in Ruhororo seemed generally among the most depressed people we met during our months of talking to Burundians (Uvin 2008). The weeks spent in the camp talking to its inhabitants had a nearly palpable heaviness. Older people fear their former neighbors, bemoan their lost children, their loneliness, their displacement. The young people had no hopes for life: no work, no capacity to get married, no access to credit, no professional training. Separation, trauma from the pogroms of 1993, and ongoing social and economic constraints, then, seem to combine to explain the different results of the people living in the IDP camp.

The fact that people everywhere overwhelmingly told us that cohabitation was good is important, for it informs us of some crucial dynamics in Burundi. One is that the current political situation of the country favors ethnic reconciliation—or, maybe more precisely, a relaxing of the importance of ethnicity. Contrary to the past, all political parties go out of their way to not present themselves as representing ethnic groups, and extremist parties have become marginal.

The second is that this answer, even if factually incorrect, reflects an image people consider desirable. Burundi is not a dictatorship like neighboring Rwanda, where only a state-imposed discourse is allowed. Hence, even if this overwhelming answer that entente is good is an image projected at outsiders, it is at least one that has widespread grounding in society, reflecting how Burundians like to think of themselves—or present themselves—after twelve years of brutal ethnic civil war.

Also illustrative of this desire to see their society as beyond ethnicity were responses to the question "Who do you admire?" A large number of answers consisted of people describing to us ordinary acts of justness and conflict resolution, or actions to defend others, all of which were special because they happened across ethnic lines. Stories like these comfort people, it seems, and demonstrate to all that a page has been turned, can be turned.

I admire a professor at his *college communal*: someone wanted to unjustly send a student out of school: this professor defended the student with the administration, even though he was of a different ethnicity than the student. (nineteen-year-old male student, IDP camp, Ruhororo)

I admire someone who discriminates against no one. Who acts for the good of others. In the IDP camp there was a leader like that. He intervened in a difficult situation to witness and save the life of a neighbor who was unjustly accused, even though he was from the other ethnic group. (nineteen-year-old female farmer, Nyanza Lac)

I admire my Hutu neighbors in my colline of birth. They remained *solidaire* when I lost my parents. (thirty-seven-year-old man, Tutsi, private-sector employee, Bujumbura)

I admire people who hid others [of different ethnic groups during the crisis], their neighbors and friends. They saved their lives. I also admire IDPs in the camp who, when they heard there would be an attack on the collines, went to warn you so you could flee. (twenty-five-year-old woman, Hutu, Ruhororo)

These statements perfectly reveal the dual truth about Burundi: Burundians clearly admire this sort of behavior and identify with it, but, equally clearly, this behavior is rare—that is precisely why it is a source of admiration. These stories do refer to past divisiveness, but they focus primarily on the capacity for surmounting ethnicity. This sentiment corresponds with the desire to avoid transitional justice mechanisms that would emphasize the negative dimensions of the ethnic divisions of the past. But there is more.

We have already referred twice to the way Burundians constantly maintain relations across great chasms of violence, class, abuse, and division. People have civil relations with the murderers of their families; separated husbands and wives, even after decades, reconnect and share all again; refugees and IDPs return home, solving most of their land conflicts between themselves. And all of this happens against a background of stunning poverty. Burundi specialists decry the level of land conflicts, involving as many as 9 percent of all households in the province of Makamba, a center of return of refugees and IDPs. But this still means that an amazing 91 percent of the population is *not* party to any land conflict, and this in a country where every square foot of land is a matter of life and death. Throughout the country, Hutu and Tutsi are living side by side again, for they were intermingled everywhere. How, then, do people manage to such an extent to reintegrate, after a decade of war, dislocation, and extreme poverty?

This puzzle becomes all the more perplexing as Burundi does not have any public rituals, mechanisms, or procedures of community reintegration or reconciliation. Not one Burundian, whether intellectual or peasant, Hutu or Tutsi, urban or rural, described to us any ceremony or rite of reintegration or reconciliation, whether traditional, religious, or state-sponsored. Instead, the process leading to cohabitation takes place ad hoc between ordinary people.

Burundians themselves talk about flexibility when they describe how this happens. What they mean by this is that they value the capacity to compromise, to go with the wind, to hide their true feelings, to move on. These are individual behaviors, anchored in the essential individual struggle for survival of all Burundians. At the same time, these attitudes and behaviors are socially valued and reproduced: Burundians are proud of this and uphold it as desirable.

There seems no doubt that this results from Burundians' profound vulnerability: they need to maintain relations at all costs, for, apart from their bodies, the little bit of social capital they have is the only thing that may make the difference between total destitution and simple poverty, especially in a context of complete absence of rule of law. The capacity to maintain relations with people who crossed you, whom you distrust, is crucial, for one never knows—they may be necessary one day. Those who exploit you today may be the only ones upon whom you can call for assistance tomorrow, and the only way to have a fighting chance is to stick with it. It is likely that this happens most from the perspective of women; it is they who depend upon and invest in these relations most.

This, then, is not the Putnamian social capital of generalized trust born out of collaboration and compromise, shared norms and expectations. Rather, it is based on such an extent of generalized, institutionalized, and internalized *distrust* (as well as insecurity and absence of rule of law) that one needs to build up the maximum amount of social relations possible, in order to survive. In a situation of insecurity and unpredictability, and in the absence of community-based mechanisms of reintegration and reconciliation, Burundians protect themselves by nurturing relations, by compromising, by maintaining a poker face of acceptance under all conditions.

The question of culture in all of this is fascinating and difficult. Burundians, for as long as we know, have been described—and describe themselves—as masters of dissimulation, of not showing their true feelings. They are proud of it and will often jokingly tell you about the fact that a no can always mean a yes and vice versa, or that they can warmly hug the man they will kill a few hours later. They treat this as a cultural feature. This theme is represented in a line of Burundian proverbs, such as "The one who doesn't lie has no food for his children." This sort of behavior is reproduced through the generations, passed on from parents who demonstrate this behavior and legitimize it to their children. As such, it becomes normal, invisible—just as our own western constructs and expectations are largely invisible to ourselves. As a result, dissimulation of true emotions serves the constant maintenance of social capital at all costs.

The possibility for orthodox transitional justice mechanisms to be divisive and to unravel the ties that form the basis of this social capital is evident. In accusing or testifying against neighbors, individuals would break with the socially preferred silence and risk ostracism, suspicion, and reprisal, along with heightening ethnic animosity in their communities and elevating barriers to the cooperation on which their survival depends. As such, supporting these mechanisms would be an act against their individual interests, in a context where most of the non-elite have nothing to spare.

Community-Based Dialogues

So far, we have documented Burundians' preference for silence. As part of the larger cultural strategy of flexibility, this is a way of maintaining social capital and daily survival for the great many of Burundi's poor. These strategies, however, do not address the exceptional fear and lack of trust that were exposed during the war. This radical social breakdown impedes normal efforts to get along and may explain why many Burundians also expressed a desire for something additional to assist them on a personal level: namely, the organization of meetings that would focus on creating conditions for renewal of relations between parties and possibly even interpersonal forgiveness, rather than truth or accusations (see Kaufman 2006:213–14 for a general discussion).

One respondent in Ruhororo described a meeting he witnessed, which was organized by an NGO and held with church leaders, to bring together freed prisoners and those who had accused them. The main positive effect of these meetings was achieved through the catharsis generated between the participants in both groups, allowing them to accept each other again.

> During these meetings, these people spoke of their life in prison. They told this to the people who accused them. They also had to relate what they did during the war. They asked pardon from these people and these people forgave

them, verbally. These meetings were something which touched the hearts of the people there. The prisoners had spent years in prison; some had been given the death penalty. For them to even see again their victims was a miracle. The moment when they accepted to ask for forgiveness really touched people. It is very important that we continue to do this in order to have a return to peace. (thirty-eight-year-old male, returned IDP, Hutu, Ruhororo)

While not all people spoke of forgiveness in this context, there existed in our conversations an undercurrent of interest in some kind of conflict-resolution dialogues that would help people to reestablish social links through recognition of common suffering. This contradicts the preference expressed by most Burundians in favor of silence and against truth commissions.

Part of this contradiction seems to arise through the difference between talking of the facts of the past and talking about their origins. Talking about the facts is about suffering and loss, destruction and displacement. For some—though clearly not for all—it can be therapeutic. It can even have the power to recreate bonds, as so much of the suffering is so similar across groups On the other hand, talking about the causes of the war—and a fortiori assigning blame, naming and punishing individuals—is divisive, as people realize that there are major divisions among them in how they see the past.

People do talk of the crisis, but they do not want to touch on the origins, because if they do, everyone will start throwing around blame. Each ethnic group will think the other started it, and it will mire people's hearts in anger. I think that talking of the crisis should only be of the lives they lived while displaced, but not to evoke the subject of the origin [of the crisis]. (thirty-eight-year-old female, Nyanza Lac)

The key insight here is that there is a major difference between talking about the facts of the crisis and about the origins of the crisis, or even more so, about culpability. Individuals frequently positively described mechanisms that are local, face-to-face, but not designed for truth and justice. Instead, these mechanisms focus on defusing tension, interpersonal healing, forgiveness, and cohabitation. Such meetings may lead to forgiveness, but they may also be useful simply in renewing social relations—a less high, but much desired achievement.

Forgiveness

Some Burundians suggested that more was possible: they spoke about local meetings where perpetrators could ask forgiveness of their victims in front of their communities. This was seen as a powerful symbol that could work to dismantle fear and distrust, and further obviate the need for prosecutions.

Many of the reasons given in favor of amnesty extended to personal-level forgiveness as well. Individually, some had already forgiven those who had harmed them, and others were willing to forgive if asked, even in the IDP camp in Ruhororo. People explained their willingness to forgive based on the exceptionalism of the crisis—the fact that during this period people were not acting as themselves. Others repeated that nothing could return their loved ones to them, so an unwillingness or inability to forgive would only continue to cause them hurt while achieving nothing. The strong religiosity in Burundi (primarily Christian) also served to focus many responses on the approach of forgiveness.

One perhaps surprising aspect was the absolute terms in which respondents who spoke of forgiveness described the effect of this process: once having been asked for forgiveness and having given it, they would no longer harbor the same fear or desire for vengeance against perpetrators. The qualifier was, again, that such forgiveness would depend on the perpetrators' manner in asking for it.

> If someone asked my forgiveness, I would be ready to forgive this person. The idea of being satisfied by this is my idea, though, not for everyone. But if I forgave this person, I would prefer that he not be prosecuted by the justice system, or that the justice system also pardoned this person. But the forgiveness would depend on how he explained himself, and on the dialogue that we would have. After this forgiveness, trust and relations would be reborn between these people and myself, and I would not be afraid of these people anymore. (twenty-seven-year-old male, Tutsi, IDP camp, Ruhororo)

> If I saw someone who did me ill, it would be normal to have negative feelings, because you remember what they did. [. . .] If this person dares to ask my pardon, I'll give it to him, but I would advise him not to do it again. If I saw him again, the next time I would not have these same feelings, because I would already have forgiven him. (forty-eight-year-old male, returned IDP, Tutsi, Ruhororo)

The basic vision of achieving conditions for forgiveness was of meetings where individuals of different groups could come together and perpetrators could express themselves, admit crimes, and ask forgiveness of the victims and the community. For many, the act of asking for forgiveness by perpetrators was a key condition. Some highlighted the importance of doing that in front of the community, instead of merely from an individual victim. Through these mechanisms, perpetrators could demonstrate before their communities their remorse and renunciation of violence against anyone.

> Some people who went to Tanzania killed and did other bad acts. For people in the site and people in the hills, it is the same situation. So what must be done is for everyone to assemble themselves in one place, and each must ask pardon of the others. This should be done on an individual basis, from a person who hurt someone to a person that he hurt. If they asked for pardon like that, people could not not forgive. (fifty-three-year-old male, Hutu, Ruhororo)

> Those who committed crimes should ask for pardon not from an individual but from the population. Because he could still do the same things to other people if he asks only for the forgiveness of the one person. (twenty-six-year-old female, Hutu, Ruhororo)

Several people suggested roles for national-level leaders, local administrators, and NGOs in assisting people to hold such meetings. In particular, religious leaders were named as being a critical avenue for exhorting their congregations to participate and to ask for forgiveness. This resonated with the large number of respondents who named their Christian faith as a key driver for accepting forgiveness as a means of reconciliation.

> Some will accept to ask for forgiveness, and some will not. There are others who should help with this process, such as the administration, the council members, and religious leaders. (twenty-six-year-old female, Hutu, Ruhororo)

> Some people would accept to apologize and others would not come forward because they would be afraid of being poisoned or hurt. If you want people to come and apologize, you must say these things in church, to insist that it is very important to go. (twenty-one-year-old male, ex–child soldier, Tutsi, IDP camp, Ruhororo)

Traditional Justice and the Bashingantahe

It is impossible to write about Burundi without discussing traditional justice mechanisms. Our field research has little new to contribute to this subject, so we will be brief. During the precolonial period, Burundi had a decentralized system of law and adjudication centered on the king and his chiefs (Laely 1997). A particular feature of this system was the existence of bashingantahe (singular: *mushingantahe*)—men designated by their community, selected on the basis of their wisdom, impartiality, knowledge, and wealth (Trouwborst 1961:148). Their role was to mediate, give advice, and propose judgments in local conflicts. The institution was non-ethnic (Naniwe-Kaburahe 2009). It was not hereditary: each person had to earn the position through his behavior, his words, his learning, and his eventual investiture by the entire community.

This institution did not survive Burundi's colonial period in its traditional form. Under the colonial administration and the later postindependence regimes, bashingantahe were increasingly nominated from above, obliged to apply formal law, and limited in their power (Dexter and Ntahombaye 2005: 14ff; OAG 2007:40ff).

At the same time, "real" bashingantahe still persist. They are often referred to by the designation "*bashingantahe investi*," i.e., those who went through the traditional investiture ceremony, as opposed to those who are just mere terms of politeness, or, now, locally elected representatives. It is not clear how many there are today (Naniwe-Kaburahe 2009 cites a UNDP study that counts 34,000 of them, which seems exceedingly high) or what their role and legitimacy is. In our conversations, a number of people identified themselves as being "bashingantahe investi," and a larger number spoke about the bashingantahe, sometimes positively and sometimes negatively.

The role of bashingantahe during the war was ambiguous. In some places, such as Busiga and Nyanza Lac, we were told that they gave advice that prevented "hot-headed young men" from killing and looting, thus maintaining peace. In other communes, most notably Ruhororo, this was not the case: the bashingantahe themselves were killed, or were simply not listened to. In some instances, we were also told about bashingantahe who participated in the violence (similar results in OAG 2007:42; Dexter and Ntahombaye 2006:15ff). The issue of bashingantahe corruption was also often mentioned (see too OAG 2007:46).

Yet all accounts agree that bashingantahe remain a potentially important source of justice for many Burundians (Dexter and Ntahombaye 2006:20ff).

They are close by, cheap and fast (OAG 2007:6). But, more importantly, our conversations reveal that the values that underlie the institution are still deeply alive among Burundians. For example, when asked "Who do you admire?" Burundians responded:

> Someone who is objective and can solve conflicts peacefully, someone who can give good advice to others. (Busiga, twenty-five-year-old farmer and part-time employee of the civil register of the zone, nine years of education)

> A person who practices justice, tells the truth, and lives peacefully together with his neighbors, who takes care of the well-being of others. (thirty-two-year-old demobilized ex-FAB, taxi-vélo driver, Ruhororo camp)

> Someone who in a conflict advises the parties without bias. (twenty-two-year-old female farmer, Ruhororo colline)

> Someone who is just and honest, who manages conflicts that are entrusted to him by others well. (Kamenge, twenty-three-year-old migrant taxi-vélo driver)

Late in the research, a translator, on his own initiative, asked a new question of fifteen young ex-combatants he found in Bujumbura: "What is a man?" Most of these people he was talking to had years of violence behind them and were of low educational level, mostly unemployed.

> I think my friends expect that I be a man of my word, a true mushingantahe, a man who takes care correctly of his family without forgetting his immediate and further-away environment. (eighteen-year-old)

> For me, a man is someone who tries to listen and understand the others, someone who is just, who doesn't discriminate and has no biases. (twenty-eight-year-old)

> To me, being a man is not simply having a woman, or having money. A man is about the *parole*: a word of honor, of truth, of wisdom. (twenty-one-year-old)

> To me, a man is a parole of honor, without lies, someone who speaks the truth and wisdom in his family and community, who is just, without biases and favoritism. (twenty-three-year-old)

In short, throughout many of the conversations, and in response to many different questions, Burundians told us not so much about specific individual bashingantahe as about the values associated with the institution. These values are clearly still deeply alive in Burundi. People admire others who behave this way; they would like to be treated that way by the authorities and anyone who has power over them; they dream of themselves living up to those standards.

As a result, in the postwar period, many Burundians and the international community have tried to restore the institution of bashingantahe, in the hope of using it as a locally appropriate mechanism for transitional justice and rule of law (Dexter and Ntahombaye 2006). The Arusha agreements, among other "cultural" stipulations, talk about the "rehabilitation of the institution of *Ubushingantahe*" (Prot. I, art. 7, para. 27). In 2005, with foreign support, the National Council of Bashingantage was created by constitutional fiat. Justice NGOs and the UN provide trainings to bashingantahe in various places and organize dialogues between them and judges and the local administration.

The current government, however, is distinctly less enthusiastic about bashingantahe (Dexter and Ntahombaye 2006; Vandeginste 2006; OAG 2007:43). As it seeks foremost to establish its full control over the territory, it is weary of a corps of people with major public roles who are entirely uncontrolled by itself—a potential parallel network of local power. Moreover, it has proven hard to "restore" an institution that has decades of weakening behind it, and whose manifestation is different from locality to locality. Still, attempts to strengthen the bashingantahe continue till this day.

Conclusion

Our conversations reveal three strong tendencies that run counter to the basic tenets of transitional justice. First, most people seem to prefer to be silent, to forget, whether out of fear, a sense of futility, a normative preference in favor of silence and flexibility, or—most likely—a combination of these factors. This preference has deep cultural and socioeconomic roots that go far beyond the strict transitional-justice debate and relate to how people have learned to cope with extreme uncertainty, poverty, and upheaval.

Second, the paradigm of prosecution and equal treatment for the same acts, no matter who committed them, is not shared by many Burundians. Most people *on both sides* see themselves as victims and the other as aggressors; each group sees its own acts as necessary for survival, while the other's acts were unjust. When people talk about wanting justice, then, they more often than not intend it to be meted out for the crimes committed by the other side. When they speak of forgiveness, most believe that it is the other side that ought to be apologizing first. For many people, in short, to the extent that they desire justice, they see it through a politicized lens. The more polarized their social or political situation, or the more marginalized they feel, the more people revert to this distorted approach to justice.

Third, our results also run counter to another dominant implicit assumption, shared by scholars and policymakers in many post-conflict countries, namely, that "the people" want western-style justice, but that "the elites" block that deep groundswell in favor of justice by their short-sightedness, arrogance, fear, or complacency. Our interviews in Burundi reveal that the strong and the weak, the powerful and the powerless, prefer partial justice, or even silence and "no justice." Deep ambivalence toward transitional justice in Burundi exists not only at the level of the political elite, but also among ordinary people. Life goes on, and social and economic relations are reestablished; beer is shared, as are benches in the church. This coexistence is a far cry from justice in any international meaning of the term, but it is a recognizable and desired goal for many people.

Fourth, people do appreciate when safe environments are created for them to talk about the hardships they faced and the fears they still have, and to reach out to others in their communities. Dialogues and workshops along those lines, organized by communal administrators, parish priests, and professional conflict-resolution NGOs are widely liked. By showing the commonality of suffering between all groups during the crisis and offering a forum where perpetrators can demonstrate their changed behavior, these cathartic processes may lead at a minimum to improved cohabitation. Under certain circumstances, for individuals, such dialogues can even lead to genuine personal reconciliation and forgiveness.

These factors together strongly suggest that only a minority of Burundians in 2006 adhere to the transitional justice agenda as proposed by the international community. There seem to be two fundamental reasons for this divergence. One is that the conditions of life of Burundians do not reflect those that are required for the international model to work. They have neither faith in the institutions of formal justice nor a strong desire to bring things out into the open. They have deeply rooted strategies for survival in situations of continuous vulnerability, lack of trust, and profound economic and, since recently, political insecurity; maintaining a minimum of social capital is under those conditions crucial. This favors flexibility and the maintaining of relations—not fixed truths and judgments. The other is that the type of acts under consideration—widespread participation in communal violence during years of fear and anarchy—does not lend itself easily to the international model. All these conclusions are tentative, but they are concordant with other social dynamics observed in Burundi, and elsewhere.

Chapter 9

"Like Jews Waiting for Jesus"

Posthumous Justice in Post-Genocide Rwanda

Lars Waldorf

I have a habitual feeling of my real life having past, and that I am leading a post-humous existence.

—*John Keats*

Urwishe abandi ntirukwibagiwe. (The death that killed the others does not forget you.)

—*Rwandan proverb, cited in Crepeau and Bizimana 1979*

Rwanda has finished the most ambitious experiment in transitional justice ever attempted: mass justice for mass atrocity. In the wake of the 1994 genocide, Rwanda resurrected and transformed an ad hoc, local-dispute resolution mechanism (*gacaca*) into a formalized system of 11,000 community courts (*gacaca inkiko*). Over the past few years, more than 100,000 lay judges have tried over one million genocide cases in those courts. Nearly every week, local communities assembled on Rwanda's verdant hills and dusty soccer pitches or gathered in fragrant eucalyptus groves and cramped meeting halls to listen as *génocidaires* offered confessions, *rescapés* (survivors) leveled accusations, and witnesses gave testimonies.

Gacaca was a proudly homegrown response to mass violence, and one that explicitly contested the international community's preference for international criminal tribunals and national truth commissions. Although Rwanda originally pushed the UN Security Council to create the International Criminal Tribunal for Rwanda (ICTR), it was the only country to vote against the

Tribunal.[1] It also dismissed proposals for a South African–style truth commission as an inadequate response to genocidal violence.

Gacaca challenged the transitional justice "toolkit" in several innovative ways. First, it suggested that customary dispute resolution practices could be modernized and scaled up to provide transitional justice.[2] Second, gacaca was avowedly local and participatory, with each and every community across Rwanda prosecuting and judging its own members for their actions in the genocide. Finally, gacaca went further than any other transitional justice mechanism in holding lower-level perpetrators and bystanders accountable.[3] In important respects, however, gacaca hewed to the transitional justice paradigm and even affirmed its two central nostrums: individualized prosecutions break the cycles of violence, and truth telling promotes reconciliation. This partly explained gacaca's appeal among many policymakers, donors, and scholars.

This chapter begins by describing gacaca and challenging the common misconception that it was "traditional." Next, I look at gacaca's evolution over the past seven years, showing how it was refashioned in response to changing government priorities, donor and NGO critiques, and local practices. I then examine the difficulties that gacaca encountered with truth telling, justice, and reconciliation on Rwanda's hills, before concluding with some broader lessons from gacaca.

Background: Genocide and Post-Genocide

The assassination of President Juvénal Habyarimana on April 6, 1994, prompted Hutu extremists to seize power, murder political opponents and UN peacekeepers, restart a civil war with the predominantly Tutsi Rwandan Patriotic Front (RPF), and unleash an extermination campaign against the Tutsi minority. The 1994 Rwandan genocide was remarkable for its speed, intimate violence, and widespread participation (see Des Forges 1999; Straus 2006). Over the course of one hundred days, extremists incited and pressured large numbers of ordinary Hutu peasants to massacre their Tutsi neighbors—and even their Tutsi family members—using machetes, hoes, and clubs. By the time, the RPF defeated the genocidal forces in July 1994, approximately three-quarters of the Tutsi population had been wiped out.[4]

After the genocide, the victorious RPF created a "Government of National Unity" that grouped together all the nonextremist political parties. However, the RPF quickly became the dominant party, politically marginalizing both Hutu democrats and Tutsi survivors.[5] While the RPF has managed the extraordinary feat of rebuilding Rwanda, providing security, and spurring economic growth, it has also become increasingly authoritarian—even after it won landslide victories in the 2003 and 2008 elections (Front Line Defenders 2005; Human Rights Watch, May 8, 2003; International Crisis Group 2002; Reyntjens 2009). Thus Rwanda does not fit the teleological transitional justice paradigm in which a post-conflict successor regime is presumed to be democratizing (Reyntjens 2004; see Carothers 2002).

After the genocide, tens of thousands of genocide suspects were arrested, often on the basis of unsubstantiated accusations. André Sibomana (1999:107), Rwanda's most courageous human rights activist, said: "For a house, for a field or a tool, people are denounced without evidence, and awkward neighbors are arrested." The mass arrests overwhelmed the devastated prison and judicial system, and, by 1999, Rwanda's courts had managed to try only a few thousand out of some 120,000 genocide detainees. The government also came under increasing pressure from international donors and international human rights organizations to improve the situation for detainees (see Sibomana 1999:108–10; Tertsakian 2008:47–50). In 1998, then Vice-President and future President Paul Kagame stated: "Presently, the maintenance of 120,000 prisoners costs US$20 million per year. . . . This cannot continue in the long-term: we have to find other solutions" (Vandeginste 1998:45).

In 1999, the government began emphasizing reconciliation. This coincided with the winding down of a brutal insurgency and counterinsurgency that had wracked northwest Rwanda, as well as the co-opting of Tutsi survivor organizations that had opposed reconciliation efforts. As a UN Special Rapporteur noted in 2000, "after five years of refusing to talk of reconciliation until justice is seen to be done, Rwandans now accept that reconciliation must be a national goal in its own right" (UN Commission on Human Rights 2000, para. 180). Through its reconciliation policies, the government seeks to (re)create the non-ethnic, harmonious society that supposedly existed before colonialism.[6] As President Paul Kagame has declared, "We are inculcating a new outlook that is Rwandan, and not ethnic" (Kagame, April 22, 2004). To accomplish this goal, the government has criminalized use of the terms Hutu and Tutsi—except when talking about the genocide. However, the government's declarations of national unity and reconciliation are undercut by its instrumentalization of ethnicity and the genocide (Eltringham 2004:97–99; Pottier 2002:111, 123–26, 130–31; Waldorf 2009a). For example, the government accused a prominent opposition parliamentarian of stirring up genocide ideology—even though he was well known for saving Tutsi during the genocide and testifying against prominent génocidaires.[7]

Gacaca

Gacaca: A Reinvented Tradition

Searching for a pragmatic, political solution to the overwhelming numbers of genocide detainees, Rwandan officials turned for inspiration to gacaca, an ad hoc mechanism named for the grass where that traditional dispute resolution took place.[8] Under gacaca, community elders (inyangamugayo, literally "those who detest disgrace") came together as needed to mediate and adjudicate family and interfamily disputes over property, inheritance, personal injury, and marital relations. "Traditional" gacaca generally did not treat cattle theft, murder, or other serious crimes, which were handled by chiefs or the king's representatives. Older men dominated gacaca, as women were not permitted to speak. Traditional gacaca could impose a range of sanctions that mostly emphasized restitution. Punishment was not individualized; rather, family and clan members were also obligated to repay any assessed judgment. The losing party typically had to provide beer to the community as a form of reconciliation.[9] In sum, "[t]he traditional objective of gacaca . . . is not to determine individualized guilt or to apply state law in a coherent and consistent manner . . . but to restore harmony and social order in a given society and to reintegrate the person who was the source of the disorder" (Reyntjens and Vandeginste 2005:118).

Belgian colonial administrators had encouraged gacaca even though colonial law did not formally recognize it. Under their system of indirect rule, the Belgians favored the Tutsi elite, appointing them as chiefs and subchiefs to govern the Hutu majority. Those, in turn, often appointed the inyangamugayo. After independence in 1962, gacaca was transformed into a "semi-official and neo-traditional" institution used by local authorities to resolve minor conflicts outside the formal justice system (Reyntjens 1990). When Filip Reyntjens examined gacaca in a Butare commune in 1987, he found that the sector conseiller (local official), assisted by the cell committee, presided over weekly gacaca sessions, hearing approximately four to five cases. Whereas customary gacaca usually involved the concerned parties, their family or clan members, and the inyangamugayo, this "semi-official" gacaca involved public hearings before the assembled local community. In a sample of 112 cases, Reyntjens found that 40 percent were quarrels, brawls, and public insults (some involving personal injuries), and 60 percent were between family members or immediate neighbors. Commune residents rarely appealed gacaca decisions to the canton courts (the lowest-level courts), but when they did, those courts took note of gacaca decisions. Reyntjens concluded that gacaca was "quick justice, a good bargain (for the public authorities as well as for those being judged), extremely accessible, understood and accepted by all, and involving a large popular participation" (Reyntjens 1990).

Following the genocide, gacaca was proposed as a mechanism for trying genocide cases. Several Rwandan scholars rejected the idea in 1995, observing, "The justice of gacaca would be incompetent in the matter of genocide because it cannot even judge a homicide case" (UN High Commissioner for Human Rights 1996:20). Rather, they proposed that gacaca function as local truth commissions to distinguish the innocent from the guilty. Meanwhile, gacaca began functioning again in several communities (Ingelaere 2008:35–36; Rose 1995). Some local officials, particularly in the eastern part of the country, revived gacaca in 1997 to deal with property disputes as refugees returned to the country and found their houses and lands occupied (Karekezi 2001:33). In addition, some genocide detainees, with the encouragement of prison officials, started their own gacaca in 1998 to hear confessions from fellow inmates (Penal Reform International [hereafter, PRI] January 2002:29–30).

As part of national-level discussions on reconciliation, then-President Pasteur Bizimungu established a commission in October 1998 to explore "a new type of arbitration court" that could try lower-level genocide suspects (see Ingelaere 2008:37). The commission's January 1999 report laid out the elements of what became modernized gacaca without ever using the term. Six months later, the government issued a report "recommend[ing] that the new judicial institutions which aim to foster a system of participatory justice be called Gacaca Tribunals (*Inkiko-Gacaca*)" (Republic of Rwanda, January and July 1999).

In 2000, the government passed a law creating approximately 11,000 community courts staffed by nearly 260,000 lay judges to try lower-level suspects for murder, manslaughter, assault, and property offenses committed during the genocide.[10] Gacaca offered significantly reduced sentences, including community service, to those convicted—particularly if they pleaded guilty. Following a lengthy pilot phase (from June 2002 through December 2004), gacaca was launched nationwide in January 2005, and trials of lower-level perpetrators finally got under way throughout the country in July 2006. Most of those trials were completed by the end of 2007. In late 2008, gacaca courts began

hearing cases involving higher-level suspects (those charged with sexual violence or having led the genocide locally). Gacaca officially ended in December
2009.

Gacaca began with a lengthy pretrial stage, in which accusations, confessions, and information were collected and compiled by 9,201 cell-level courts.[11]
Those courts eventually ranked the accused according to the severity of their
crimes and sent their dossiers to the appropriate jurisdictions for trial; 1,545
sector-level courts tried those accused of murder, manslaughter, and assault
during the genocide, handing down sentences ranging from five to thirty years.[12]
Suspects who confessed earned reduced sentences and then served half of those
sentences doing community service. Another 1,545 courts at the sector level
heard appeals from those judgments. The 9,201 cell-level courts also tried those
accused of property crimes and made restitution awards—unless the parties
had already reached amicable settlements.[13] Those cell-level courts more closely
resembled "traditional" gacaca (see Waldorf 2009b).

Gacaca is often portrayed as "traditional," much as the South African Truth
and Reconciliation Commission supposedly reflected an authentic expression
of African harmony (*ubuntu*). In his public speeches, President Kagame promoted gacaca as a "traditional participatory system" (Kagame, April 22, 2004)
that "had served us well before colonialism" (Kagame 2005). At a July 2008
conference in Kigali, the Minister of Justice stated: "Rwanda had to step back
into its past to find a solution for its present predicament" (Workshop on
Rwanda's Move Towards Commonwealth Membership, Kigali, August 5, 2008).
In fact, gacaca bore no resemblance to customary dispute resolution other
than the name.[14] For one thing, genocide gacaca was a state institution intimately linked to the state apparatus of prosecutions and incarceration, and
applying codified, rather than customary, law. This was recognized by its official title: inkiko-gacaca, or gacaca courts. Second, modern gacaca courts
were judging serious crimes and meting out prison sentences, whereas "traditional" gacaca mostly resolved minor civil disputes with restitution awards.
Third, the inyangamugayo were elected, comparatively young, and nearly
one-third women, rather than the male elders of the past.[15] Fourth, traditional
gacaca hearings involved only the parties and the inyangamugayo; they were
not held before the entire community. Finally, "[t]he main difference between
the traditional and the new systems is probably the destruction of the social
capital that underlies the traditional system" (Reyntjens and Vandeginste
2005:118).

Gacaca may be the Rwandan government's best-known (re)invented tradition, but it is far from the only one. Since 1999, the government has named several policies and programs after Rwandan traditions.[16] For example, the government's National Unity and Reconciliation Commission calls its re-education camps "*ingando*" after the traditional Rwandan palavers, even though the new camps owe more to Uganda's *chaka-mchaka,* which teach youth the tenets of Yoweri Museveni's one-party state, as well as the use of firearms. Such ersatz "traditions" bestow cultural legitimacy on government programs, while, at the same time, insulating them from donor criticism. Anticipating criticism from Human Rights Watch at a June 2008 conference on the judicial sector, the Rwandan Minister of Justice declared "Gacaca is Rwandan culture" (International Conference on the Impact of the Judicial Reforms, Kigali, June 17, 2008)—even though he once privately told me how he helped come up with the idea for gacaca.

Gacaca's Evolution

Gacaca evolved considerably over its seven-year lifespan as it ran the gauntlet of legal amendments, official pronouncements, shifting priorities, donor worries, NGO critiques, practical hurdles, and local resistance. As a high-ranking justice official told me in mid-2006, gacaca was a work-in-progress: "Gacaca is not a textbook. We are writing the book as we practice it. Sometimes we change the paragraph before we write the next one." From 2000 through April 2009, Parliament amended the gacaca law five times, and the National Service of Gacaca Jurisdictions (SNJG) issued fifteen instructions modifying gacaca.[17]

During the past seven years, gacaca was altered in several fundamental ways. First, it had to be dramatically revised to keep its promise of reducing the enormous number of genocide detainees (approximately 100,000 when gacaca began in mid-2002). The pretrial phase resulted in an avalanche of accusations that eventually added up to more than one million cases, including some 450,000 accused of violent crimes.[18] As the prisons started filling up again with those convicted in gacaca, the government took several creative steps. It began by reducing the overall length of sentences and increasing the proportion of time to be served doing community service. More radically, SNJG's executive secretary decreed in mid-2007 that convicted génocidaires would do the community service portion of their sentences *before* doing jail time.[19] As a result, the prison population had stabilized at about 58,000 in mid-2008. The government is eventually expected to issue pardons, so that hundreds of thousands are not forced to go to prison after they complete their community service.

In the second major change, gacaca was simplified and streamlined to speed up the process as the government, donors, and population wearied of the weekly sessions. For example, the government made gacaca's information-collection phase more efficient in 2005 by delegating the task to local administrators—even though that was never authorized by the gacaca law and the administrators had received little or no training.[20] As Avocats Sans Frontières (ASF) (2005:1–2) and Penal Reform International (2008) have clearly documented, gacaca sacrificed quality for quantity when it came to trials.[21] Similarly, a donor representative told me in 2006 that the government "is completely focused on the organization and logistics of [the trials]—and the quality is forgotten."

Third, gacaca became less participatory and more coercive over time. Public interest flagged as proceedings dragged on.[22] During one gacaca, a participant plaintively observed: "Let me point out that this number here in gacaca is small compared to the number of people who used to go for attacks when an alarm was made" (Southern Province gacaca, January 2003).[23] Most Rwandans could ill afford to spend the day neglecting their fields or forgoing itinerant labor.[24] Also, many (including Tutsi survivors) foresaw few benefits from gacaca. Nonparticipation sometimes became just another everyday form of peasant resistance to state authority (see Scott 1985:xvi–xvii). Local officials and gacaca judges started with persuasion and finished with coercion. Government officials closed shops, rounded up the population, and fined (or threatened to fine) late arrivals and absentees (Avocats Sans Frontières 2005:4 and n. 9; LIPRODHOR 2005:31; PRI 2003a:32, 41, 62, 70, and 73, 2006:43; Rettig 2008:37). The 2004 Gacaca Law reinforced gacaca's coercive aspect by making attendance compulsory (2004 Gacaca Law, art. 29). In a 2004 meeting of donors and NGOs, a gacaca spokesman stated that a person who does not participate in gacaca risks being "mistaken for a génocidaire" (pers. comm. to author, June 22, 2004). Even increased coercion did not always work. At one gacaca I attended, the sector conseiller eventually ordered the *nyambakumi* (local officials in charge of ten households) to round up people for gacaca, telling the crowd: "It is a shame to have people who do not want to come to gacaca. We also have visitors who have come from Kigali, and I do not know if they are going to see something [gacaca] with this number of participants." A half-hour later, laughter rippled through the assembled crowd as they saw farmers on an adjacent hill running to hide in banana groves (Eastern Province gacaca, September 2005).

Fourth, the government reneged on gacaca's early promise to compensate genocide survivors. Gacaca courts dutifully tallied up human and material losses during the genocide. Under the 2001 Gacaca Law, those lists of damages were supposed to be transmitted to the Compensation Fund so reparation payments could be made to survivors. However, the 2004 Gacaca Law put off the issue of compensation, and as of April 2009, the compensation fund has still not been created. While cell-level gacaca courts awarded restitution in cases of property theft and destruction, most perpetrators were too impoverished to repay the full value of the goods stolen or destroyed (PRI 2007; Waldorf 2009b).

Finally, gacaca quickly became "victor's justice." In its early pilot phase, participants occasionally demanded justice for family members allegedly killed by the RPF forces. In response, the government removed gacaca's jurisdiction over war crimes in 2004. That accorded with the government's reluctance to try its own soldiers for war crimes—or to allow the International Criminal Tribunal for Rwanda to try them (Human Rights Watch, July 24, 2008:89–94; Peskin 2008:186–231).[25]

Looking back, the government's willingness to continually adapt gacaca in the face of difficulties is striking—all the more so, given its authoritarian tendencies and the timidity of international donors. It is helpful to look at two examples in more detail. When the evidence-gathering and indictment phase ended in 2006, there were more than 300,000 people accused solely of property offenses (Service National des Juridictions Gacaca [hereafter, SNJG] 2006).[26] That enormous number of suspects prompted a further amendment to the gacaca law in 2007: all genocide-related property crimes were required to go through mediation first, and only if that failed would cases be heard by gacaca courts.[27] The government justified that pragmatic shift in terms of reconciliation. For example, the SNJG, which is charged with administering gacaca, stated that mediation "will show that the authors of these offenses are conscious of what they have done and repent" (SNJG 2006:3). In fact, perpetrators understood that "the refusal to settle is considered a lack of will to reconcile which must be punished severely" (PRI 2008:76). Furthermore, both sides pragmatically recognized that while gacaca courts might award higher restitution amounts, those convicted would not be able to pay those amounts (ibid.:72).

The most controversial change to gacaca was the 2008 law's transfer of more serious genocide cases—including an estimated 6,000–7,000 rape cases—from the national courts to gacaca's 1,545 community courts.[28] In the discussions around the initial gacaca law in 2000, Rwandan women's and survivors' organizations successfully pressured the government to class rape among the most serious crimes—the so-called Category 1 crimes—to be tried in national courts.[29] As accusations in gacaca ballooned, the government came under pressure to narrow the scope of Category 1 crimes to reduce the burden on the national courts. In mid-2006, Domatilla Mukantaganzwa, Gacaca's executive secretary, insisted to me: "Rape is going to stay within Category 1 because rape has been used to eliminate the Tutsi group within the country." The 2008 law kept rape in Category 1 but moved the trials to gacaca courts, where they were held in camera. A female NGO staffer expressed frustration with this change after a mid-2008 presentation by Gacaca's executive secretary:

> Rwandans are frustrated, but we shall bear it. . . . Judges are not professional so we can't ask them to keep professional secrets. So that means all the things the women are saying will be on the streets the next day. We asked that those people accused of raping should appear in the classical courts. (Conference on the Tutsi Genocide, Kigali, July 2008)

The executive secretary insisted that "the victims made the choice" to have their rape trials transferred to gacaca (Conference on the Tutsi Genocide, Kigali, July 2008).[30] In fact, representatives of women survivors were consulted only after the decision had been taken. A Tutsi rape survivor told me in mid-2008 that she would not take her case to gacaca, because she did not want her neighbors to know she had been raped.

Gacaca on the Hills

Large billboards advertising gacaca dotted Rwanda's roadsides for several years. The photo showed nine gacaca judges—with sashes sporting the national colors (green, yellow, and blue) and the word inyangamugayo—looking intently at a seated assembly of men in second-hand T-shirts and women in vibrant pagnes. The scene became a familiar one in everyday life, except for one false note: every member of the assembly had their arms outstretched—like obedient schoolchildren—asking to be called on. The billboards read "Inkiko Gacaca: Ukuri, Ubutabera, Ubwiyunge" ("Gacaca Courts: Truth, Justice, Reconciliation"). They captured the government's and international donors' high hopes for gacaca, while communicating the transfiguring tropes of transitional justice: truth would lead to justice, and justice, in turn, would lead to reconciliation. Out on Rwanda's hills, however, gacaca confounded those expectations as it was reshaped, resisted, and appropriated by local actors.[31]

Truth

> Amagambo aratinywa aliko ntiyica nkicumu. (Words kill, but they do not kill like a lance)
>
> —Rwandan proverb (Crepeau and Bizimana 1979:91)

Gacaca was meant to encourage truth telling on Rwanda's hills, but the occasional truths were often accompanied—and at times submerged—by the silences, evasions, half-truths, and lies. At one gacaca hearing, a sector conseiller berated the assembled crowd for its silence:

> It is impossible that 20,000 people were killed by ten or twenty people only.... You don't want to tell us. Don't you know that whoever doesn't tell what he knows will be punished? ... It is in fact a way to identify the real killers of these people so that peace and unity comes back in our society. Some say it is impossible. It will be impossible if you don't talk.... Many claim that they were sick or absent. Now who did the killings? (Southern Province, October 2002)

In another community, a gacaca official told the crowd: "Many people claim the former bad regime made them participate in genocide, but now who is making you stop telling what happened?" People did not speak for any number of reasons: fear, mistrust, complicity, indifference, and disobedience. Silence was often a means of self-preservation. Survivors and perpetrators frequently live side by side, and they fear retaliation, one from the other.[32] Under the 2004 Gacaca Law, judges imposed fines and prison sentences on some who kept silent (Avocats Sans Frontières 2005:4 and n. 9; PRI 2005:32, 41, 62, 70, 73). Still, the silences remained pervasive and persistent enough that they earned the name *ceceka,* or "pact of silence" (see Rettig 2008:40–41).

Even when people did speak up, it was never clear whether they were telling the truth. False confessions and false accusations abounded. Gacaca hearings usually opened with the presiding judge or local official inviting people to come forward and confess their crimes, while reminding them that those who confessed before being accused would get the largest sentence reductions. Perpetrators had obvious incentives to confess to lesser crimes in the hopes of receiving lighter sentences and earlier releases. As the former president of IBUKA, the largest survivors' organization, worried: "It's not the truth that matters for them: the pure objective is to get out of prison" (Antoine Mugesera, CLADO Conference on Gacaca, February 14, 2003).[33] Inside the prisons and on the hills, there was a lively market for accusations and confessions—an amoral economy of guilt (see Avocats Sans Frontières 2005:11; Tertsakian 2008:396–97, 412–15). The expression *"kugura umusozi"* ("buying the hill") was used to describe the situation in which one person was paid to confess to the crimes committed by others. In most of the trials I observed, survivors challenged the perpetrators' confessions as inaccurate and incomplete (see Avocats Sans Frontières 2005:10). Whether confessions were accepted or not seemed to depend in part on the composition of the gacaca courts. In one sector in the Northern Province, the survivors who controlled the court regularly rejected confessions and sentenced defendants to lengthy prison terms (usually twenty-five years) without the possibility of doing community service.

Just as some used the genocide opportunistically to settle personal scores that had little to do with anti-Tutsi ideology (Straus 2006), others subsequently used gacaca to serve their own ends (see Kalyvas 2006). False accusations of genocide quickly became "weapons of the weak" in land, inheritance, and family disputes (Burnet 2008:187; Rettig 2008:39), a new addition to the familiar arsenal of everyday violence on Rwanda's hills, alongside rumors, witchcraft, and poisonings (*abarozi*).[34] A prominent Rwandan academic acknowledged, "There are survivors who visibly lie and other survivors say so. . . . Family members denounce their own kith and kin over land—the demographic pressures come into play" (CLADHO Conference on Gacaca, Kigali, February 14, 2003). In a few cases, survivors confessed to making false accusations, although it was difficult to know whether they had been bribed or intimidated into withdrawing their accusations (PRI 2002a:27).

Gacaca's insistence on public truth telling was fundamentally at odds with rural Rwanda's "pervasive" culture of secrecy (Lame 2005:14; Ingelaere 2007: 22–24). Practices of concealment and dissimulation have their origins in the region's turbulent history and remain a widespread means of responding to perceived danger in the present, as anthropologist Lame details:

> Secrecy persisted as a cultural habit well beyond pre-colonial and colonial Rwanda, where people, subjected to a climate of constant insecurity, were at the mercy of capricious chiefs whose intrigues affected their lives. . . . The habit of secrecy continues in the most ordinary circumstances: one's dwelling place is mentioned evasively, and the rooms of a house are set up so as to conceal the state of one's provisions. (Lame 2005:14–15)

"Ritualized dissimulation" (Wedeen 1999:82) under successive authoritarian states also enabled people to keep their true thoughts private. Another anthropologist described Rwandan society as "administrative groupings of nuclear families, devoid of a collective spirit and rife with suspicion" (Pottier, quoted in Eltringham and Hoyweghen 2001:218). Still today, most rural Rwandans prefer to live in scattered households on hillsides rather than in villages. Furthermore, transparency and directness are considered undesirable and foolish traits: they put oneself and others at risk and undermine social relations (Overdulve 1997:279–80, 282).

Several authors claim that gacaca created space for local dialogical truths and reconciliation (e.g., Clark 2007:55–58, 2009:314–15; Ngoga 2009:327; Wierzynska 2004:1962). However, this ignores how gacaca testimonies and silences were shaped by "the micropolitics of local standing" (Moore 1992:11, 42). On Rwanda's hills, people were more concerned with demonstrating loyalty to kin and patrons than with truth telling (PRI 2006:1; see Moore 1992: 37–38). For example, a woman refused to answer questions about her son in gacaca, saying: "If my son participated in the genocide, it is his affair. Me, I cannot be a traitor to the family which gave me milk" (Gitarama gacaca, October 2002). Such micropolitics played out against the backdrop of pervasive secrecy, mutual suspicion, and occasional denunciation. Thus, a team of Rwandan researchers found "the sentiment of not wanting to attract enemies (*kutiteranya*) prevailed within the general population" during gacaca sessions (Karekezi 2004:79).

Justice

Genocide is too heavy for the shoulders of justice.

—*Zarir Merat, head of mission, Avocats Sans Frontières–Rwanda*

From the beginning, it was clear that gacaca would depart radically from international norms for fair trials, most notably the right against self-incrimination and the right to defense counsel (see Amnesty International 2002; UN Human Rights Committee 2009:para. 17). Gacaca courts were not excused from those standards by virtue of their supposedly "traditional" nature. For the African Commission on Human and Peoples Rights has made clear that "[t]raditional courts are not exempt from the provisions of the African Charter relating to fair trial" (African Commission 1999). Much of the scholarly commentary on gacaca focuses on whether Rwanda's specific post-genocide circumstances justified such derogation from basic human rights principles (e.g., Clark 2007;

Longman 2006; Sarkin 2001; Tully 2003; Uvin 2001).[35] A Special Representative of the UN Human Rights Commission put the issue starkly:

> The question facing Rwanda's international partners is relatively simple: Do they grasp the nettle and participate, on the grounds that anything is preferable to the abuse [of then 120,000 detainees] in prisons, or do they hold firm to established legal principles [for fair trials] and stay aloof, thus increasing the likelihood that gacaca will fail? (UN Commission on Human Rights 2000)

By and large, Rwanda's international partners chose to back gacaca through financing and technical assistance.

Even as gacaca departed from some fair trial norms, it simultaneously reaffirmed many others. The various gacaca laws, directives, and manuals emphasized procedural due process (e.g., the right of defendants to confront their accusers) and the independence of the judges (e.g., they deliberated in camera). Unlike Amnesty International, which condemned gacaca with reference to the international human rights covenants ratified by Rwanda (Amnesty International 2002), Avocats Sans Frontières more convincingly critiqued gacaca by pointing to the way those courts failed to conform to the human rights protections guaranteed by the gacaca laws and directives. ASF documented how both gacaca trial courts and appeals courts did not allow sufficient examination (and cross-examination) of defendants and witnesses, and did not provide reasoned judgments and sentences (Avocats Sans Frontières 2005:22 and n.46; Avocats Sans Frontières 2008). In my own observations, gacaca judges rarely set forth their reasoning and evidentiary findings, making it difficult to assess the fairness of their judgments and the legality of their sentences. There are two main reasons why gacaca courts failed to meet their own minimum standards: inadequate training and little financial compensation for the poorly educated judges, and government pressure on judges to try cases quickly.

Inevitably, gacaca judges were not independent and impartial, given their family and neighborly ties with accusers, defendants, and witnesses; their personal knowledge of events; and their personal stakes in the outcomes. They were also susceptible to pressure or corruption from the community, local elites, and government officials (PRI 2008:44–50). Numerous judges had to be removed after themselves being accused of genocide (PRI 2004b:77). One gacaca president complained to me that genocide survivors falsely alleged he had been bribed when he proposed further investigations against a particular suspect they had accused.

Most ordinary Rwandans I have met, whether in the capital or on the hills, do not believe that gacaca delivered justice. Many Tutsi survivors deeply resented gacaca. A representative of AVEGA, the leading organization of women genocide survivors, told a public gathering early on: "Gacaca is for liberating the prisoners. It's a sort of hidden amnesty" (Coexistence Network meeting, Kigali, July 23, 2002). Another Rwandan told me: "Rescapés [survivors] are convinced that there is no justice, because they wish that everyone is in prison. They think that the government has decided to give pardon. Rescapés have a spirit of resignation."[36] Once on my way back from a gacaca, I gave a lift to an elderly survivor. When I asked him what survivors thought of gacaca, he responded, "We are waiting for gacaca like Jews waiting for Jesus."

Many Hutu also see gacaca as unjust, but for very different reasons. Some argue that gacaca elicited false confessions from innocent people grown weary of being unjustly detained for many years. Others see gacaca as "victor's justice," because it focused exclusively on the genocide against Tutsi (African Rights 2003:24–26; Longman and Rutagengwa 2004:176; PRI 2004:44–47; Rettig 2008:40). For example, one Hutu man stated:

When we fled the genocide in 1994, we left behind many of our relatives. When we came back, they were nowhere to be seen. But in gacaca they are not mentioned. People are always talking about the Tutsi who died. But what about Hutu? How come those who killed Hutu are not prosecuted? (Internews 2005)

During gacaca, people occasionally talked about the suffering of Hutu refugees in the DRC, Hutu suspects in overcrowded prisons, and Hutu victims of RPF killings, only to be cut off by local officials and gacaca judges. In a gacaca I attended in 2002, two judges stood at the end of the session and described how RPF soldiers "disappeared" their family member. When they asked why gacaca could not try the case, an official explained, "Gacaca treats uniquely the question of genocide," and told them to take their complaint to the local officials or the military courts (Southern Province, July 2002).

Remarkably, in 2004, the government agency charged with gacaca acknowledged that some Hutu and Tutsi perceived gacaca as unjust:

There are those who have responded that the genocide survivors are not satisfied with gacaca because the sentences that it envisages do not reflect the gravity of crimes of genocide. Equally, the perpetrators who are now freed do not appreciate gacaca because in the course of proceedings, their roles might be revealed. There are even those who feel marginalized by gacaca because they do not judge the common crimes committed during the war, that is between 1990 and 1994, and even those in 1998 in the north of the country [during the counterinsurgency]. (SNJG 2004)

Reconciliation

Urwagwa ntirukura urwangano mu nda.

—*Banana beer does not lift hate from the stomach: Rwandan proverb*

(Crepeau and Bizimana 1979:552)

As for saying that you will not forgive him, or that you will not do this or that, that is very bad. Whether you like it or not, the law is the law.

—*Jean-Marie Mbarushimana, then Prosecutor General of Nyabisindu*

(Quoted in PRI 2002:23)

The Rwandan government created unreasonably high expectations when it promised that gacaca would foster reconciliation. Those expectations were unrealistic given Rwandan cultural norms, which privilege secrecy and guarded emotions. Gacaca, like the South African TRC, leaned heavily on the modern (and largely western) notion that truth telling is therapeutic for individuals as well as for local and national communities. For example, the Executive Secretary of the National Unity and Reconciliation Commission contended: "The encouragement of truth telling and confession in return for commutation of a sentence is cathartic and heals" (Ndangiza 2008). Yet there is scant empirical evidence for the healing powers of truth telling (see Wilson 2001; Stover and Weinstein 2004). Reconciliation also seems too much to ask of people—especially survivors—only sixteen years after genocide. Yet gacaca did not just fail to reconcile; it actually made it more difficult, as the uneasy coexistence among neighbors was up-ended by accusations and counteraccusations.[37]

Gacaca was supposed to produce public narratives of repentance and forgiveness on Rwanda's hills. In fact, I heard very little of either in gacaca sessions. This was partly cultural, as Rwandans consider it shameful to express emotion in public (Overdulve 1997:279–80, 282). Génocidaires confessed their actions, but not their motivations, and described themselves as lacking agency (see also Straus and Lyons 2006:21–22). For example, one confessed génocidaire recounted, "Evil came in me and I killed them" (Southern Province 2002). Perpetrators mostly made "formulaic" apologies, asking forgiveness from survivors and the Rwandan people (see Karekezi, Nshimiyimana, and Mutamba 2004:79; Burnet 2008:181).[38] Not surprisingly, then, many survivors were unforgiving (see Avocats Sans Frontières 2005:10). One survivor asked, "How can one pardon these people who lie?" After one confession in gacaca, the mother of a child who was killed responded angrily, "Don't ask me for forgiveness" (Southern Province January 2003). Survivors did not simply refuse to forgive, they often challenged the confessions as untruthful or incomplete in the hopes of persuading judges to hand down maximum sentences. Gacaca sessions were sometimes divided along ethnic lines, with Tutsi survivors sitting apart and doing most of the talking, while their Hutu neighbors looked on silently (see PRI 2003b:36, Penal 2003a:24–27, 33, 37; Karekezi, and Mutamba 2004:79).

Gacaca proceedings heightened fear, suspicion, and interethnic tensions in several communities (Burnet 2008:186–88; Ingelaere 2007:22–24; LIPRODHOR 2005:110; PRI 2003a:24–25; Rettig 2008:42–44; see Stover and Weinstein 2004:323). One gacaca president warned, "I don't want you to open gacaca in the beer places where you end up fighting" (Southern Province January 2003). Some neighbors intimidated survivors and witnesses so they would not testify in gacaca. One confessed perpetrator told a gacaca court:

> I am very threatened by having dared to speak the truth. Is it really possible that I participated in the massacres alone! Why am I threatened by the people who accompanied me in the massacres?

A common form of intimidation was to throw stones on roofs at night. Hundreds of survivors and witnesses were also killed (LIPRODHOR 2005:46–48, 50; PAPG 2004; PRI 2004b:50–54). More corrosively, illnesses and deaths were often blamed on poisonings and gacaca, generating a vicious cycle of rumors. From February through April 2005, an estimated 19,000 Hutu briefly fled Rwanda as rumors spread that the government had built a machine for grinding up Hutu accused in gacaca.

The government's National Unity and Reconciliation Commission conducted attitudinal surveys to measure social cohesion in Rwanda. Some specific findings undermine claims that gacaca has promoted trust and reconciliation:

Almost two-thirds of the general population believes that witness accounts on either side, the prosecution and the defense, cannot be trusted. An overwhelming number of prisoners (83%) do not believe in the truthfulness of prosecution witness accounts and a large number of survivors (77%) have doubts about statements made by witnesses for the defense. . . .

Forty-six percent of survivors also feel that it would be naive to trust prisoners in the future. A majority of genocide survivors also feel that public testimony during the gacaca aggravates tensions between families (76 percent) and that the families of those found guilty of crimes of genocide will always feel resentful (66 percent). Prisoners reject the latter argument (63 percent) but agree that testimony during gacaca aggravates tensions (71 percent) (National Unity and Reconciliation Commission 2008:5–7).[39]

In response to this study, one Rwandan woman at a 2008 conference in Kigali asked gacaca's executive secretary, "Are we rehabilitating our society really? . . . [The NURC study] showed that gacaca is the number two cause of conflict after the ideology of genocide" (Conference on the Tutsi Genocide, Kigali, July 2008).

According to the transitional justice paradigm, criminal trials are supposed to break the cycles of violence, because the individualization of responsibility avoids collective guilt. A Rwandan representative of Avocats Sans Frontières captured this when he told me: "It is also good for peaceful coexistence when the truly guilty are known. . . . Those Hutu who did nothing . . . are now cleaned of the common feeling of guilt." In fact, however, gacaca trials appear to have reinforced each group's feelings of collective victimization, making it harder to see past their own suffering to comprehend the suffering of the other group.[40]

Overall, gacaca imposed collective guilt by generating accusations of genocide against perhaps one million Hutu—a quarter of the adult Hutu population (SNJG 2008a:19).[41] Thus gacaca has reinscribed the ethnic labeling of the past (Hutu–Tutsi), using new labels (génocidaire–victim) (see Eltringham 2004:-72–99). The government further reinforced this by meting out collective punishments against communities in which survivors have been threatened or injured (Human Rights Watch 2007).

Conclusion: Gacaca and the International Community

Although gacaca has been a new addition to the transitional justice toolkit, it has not fundamentally challenged the paradigm itself. Rather, gacaca conforms to the trinity of that paradigm: truth telling, individualized punishment, and reconciliation. Yet local responses to gacaca have challenged those foundational assumptions in crucial ways, frustrating claims that gacaca has promoted truth, justice, and reconciliation.

International donors and policymakers were largely inattentive or dismissive when it came to those local responses to gacaca.[42] After the Rwandan government criticized Penal Reform International's action research on how local communities viewed gacaca, the UK's Department for International Development cut its funding to PRI. Even when it became apparent that gacaca would swell the ranks of the accused and worsen ethnic tensions, most donors kept on financing it. This perplexed a former head of mission for PRI: "Gacaca was designed in 1998–1999 to deal with 130,000—no more. No one dared to think 1 million could be judged. . . . No one has been traumatized by this figure—not the government and not the donors."

Similarly, international policymakers continued lauding gacaca long after its failings came to light. The prosecutor of the International Criminal Court has repeatedly suggested that states might be able to preclude ICC investigations and prosecutions by adopting a gacaca-like model (see Colloquium of Prosecutors 2004). He gave a spirited defense of gacaca when I raised concerns about it at a workshop in late 2005 (Conflict-Mapping Workshop, Harvard Law School, November 2005). The United Nations also praised gacaca in 2006 for having "helped bring Rwandan society together to rebuild trust, share the truth about the genocide and provide access to justice to the public" (UN Office of the High Representative for Least Developed Countries 2006:130).

International support for gacaca cannot be explained solely by reference to what has been cynically termed Rwanda's "genocide credit" (Reyntjens 2004:-199).[43] It also reflects disillusionment with expensive and inefficient international tribunals, belated appreciation for national and local responses to mass violence, a romanticizing of the "traditional," and wishful thinking about an "African renaissance." President Kagame has skillfully played on all these themes in some of his speeches:

> First of all, we must recognize that . . . there can never be a "one-size-fits-all" prescription for conflict resolution. . . . Second, any approach to conflict resolution must be locally driven, people-centred and people-owned. . . . Third, we Africans must learn to find African solutions to African problems, and only invite the international community to complement our own efforts. (Kagame 2005)

Seduced by such rhetoric, some policymakers and scholars have looked to gacaca for guidance on how to adapt local dispute-resolution mechanisms to accomplish transitional justice in other post-conflict African states, such as Burundi, Uganda, and the Democratic Republic of Congo.

Gacaca offers several lessons for transitional justice—although not the ones that most policymakers and scholars want to hear. First, it points up the need to interrogate local, populist mechanisms more closely and to distinguish clearly between those produced bottom-up by communities from those imposed top-down by states.[44] Gacaca looks awfully familiar when compared to other disappointing experiments with state-imposed informalism in many postcolonial states in Africa and Asia, which also resulted in increased formalism, decreased popular participation, and increased state coercion (Merry 1993; Stevens 1999). Second, Rwanda's experiment with gacaca suggests that local dispute-resolution mechanisms will be driven in new—and often problematic— directions where they are captured and co-opted by the state. Finally, where people have reason to fear the government and/or their neighbors following communal violence, and where constraints against truth telling have developed as a historical response to danger, public truth telling within communities may expose people to serious risks and will be subject to resistance and reworking.[45]

PART IV

Practicing Place-Based Justice

Chapter 10

Weaving a Braid of Histories
Local Post–Armed Conflict Initiatives in Guatemala
Laura J. Arriaza and Naomi Roht-Arriaza

Our children didn't know what happened to us, and we have no political power. So four years ago we started our own process of reconstructing what happened; we decided to dedicate one day a month to this effort; now there are some 400–460 of us working on it. We have made local maps, we've worked out the time lines of how the army attacks happened and knotted them onto ropes so everyone can understand. When each community contributes its knotted-rope time line, we create the braid of how the conflict took place in our region.[1]

From 1960 to 1996, some 200,000 people were killed in Guatemala in the course of waves of government repression and armed conflict. In 1996, peace accords between the government and a coalition of guerrilla groups promised extensive reforms. Two truth commissions have established a historical record of the nature and consequences of the conflict. Currently, an ambitious although troubled National Reparations Program has distributed checks to some widows and other victims of the conflict, and has begun a series of pilot projects to distribute communal reparations in some of the most affected and poorest regions of the country. A few trials in notorious cases or against low-level defendants have resulted in convictions, although the justice system remains compromised and ineffective. Particularly notorious police units were disbanded and the army reduced in size after the peace accords. The government and the guerrillas—but not the army—have apologized for their role during the armed conflict. In sum, despite limitations and halfway measures, Guatemala has enacted many pieces of the "transitional justice" agenda. Yet it is not clear how much difference these efforts—while necessary—have made in people's daily experience. Just over ten years after the peace accords, Guatemala remains a deeply wounded society.

Two main factors help to explain why these efforts have not translated more fully into changes in lived experience and perception. The first, which is largely beyond the scope of this paper, is the continuing lack of social and economic justice. People are poorer than ever, crime and insecurity are rampant, an exclusionary political system continues to be dominated by ladino elites,[2] racism and discrimination against the Mayan majority persist, and the economy is largely dominated by large landholders, drug dealers, and various types of organized crime.

The second, which is our focus here, is that national-level initiatives, by themselves, are insufficient to capture the meaning of the conflict for people living in specific villages, towns, "hills," or other local spaces, whose experience may vary widely from that of people elsewhere in the country. When it comes to post–armed conflict interventions aimed at reconstructing a shattered society, international and national policymakers have treated countries as an undifferentiated whole. In part this is due to their emphasis on reconstructing and strengthening the state and on establishing or reinforcing global norms;[3] certain kinds of tasks can be carried out only on a uniform basis, by a national state.[4] But such efforts ignore the different ways in which people in different localities experienced the conflict, as well as existing local dynamics aimed at reinforcing or transforming the power relations that are often most relevant to people's lives. This is especially true given the distance and perennial weakness of Guatemala's central state. In transitional justice as elsewhere, all politics is local.

We are not simply arguing that national-level initiatives should have a regional aspect or component—something that has been done.[5] Nor are we simply advocating the use of "traditional" or local justice processes, as has been suggested in northern Uganda and elsewhere. Rather, we posit that those assessing past efforts and contemplating new ones should seek out and examine independent initiatives arising from the local environment as an integral part of the post–armed conflict justice landscape. Such local efforts often precede formal national programs, and they can also follow on or extend such programs, making them more locally relevant. They often look very different from national initiatives and are particularly important in unraveling the complexities of local power dynamics and tying initiatives regarding the past with current concerns. They may also more easily tap into the agency of survivors and be less prone to large-scale patronage and corruption. At the very least, national and international initiatives should strive to be aware of, and not to undermine, such local processes.

Part 1 of this chapter describes the nature of the conflict in Guatemala. Part 2 explores the possible advantages, and roles, of a focus on local efforts at social reconstruction and transformation, focusing on truth-telling, justice and dispute resolution, and reparations, respectively.[6] Part 3 concludes that such efforts should be more systematically identified and supported in a post-conflict setting, both as building blocks and complements to a national approach, and that assessments of the reach of post-conflict justice efforts should include these types of initiatives within their parameters.

The Complexity of the Armed Conflict and Its Aftermath

The conflict in Guatemala began, depending on whom you ask, with the Spanish invasion in the sixteenth century, with the overthrow of the democratically elected Arbenz government by CIA-backed mercenaries in 1954, or with the rebellion of young army officers against the resulting dictatorship in 1960. In practice, most of the violence at issue today stems from selective state repression of outlawed opposition parties, trade unions, peasant leagues, student organizations, and similar groups in the 1970s. In the 1980s the violence escalated, as the army put down the resulting armed revolutionary movements, especially those that had grown roots among the indigenous population of the western highlands. The army carried out bombings, massacres, scorched-earth policies, the hunting down of refugees, and the concentration of survivors in army-controlled "model villages." Most of the victims were Mayan peasants: according to the UN Truth Commission (Comisión de Esclarecimiento Histórico, or Commission on Historical Clarification [hereafter, CEH]), acts of genocide against Mayans were carried out in at least four areas of the country (CEH 1999; see also Carmack 1988; Sanford 2003). Of the killings, disappearances, torture, and destruction, the CEH found the army responsible for 93 percent, with the guerrillas responsible for a number of massacres and more selective killings. Over six hundred villages were completely destroyed, sometimes with no survivors. Women were raped on a massive scale; children and old people were targeted as bearers of culture; crops, forests, and animals were destroyed. The effects were devastating throughout a broad swath of the country.

Layered on top of this violence committed by the organized state against its own people are a host of complexities. The country is divided into over twenty language groups that inhabit different although overlapping regions, mountainous valleys with little communication between them, and different histories, social composition, and cultural practices. In some areas, Mayan communities lived next to ladino ones, while in others a ladino minority held local economic and/or political power within a largely Mayan town or dominated a county seat surrounded by Mayan communities; in still others there were no ladinos. In some areas, land or water disputes were at issue, as were rising tensions between Catholics and evangelical Christians or between traditionalists and modernizers. In fact, the contours of the conflict varied widely throughout the country, with some regions, such as the largely ladino eastern region of the country, remaining relatively untouched by the 1980s political violence. Other areas were massively attacked or wiped out entirely, and still others experienced more selective state attacks on community leaders.

The army played on and exacerbated these preexisting divisions as well as personal feuds, for example by issuing ID cards allowing freedom of movement to evangelicals but not Catholics (who were widely viewed as supporting the insurgency). Army repression was aimed at replacing traditional religious and civic authorities with people aligned with the military, who benefited by their association, obtaining the lands (and sometimes widows) of those killed. Most importantly, the army created paramilitary forces known as Civil Defense Patrols (PAC, Patrullas de Autodefensa Civil). These forces served as the eyes and ears of the military in their villages and were used as cannon fodder to sweep areas where the army believed there was guerrilla activity. They also committed many of the atrocities of the period, including some of the worst massacres. Some PAC members voluntarily took advantage of army sponsorship to settle old scores with neighbors or neighboring villages or to amass wealth and local power. However, substantial numbers of civil patrollers were made up of Mayan men who were intimidated or forced to join on pain of death or who joined in an effort to save their communities from worse destruction. Most PACs were indigenous, while their commanding officers were ladino, often local military commissioners. Thus "society was transformed by the army's coerced integration of the rural indigenous majority into its counter-insurgency design, with negative effects for indigenous and religious practices" (Sieder 2001:165).

Like most internal armed conflicts, the Guatemalan had both "vertical" (state/citizenry) and "horizontal" (neighbor/neighbor) aspects, but the relative weight of each varied among localities. In part, this was a question of timing: some communities were active in support of insurgent forces, while in other areas the guerillas had already been wiped out or had fled before the army came in, and the killings and destruction were more in the nature of reprisals for opposing the government. Adding to this complexity is the net of complicities, betrayals, and duress designed by the army to tear apart the bonds holding communities together. Many families had members in both the guerrillas and the PAC, and many were forced to collaborate or to betray family and friends. PAC members were told that if they did not adequately repress the local population, they themselves would be killed as presumptive insurgent sympathizers. The army in a number of cases forced PAC members to publicly kill other PAC members as supposed guerilla collaborators (CEH 1999:43, 53). Worse, in other cases, PAC and the army together forced villagers, and sometimes an entire village, to participate in the public killing or torture of their neighbors or in desecration of their bodies (CEH 1999, case 107; REMHI 1998:35.) These types of events, which are not of course limited to Guatemala but are common to many recent conflicts, continue to divide and traumatize communities even years later.

In the postwar period, conflicts within and between communities continue, exacerbated by the newly exalted position of some ex-PAC members as compared to the almost uniform destitution of their victims. Populations are heterogeneous: certain regions are now heavily populated by communities in which residents never left, while other regions house refugees who returned to their old communities or were forced to make their homes in new places, creating tensions with existing residents (Cabrera 2006:85–91). Sometimes, returning refugees found others in their homes and lands (Manz 2004). In some communities, everyone is a massacre survivor. Local structures of power are also heterogeneous: in some communities local power is held by ex-PAC members; in others some traditional authorities have been reconstituted, and in still others new political forces, including evangelical pastors, justices of the peace, or activists linked to national Mayan organizations, have emerged. Fear of continued violence contributes to silence about the past, sometimes even within families, and has been manifested in myriad types of social dysfunctionality, from lynchings to somatic illnesses. It is this degree of variation and complexity that make international and national-level responses inadequate and, to some degree, irrelevant at the local level, and that require further exploration of local-level responses.

Adding in the Local: Initiatives in Truth Seeking, Justice, and Reparations

A common attribute shared by all kinds of local responses to past atrocities is that they are best able to ensure "a comprehensive community-based approach that includes the opinions and ideas of those whose lives have been most directly affected" (Fletcher and Weinstein 2002:638). In addition, such responses tend to be more agile than national or international efforts, which because of their scope and complexity may come after—or end before—local communities have engaged in their own form of (just or unjust) recomposition.[7] Rather than the separation into truth telling, justice, reparations, and commemoration that predominate in discussions of the transitional justice "toolkit," these local initiatives combine elements of all these things. Almost all share certain characteristics: an emphasis on local (here, Mayan) cultural and spiritual practice, a connection to present-day issues, material and labor contributions by the beneficiaries, and tailoring to the specific needs of the place and people. Such local responses can help compensate for some of the limits of other forms of post–armed conflict or transitional measures.

We consider three different post–armed conflict interventions: truth seeking (generally through truth commissions or truth and reconciliation commissions), criminal prosecutions, and reparations programs. We recognize that post–armed conflict social reconstruction may have other aspects. In particular, it may be important to focus specifically on creating some kind of dialogue, mutual recognition, or other processes to knit back together the fabric of community deliberately destroyed or damaged by armed conflict. This is especially key where communities turned on each other or on themselves ("horizontal" conflicts), where the wealth and power disparities between the two sides are less salient, and where former enemies need to continue to live side by side. Community healing, it seems, is not an automatic consequence of truth telling, or even justice, although both might be components of it. Rather, it is a very context-specific exercise, which may involve ritual, religious practices, public discussion, apology, vetting, punishment, and/or reparations.

Truth Telling

As mentioned, Guatemala had two major investigative commissions. The first, organized by the Catholic Church, used some seven hundred bilingual lay Catholic statement takers to interview people throughout the highlands around a number of open-ended themes. They collected over five thousand testimonies and produced a four-volume report, *Guatemala Never Again*, that details the kinds of violence, the effects, the history and, where possible, the names of both victims and perpetrators. (REMHI 1998). The 1998 REMHI report was intended to both feed into, and set a standard for, what was expected to be a much weaker official truth commission.

The official commission, composed of German law professor Christian Tomuschat and Guatemalans Alfredo Balsells Tojo, a lawyer, and Otilia Lux, a Mayan educator, had a very short period in which to document and analyze thirty-six years of conflict, and a mandate that required the commission not to individualize responsibilities. From this weak and much-criticized start (Sieder 1998; Wilson 1998), the recommendations and conclusions turned out to be far stronger than had been expected by most human rights organizations, in part due to pressure from civil society groups and the existence of the REMHI report. The CEH also, importantly, found that acts of genocide had been committed in at least four areas of the country.

Nonetheless, although the reports were extensive and alluded to the magnitude of the effects of *la violencia,* they do not—could not—cover all the victimized communities or all the local experiences. A truth commission (TC), at least one dealing with large numbers of violations, has inherent time, budgetary, and space limitations. It must pick and choose illustrative and exemplary cases; not everyone will see their experience reflected in the report. At most, there will be a listing of their community or of the names of the known victims. Moreover, the commission must, by necessity, pick its illustrative cases based on the amount of evidence available, with the result that they will not be the cases involving the worst violations, where there may be no survivors to bear witness or even to list the dead. Nor will they necessarily be the most common types of violations, since a search for illustrative cases may fail to consider all the places where broad patterns repeat again and again. Thus, in cases of massive violations, a truth commission report, no matter how well researched, will provide only a general, not a personal, "truth" to many.

Moreover, a short-term truth-seeking endeavor cannot hope to garner widespread trust among people of a deeply traumatized society, and thus the testimonies taken may be from those less affected or more articulate, or from members of organized groups. Furthermore, without reaching all sectors of society, a partial, fictionalized, or exaggerated past of a few may become the official narrative through the TC process (Zur 1998:179). People in dire economic straits facing investigators who take testimony or hold hearings for a few days will naturally tailor their testimony to those aspects they hope will result in support or assistance. Even under the best of circumstances, a TC can only hope to portray a snapshot of memory at a particular moment and cannot capture the processes of memory changing over time (Halbwachs 1980; Jelin 2003). Nor can a one-time opportunity to give testimony (whether public or privately) substitute for long-term rehabilitation of survivors. For these, longer-term local processes are needed.

In several communities hard hit by massacres, community members and supporters have developed variations on community museums and historical memory recovery initiatives. Community museums exist in Rabinal (Baja Verapaz) and Santiago Atitlán (Sololá), sites of extensive massacres and repression and local areas where survivors have been particularly well organized and proactive. The museums are generally designed by local groups and include exhibits of the local customs, traditional knowledge, and history as well as references to the massacres and destruction. They provide a combination sanctuary, meeting space, and place to both celebrate the community's resources and resilience and commemorate its losses, tying together the past, the rupture of the conflict, and a new emergence.

The historical memory initiative, spread throughout Quiché province and other parts of the country by word of mouth, attempts to piece together the effects and history of the internal armed conflict within a community. It uses discussion and participation in communal map making of how the conflict progressed in that community, and the weaving of a rope-braid representing the community's historical time line. Begun in 2004 by former inhabitants of Popular Communities in Resistance (Comunidades Populares en Resistencia, known as CPRs) and community leaders, the initiative does not follow the logic of traditional programs or projects that have a beginning, a middle, and an end. Rather, it is fueled by the participants themselves and is ongoing for as long as the community members' discussions and debates over the facts of their community's experience continue. Funding is limited to donations from the community itself and individuals in solidarity with the initiative's methods. To date, this initiative has begun in about twenty-five communities. Local leaders facilitate the initiatives along with a team that moves between Quiché and the capital.[8]

From its inception, the initiative worked to reconstruct a community's narrative using tools that were low-cost, widely available, and familiar to participants who may not read well or even speak the same language: paper for maps and thin rope for time lines. Each participant has a rope the length of their own choosing, which becomes a time line by tying knots wherever they consider they lived an important moment, for example when a family member was killed or they were forced to flee. They create time lines for their own life individually, and collectively create general and topical time lines for the community, ranging from the agricultural history of the area to the unfolding of the internal armed conflict. Multiple rope time lines can then be braided together, creating a visual representation of the key developments in the region. Maps of the area, including the location and sequence of events where important developments took place, are drawn and redrawn during community-wide discussions. The project involves physical mapping of how the community used to be, which is especially important in an area where existing villages were burned to the ground and reconstituted, and new generations have no sense of what the prewar community looked like. It also involves tracing how the military campaigns in the area took place, where people were killed, where the survivors fled, and also how the community resisted and created new ways of surviving (markets, temporary housing in the jungle) in the face of military persecution.

The facilitators spark discussions and systematize the information collected through computer documents and video recordings, but it is the community members who drive the initiative's direction and its ultimate goals on how to use their newly documented and synthesized historical memory. Without formal funding (with its grant reviews and deadlines), the initiatives are free to move at the pace that community members prefer. This permits them to make allowances for work, weather, and whatever other incidents arise that make it impossible to meet collectively for a certain period of time. The structure of the initiatives also means that there is no "director," but rather respected community leaders who facilitate the gatherings but are not responsible for a final product or project findings. In fact, the structure of the initiative does not lend itself to a "final ending," but rather to ongoing dialogue within the community.[9]

Justice and Conflict Resolution

Human rights advocates increasingly insist that those who are responsible for massive atrocities should be brought to justice. In the last decade or so, an array of international and hybrid courts have been set up where national justice was judged unavailable or untrustworthy. At the same time, millions of dollars have been spent reforming, modernizing, streamlining, and otherwise attempting to improve domestic judiciaries, prosecutor's offices, and police forces. Although some things have improved, in most post–armed conflict countries, including Guatemala, the justice system remains a poor venue for those seeking justice.

Years of repression and armed conflict drain legitimacy as well as resources from judicial systems. Judges, prosecutors, and lawyers are killed, are forced into exile, or survive through complicity with the regime. Post-conflict, judges and lawyers involved in human rights-related cases continue to be subject to threats as well as tempted by corruption and bureaucratic inertia. In Guatemala, even twenty-five years later, investigation of massacres can lead to threats. These are problems that cannot obviously be solved at a local level.

However, even before the years of armed conflict, the majority of poor, rural, Mayan Guatemalans did not see the justice system as a source of rights vindication. Instead, they saw it as at best irrelevant and at worst an incarnation of the discrimination and oppression to which, since colonial times, they have been (and are) subject. Even now, proceedings are opaque, held in a language that most speak imperfectly, and Maya are treated with disrespect and contempt throughout the system. Only the poor go to jail, but when crimes are committed against them suspects are hardly ever found. Variants on this situation are common to many post–armed conflict countries. It is unrealistic to expect even the best set of anti-impunity and judicial reform measures to reverse the centuries of warranted distrust of formal legal systems.

The Guatemalan legal system by and large has not mustered the political will to prosecute crimes arising from the internal armed conflict. Indeed, a case against members of the military high command alleging genocide has languished in the courts since 2001, because the prosecutor's office has been unable or unwilling to push it forward. The Constitutional Court in December 2007 found that the local courts should not honor a request for extradition of these high-ranking defendants to stand trial in Spain for genocide, pursuant to an investigation initiated under Spain's universal jurisdiction law (Roht-Arriaza 2008). While the cases remain open in both Guatemala and

Spain, it is unclear whether either will ever result in a full trial of the top leadership.

A focus on the top of the chain of command, the approach favored by international and hybrid tribunals, creates its own difficulties. Focusing on leaders and organizers makes sense from a standpoint of both limited resources and moral culpability. However, it is often quite unsatisfying for victims. The army high command, even though survivors recognize its ultimate responsibility and may want to see its members prosecuted, may be as much of an abstraction as the state itself from a ground-level perspective. Rather, people are often most interested in seeing in the dock those they saw and heard giving orders and committing atrocities: only then does justice take on a real face. Those who participated in and organized terror locally and who continue to enjoy impunity are often still "the most powerful local members of the local apparatus of repression" (Sanford 2003:269). It is galling and disturbing to have to live among such people, to see them flaunt their power (and often, wealth) and to feel permanently silenced and threatened by their very presence. Even issues unrelated to the past armed conflict become entwined with the power relations arising from that period. For people to perceive a change in their daily lives, those people need to be removed from the scene.

An example of the local complexities of justice comes from the attempts to prosecute those responsible for several 1982 massacres in the village of Río Negro near Rabinal. A group of soldiers from the local army base commanded by Captain Jose Antonio Solares led some forty civil patrollers from the nearby village of Xococ in the massacres. Several hundred villagers were killed (including at least 107 children), houses and possessions were burned, and eighteen children were selected as war booty to be slaves in the homes of PAC members. Unlike other cases, here apparently the Xococ civil patrollers acted knowingly and voluntarily, in part because of preexisting tensions over land in the area. After many years, survivors asked for exhumation of the bones of those killed and filed a criminal complaint against the military and against twelve PAC members, including three Xococ PAC leaders. The 1998 conviction was overturned by the regional appeals court, which also ordered the cases closed. A second trial, involving judges imported from outside the region, eventually resulted in a murder verdict against the three PAC leaders and a decision to reopen the remaining cases. An initial death sentence was commuted to life imprisonment (Dill 2005). In the remaining cases, five PAC members were sentenced to a total of 780 years for the killing of twenty-six victims in May 2008. They were also sentenced to pay reparations to the victims' families (Prensa Libre 2008).

As Kathleen Dill points out, the local trial proved problematic for sorting out the relationship between national and local justice. National groups were more interested in focusing on the national military leaders—those most responsible—and had insufficient resources to support both local and national investigations. Community organizations in the area, on the other hand, were far more interested in prosecuting the local PAC leaders, both because they were the visible face of repression and because of their continuing threats to communities in the region. Also, talking about the role of the PAC might open up a conversation about the different levels of coercion and complicity in Xococ and other nearby villages.

The focus solely on national prosecutions may make justice advocates miss important opportunities. In the Río Negro case, for example, once it became clear that arrest orders would be issued against the PAC leaders, they reportedly entered into negotiations with a local victims' group. The PAC leaders wanted the victims' group to support leniency in sentencing; in exchange, the victims' group wanted the men to admit their role and to testify as to who had given the orders to massacre the villages. In effect, the PAC leaders named Captain Solares, and the victims supported commutation of the sentences. A focus simply on high-level prosecutions would miss opportunities like this not only to build cases from the bottom up, but also to meet other important objectives of social reconstruction.

On the other hand, a focus solely on local prosecutions often runs up against exactly the local power dynamics that make such efforts so important. So, for example, it took seventeen years and three attempts for a local court to convict notorious PAC leader Cándido Noriega of murder, due in part to threats to judges and prosecutors. In Colotenango, in the country's far north, a mob of ex-PAC members surrounded the jail and freed convicted PAC leaders, who promptly absconded. It has taken five years, from 2003 to 2008, for the first trial involving forced disappearances during the armed conflict to get under way against a local military commissioner in Choatulúm, Chimaltenango Province. It is unclear how far the prosecution can go, given reports that the defendant, free on bail, has according to news reports been threatening witnesses. This is not a reason to abandon such efforts, but perhaps to buttress them with national and international resources.

Criminal prosecutions cannot adequately grapple with the ambiguities, mixed motives, and shades of gray that color most conflicts. Criminal justice requires categorization as perpetrator, accomplice, or innocent witness. It does not deal adequately with bystanders (Fletcher 2005) and deals even less well with the kinds of forced complicity described above. As discussed, the dynamics of the victim/perpetrator relationship varied greatly in Guatemala; in some places the roles were blurred, while in others crimes were clearly committed by outsiders in uniform. Moreover, the roles varied over time; shifting allegiances and mixed motivations were common. While the few cases involving PAC leaders that have come to trial so far seem to target individuals who acted voluntarily and intentionally, neither trials focused on the military high command nor those of PAC leaders will necessarily bring out the perverse dynamics of the PAC system or allow discussion in places where roles were blurred and complicated. But local trials of local perpetrators are more likely to do so.

In societies where formal legal systems do not work for the majority, other forms of dispute resolution exist. These forms, under the names of "traditional justice" or "customary law" vary among regions, and often from place to place. Guatemala's Mayan communities, for example, have long had minor disputes settled by their own authorities, be they religious or secular (*cofrades,* Mayan priests or "indigenous mayors"). The survival or revitalization of these traditional authorities, or their replacement by other kinds of authority, varies from one municipality to another. While it is important not to romanticize traditional justice, which can be arbitrary, patriarchal, and/or coercive, a focus on local justice can take into account these cultural variations and can tailor dispute resolution mechanisms to forms that resonate with local populations and are recognized as their own.

A number of locally based organizations are attempting to use old, revived, and reformed Mayan practices for resolution of present-day disputes. In part, this work is driven by the persistence of tensions around land and resources, and in part by burgeoning domestic violence and common criminality, which has in turn spawned incidents of lynching. It is also perhaps an attempt to reappropriate and revert the use of Mayan symbols and beliefs by the military, which tried to create the belief that the military embodied the spirits of the mountains (Wilson 1999). It is also driven by the continuing dysfunction and discriminatory practices of the formal justice system. By tailoring their mediation and dispute resolution techniques to both the culture and the underlying issues and history of each zone, these groups are setting the stage for a new relationship within communities, where disputes are potentially settled peacefully, but also equitably. They are also beginning to redefine the relationship between justice and the state in a multicultural society, through methods that have not yet—but may eventually—play a role in resolving disputes over the past.

Some of the conflict resolution work involves dealing with individuals accused of stealing, wife beating and other crimes (although generally not homicide or rape). With regard to justice, Mayan beliefs stress that the goal in dealing with those who have committed crimes is getting them to understand their mistakes and reintegrating them into the community, not punishment. The goal is to make the individual recognize that he or she has done something unwarranted (*awas*, which means both "crime" and "sin") and that the person needs to develop "shame" or a social conscience. This usually involves a public meeting including the family, victim(s), and whoever else may be affected. Sanctions may include public discussion and acknowledgment by the wrongdoer or, in serious cases, whipping with a tree switch (explained as releasing positive energies rather than as a punitive measure) or temporary or permanent banishment or ostracism. While highly controversial from the standpoint of international human rights law, such methods are considered highly effective by some traditional community leaders but are also contested, both as to their authenticity and their appropriateness. In cases of conflicts between communities, dialogue and mediation take place in mass meetings of both communities, preceded by careful preparation with religious (Mayan and Christian) and secular leaders.

We found little evidence that these Mayan cosmovisión-based dispute resolution practices have been applied to tensions arising from the legacy of the armed conflict itself, rather than current disputes. In part, this is a timing issue: after more than twenty years from the worst massacres, people in many places no longer base their identity solely on their status as victim or perpetrator, and although those tensions persist, they have been joined by newer sources of tension—economic, familial, religious, or political—that often involve different groupings. While in some senses "too late," in another it may be "too soon," as the local power relationships between former perpetrators and their victims continue largely to favor the first group. Ex-PAC members and army representatives continue to wield economic, political, and military power locally, and continue to be able to threaten others. Unlike in other places, these people have no interest in reintegration into a community or in acknowledging their past acts, so there are no grounds for invoking any local dispute-resolution process. The potential is there: we were told of a case in which a Kich'e widow invoked the help of a Defensoría Indígena to claim the return of land stolen by a PAC member years before. But whether the techniques of dialogue and mediation used to deal with thievery and thuggishness can deal with the sequelae of plunder and massacre is still an unknown.

Reparations

In the wake of large-scale violence or repression, reparations can provide one of the most tangible manifestations of a government's recognition of victims' dignity and rights, and of its commitment not to repeat past wrongs. In an extremely poor country, reparations also have a chance to make a real difference in the lives of those who lost everything. Reparations can be material or symbolic, individual or collective (Roht-Arriaza 2004). According to the 2005 UN Principles on the subject, reparations can include restitution (of property, jobs, pensions, good name, etc.), physical and mental rehabilitation, economic compensation, and a wide range of guarantees of nonrepetition, including commemoration, legal and political reforms, and access to justice (United Nations 2005).

In practice, however, when faced with poor societies, a weak state, and many victims, reparations programs confront substantial challenges. The state may not be in a position to efficiently and fairly administer programs involving a great deal of money or the creation and administration of the public goods that in other places have been labeled "collective reparations." After a prolonged conflict, societies are in some degree of disarray, government is either dysfunctional or overwhelmed or both, and past patterns of patronage or group-based politics may persist. There may be, as in Guatemala, little or no tradition of a democratic process and still less administrative capacity, along with a long history of self-dealing, the capture of popular organizations, corruption, influence peddling, and the like, exacerbated by the transformation of criminal and intelligence networks into organized crime rings (Peacock and Beltrán 2003). Into this scenario comes a short-term burst of foreign aid money for both government and NGOs, one that after a few years will subside in favor of the next troubled post-conflict country. There is also an unhealthy tradition of centralization of both government and NGOs: by working mostly from the capital, organizations run the risk of misunderstanding community needs and realities, putting extra burdens on potential beneficiaries, as well as of stretching limited resources too thin. Guatemala has been a recipient of large amounts of both post-conflict and "development" aid, and its generally weak civil society has been particularly prone to the dangers of external funding and the "NGO-ization" of social movements. Trying to create large-scale social reconstruction projects in this context risks having them collapse into in-fighting over patronage and spoils, administrative disarray, and cynicism. Moreover, cultural and conceptual issues may bedevil reparations programs.

Guatemala's considerable efforts at reparations illustrate some of these difficulties. The CEH recommended a national reparations program, but while one was conceived in 2002, political opposition stalled its implementation until 2004. On paper, the National Reparations Program (Programa Nacional de Resarcimiento, PNR) sounds impressive. It has a ten-year mandate, with a planned annual budget of 300 million Quetzales (about $37.5 million). The PNR also in theory proposed to approach reparations from five integrated angles: material restitution, individual economic reparations, cultural restitution, victim dignification, and psychosocial reparation.

In practice, difficulties arose. Civil society organizations, initially on the governing board, fought bitterly among themselves, stalling implementation. To compound matters, the reparations issue became conflated with the question of payments to former PAC members for services rendered to the military. Organized and vocal groups of ex-PACs claimed that the state owed them millions of dollars in unpaid wages and reparations for their own suffering during the internal armed conflict. Former President Portillo agreed to pay but only partially did so. With the creation of the PNR, many ex-PACs saw it as an opportunity to pressure the government to include them as a group to which the PNR should provide reparations. This outraged the victims' groups, and the government finally agreed to exclude PACs from the PNR but pay them from a separate fund. From a grounds-eye view, it looked to many people as if the government was distributing checks right and left; all efforts to use reparations as a means of dignification of victims rather than a simple handout were lost in the infighting and confusion over who constitutes a "victim" and why.

In 2005 the executive branch of the government changed the governing structure of the PNR, eliminating the direct participation of civil society and reducing the Commission to five government representatives. This streamlines the work of the PNR by allowing it to make quicker decisions and act more efficiently but risks making it more difficult for survivors of the internal armed conflict to voice their opinions to the Commission. It also opened sixteen regional field offices throughout the country in 2006 to gather and receive applications for reparations from individual survivors, and created nine mobile teams to facilitate applications from those who are unable to reach, or are unaware of, the regional offices. The focus throughout these reforms, until recently, has remained on individual economic reparations. As a result, many have criticized the PNR of being a divisive instrument of the state, intended to favor the ex-PAC members, divide survivors, and create conflicts over money, thereby distracting them from their search for justice and accountability.[10]

Smaller amounts distributed to a lot of different groups at the local level, with adequate training and accountability, stand a better chance of avoiding these problems. By staying smaller, or at least having decentralized offices and budgets, agencies and groups are less likely to fall victim to the interorganizational, patronage, political, and even security problems that access to large amounts of money can reap. Decentralization is now recognized as a component of responsive, responsible public administration. Indeed, the current Commission, appointed by President Álvaro Colom, has moved toward a more decentralized approach. A pilot project begun in May 2008 focuses on communal reparations in the poorest regions of the country and among those most affected by the internal armed conflict. Under this new focus, the communities and the PNR work together to create an integrated reparations package, focusing largely on community development, psychosocial programs, and victim dignification. Individual economic reparations would become a final step, rather than a first one. The Commission has also proposed to reorganize the regional offices, charging them with the task of proactively seeking survivors and working with them to create integrated reparations packages. It is too early to know whether this approach will be successful. Meanwhile, the distribution of checks continues.

On the other hand, localized reparations projects do mean that uniformity will be sacrificed, and that resources may flow to the most organized or most compelling places but not to others. We suggest that, given the conditions we describe, this will happen even under a nationally administered scheme, with the difference that communities will have less ownership of the process, and middlemen (be they bureaucrats or consultants) will take a greater cut.

A parallel critique of reparations in Guatemala has been the focus on monetary compensation in general. In interviews, several beneficiaries explained that because the life of their family members has no price, it was highly problematic to frame "resarcimiento" in terms of paying for the loss of life, creating feelings of guilt and dissatisfaction. On the other hand, beneficiaries felt that the government paid inadequate attention to material reparations, especially for the loss of their homes, material possessions, animals, and crops (Viaene 2007). Indeed, it is striking that a quarter-century later victims can still recite how many pots, hoes, chickens, or rows of corn they lost in the conflict. They also felt that the nature of a reparatory process had been lost, because there was insufficient discussion and negotiation between those offering and those accepting the reparations, rather than a bureaucratic documentation procedure leading to receipt of a check. In the Mayan tradition, making good for wrongdoing involves just such a process of negotiation and acceptance.

Other types of reparations, both preceding and under the auspices of the PNR, may be less problematic. For example, communities have taken the lead in the exhumation and reburial of those killed during the conflict. Guatemala is riddled with clandestine and unmarked graves. Part of the military's strategy of terror was to leave bodies in town squares and along the sides of roads, and to prohibit family members from recovering or properly burying those killed. As is true in other places, the lack of appropriate burial ceremonies and of a place to mourn and remember the dead has been a source of anguish (Stover and Shigekane 2004:95), especially since the local culture posits a continuing relationship between the dead and the living that requires proper attention to the dead. As elsewhere, one of the most common needs of survivors is to recover the body and rebury it with the appropriate (Catholic, Mayan, Protestant, or combined) ceremonies.

Since the early 1990s, several groups of forensic anthropologists have been hard at work exhuming clandestine gravesites; over eight hundred have been discovered so far, with years' more work to go. These exhumations are not simply technical affairs but have deep connections to community mental health and commemoration efforts as well as to local justice processes. The process requires extensive preparation of family members (both for finding the remains and for the risk of not finding them) and has often become a collective task of a community. Community members provide food for forensic anthropology teams and help with digging and erecting the temporary structures needed for a major exhumation.

Exhumation of a clandestine grave cannot proceed without the presence of the Public Prosecutor's office or a judge, and the identification of bodies, by law, triggers a criminal investigation. (In practice very few identifications actually lead to a criminal complaint being filed, much less pursued). For local communities where PACs were involved in the crimes, the tie-in to the criminal justice system raises the stakes, since the judicial authorities are there to take statements from witnesses who may well implicate individuals still living in or near the area. A pending exhumation often leads to renewed threats against victims' families and local social activists, and potential sabotage to the forensic anthropologists' work. On the other hand, the presence of judicial authorities may impede the ability of communities to use the exhumations as a moment for acknowledgment of wrongdoing. While there have been several anecdotal accounts of former PAC members and supporters helping out at, or even showing remorse toward, victims' families in the course of exhumations, any public acknowledgment of responsibility for the crimes would lead to an automatic duty on the part of the Public Prosecutor or judge to file a criminal complaint against the individual(s) involved. So PAC members generally hold their peace.

Once bodies have been exhumed and, where possible, identified, many local communities have organized massive public reburial ceremonies. These have been moving, impressive affairs, where hundreds of people turn out to accompany the coffins of the dead to the burial ground, prayers are said, food and memories are shared, and a marker or memorial has been erected to mark the names of those buried there. Where no bodies have been recovered, plaques, markers, or memorials have been set up at the massacre sites or other places with symbolic significance. These memorials, sometimes with large crosses, others with Mayan altars but always listing the names of the dead, can become quite elaborate as well as contested. For example, in 1995, members of twenty-eight communities from Alta Verapaz pooled their resources to erect a giant cross with plaques listing the names of 916 massacre victims in the village of Sahakok; the initiative was sparked by dreams of local elders.[11] Outside Rabinal, the Río Negro memorials involve a series of murals depicting the massacres (described above) and several different markers with victims' names. After a first, modest memorial was pulled down by civil patrollers from Xococ, the village associations rebuilt a bigger concrete memorial, and again inscribed it with the names of murdered villagers, adding that they were "killed by the civil patrollers from Xococ." Similar murals exist in Comalapa and other towns of the Chimaltenango area. These often constitute the first community recognition of local history.

In other places, the community has built culturally appropriate monuments. In Panzós, Alta Verapaz, the Monument for Peace and Tolerance sits adjacent to the site of the 1978 massacre victims' mass grave. The site was exhumed in 1997, the victims reburied by their families in a mass interment ceremony a year later. The monument is an open-air chapel, thus incorporating both the Mayan tradition of connecting with the natural world and the Christian tradition of praying inside a chapel. Furthermore, the monument has one Christian cross in the front and an offerings altar, which was specially designed in a truncated elliptical form to represent the interrupted lives of the slaughtered men, women, and children. Adjacent to the Christian altar, directly over the site of the former clandestine grave, is a second altar for Mayan ceremonies. Community members who sacrificed workdays in order to participate carried out the bulk of the monument's construction. The altar and chapel's integration into community events demonstrates how a memorialization effort can genuinely become incorporated into a community.

These initiatives arise from and are organized and financed locally, sometimes with support from national NGOs, local community organizations, or religious authorities. Because they arise from local, deeply felt initiatives, they are protected and "owned" by community members. They stand in stark contrast to the lack of any kind of national memorial relating to the armed conflict; although individual plaques marking where victims were killed dot Guatemala City, there is no prominent central marker or memorial, and a planned museum has not yet opened its doors.

Exhumations and reburials are stressful for survivors, reviving old memories and traumas. In some communities, people have never spoken of what happened to them, even within their own families; this is especially true of women victims of sexual violence. A number of groups have developed methodologies for working with communities before, during, and after exhumations to combat the culture of fear developed over years of terror and to allow people to begin to speak of, and make sense of, their experiences. Accompaniment programs and individual and group mental health programs emerged as a response to the perceived needs that followed the thirty-six years of conflict in Guatemala. Much of the success of these programs lies with how much the community trusts them. Trust in Guatemala is built by demonstrating that the organization will not abandon the community—as the government and the guerrillas both did during the internal armed conflict—thereby making the program an enduring one. For this, the organization must be embedded in a local area.

A number of psychosocial intervention programs are firmly grounded in Mayan cosmovisión, an abstract term that incorporates philosophy, ideology, and history. Each community interprets the specificities of Mayan cosmovisión differently, and in some places more memory exists of the old ways of doing things than in others, where specific rituals need to be reinvented. Key elements to Mayan cosmovisión include the belief in place-based spirituality related to the local landscape; the interconnectedness of nature, people, and ancestors; and deference to elders. Dealing with trauma involves a close relationship among the body, the mind, and the spirit world (Viaene 2007; Wilson 1999). In the context of exhumations, fire-based ceremonies are often used to cleanse survivors of guilt and to communicate with those who were killed (Domingo Hernandez, interviews, Guatemala City, July 2004, March 2008). By incorporating Mayan traditions into their work, these organizations are more accessible to community members who might otherwise be skeptical of a program that relates back to the internal armed conflict. At the same time, most organizations working with Mayan rituals do not work solely on post-conflict trauma but also incorporate either a focus on new forms of dispute resolution (see above) or a focus on health, education, and empowerment. The focus is not on survivors solely as victims, but as bearers of a valuable history and continuing culture.

Conclusions

These local-level initiatives can tailor their strategies to the unique experiences of each geographic region and community. They can foster the integration of cultural practices, promote participation and a sense of ownership, and thus make such initiatives sustainable beyond the short window of external project financing. They can begin to bring about a cultural shift. Most of these initiatives combine a number of the often-enumerated goals of transitional or post–armed conflict justice, but they also connect the past to present-day struggles and exist without the tight time frames of national-level interventions and with material support from those directly involved.

Still, working locally creates certain dilemmas. It is not clear whether such initiatives, because they are so place- and culture-specific, can—or should—be "scaled up" beyond their local origins. Those designing post-conflict social reconstruction policies tend quite naturally to want to reproduce successful experiences, but these may be so sui generis that no such reproduction is possible. Rather, the best outsiders can do is to investigate carefully the existence and extent of such local initiatives and try to avoid working at cross-purposes with them. Anything else, as we have seen with the Rwandan gacaca courts, will twist their meaning beyond recognition. The existence and nature of such local practices may provide important clues as to what will, or will not, resonate at a national level, what kinds of "reconciliation" have already happened, and what remains to be done. The careful documentation and study of such practices is also important to assess the success or failure of a "transition," as well as to elicit what people understand to be justice.

At the least governments, international agencies, and transitional justice practitioners can aim to "do no harm" and to make sure space exists for these practices. Thus an amnesty law or de facto amnesty may preempt local attempts at dialogue by giving one side of the conflict impunity and consolidating the existing local power imbalances. A poorly thought-out reparations program that simply distributes checks can exacerbate community tensions, making the local rebalancing that is essential to felt reparation more difficult. In prosecutions as well, national and international or transnational prosecuting authorities need to consider not only the national impact but also what impact, if any, investigation or arrest will have locally. The same is true of land and household goods restitution and vetting of local military, police, and political officeholders. Local power dynamics need to be investigated and taken into account, so as not to simply reinforce or exacerbate existing inequalities.

In designing national post–armed conflict initiatives, space can be left for local precursors or follow-ons. Thus, for example, a truth commission can identify and support efforts, either preexisting or generated as a response to the call for testimony, to deepen local understandings of what happened, through community mapping or community museums. Often the chance to speak to an official commission will provide a mobilizing spark for communities, whether it takes the form of gathering or rehearsing their testimony or of organizing hearings or statement taking. Those efforts should not be seen simply as preparation for the overall national report, but also as starting points for ongoing local initiatives. Similarly, exhumations are not simply about recovering bodies, or even about preparing judicial cases, but can be starting points both for commemorative activities and for local psychosocial intervention work.

Finally, a local focus might prompt some reevaluation of timing and funding for transitional justice initiatives. The time frame would have to be considerably longer, thought of in terms of decades and generations, not short-term "fixes." Decentralization and responsiveness to bottom-up initiatives with small quantities of funds to complement local material support (in kind, through labor, through contributions), rather than large-scale, short-term megaprograms, would align post–armed conflict initiatives with much thinking in the development area. Keeping things small might more easily create opportunities for local residents (even very poor ones) to contribute part or all of the financing of "their" projects. And the focus would be on ongoing processes, not necessarily end products.

We are not arguing that national or international initiatives should be abandoned—simply enriched and more carefully calibrated, taking into account both the wisdom and the conflicts that exist locally. The lessons learned regarding the importance of a localized approach to social reconstruction underscore the role of local communities as cornerstones of wider-scale human organizations, and the ways in which different post–armed conflict strategies work together. Without the building blocks carefully understood and differentiated, larger-scale attempts at social reconstruction will surely crumble.

Chapter 11

Dealing with the Past when the Conflict Is Still Present

Civil Society Truth-Seeking Initiatives in the Israeli-Palestinian Conflict

Ron Dudai and Hillel Cohen

Using the term "dealing with the past" in relation to the Israeli-Palestinian conflict is bound to raise some eyebrows. This term, usually seen through the prism of transitional justice, is associated with mechanisms, ranging from the South African Truth and Reconciliation Commission (TRC) to the International Criminal Tribunal for Rwanda (ICTR), that are set in a transitional or post-conflict stage. In other words, first a conflict is resolved or at least transformed, and only then does a project of dealing with the past begin. And while there are many conflicting observations about the current Israeli-Palestinian situation, the one thing about which everyone would agree is that it is not post-conflict.

Nevertheless, as this chapter will show, several projects of dealing with the past are already taking place in the area: these projects illustrate that there are circumstances in which dealing with the past could—and perhaps should—begin even before the conflict is resolved. This conclusion requires a conceptual modification, a broadening and "thickening" (cf. McEvoy 2007) of our understanding of the transitional justice field (as both practice and theory), and in particular a perception of civil society initiatives, not just official endeavors, as important mechanisms for dealing with the past.

It should be emphasized that in developing these ideas we have, like many transitional justice scholars, followed practice with theory, not the other way around. We noticed that many new initiatives in the Israeli-Palestinian setting share attributes with transitional justice mechanisms (even if their initiators do not always view themselves as engaging in "transitional justice"), and then located these projects within a broad transitional justice framework. While some of these initiatives echo familiar methods of transitional justice elsewhere, they often developed new variations, which do not always correspond to the international "toolkit." Indeed, such "toolkit thinking" is not always helpful in approaching local cases, as this volume suggests, and there is a need to think in place-based terms about what can be used (and *how* it might be used). This chapter follows on from this insight.

Many of these activities take place below the radar of international observers and may look surprising against the background of the normally bleak reports from the area. As we will elaborate below, these days one can find former Palestinian militants and former Israeli soldiers coming together to talk about their past violent activities; Israelis and Palestinians who lost relatives in the violence meeting to discuss their narratives of the conflict; and schoolteachers from both sides who together design joint textbooks about the conflict. While the overall situation in the area is indeed bleak, these activities are worth attention. In this chapter, we seek to document and analyze them.

In the next section we will present our framework, including a few remarks on transitional justice and dealing with the past, a comparative overview of civil society initiatives that focus on dealing with the past in other countries, and a short justification of the importance of dealing with the past in the Israeli-Palestinian conflict. Following this, we will offer a mapping of existing initiatives in the area. We then move to analyze certain aspects of these initiatives, such as their genesis and their activities. Finally, we will discuss some lingering dilemmas, such as whether these activities should deal with past violence by *both* sides, and in concluding we will briefly discuss the question of their impact—or lack thereof.

In addition to secondary sources and materials published by these initiatives we have relied on interviews and informal conversations with key activists in the area. We also draw from our own involvement in civil society groups, including some of the initiatives described below.

Theoretical and Comparative Framework

From "Transitional Justice" to "Dealing with the Past"

While the term *transitional justice* is now firmly established, it actually can be an inaccurate and sometimes misleading label. First, the term *justice* is loaded, and often overambitious. For example, many victims feel that receiving compensation for the death of their loved ones or learning the true facts about their relatives' death, as important as they are, do not constitute "justice." For others justice will be associated with economic equality or with achieving self-determination, not with institutions such as truth commissions. Using the term *justice* can place the bar too high and create false expectations or resentment when in reality the ambition is much lower—for example, to establish a common understanding of the facts about past abuses.

Second, the term *transitional* can also be unsuitable. As Roht-Arriaza (2006) notes, the common perceptions of "transition" imply "a defined period of flux after which a post-transitional state sets in," whereas in reality transitions can often be longer and more fragmented processes. More specifically, Ni Aoláin and Campbell (2005) argue in their work on Northern Ireland that "paradigmatic transitions" should be distinguished from transitions in "conflicted democracies"—where a state with at least internal procedural democracy engages in abuses elsewhere, such as Britain and the conflict in Northern Ireland, or, it can be added, Israel and the Palestinian Territories. In such cases, the transition would be less linear and more complex and fragmented.[1]

Moreover, unpacking the concept of transitional justice into its various components—such as trials, compensations, truth, release of political prisoners—reveals that at least some of them have a potential to take place, even if in modest forms, before a transition is completed (for example, before a full peace treaty is signed or implemented). From this perspective, the use of the term *transitional justice* might end up inhibiting discussions on such mechanisms *during* a conflict, as it implies that they can take place only after—or during—political transitions. While in most cases these mechanisms are more likely to be effective during or after a transition, a political transition need not be a precondition for all measures.

For these reasons we prefer to use the term *dealing with the past* (e.g., Bell 2003, Boraine et al 1994) as a less ambitious but more accurate and down-to-earth term. Of all the elements in the transitional justice "package"—accountability, reforms, reparations, truth, and so on—the focus here is on the "truth" element. For various reasons outlined below, this is the element most likely to be taken up by civil society and to begin before a formal transition is completed. It is, in addition, one of the most acute issues in the Israeli-Palestinian context.[2] Before our focus shifts to the Israeli-Palestinian setting, we will next examine the ways in which civil society organizations have engaged with truth seeking elsewhere in the world.[3]

From Truth Commissions to Truth Seeking: The Emerging Role of Civil Society Initiatives

Truth commissions have been established, in various forms, in close to forty countries, attracting huge attention from policymakers, activists, academics, and journalists. These commissions normally engage in an examination of past abuses and violence (resulting in a published report), provide a platform for victims—and in some cases perpetrators—to tell their stories (sometimes through public hearings), recommend reforms, and contribute to reconciliation. Hayner provides probably the best-known definition of truth commissions (2001:14): they focus on the past; investigate patterns of abuses rather than one event; are temporary bodies that end their existence after a limited period of time; and are bodies that are "officially sanctioned, authorized or empowered by the State." This last element of the definition is particularly important in our context, as it excludes civil society-led projects.[4] In another authoritative study of truth commissions, Freeman mostly echoes Hayner's definition but goes even further to emphasize that any "non-state" inquiry should not be considered a truth commission (2006:18).

Being officially established by the state gives truth commissions several important advantages over civil society initiatives. It allows a commission to gain easy access to official records and at times to compel people to testify through subpoena powers—powers that NGOs lack. It also allows the commission to operate in relative safety, and most likely to have more budget and resources than a civil society project. Finally, its official status (especially when the body is established by a democratically elected leadership) often gives a commission better legitimacy, public trust, media interest, and impact for its report and recommendations.

While these advantages are important, this definition of truth commissions might (whether consciously or not) impede sustained engagement with other forms of truth seeking available to civil society organizations. In situations where an official commission is unlikely, or where an existing commission's mandate is deemed to be compromised, civil society initiatives, their shortcomings vis-à-vis official commissions notwithstanding, do have the potential to play an important role. It is important to note, however, that comparing civil society initiatives to ideal-type truth commissions is not always helpful, especially where the political climate makes the establishment of an official commission unlikely. The potential of such initiatives should be weighed in relation to existing reality, not in comparison to unattainable hypothetical official commissions. Moreover, given that the truth-seeking element of transitional justice is broader than the work of official truth commissions alone, sometimes civil society will have important advantages over truth commissions. Thus truth-seeking civil society projects should be evaluated on their own terms, not as a second-best alternative to truth commissions (see Arriaza and Roht-Arriaza, this volume).

Although several works have examined the contributions of NGOs to official truth commissions (Backer 2003; International Center for Transitional Justice 2004), cases in which civil society itself engages in truth seeking have received comparatively little attention: the only systematic study seems to be the recent article by Bickford (2007). Such civil society efforts may be divided into contexts in which they accompanied or followed official commissions, and contexts in which they represent the only attempt to confront the past.

Perhaps the most prominent example of the first type is the Recovery of Historical Memory Project (known as REMHI, for its Spanish acronym), which took place in Guatemala in 1995–98 (Arriaza and Roht-Arriaza, this volume; Ballengee 1999). Less well known, however, are the "caravans of truth" (caravans de verite) organized by civil society in Morocco: these followed the official commission, organizing public hearings and documenting victims' stories (Freeman 2005). Finally, in South Africa civil society organized several follow-up activities to the TRC. These include, among others, the Institute for Healing of Memories (IHM), which brings together South Africans from various backgrounds for sessions of "testimonial dialogue,"[5] and an Internal Reconciliation Commission (IRC), established at the University of the Witwatersrand to examine the legacy of past discrimination and racial division and to aid institutional transformation (Gready forthcoming).[6]

In the second type of civil society effort, more relevant to our context, no official commission has taken place. In Brazil, for example, a group of lawyers, coordinated by the World Council of Churches, produced a comprehensive report (titled Nunca Más, "never again") about the military junta, which proved that the army was engaged in systematic torture (Weschler 1990). This report became a best seller and had lasting effects on Brazilian society, receiving (like that produced by REMHI in Guatemala) as much attention—if not more— than an official report would have. A second prominent example is that of the Russian NGO "Memorial." It was established in 1988, when it seemed clear that no official mechanism would confront the legacy of past Soviet abuses, in particular the Stalinist purges and gulags. It has engaged in the systematic collection of evidence about Soviet abuses, including interviews and recording of oral history, has produced statistical records, attempted to identify individual victims, and investigated mass graves and former detention camps. This organization is still active today and continues its tasks.[7]

Other civil society projects have focused on the community level. An interesting example comes from the United States. In Greensboro, North Carolina, members of local civil society established the Greensboro Truth and Community Reconciliation Project (GTCRP) to examine the legacy of race relations in the area, especially an incident from 1979 in which Ku Klux Klan members killed several civil rights activists. The GTCRP conducted independent investigations, held public hearings, and published a report. Whereas an official truth commission covering the entire legacy of racial discrimination in the United States seems unlikely, the GTCRP was able to at least partly perform this task in one locality.

Another well-known example of a community-focused truth-seeking project led by civil society is the Ardoyne Community Project (ACP) in Northern Ireland—a context in which thus far there has been no official truth commission. This project began well before the recent political breakthrough in Northern Ireland and focused on political violence during the "troubles" in Ardoyne, a small community in north Belfast (population of 6,000) in which a hundred were killed during the conflict and many more injured and arrested. Participants interviewed the family members of those who were killed during the violence, and collected other oral testimony. Their report—"Ardoyne: The Untold Truth"—was published in 2002 (see Lundy and McGovern 2005). The ACP, like the project in Greensboro, demonstrates some advantages of civil society initiatives: because they focused on small communities, they could achieve much more within their locality. No countrywide commission, for example, would have been able to interview all the relatives of victims in Ardoyne as the ACP did.

The last example here, also from Northern Ireland, is a recent initiative of the NGO Healing through Remembering (HTR), which organized a "national day of private reflection" in June 2007. This organization invited individuals "to reflect, individually and privately, upon the conflict in and about Northern Ireland" and organized several activities around this reflection day.[8] While national days of commemoration in the context of past wars and violence are fairly common worldwide, they are normally initiated by governments; the HTR initiative is an example of how, when leaderships are reluctant to initiate such activities, civil society can partly fill the vacuum by taking the lead.[9]

As this overview illustrates, civil society has developed rich and lively efforts to deal with the past in several diverse contexts, with or without the presence of parallel official truth commissions. While some of these projects borrow consciously from the vocabulary of transitional justice (e.g., the Greensboro project), others were developed more independently (e.g., Memorial). They have operated in contexts in which the political climate was not conducive to official commissions (Brazil, Northern Ireland), in transitions from authoritarian to semi-authoritarian regimes (Russia, Morocco), and in incomplete or unrecognized transitions (the U.S. South). Their activities mostly replicate those undertaken by official commissions, such as producing reports, conducting public hearings, or meticulously documenting past abuses. Whether as a cause or an effect of civil society involvement, many of these initiatives have been focused not on a statewide record but on a small community (Greensboro, Ardoyne, the University of the Witwaterstand).

The Importance of Dealing with the Past in Israeli-Palestinian Conflict Transformation

Before proceeding to address civil society initiatives in our area, this section will briefly demonstrate the importance of the past in Israeli-Palestinian relations. During and after formal bilateral Israeli-Palestinian peace negotiations (the Oslo-to-Camp David process, 1993–2001), attempts to deal with the past were almost completely absent from official discourse and practice. Uri Savir, one of Israel's chief negotiators, reports that early on in the first round of negotiations, participants tacitly agreed that confronting the past would be futile. Savir (1998) describes his first meeting with Abu-'Ala, one of the Palestinian chief negotiators (and later a Palestinian prime minister): the two, according to Savir, started arguing over who did what to whom in the 1948 war but soon realized that these kind of arguments would not advance the negotiations. Savir describes the insight that arose: "Never again we would argue about the past. This was an important step, for it moved us beyond an endless wrangle over right and wrong. Discussing the future would mean reconciling two rights, not readdressing ancient wrongs" (1998). Indeed, "during the early negotiations of the Oslo Accords, the negotiators decided not to debate historical issues, realizing that neither could convert the other to its view of the past"

(Quandt 2005:15). Sandy Berger, who was a senior member of the American team in the Camp David negotiations, expressed a typical view when he wrote that "the key is to get them to focus on the future and not the past" (quoted in Dudai 2007b).

However, this approach is acutely misguided in relation to the Israeli-Palestinian case. While collective memories and different understandings of the past play a role in many ethnic conflicts (Cairns and Roe 2005), the Israeli-Palestinian conflict is one in which these issues are truly prominent. Memories of abuses and perceptions of exclusive victimhood play a huge role in both Israeli and Palestinian society and adversely affect their ability to reach a political compromise (Dudai 2007a); collective denial of the other side's suffering is also ingrained into both sides' consciousness (Cohen 2001). As Palestinian academic and former Labor Minister Ghasan Khatib (2005) observes, "the narratives that inform Palestinians and Israelis are important and dangerous components of the Israeli-Palestinian conflict that are rarely touched upon by those who are trying to bring it to an end." As he adds, it is difficult to see "a lasting peace agreement without dealing with these contradicting narratives" (ibid.).

The decision not to engage with the past has had several specific effects. First, it has hampered the potential to successfully negotiate agreements on substantive issues. Bell argues that in many conflicts there is also a "meta-conflict," or "a conflict on what the conflict is about" (2000:15); this is certainly true for the Israeli-Palestinian conflict, where the "meta-questions" such as who was the initial aggressor and who acted in self-defense—limited both sides' ability to deal with (for example) the Israeli settlements in the West Bank or the Palestinian refugees. These issues cannot be resolved on purely technical and forward-looking terms without engaging with each side's narratives and historical sensitivities (Agha and Malley 2001; Quandt 2005). Another problem created by this omission is that it sustained each side's self-perception as eternal exclusive victim. This helped to derail the peace process with each violent attack by either side, which was perceived by the other as one in a long historical chain of violent attacks, thereby confirming that all members of the other group do not—and never did—seek peace (Dudai 2007b). Only a more complex collective engagement with the past can transform this situation and reduce the levels of animosity between Israelis and Palestinians—a reduction that is a precondition for the success of a peace process. Finally, on a deeper level, the peace process can succeed only if both sides recognize the humanity and legitimacy of the other—a step that necessitates an honest confrontation of the past and taking responsibility for past abuses (Jamal 2001); or, in the words of Rouhana, "genuine reconciliation requires facing historical truths, taking responsibilities for past injustices" (2006:127). While peace processes cannot be reduced to attitude change, this case nevertheless demonstrates the importance of such a change. To sum it up in modest terms, "a greater appreciation of the separate truths that drive Israelis and Palestinians could plausibly contribute to conflict reduction" (Rotberg 2006:2).

Reaching this insight is, of course, just a first step; the question remains how to make it concrete. The rich international legacy of transitional justice mechanisms, with the notable cases of the truth commissions in South Africa, Chile, or Argentina, provides some inspiration, but it could also inhibit concrete discussions. All these famous cases were established in an official way, a condition that could become real only in a post-conflict stage—a stage that is only a distant future scenario for Israelis and Palestinians. The alternative, advocated here, is to look at the potential of civil society to deal with the past even when the conflict is still present (and to rely on the comparative repertoire of the civil society projects sketched in the previous section). Such civil society engagement could pave the way to more official mechanisms once successful negotiations take place (Dudai 2007a); but it can also, we suggest, serve as *a conflict transformation tool in itself.* Adam and Moodley argue that "while truth commissions are normally established after violence ceases, in the Middle East the process could pave the way toward the end of violence and renewed negotiations by narrowing opposing meta-narratives" (2005:162). This sequence depends, however, on the involvement of civil society. Such civil society initiatives will never solve the Israeli-Palestinian conflict in themselves and will not even complete the task of dealing with the past. Yet given the dire current reality in the region, even the potential for a limited contribution is highly important.

Dealing with the Past in Israel/Palestine: Mapping Initiatives

Defining Initiatives That "Deal with the Past"

Defining which initiatives should fall under the heading of "dealing with the past" or "transitional justice" in the Israeli-Palestinian case is not a straightforward task. In the context of defining human rights organizations, Bell and Keenan (2004) suggest using the self-definition of the organization's members. In our case, this approach would not be very helpful, as many of the activists involved do not view themselves as engaged in "transitional justice."[10] While terms such as *human rights* or *conflict resolution* are firmly incorporated in the language of Palestinian and Israeli activists, as well as of the general public, the terms *transitional justice* and *dealing with the past* have not yet been popularized in the Israeli-Palestinian setting. They have not fully entered the language of organizations or the public and do not serve as established signifiers of this line of work.[11]

Initiatives that deal with the past are also not commonly seen as a distinct category of civil society activity in the Israeli-Palestinian case. For example, in their overview of Israeli-Palestinian civil society activities, Dajani and Baskin list eleven categories of work (e.g., advocacy groups, dialogue groups, cultural activities, Track II negotiations, or professional meetings) but do not mention "dealing with the past." It might also be that since efforts to deal with the past usually take place after the conflict has been transformed, these initiatives in the Israeli-Palestinian case are yet to be recognized as such by international observers. For example, in his overview of civil society truth efforts worldwide, Bickford (2007) does not mention any Israeli-Palestinian examples. Nevertheless, we argue in this chapter that the initiatives outlined below should be seen as a distinct form of civil society activity in the Israeli-Palestinian context.

Bickford refers to similar initiatives elsewhere as "unofficial truth projects," which he defines as follows:

> (1) they are geared towards revealing the truth about crimes committed in the past as a component of a broader strategy of accountability and justice; (2) in their effort to do so, they self-consciously or coincidentally resemble official truth commissions that have been created in countries as different as Chile, Morocco, South Africa, Sierra Leone, and East Timor; but that (3) these particular efforts are rooted in civil society—hosted and driven by human rights NGOs, victim groups, universities, and other societal organizations—and are not primarily state-based efforts. (2007:994–95)

This definition will be broadly followed in this chapter, with certain modifications. We view civil society truth-seeking initiatives somewhat more broadly than Bickford's definition of "unofficial truth projects" and will include activities beyond those normally associated with official truth commissions, such as the production of joint school textbooks about the conflict by Israelis and Palestinians. In this chapter, the initiatives we discuss focus on engaging with the past of the Israeli-Palestinian conflict; this engagement is conducted in a framework of broad political commitment to peace and conflict transformation, and through some form of group effort (thus historical studies that are done for their own sake will be excluded, as well as individual work by historians or journalists). A further way to elucidate such initiatives is through contrast to other types of civil society work, such as human rights NGOs, political protest groups, humanitarian organizations, or Track II projects—all of which focus on the present or the future rather than on the past.

It is important to note that because in both societies commemorating the victims of one's own side has long been a legitimate and encouraged activity, we will examine only initiatives that either deal simultaneously with the actions of both sides or those in which one side deals with the victims of the other. Thus we exclude Israeli initiatives that commemorate only Israeli victims and Palestinian crimes, and Palestinian initiatives that commemorate only Israeli crimes and Palestinian victims.[12]

An Overview of Organizations

In general, the following groups and initiatives are not part of the mainstream publics in both Israeli and Palestinian societies, although this is much more marked on the Israeli side.[13] For example, the Palestinians in the "Combatants for Peace" initiative discussed below maintain contacts with Israelis, recognize Israel, and support nonviolence. This is of course far from an uncontested consensus among Palestinians. But at the same time, many of them are members of the Fateh movement (the dominant force in the West Bank and in the official Palestinian Authority, as opposed to the currently Hamas-led Gaza Strip) and belong to the wing that opposes the armed struggle. Thus they have good relations with some officials in the Palestinian Authority, including the office of President Abu Mazen. As a result, some Palestinian officials participate in and support the activity of this group. On the other hand, Israeli officials actively try to prevent some of this group's activities: the ministry of foreign affairs instructed its embassies to use its influence on Jewish communities and student organizations abroad, demanding that activists of this group and similar organizations should not be invited to lecture. In the West Bank, tours organized by these movements are frequently blocked by the Israel Defense Force (IDF) or the police. This derives from the fact that those activists agree with the demand of ending the Israeli occupation, and present the occupation as the main reason for the conflict—a claim the Israeli government robustly denies.

Combatants' Groups   The position of former combatants is particularly important in attempts to influence societies to confront the past, and in many transitional contexts toward democracy, stability, or peace, ex-combatants have played an important role (see McEvoy, Mika, and McConnachie, forthcoming). In both Israeli and Palestinian society, combatants have an elevated status in public opinion, which enhances their message. We outline two major ex-combatants' groups here: Combatants for Peace and Breaking the Silence.

Established in 2005, Combatants for Peace consists both of former soldiers and officers in the Israeli Army (the IDF) who later, as reserve soldiers, refused to participate in army activities in the Occupied Territories, and of former Palestinian militants (mainly members of Fateh), who in the past took part in violence against Israel, were prisoners in Israeli jails, and now call for nonviolence. Their founding statement is: "We all used weapons against one another, and looked at each other only through weapon sights; however today we cooperate."[14] This group holds public meetings of a semiconfessional nature in which its members—both a Palestinian and an Israeli—share their narratives of the past: how they became involved in violence, details of the violence they inflicted, and their paths to nonviolence.[15] On some occasions this group invites Palestinian officials to attend their meetings. In a session in Jericho in April 2007, for example, the Palestinian district's governor, the mayor, the chief of the local police, and the head of the Palestinian negotiation team, Dr. Sa'eb Ariqat, attended and talked with the mixed audience. This is not the case in meetings held inside Israel, where the group is not recognized, let alone supported, by Israeli officials.

Another group of ex-combatants, Breaking the Silence (Shovrim Shtika in Hebrew), consists only of Israelis, mostly young soldiers who recently finished their compulsory service in the army. They aim to bring to the attention of Israeli society abuses committed by the army in the recent past of the second intifada. Beginning with a handful of discharged soldiers who shared their own stories from the West Bank, this group has since interviewed hundreds of soldiers and disseminated their unedited testimonies using their Web site, booklets, exhibitions, lectures, and tours. They define their goal as follows: "Israeli society must confront what's being done in its name and acknowledge the price of the reality to which it sends its sons and daughters."[16] This group also conducts "Tours of Breaking the Silence" in the Palestinian city of Hebron (which is partly under Israeli control), in which they told thousands of Israelis of their past experiences as soldiers. These tours were blocked by the Israeli police and IDF officers in Hebron, however. Only an appeal to the Israeli Supreme Court in May 2008 forced the army to enable their continuation.

While Israeli "peaceniks" are often attacked as being naive or even traitorous, such allegations cannot be so easily directed at former combatants, many of them veterans of elite army units. The same is true regarding the Palestinian members of Combatants for Peace, who have special status as former militants and ex-prisoners: thus their message cannot be easily sidelined by their compatriots. As Bassam Aramin, a member of the group, said: "We get respect in the Palestinian street, since we paid a price in prisons."[17]

Victims' Group   Another category with elevated status in both societies is that of victims of political violence, especially bereaved people who lost loved ones in the conflict. The Parents Circle/Bereaved Families Forum is a group of Israelis and Palestinians that lost relatives in the conflict and together advocate peace and nonviolence. This organization was established in 1996 and has been focusing on advocacy for peace. Recently, it started a project of dealing with the past, titled "Knowing Is the Beginning," in which dozens of members come together to share and discuss their personal and collective narratives of the conflict. In the first stage of this project, participants (Palestinians and Israelis) learned about both nations' collective narrative of the past and together visited sites of Palestinian villages that were destroyed in the 1948 war, as well as Yad Vashem, the Israeli holocaust memorial museum. In a subsequent stage the group moved to discuss family narratives and personal stories from the past of the conflict (Sharom Mishayker, interview with author, BFF, June 2007).[18]

Educational/Academic Projects   At least three projects that deal with the past have an educational/academic character. PRIME (Peace Research Institute in the Middle East) was founded by two academics, an Israeli and a Palestinian. Its main activity is a dual-narrative history project titled "Learning Each Other's Historical Narrative in Israeli and Palestinian Schools."[19] This project aims at engaging teachers on both sides in an entirely new collaborative process for teaching the history of the region, in which students in each community are exposed to the other's narrative of the same set of events (for more detail, see Adwan and Bar-On 2004). The first booklet, literally displaying a dual narrative placed on the right and the left of each page of Israeli-Palestinian history before 1948, has already been produced.[20]

A second project, conducted jointly by the Israeli Van-Leer Institute in Jerusalem and the al-Quds Palestinian University in East Jerusalem, aims to promote knowledge of the other's narrative. After a series of meetings between Israeli and Palestinian graduate students, who heard lectures on different historical topics from Palestinian and Israeli scholars, project members chose four topics and produced four booklets for high school students, with guides for Israeli and Palestinian teachers. Each booklet consists of Israeli and Palestinian narratives, in both Hebrew and Arabic, of the war of 1948, the refugee problem, the settlements, and Jerusalem: all central issues in—and obstacles to—Israeli-Palestinian relations. Finally, another book, titled *Shared Histories* (published by Pogrund and Salem, 2005), was the outcome of several workshops that brought together leading Israeli and Palestinian historians, academics, and journalists (e.g., Salim Tamari, Manuel Hassassian, Meron Benvenisti, Moshe Ma'aoz). They discussed both sides' narratives of key events in early phases of the conflict. Each book includes interventions on each topic by a Palestinian and an Israeli, followed by a polyphonic discussion of the joint group. The premise of this project is that "how the two sides understand—and misunderstand—their own and the 'other's' history has a profound influence on their ability—and inability—to make peace" (ibid.:1).

Activist Group   Perhaps the most publicly well known among the groups discussed here is Zochrot (in Hebrew, the feminine form of "remembering"). This is a group of Jewish-Israelis who seek to bring to Israeli society the memory of abuses committed by Israel against Palestinians in 1948 (the common Palestinian term to describe these events is the Nakba, meaning "the catastrophe" in Arabic), and to make Israeli society confront this legacy.[21] Zochrot uses diverse methods, printing publications in Hebrew, producing maps that include the sites of Palestinian villages or neighborhoods from which occupants were displaced in 1948, conducting tours to these sites, and organizing workshops and lectures with different groups of students, teachers, social activists, and so on, who want to learn about the Nakba. An additional activity—placing commemorative and informational signs at sites of displacement—became the trademark of this group. Zochrot works:

> to make the history of the Nakba accessible to the Israeli public so as to engage Jews and Palestinians in an open recounting of our painful common history.

We hope that by bringing the Nakba into Hebrew, the language spoken by the Jewish majority in Israel, we can make a qualitative change in the political discourse of this region. Acknowledging the past is the first step in taking responsibility for its consequences.[22]

Dialogue Group   Finally, the Ya'ad-Mi'ar group, which consists of Jewish-Israelis and Palestinian citizens of Israel, engages in dialogues about the past. Mi'ar was a Palestinian village until its inhabitants were uprooted during the 1948 war. They became "internal refugees" in nearby villages, and their land was transferred to the state. Ya'ad is a Jewish village in the north of Israel built on former agricultural lands that belonged to Mi'ar. An area between the two villages, the site of Mia'r's old cemetery and the remnants of a few buildings, were left untouched for decades until a local authority planned to build a highway through it. Members of both villages opposed the plan (originally for different motivations) together, which has led to an initiative to conduct a joint dialogue group consisting of members of both villages. This dialogue focused on collective and personal narratives of the past for these two communities (Back 2006).

Analysis

Origins and Actors

It is quite remarkable that so many initiatives that deal with the past already exist at this stage of the conflict. How might we account for this trend? One explanation could be simply that awareness of the negative effects of neglecting this angle during the Oslo process has spread. Another could be that knowledge of transitional justice mechanisms elsewhere in the world has filtered into the area, even if in a belated and fragmented manner, especially in the academic circles that were behind some of these initiatives.

Additionally, some Israeli activists' energies might have been channeled toward these activities as other avenues were closed or became unattractive. For various reasons the political system in Israel has reached stagnation, with a series of national unity governments, a lack of clear differences between the major parties, and a collapse of the main left opposition parties. All of these developments make party-political activities unappealing. While during the 1980s and the 1990s extra-parliamentary peace organizations were able to attract thousands (and at times tens of thousands) of demonstrators on a fairly regular basis, this is no longer the case, and participation in movements such as Peace Now has waned. Human rights organizations, as well as think tanks or Track II activities, require professionals and do not offer many opportunities to volunteers. The above combination of circumstances, aided by a general sense of frustration and hopelessness regarding civil society's ability to affect the present situation, may have channeled energies toward the projects described here. In addition, it should be noted that, in contrast to many other conflict situations, oppositional civil society can work in relative freedom in Israel, as official harassment by the government is (comparatively) very low.[23]

Many of these initiatives seem to have their origins in spontaneous processes, often starting almost by chance. Zochrot began when its founder started placing signs on the sites of several destroyed Palestinian villages, without planning to start an organization. Attracting attention and sparking a debate, his initiative was transformed into a professional organization (Eitan Bronstein, interview with author, June 2007). The Ya'ad-Mi'ar group also started as a result of a chance development: the struggle against the planning authority. Shovrim Shtika was generated by the frustration of several individual soldiers who gave press interviews, and who also, it seems, did not plan to found an ongoing movement. In the case of Combatants for Peace, the practice of focusing on personal narratives emerged during the group's consolidation and was not a preconceived concept (Zohar Shapira, interview with author, Combatants for Peace, June 2007). In one of Ron Dudai's early interviews with a Combatants for Peace member, after hearing about the organization's methods he raised the issue of similarities with transitional justice approaches in other countries and asked whether they were inspired by these. Slightly impatiently, the interviewee finally said: "Look, this is the Middle East. We don't do comparative research. Someone thought, 'It's a good idea,' phone calls were being made, we've started rolling; that's it" (Avichai, interview with author, June 2007). This refreshing answer can be seen as an indicator of the strength and viability of this organization—beginning not with an imitation of something from abroad, but with an implicit understanding of the importance of these actions. It is important to note, however, that some of these projects, such as PRIME and Shared Histories, do seem to have started in a more premeditated way, consciously echoing and inspired by transitional justice activities elsewhere in the world.

Methods

While some of the groups described above report and document past human rights abuses, these activities are much less central than in many other contexts (such as the civil society work in Brazil mentioned above). Given that conventional human rights activism, academic historical work, and journalistic reporting already operate without major constraints, the focus of these groups is less on factual documentation and more on personal stories, testimonies or narratives, oral history, and the transplantation of known facts into a new dual-narrative format. These personal narratives, as we have seen, are disseminated in a variety of ways, including printed publications, Web sites, exhibitions, lectures, and public meetings. Mostly, these take a format very different from that of human rights NGO reports. Although, for example, the booklets produced by Breaking the Silence include testimonies of abuses by soldiers, these are meant to speak for themselves and are not complemented by legal analysis in the manner of reports by human rights NGOs. In addition, members of Breaking the Silence are much younger than the staff of the established NGOs and are not yet "professionals": most are in their early twenties and have not yet (or have only just) entered their university studies or careers. The members of Combatants for Peace are not employed by the group but participate in its activities on their own expenses and time. It should be stressed, however, that members of these two groups coordinate their activities with each other as well as with established NGOs, such as B'Tselem, when they see it as advantageous for their purpose. Some of the other initiatives, like Zochrot, also rely on paid staff in addition to volunteers and have a more established character.

Another difference concerns the production of new school textbooks as a method of dealing with the past. The reform of textbooks has thus far been in the margins of the transitional justice field (see Cole 2007): although curriculum change has occasionally been dealt with in the literature (e.g., Freedman et al. 2004), this issue does not feature prominently in the common "menus" of transitional justice work.[24] The attention paid to this issue by some Israeli-Palestinian groups, developed somewhat independently from the mainstream of transitional justice, attests to its urgency (perhaps in line with other calls to focus on textbooks worldwide—see Cole 2007). In both Israeli and Palestinian schools, teachers usually use textbooks with biases and stereotypes, offering narratives of the past in which the "enemy" has committed nothing but atrocities, whereas one's own side is nothing but an innocent victim. Though there were a few changes in this regard, mainly after Oslo agreements (see Moughrabi 2001; Podeh 2002), the "traditional" narratives still predominate. Reforming the textbooks, integrating elements from the Palestinian national narrative into the Israeli curriculum and vice versa, could have an important role in the process toward truth seeking and acknowledgment.[25] The very process of producing these books is important in itself: in addition to state-sponsored changes, civil society organizations initiated joint workshops of Israeli and Palestinian teachers and historians who deliberate these issues, and in which the participants themselves experience a significant development. The novelty of having a dual narrative makes these textbooks interesting reading for adults as well as school students.[26]

Public tours are also a less conventional method in transitional justice activities (or human rights advocacy) elsewhere. As we have described, Zochrot uses tours to sites of destroyed Palestinian villages or of battles/massacres from the 1948 war, with refugees serving as guides, as a means to convey the past to Israeli society. Breaking the Silence, in addition, operates tours to areas of the West Bank, where ex-combatants serve as guides, explaining about abuses by the Israeli army. (Tours in general have become a popular tool of human rights organizations in the area: there are also tours of East Jerusalem, and tours to the West Bank Wall/Barrier). In this age of internet and information technologies, one might have expected that getting people on a bus and going on a tour for several hours would not be a sustainable option, yet these tours have proven to be an important method.

All these methods—conveying personal testimonies of known events, creating dual-narrative textbooks, tours guided by victims or ex-combatants—seem to respond to the particular situation in the Israeli-Palestinian context. The facts of the past are usually commonly known; the problem lies in the intricate ways in which individuals and societies manage to deny them in practice (Cohen 2001). These activities, then, are less about producing new facts and new knowledge, and more about creating "acknowledgment" (ibid.).

Dilemmas

Should Activities Look at Actions of Both Sides of the Conflict?

As discussed above, some initiatives, such as Zochrot and Breaking the Silence, engage only with abuses by Israelis, whereas others, such as Combatants for Peace, at least in theory cover both sides. This opens the question of what is the right course. This dilemma is based on the asymmetry in power relations between Israelis and Palestinians: Israel is the stronger force, the occupier, whereas the Palestinians are victims of the occupation (and of discrimination within the borders of Israel). For some, this asymmetry leads to the conclusion that dealing with the past should focus exclusively on Israeli abuses. However, any confrontation with the past must be honest and complete, and cannot ignore the various abuses committed by Palestinians during their struggle, most notably the systematic pattern of attacks against Israeli civilians. These attacks have reached a record with the suicide bombings of the second intifada but have been a feature of the conflict since before 1948—as, of course, were Israeli attacks against Palestinian civilians. The challenge is to look at both sides without creating a false balance, or in other words to confront Palestinian abuses without distorting the structural issue of occupation. An important analogy in this context is the scope of the South African TRC: while finding that the structural issue in that country's past had been apartheid, and that the struggle of the liberation movement was justified, it also condemned abuses committed by anti-apartheid organizations (which included attacks against white civilians, against supporters of rival anti-apartheid groups, and against suspected collaborators with the apartheid regime). Without creating a balance between apartheid and anti-apartheid, the TRC managed to convey the message that the ends do not justify the means. Such an approach should guide the efforts in the Middle East. The important issue is reciprocity—the willingness of Palestinians to confront their own crimes and mistakes—rather than balance.

It should be added that for some the choice of focusing only on Israel is tactical: some Israelis feel comfortable and confident to call their own society to account, but not the other side's (Eitan Brunstein, interview with author, June 2007). There are also numerous practical and political challenges in arranging for joint activities, and at times some Palestinian civil society groups even declared a boycott on joint activities with Israelis (on this and other issues of joint activity, see Cohen 2007:137–49). Another concern relates to the problematic legacy of joint "people-to-people" activities during the Oslo period, which often ended up as purely "feel-good" enterprises, disengaged from the political reality (Tamari 2006). These considerations are valid. However, unconditional solidarity with Palestinians by Israelis does not seem a fruitful way to engage with the past.

Should the Goal Be One Common Narrative?

For many observers, the starting point of the discussion is that both sides have two contradictory narratives,[27] which creates an impediment for peacemaking. The question is how to respond to that situation: should the ambition be to create, at the end of the process, one broadly shared narrative? Or perhaps the ambition should be different: to reach a situation in which both sides recognize the legitimacy of the other's narrative, without necessarily accepting it as the full objective truth.

The aim, it is argued here, should not be to convert one side to the narrative of the other or to create one common history that would somehow merge the two narratives. Rather, the goal should be to acknowledge both narratives, to make each legitimate in the eyes of the other. This is not meant as a postmodern affirmation of all versions as equally valid: some facts must be recognized. An oft-quoted articulation of the goals of a truth commission is "to narrow the range of permissible lies" (Ignatieff 1996). A similar goal should apply to Israeli-Palestinian discourse; perhaps the gap between the two narratives should be reduced, and some events and policies no longer denied. But exact agreement on the meaning of such events is unattainable, and perhaps unnecessary. The point is to accept that the other has its own legitimate, coherent, and meaningful historical narrative, and that the existence of an alternative narrative does not necessarily pose a threat to one's own side. It should also be emphasized that one does not have to accept the historical interpretation of the other side as authoritative in order to empathize with the other's suffering. Hence, one can empathize with the suffering of a refugee without necessarily accepting that refugee's version of who was responsible for the suffering.

The basic issue of vocabulary can serve to illustrate this point. Perhaps the most prevalent example is that of the events of 1947–48, which are termed the "war of independence" by Israelis, and "Nakba" by Palestinians. It seems ludicrous to expect that all Israelis or Palestinians will adopt the other side's term; and it is perhaps equally unhelpful to demand that both adopt some sterile term such as "The 1948 War" (the term used in this chapter). Each should be entitled to use its own narrative: the goal, ideally, is that Israelis would not be scared when Palestinians use the word *Nakba* in their company, and Palestinians would accept that Israelis would probably never disavow their own term. The plural in the title of the "Shared Histories" project is an important indication of such an approach.

The Role of International Influence

A final, tentative, question is whether adopting the international framework of "transitional justice" would be fully beneficial for these activities. As we argue above, many of these initiatives started as an organic idea, an indigenous and spontaneous development in response to the specific situation in the area. But what happens when organic, spontaneous, and indigenous projects that start with grounded understandings meet up with the preestablished international framework of transitional justice, with its own vocabulary, structures, and money? What would happen when enthusiastic and well-meaning consultants, officers of funding agencies, or law school interns from Europe and North America come to work in the area after "smelling" transitional justice beginnings?

The usage of the international terminology of transitional justice has some contradictory effects. On the one hand, it helps the Israelis and Palestinians involved in such activities feel part of a larger international community, with shared values, and, moreover, with some historical successes. As these activists, at least on the Israeli side, are often isolated and in the margins of the mainstream, it gives them the feeling of a community and eases their political loneliness. Some people and institutions in Israel use this language already; they feel that they are part of the international community from their very beginnings and see their role as intermediates between Israel and the West. On the other hand, the very use of international language (let alone funding) positions these groups in an unpopular corner: one of the main debates in Israeli and Palestinian societies concerns giving up "authentic values" and adopting "foreign" ones instead. In this context, international language might alienate the mainstream of society, or at least the conservatives among them.

A further concern relates to the role of funding agencies. Most peace and human rights initiatives rely on funding from abroad (from foundations such as the Ford Foundation, the EU, foreign governments, etc.). These sometime affect the practice of organizations. As Hermann (2006) writes in her overview of peace organizations in Israel, new organizations "often were not only supported by external donors but their structure and mode of action were strongly influenced by donor suggestions." This echoes De Waal's concept of "donorism": the way ideas follow money, rather than the other way around.[28] There is a concern that in order to get funding, individuals and organizations will phrase their activity in a way that appeals abroad—especially in the case of transitional justice, which is very prominent among many leading organizations in North America and Europe. For example, it can mean adopting key words such as reconciliation, which are perhaps premature and unfitting to the situation of the Israeli-Palestinian conflict. This can also be a product of involving consultants and academics from abroad, who are well versed in the transitional justice repertoire but do not always have sufficient understanding of the specific, complex—and sometimes peculiar—conditions in the Israeli and Palestinian societies, and who through advisory roles (and sometimes the ability to fund) may influence organizations to direct their activity in line with international frameworks.[29]

A third concern derives from the popularity of the initiatives discussed in Europe and the United States. Partly because of their need to raise funds, partly because of their wish to be out of the region for a while, and partly out of the need to meet supportive rather than hostile audiences, some members of these initiatives may prefer to lecture abroad and neglect the harder challenges at home. It is also important, however, to acknowledge the benefits to local groups of learning about international examples and structures. The final point remains, nevertheless, that donors, consultants, and NGOs from abroad must emphasize humility and be sensitive to the peculiar situation of Israelis and Palestinians. They should refrain not only from imposing, but also from overly "marketing" mechanisms that may have worked elsewhere but might not be appropriate for the Middle East. It is also important to point out that such interactions should be a two-way learning process: those in major U.S. and European organizations could learn from, not just teach, local civil society organizations.

Before concluding this chapter, we wish to emphasize again that although our focus was primarily the Israeli-Palestinian case, the themes raised here—especially that of the role of civil society and the possibility of engaging with the past before a transition—may have broader applicability. We hope that this chapter has relevance beyond this particular case, and that it may contribute to the analysis of and prognosis for other conflict situations.

Conclusions: Appraising the Impact

As with most cases of human rights or transitional justice initiatives, the final question must address the impact or success of the initiatives described above. This question should be contextualized and answered in a nuanced way.

On the one hand, it is important to note that the dedicated activists who spend most of their time working on these issues probably number a few dozen, and in any case no more than a few hundred. With ten million Palestinians and Israelis living in Israel, the West Bank, and Gaza, this is just a beginning. Yet these numbers can mislead: there are plenty more people who occasionally participate in activities, come to tours or public meetings, are exposed to publications, and serve as a much wider circle of supporters (Eitan Bronstein, Zochrot, and Zohar Shapira, Combatants for Peace, interviews with author). These people, in turn, may influence their friends, families, and associates, while numerous others are exposed to these activities through the media.[30] In any case, the number of active supporters and the volume of activities become much more impressive when one considers that not only is the current situation in the area far from a transition, but in fact the conflict is still ongoing, with high levels of animosity and no effective negotiations between the two sides. If in this situation we witness all these initiatives, the numbers could become much higher if a more positive atmosphere, even short of full peace, were to prevail.

But while events organized by Combatants for Peace draw growing numbers of participants, they also generate criticism from the right-wing side of the political map, as well as from many ordinary people. When this group organized a commemoration of both Israeli and Palestinian victims of the conflict for the second time in 2008, on the official Commemoration Day for Fallen Israeli soldiers, this attracted hundreds of people. But it also generated hundreds of negative responses in "talk-backs" in the newspapers and Web sites that reported this event. In a way, provoking such responses is also important: even if there is not broad agreement with the message, such an event at least turns the official narrative of the past into a question that needs to be answered, rather than something that is unreflexively accepted. Yet in the final account it is important to acknowledge that these activities, currently, are at the margins of Israeli society (and in a different way, of Palestinian society).

It is also important not to become overenthusiastic and to remain aware of the inherent limitations of civil society. For example, Israeli members of the initiatives described here might come to agree with the demands of the Palestinian members regarding the release of Palestinian prisoners from Israeli prisons, but they are powerless to actually achieve this—unlike officials of the state. A similar point can be made about apologies and acknowledgment: while victims may be encouraged to hear these from the other side's civil society, the effects of a governmental apology for past human rights violations, or at least an official acknowledgment, would be, of course, stronger. Thus, civil society can contribute to a process of dealing with the past but, even at its best, cannot serve as a full substitute for official governmental mechanisms. In addition, while locally based civil society initiatives—whether in transitional justice, human rights, or peacebuilding—do often have the potential to spread and gradually affect high-level policymaking, the term "bottom-*up*," used so often in the literature (and indeed in this chapter), is a wish rather than an accurate description of many of these projects. Frequently, the accurate description should be "bottom-*bottom*," as the initiatives often do not break from their immediate circles and influence society's leadership. Even such "bottom-bottom" initiatives play a very important role, however. Among other things, they give all those people who are ready to hear the "other" voice an opportunity to do so—which the state does not. They also give those from both sides who wish to air their feelings, to "confess," to publicize their regret, a space in which it is legitimate and desirable to do so. But one should not assume that such activities will *automatically* succeed in influencing policymakers.

As we pointed out above, these initiatives should be seen as performing two tasks. First, they are part of an effort of conflict transformation, contributing to a broad societal and cultural process that might hopefully pave the eventual way to successful negotiations between the Israeli and Palestinian leaderships. Second, if and when such successful negotiations are achieved, the earlier civil society work could serve as a foundation for official mechanisms of dealing with the past.[31] It is evidently too early to measure impact in either of these processes. No realistic observer would expect the organizations discussed above to change the prevailing state of mind in the Middle East in any short period of time. Such changes happen in a gradual and fragmented way. Nevertheless, as Hermann (2006) argues, although peace and conflict-resolution civil society organizations in Israel tend not to directly affect specific policies or decisions, "they are much better at laying the groundwork for cognitive changes and introducing new options for the national repertoire." That is exactly the potential of the organizations discussed here, a potential that will be tested over time.

In the more immediate term, however, the mere existence of these initiatives in these difficult times is critical in itself, sending an important message that it is indeed possible for Israelis and Palestinians to confront past abuses and suffering. They thereby present an alternative to the current mainstream discourse, building trust and keeping open the channels of communication between segments of both societies. Their members include ex-combatants, former prisoners, academics, schoolteachers, human rights activists, and bereaved families from all walks of life; they use diverse methods, and range from professional organizations with budgets and paid staff to loose movements based on volunteers. They all create what might be described as a "small niche of sanity." Within each group, serving as a potential microcosm of the Israeli-Palestinian world, a significant process of conflict transformation and confronting the past has already taken place, demonstrating to their societies, amidst the violence and animosity, that such a process is feasible. Even if that is all they will achieve, that is already considerable.

Chapter 12

Local Transitional Justice Practice in Pretransition Burma

Patrick Falvey

Burma is headed for a transition, and Burma's military government, the State Peace and Development Council (SPDC), is directing the process. Over the next few years, the regime's plan is to implement its "roadmap to a democracy," securing a continued leading role in Burmese political life for the Burmese armed forces, known in Burmese as the Tatmadaw, under a facade of a transition to democracy. Within this context, transitional justice becomes relevant in preparation for any cracks in that facade that may emerge. In addition, as several of the other chapters in this volume demonstrate, consideration of justice in a "transitional period" may benefit from an expanded, long-term conceptualization of the boundaries of transition.

No system of repression is fully effective, and resistance to the military's violence has existed since military rule was established in 1962. This chapter analyzes local transitional justice initiatives that aim not only to catalyze democratic change in Burma but also to prepare for the challenges that will emerge under democratic rule. Those initiatives—community-based human rights documentation and transitional justice trainings—demonstrate a localized transitional justice framework that seeks to draw from the field to support a place-based, grassroots approach to justice. Such a framework raises the question, "What do local actors mean by 'justice'?" This paper also explores a range of local actors' responses to that question and emphasizes the importance of considering the concept of justice before a transition begins in Burma.

These local initiatives draw on comparative cases where the social and political momentum to seek justice for past atrocities has been stalled (as in Argentina) or delayed (as in Cambodia) but then gained speed decades later.

Taking the long view, then, in this pretransition setting, the initiatives explored in this chapter aim to further the goals of seeking truth, gaining justice, and ending impunity. The meanings of these concepts vary across cultures, and even from person to person. For one, justice may connote a trial where a perpetrator is found guilty, while another may view equal access to quality education as a justice issue. Similarly, for some people seeking truth means gathering evidence by, for example, writing down people's stories of suffering and resistance. For others, the most important aspect of seeking truth is having those experiences acknowledged in an official manner. The early involvement of local actors in defining those goals may lead to the development of a transitional justice policy that is more effective in addressing the priorities and concerns of those people most affected by the violence.

Toward these ends, this paper identifies the importance of taking the long view and localizing transitional justice through place-based engagement and broadening understandings of justice through this engagement. This chapter examines local initiatives that have an eye on, but are not waiting for, a future transition—human rights documentation and trainings that explore scenarios for change. It then turns to look at justice through a diversity of local views and considers the power dynamics inherent in assessing those views.

Background of the Conflicts

The story of the conflicts in Burma is, in many ways, the same story about conflicts in many other societies: colonial rulers who drew new national borders, uniting groups that previously did not have a shared identity but are now bound together; violent clashes over access and control of natural resources; rulers bent on exploiting ethnic differences; and harsh restrictions on personal freedoms that force dissent underground.

Under military rule since 1962, the regime's opponents have suffered atrocities that many analysts consider crimes against humanity, including forced labor, forced relocations, extrajudicial killings, rape, and political imprisonment, among other abuses.[1] Generally speaking, people in urban centers in central Burma who participate in demonstrations or are seen by the regime as potential organizers of resistance are under constant threat of intimidation, physical and mental torture, and long prison sentences under inhumane conditions. This threat is all the more pronounced since the crackdown on monk-led mass demonstrations in September 2007. People in the rural areas of the plains endure forced labor and can be taken as porters to accompany military battalions and carry their supplies. People in areas where fighting continues are subjected to forced labor, forced relocations, torture, rape, killings, and having to serve as human minesweepers (Fink 2001). For many people throughout the country, economic hardship makes mere survival a daily challenge.

The most commonly known figure opposing the regime is Daw Aung San Suu Kyi, General Secretary of the National League for Democracy (NLD) and 1991 Nobel Peace Prize laureate. The NLD won over 80 percent of the parliamentary seats in the 1990 national elections, which the military never recognized. For people who like clear lines between virtuous and evil, "the Lady versus the Generals" is an appealing myth. In reality, there are two major conflicts, distinct but related, in Burma. One is the struggle for democracy, with the NLD leading the opposition, strongly allied with a movement of students and former students, artists, and, since mass demonstrations in August and September 2007, Buddhist monks. The other struggle is for ethnic nationalities' rights, variously termed autonomy, self-determination, or independence depending on one's political hue.[2] While distinct struggles, many prodemocracy activists recognize the issues of the ethnic nationalities as essential in the push for democracy, and many ethnic leaders view democratic governance as a vital tool for ensuring their rights.

Administratively, Burma is divided into seven divisions and seven states. These divisions are largely populated by the Burman majority and lie geographically in a central valley. The seven states—Karen, Kachin, Chin, Shan, Karenni, Mon, and Arakan—each carry the name of its largest ethnic nationality. Together, these states form a mountainous horseshoe along Burma's borders. About two-thirds of the population of approximately fifty million people is ethnically Burman. Ethnic nationalities are the dominant population in at least half the territory of Burma, speaking over a hundred different dialects.

During precolonial times and even under British rule, ethnic nationalities controlled their own polities away from Burman rule and have since sought political arrangements reflecting that autonomy. The British agreed to grant independence on the condition that the political status of the non-Burman groups be resolved, a condition that was hindered by the assassination of independence hero General Aung San, who had forged the tenuous "Panglong Agreement" with a range of representatives from Shan, Kachin, and Chin ethnic nationalities to develop a political system acceptable to all (Fink 2001).[3]

Following independence in 1948, Prime Minister U Nu led a democratic government for a decade. However, ethnic nationalities along the country's borders had growing concerns about the central government's exploitation of their natural resources and its nationalist vision, favoring the dominant Burman culture, including Burmese language and Buddhism. The government did very little to promote development outside of Burman-dominated areas, and U Nu sought to make Buddhism the state religion. Soon, the Kachin, Shan, Karen, and other nationalities took up arms and launched a civil war, or more accurately, civil wars, threatening dissolution of the union. Following a period as head of a caretaker military government from 1958 to 1960, General Ne Win staged a coup d'etat in 1962, prompted by a conference on federalism that U Nu agreed to attend with ethnic leaders to consider renegotiating the powers of the ethnic states (Smith 1999:195). The military has ruled Burma since then.

After the 1962 coup, Ne Win implemented the "Burmese Way to Socialism," a mix of Marxism, Buddhism, and Burmese nationalist ideology that also closed Burma's borders almost completely, isolating Burma from the rest of the world. He also nationalized industry, and state enterprises were notoriously corrupt, inefficient, and unproductive. Regarding the ongoing ethnic conflicts, official rhetoric insisted that federalism would inevitably lead to anarchy, and only the armed forces could prevent such chaos (Smith 1999:195). In response to periodic shows of resistance to the repression, usually led or supported by students, the Tatmadaw did not hesitate to brutally repress unarmed citizens in central, Burman-dominated areas of Burma (Callahan 2003:223).

Outside of Burman-dominated areas, ethnic armies continued to defend areas under their control, and the Tatmadaw carried out counterinsurgency campaigns against them and the local populations. The brutality polarized the already violent relations between the ethnic nationalities and the military government. According to political scientist Mary Callahan, the regime viewed any group opposing its rule as an enemy of the state. Therefore, it sought to annihilate any opposition rather than addressing legitimate political concerns through negotiation, compromise, or accommodation. Callahan argues that the ruling junta are first and foremost army commanders who view political problems only through a military lens (Callahan 2003:2–20).

By 1987, Burma's economy was in a steady decline, gaining it a "least developed country" designation by the United Nations. The regime's isolation cut it off from the economic growth in the Southeast Asian region. In March 1988, a skirmish in a Rangoon tea shop erupted between college students and local youth, including the son of a government official, about the music the tea shop was playing. Following further clashes with the police, a student named

Phone Maw was killed, sparking a series of student demonstrations that drew on the broad discontent throughout Burma. On July 23, Ne Win unexpectedly announced he would resign, but demonstrations continued. A nationwide people's uprising on August 8, 1988, drew violent reaction from the military, whose troops fired on the unarmed crowds. The military then retreated, and with security forces suddenly absent from the streets, the ensuing six weeks, while chaotic, also saw the sudden emergence of civil society, hundreds of new uncensored circulars, and heated debates within the prodemocracy movement about ways forward. Just as it seemed a unified prodemocracy front would emerge, the military staged an "auto-coup" and cleared out strike centers, shooting anyone who resisted and killing hundreds (Fink 2001:51–63). Renaming itself the State Law and Order Restoration Council (SLORC), the military declared itself a transitional regime and promised multiparty democratic elections.[4]

The SLORC changed Ne Win's policy of isolation and began allowing foreign investment. When they held elections in 1990 and were overwhelmingly voted out of power, however, the regime refused to recognize the results of the elections. The SLORC also negotiated more aggressively with the armed ethnic nationalities throughout the 1990s and reached ceasefire agreements with almost all of them.[5] Burmese scholars Zaw Oo and Win Min suggest that with the ceasefires the SLORC was "hoping to neutralize certain ethnic resistance groups and to weaken the armed ethnic movement over time, without having to agree to a political settlement" (2007). The SLORC renamed itself in 1997, becoming the State Peace and Development Council (SPDC).

"Transition"

Since before the 1990 elections, the ruling military junta has maintained that it is a transitional regime willing to transfer power after the drafting of a new constitution. It claims to be directing a transition to "disciplined-flourishing democracy" through a seven-step roadmap, which began with the convening of a national convention in 1993, leading to the drafting of a new constitution that was put to a national referendum in May 2008, followed by national elections slated for 2010. According to SLORC Declaration No. 11/92 (SLORC 1992), the national convention process, stalled and reconvened for fourteen years, aimed to "lay down the basic principles for the drafting of a firm and stable constitution." The SPDC mandated six objectives on which the constitution would be based. Noteworthy among those guidelines is the sixth objective, outlined in SLORC Order No. 13/92 (SLORC 1992), "For the Tatmadaw to be able to participate in the national political leadership role of the State." In addition, the SPDC hand-picked most delegates for the national convention, and convention organizers muted open debate and discussion (Arnott 2004; United Nations 2004b). The NLD eventually refused to participate in the convention, criticizing the process for its lack of democratic standards (National League for Democracy 1995, 2004). The national convention concluded with little fanfare in September 2007, just before the crackdown on mass demonstrations. The SPDC announced a referendum for May 2008, released the final draft of the constitution, and slated elections for 2010.

As details emerged of the actual content of the constitution, the undemocratic nature of the "transition" became obvious. The constitution designates 25 percent of the parliament seats to be occupied by military personnel, appointed by the commander-in-chief. The judiciary lacks independence, and ordinary courts are allowed no jurisdiction over armed services branches or personnel, and most provisions that articulate citizens' rights contain exceptions that could exclude opponents of the regime of those rights. The 2008 constitution also includes provisions for declaring a state of emergency that would legalize rather than prevent an extended period of dictatorship. Finally, the constitution contains daunting requirements for the passage of amendments—approval by 75 percent of the parliament and by 50 percent of the public in a national referendum—dashing prospects for treating it as a first step in a democratic direction. On the whole, the 2008 constitution seeks not to open the door for democratic reform but aims to preserve the military's hold on state power.

Before the August and September 2007 demonstrations, and with the failure of the 1988 demonstrations to wrest control from the military and the defensive nature of the armed resistance, most mainstream political actors and observers believed a negotiated settlement would be the most likely scenario for a transition to democratic rule. They held this view while also recognizing that the regime's main goal was to retain state power. This assumption of an elite-driven negotiated settlement began to lose traction in the lead-up to the May 2008 referendum, with many analysts beginning to view the regime (or at least the SPDC supreme commander, Than Shwe) as impossible to negotiate with (Min Zin 2008). The Tatmadaw has continued armed attacks, not only on the eastern border but also against ceasefire troops on the northern border that have resisted the regime's efforts to bring them under its direct command before the 2010 elections (Kramer 2009). These attacks, along with the harsh sentences handed down to the activists who organized the 2007 demonstrations and the ongoing house arrest of Daw Aung San Suu Kyi, make prospects for negotiations appear dim indeed.

Given the restrictions on open political discussions, the process of setting an effective transitional agenda and ranking priorities is rife with difficulties. Transitional justice is a particularly delicate topic among the prodemocracy movement, and has been since 1988, as there is a common perception that equates justice with revenge. Following the NLD's 1990 election victory, in an interview with a foreign journalist, NLD leader U Kyi Maung made a reference to Nuremberg-style trials in discussing Burma's transition (Faulder 1990). In a July 1990 speech, General Khin Nyunt confronted U Kyi Maung publicly about this statement (Working People's Daily 1990). Many observers point to this incident as a major indication of the military regime's fears in turning over power to the NLD.

It is reasonable to believe that the generals are worried about being held accountable for the violence they have inflicted, and so will never agree to give up power if they fear retribution by the people. In fact, the 2008 constitution includes an immunity clause, effectively providing a self-amnesty for the regime. Chapter XIV "Transitory Provisions," Article 445 states, "No proceeding shall be instituted against [either individuals or groups who are members of SLORC and SPDC] in respect to any act done in the execution of their respective duties." Many people engaged in the prodemocracy and ethnic rights movements assume that public discussion about accountability for human rights abuses will polarize any potential political dialogue, tantamount to backing the ruling military junta into a corner (Sein Beida 1996; Smith 1999:415).[6] NLD leader Daw Aung San Suu Kyi seems to have taken a softer stand on the issue. In a 1999 videotaped interview smuggled out of Burma, she was asked to give some final words. She said, "I do believe that justice will prevail in the end. But don't forget that justice has always . . . to be tempered by mercy. So when your side prevails, don't be unmerciful to your opponents because there's none of us who could do without mercy" (Altsean-Burma 1999).[7]

The demonstrations in 2007 held potential for forcing the military to the negotiating table. In response to criticism for the violent crackdown, the SPDC wrapped up the national convention and pointed to this milestone as evidence of its progress on the roadmap (Human Rights Watch, April 30, 2008). They then finalized the constitution, organized a national referendum to approve it, and slated elections for 2010. The referendum was held despite the humanitarian crisis caused by Cyclone Nargis, which hit the former capital Rangoon and the Irrawaddy River Delta on May 3, causing tens of thousands of deaths and affecting 2.4 million people (Center for Excellence in Disaster Management and Humanitarian Assistance 2008). This movement along the roadmap points less to a genuine willingness to facilitate a transition than to the military regime's insistence on securing its long-term role in the political leadership of the country.

Taking the Long-term View of Transitional Justice

Since the 1962 coup, Burmese military leaders have insisted that the military is the only institution capable of holding the country together. The junta promotes itself as a unifying force, when in fact their military-based approach fuels the conflicts, a situation of "internal colonization" (Tharckabaw 2000). Much of the advocacy that comes from opposition groups, in the form of human rights reports, lobbying at the UN, and consultations on governments' policies toward Burma, point to the military leaders, part of the state institution, as the perpetrators of violence. Where an ethnic component exists in their analysis, it is in the military's targeting of members of ethnic nationalities with alleged links to ethnic armed opposition. In interviews I have conducted with members of ethnic nationalities about human rights violations, victims and witnesses frequently say "the Burmans arrived . . ." and, upon request for clarification, state that by "Burmans" they mean military troops.

On the other hand, the political opposition includes students and monks, many of whom are Burman, as well as ethnic nationalities organizations. Many leading civil society umbrella groups, such as the Women's League of Burma, are comprised of both Burman and non-Burman members. Shallow analysis of the complexities of the conflicts could easily conflate them to be "age-old tribal conflicts" rather than a multilayered set of power dynamics. In contrast, a place-based engagement that starts with how communities affected by the violence talk about and understand the conflict can lead to better transitional justice policy and practice. Initiatives that develop from that impulse have emerged with a view toward long-term justice.

NGOs and community-based organizations on the Thai–Burma border, keen to build trust among ethnic groups and to develop innovative ways to address the conflicts, began transitional justice programs in 2001, at a time when Daw Aung San Suu Kyi was freed from house arrest (temporarily, as it turned out) and prospects for a negotiated transition seemed more likely than they had since the 1990 elections.[8] These initiatives drew heavily on comparative cases of transition and analysis of emerging trends in transitional justice, including postrepression settings such as those in South America's southern cone, and the growing prevalence of international courts, especially the ad hoc tribunals for Rwanda and the former Yugoslavia. These projects—human rights documentation and trainings that analyze developments in transitional justice and Burma's current events—began from the principle that grassroots communities that have suffered under military rule *can* and *should* have a role in defining the terms of the transition. At present, grassroots communities have little access to policy decisions, but through transitional justice projects they can gain the tools to develop their own response to the violence and strengthen their hand as they seek to contribute to the political process.

Place-Based Engagement: Documentation, Truth Seeking, and Trainings

Despite the unpredictability of a transition in Burma, some sectors of Burmese civil society see transitional justice initiatives as an urgent, if little-recognized, need. Their work includes trainings and advocacy involving former political prisoners, legal experts, and organizations involved in human rights documentation, environmental activism, and development. The organizations with bases in neighboring countries operate cross-border and with underground activists inside the country. Cooperation between local actors and the international community aims to have a positive effect on the push for a transition to democracy in Burma and to bring some innovation to the transitional justice field. However, as evidenced in many of the chapters in this volume (on Uganda, Sierra Leone, and other countries), the international community's priorities often diverge from those of the local communities.

As communities from Burma aspire to end military rule, one can predict that the legacy of human rights abuses will become a contentious issue. A key strategy toward developing a culture of human rights entails the empowerment of communities to have a say in the policies that affect them. While working at HREIB from 2001 to 2007, I organized transitional justice trainings— usually five-day courses that include comparative case studies—that addressed the question of localizing transitional justice. How have local communities in Argentina, Uganda, and Timor-Leste pursued their agendas for justice, not only in relation to the perpetrators, but also amid often competing local, national, and international agendas? What lessons can women's groups, youth groups, political parties, and former political prisoners gain from these comparative cases? While the answers vary depending on the group, one consistent answer from community-based organizations that have taken transitional justice trainings has been "human rights documentation."

Human Rights Documentation

Many Burmese human rights organizations see a broad and systematic accounting of human rights violations as the first step on the path to dealing with a history of suffering. The opposition movement uses human rights data as a tool to appeal to the international community for assistance and to motivate people inside Burma to resist the regime. Activists also plan to use the data in a transitional setting to promote accountability. Such a historical record will reveal the structure that allows that impunity and will implicate the people involved, providing the basis for dismantling that structure. It will also reveal the heterogeneity of histories of violence in Burma, and so contribute to a process of localizing transitional justice.

In 2003, disparate local Burmese groups developed a network of organizations engaged in human rights documentation, the Network for Human Rights Documentation—Burma (ND-Burma).[9] Members of this network collaborate with one another on human rights trainings, data management, and advocacy strategies. Through collaboration, this network has standardized data collection and management methodologies. Standardization runs the risk of reducing and limiting actors' voices by, for example, encouraging statement taking that focuses on a person's experience as a victim of violence rather than as a survivor who has suffered violence but also resisted, and who has important things to tell outside of the experience of violence that a statement taker is inquiring about (Wilson 2001). To lessen the risk of reducing and limiting the survivors' and witnesses' voices, ND-Burma fieldworkers use general guidelines (rather than highly structured questionnaires) to conduct interviews. To organize their data, they use Martus software, which contains fields for both quantitative and qualitative data input.[10] With higher-quality data, local actors aim to take a greater role in how the data are used.

One of the challenges that local human rights actors face is the accusation of bias. The 2002 publication by the Shan Women's Action Network (SWAN), "License to Rape," brought unprecedented international attention to the issue of sexual violence by the military in Burma. In the immediate aftermath of the publication, SWAN was inundated with requests from western journalists, international nongovernment organizations, and government officials from countries supporting the prodemocracy movement. All of them wanted to conduct their own interviews with Shan rape survivors to verify the information in "License to Rape." Because local Shan women had interviewed other local Shan women, the analysis was allegedly biased. SWAN initially agreed to some of the requests, since international attention to the situation was one of the goals and the women who provided testimony for the report shared that goal. However, SWAN members began shielding the rape survivors from more interviews when the survivors expressed concerns about the negative effects that retelling their traumatic stories was having on them. The lesson learned from this situation for ND-Burma, which formed soon after, was that community-based human rights documentation will always be open to the accusation of bias. The challenge, then, is how to collect and organize data using rigorous methodology so that the analysis is believable and will stand up to accusations of bias, and to do so in a way that does not reduce a person's voice to merely his or her experience of victimization.

Activists involved in this network believe that their advocacy efforts will be strengthened through collaboration on human rights documentation. For example, a report on forced relocation in five districts in Mon State, Burma, would likely lead to very little international attention, while a report with data from ten different areas of Burma citing similar trends in violations would contribute significantly to international advocacy efforts, which include pushing the United Nations Security Council to take action on Burma as a regional threat to security,[11] sanctions to cut off financial support for the regime, and pressuring Burma's neighboring countries to bring diplomatic pressure to bear. (The efficacy of all of these strategies is another discussion altogether.)

Since that opening seminar, the network has invested a substantial amount of time informing one another about the local contexts in which they are operating, leading to practical strategic discussions on how to better carry out human rights documentation. In 2009 and 2010, the network is focusing its attention on arbitrary taxation, because they discovered over time that the fees imposed for health care, education, travel, agricultural production, and various everyday activities were slowly and persistently making life increasingly difficult all over Burma. ND-Burma does not believe that "arbitrary taxation" is on any UN agency's agenda for Burma; no international NGO is requesting information from the network on the topic. But arbitrary taxation has become a priority for ND-Burma, largely because its members engaged in exchanges about the local experiences of the communities in which they work. They have set their priorities based on this localized recognition of livelihood issues affecting people in Burma, male and female, rural and urban, Burman and non-Burman alike.

Truth Seeking and Protest

While community-based organizations work cross-border to gather information in areas of fighting and ceasefire zones, local actors inside Burma have also initiated truth-seeking measures. Public discussions about the human rights situation became more common in the lead-up to the 2007 demonstrations, with the impetus coming from the '88 Generation Students group, a network that was recently formed in Rangoon and led by former political prisoners who had been student leaders during the 1988 demonstrations. Upon their release from prison in 2004, these leaders urged civil disobedience through a series of innovative campaigns in 2006 and 2007. A petition campaign calling for the release of political prisoners and for a genuine national reconciliation process garnered over 500,000 signatures, which were sent to the SPDC and various UN agencies. Tens of thousands of people participated in a weekly multireligious prayer campaign, with participants wearing white and holding candlelight vigils in their places of worship. The '88 Generation Students leaders also traveled outside of Rangoon to speak at public gatherings, and they regularly visited families of political prisoners to combat the stigma and isolation many of them feel.

In 2007, the '88 Generation Students organized the "Open Heart Campaign," encouraging Burmese citizens throughout the country to write about their everyday grievances with military rule. They received over 2,500 letters. In their 2008 report on this campaign, the '88 Generation Students found that the majority of grievances related to "the costs of living, business, education, and health." Although the leaders were detained in September 2006 (and subsequently released in January 2007), and over a hundred activists were arrested in a June 2007 crackdown, the success of these campaigns suggested a renewed courage among the general population to risk airing their grievances and general views on the problems facing their country, still under military rule (Lintner 2007).

Those grievances burst out into full-blown demonstrations in August 2007, when the SPDC announced on August 15, without warning or explanation, a fuel price hike that raised diesel and petrol prices by 100 percent and natural gas by as much as 500 percent. The ripple effect through the economy was almost immediate, with commodity prices increasing dramatically and day workers struggling to pay higher bus fares to travel into Rangoon to find work. From the initial demonstrations that begin on August 19 to the crackdown that began in the early hours of September 26,[12] one of the main demands of the demonstrators was "national reconciliation." During a demonstration I accompanied on September 25, every person I asked explained that "national reconciliation" referred to the call for dialogue between the SPDC and opposition forces. The subsequent crackdown, followed by the severe restrictions on assembly and expression in the lead-up to the national referendum, lays bare the SPDC's insistence on a one-way "dialogue."

If truth telling becomes an aspect of a transitional justice policy in Burma, it will emerge from a legacy of severe restrictions on open expression. It will also have to face the challenges that may accompany that legacy, including an ongoing culture of fear or its other extreme, a chaotic naming-and-shaming process that could lead to vengefulness. ND-Burma's activities and the '88 Generation Students' "Open Heart" campaign aim to lay the groundwork for future truthtelling measures. Ultimately, they hope that giving license to the urge to have grievances aired and acknowledged will go a long way toward harnessing the legacy of violence to develop a democratic and less violent society.

The transitional justice field has been greatly influenced by the Latin American transitions in the 1980s and 1990s, where the nature of state violence was obscured through the tactic of "disappearing" dissidents (and suspected dissidents). Truth telling then became essential to the transition process, because one of the primary demands of the victims, families of victims, and survivors was to know what had happened to their loved ones (or in some cases, to themselves) (Arthur 2009). A formal public airing of the truth through an official truth commission may not be the most effective measure in every setting to deal with past human rights violations. But in Burma's case the effectiveness of ND-Burma in bringing together community-based organizations of different ethnicities and the success of the '88 Generation Students to encourage public expression of discontent, particularly through the "Open Heart" campaign, suggest that a truth-telling measure, whether official or unofficial, may be one way to effectively address that legacy of violence.[13] These groups' strategies are rooted in their communities' experiences of violence. When the time comes to develop policies to address the legacy of that violence, however, a localized transitional justice will need to take seriously not only the regime's violations of civil and political rights, but also the structural violence of widespread economic hardships that groups like ND-Burma and the '88 Generation Students have identified as priorities in their communities.

Trainings

Truth seeking among Burmese groups is an activity that lends itself easily to future transitional justice measures. But still the question remains: how and when will a genuine transition occur? In various gatherings—workshops, press conferences, and meetings—political opposition leaders have expressed their concern that the military will refuse to come to the negotiating table if they feel threatened, and so do not want to discuss "justice." They also want to avoid outside scrutiny of their roles in their own communities.[14] These views ignore the perspectives of victims and survivors, as well as the complexity of the transitional justice field, and are not necessarily rooted in local perspectives.

An example serves to demonstrate this point, taken from a presentation I gave at a 2004 conference on transitional justice in Chiang Mai, Thailand. To open my presentation, I outlined two scenarios, contrasting the experiences of an urban former political prisoner and a rural farmer. I asked, "In a future democratic Burma, how might a male student activist from a city react if he met the former soldier whom he saw kill a close friend? And how would an ethnic minority woman react if, in the local market, she came across the former soldier who raped her?" The fifty conference attendees, who ranged from interns to elected members of parliament (in exile), gave their input, which spanned a wide range of options, including avoidance, violent revenge, and trials. A rich discussion ensued about why each victim's reaction might be different. A final comment came from a male leader from the ethnic group referred to in the rape case. He asked if, in the scenario, the perpetrator of rape was of the same ethnicity as the victim or Burman. I responded by asking if his answer to the question would differ depending on the rapist's ethnic identity. Indeed, it would: the Burman would need to be held accountable in a court of law, but if the soldier were the same ethnicity as the victim, then it would be an "internal matter," implying that nothing, in fact, would need to be done.

This anecdote speaks to the need to take a nuanced view of "the local." The political leader was from the same ethnic group as the hypothetical female rape survivor. Because of that shared ethnic identity, does his view represent the "local voice," despite the power dynamics around gender, age, and education between him and the rape survivor?

Recognizing this dynamic, local organizations have developed trainings to consider possible transitional scenarios in order to explore what a localized transitional justice might look like in a future Burma. Until 2007, I worked with a local Burmese organization, the Human Rights Education Institute of Burma (HREIB), conducting trainings to foster broader understanding and a more nuanced approach to transitional justice among community-based organizations.[15] In the trainings we used various case studies and activities to deepen understanding of concepts such as "truth," "reconciliation," and "impunity."

On the final day of a typical five-day training, participants engage in a transition simulation. The trainers take on the role of the military regime, and the training participants, full of new ideas from the previous four days, are told that secret negotiations for a transition in Burma have been nearly successful, but the sides have reached a stalemate on what to do about past human rights violations. The training participants are then appointed as the opposition's negotiating party on the issue, and they must come up with an offer to the regime on the following five transitional justice issues: truth seeking, prosecutions, reparations, institutional reform, and commemorations. In the role of the military regime, the trainers take a hard line, refusing trials, limiting truth seeking to identifying victims only, and dismissing any significant institutional reform. The negotiations continue, usually for the entire day, until an agreement or a final impasse is reached.

More often than not, the activity ends in a successful impasse, "successful" because the goal of the activity is neither agreement nor impasse, but rather for the training participants to think through the complexities of each of the transitional justice measures and to decide for themselves and their communities what the best policy would be. Many times during the postactivity discussion, emotional participants will say that they imagined going back to their communities and saying one of the following two statements: (1) "The war is over and we will soon have elections, but we cannot openly discuss the past, and some military leaders will probably be elected and maintain some control over our village"; or (2) "You will continue to suffer forced labor, and our village will probably be attacked and forcibly relocated again, because I thought we should not allow the perpetrators to be given a blanket amnesty." The activity is successful when participants understand for themselves at what level they will compromise, or decide to go back to their community to spark discussions on these issues.

This approach to learning about transitional justice is very different from the top-down approach that often characterizes human rights and transitional justice "sensitization" activities and workshops, many of which discount local understandings and are aimed at getting buy-in and participation in an already-established mechanism or program (Englund 2006; Shaw 2005, 2007). In contrast, the HREIB trainings encourage community-based organizations to consider comparative cases within the context of their communities' experiences and priorities. The very uncertainty of how and when a genuine transition will occur provides an opportunity to develop a transitional justice that is more locally attuned, and could result in better policy and practice when an actual transition emerges.

A Broadened Understanding of Justice

One important lesson learned from other societies that have experienced a transition to democracy is that different parts of society (e.g., rural and urban, male and female) experience different types of human rights violations (Ross 2003a and this volume). Their own standpoints, histories, and cultural ideas influence their understandings of those experiences, moreover, differently shaping their ideas of how justice should be obtained. For example, a male student activist who suffered torture and fled to Thailand may have very different ideas of justice from those of a female Karenni villager who has been displaced from her land, endured forced labor, and had a relative tortured and killed by the military. One may prioritize financial reparations, the other prosecutions. The complexity of the situation in Burma demands a thorough inquiry into how communities in Burma have suffered and what ideas they have about justice and reconciliation. Any transitional justice policy needs to take into account the diversity of Burma and the diversity of the suffering, but also the related variance in ideas about justice, peace, and reconciliation.

It must also confront differences of emphasis between the international community and local communities in Burma. The majority of grievances reported to the '88 Generation Students' Open Heart Campaign concerned "the costs of living, business, education, and health." ND-Burma's attention to the priorities of their own local communities has directed them to a focus on arbitrary taxation. The 2007 demonstrations were triggered by the sudden, unannounced fuel price hikes that exacerbated existing economic hardship throughout Burma. While socioeconomic justice in Burma does not receive the same attention that the UN and international NGOs give to political and civil rights abuses, it forms a priority for communities within Burma and must therefore become a central part of a broadened concept of justice to be addressed in a transition.

This inquiry into varying ideas about justice will be particularly important if the regime is able to push forward with its "transition to a discipline-flourishing democracy," creating a facade of transition while maintaining control (and so, impunity) after the 2010 election. If demonstrations eventually erupt again, people are likely to seek a measure of "street justice" if measures are not developed to address past human rights violations. Indeed, amid the chaos of the 1988 protests, reports circulated that protestors had beheaded three policemen, and that monks had held trials of military intelligence officers, who were then murdered by crowds in the streets. Others reported that the more optimistic activists were preparing to put the dictator Ne Win and others in the ruling military clique on trial (Smith 1999). One of the incidents that motivated demonstrators in the 2007 demonstrations was the attack on three monks in the central Burma town of Pakkoku. Following the incident, monks in the town called for an apology for the violence against their fellow monks and held several government officials hostage in retaliation. Anger toward the government was heightened after they carried out a violent crackdown against demonstrators, which according to the UN, entailed killing or disappearing dozens (including monks) and detaining or arresting between three thousand and four thousand people (United Nations 2007).

In addition to calls to hold the SPDC accountable for the human rights violations that military personnel have committed, Burmese opposition groups are also beginning to discuss human rights violations that armed opposition groups have perpetrated. In the five-day transitional justice trainings discussed above, trainers have begun addressing this issue with participants from armed opposition groups. From interviews I have conducted with individuals in key sectors to address these issues, two people in particular gave a sense of the need for justice measures in a transition.

First, in 2006 a thirty-five-year-old member of an opposition army discussed with me the logistics of a truth commission. When asked if he thought his armed group should be held to account for violations they have committed, he enthusiastically said yes. Now a commander, he said, "I would like to testify at a truth commission, but as a victim." He had been recruited twenty years earlier, at the age of fifteen, and knew that the recruitment of child soldiers is a major human rights violation. "I am loyal to (my organization) and want to keep fighting for my people," he said. "But I also regret that I never had the chance to finish my education." When asked what outcome he would want from testifying before a truth commission, he said he simply wants acknowledgment that he should not have been taken as a soldier at that age.

In another interview, in 2002, a leader within the prodemocracy movement explained the need for a transitional justice mechanism, saying "I want some way— a truth commission, a trial, or any public forum—to face my accusers." In 1992 near the Burma–China border, local commanders in his armed organization summarily executed fifteen of their own soldiers, accused of being spies. He said, "I wasn't there, but there are people who accuse me of ordering the killings or who say I was protecting the perpetrators." This leader has strong political aspirations and said he wants a measure to face his accusers and explain his views on what happened, in order, he says, to restore his political reputation.

Interviews and focus groups that I have conducted with former political prisoners, all torture survivors, have revealed their experiences and views on transitional justice. This population is, generally speaking, well-educated, politically engaged, and keen to play a role in national politics in Burma. One former political prisoner, now living on the Thai–Burma border, explained his views in an interview in 2000. He had participated in the 1988 demonstrations and soon after was targeted by the military intelligence for his involvement in student organizing. He spent over seven years as a political prisoner between 1990 and 1998, enduring torture and isolation before fleeing to Thailand to avoid being arrested a third time. When asked about prospects for transitional justice, he said, "Can we persuade the people, the angry people, not to harm [the military leaders]? There are many people, so many people are very angry with them. Many people want to kill them." He then explained the challenge of reconciling practical realities with his feelings as a torture survivor:

> The most important thing is to transfer [power to] the elected party. And if they [the SPDC] are willing to work together with us for the country, we agree for that. If the situation allows us to have a truth commission, we will do that. So at that time, if the situation does not allow us, we should give in to them. . . . [But if we have the chance] to inquire into the true situation of what they did in the past, we will publicize it. We will take them to the court, and the judge will decide whether they should be in prison or not. According to the law, he should give them the death penalty. According to the law.

As the interview progressed, his comments moved away from his views as a political pragmatist and became more personal.

> They tortured us like this. So if we had the opportunity, we would tell that publicly. At that time, I didn't do anything to them. So then I will charge them in a court. The judge will decide. . . . Now [if] I had an opportunity, I would tell my story publicly. So one day I think they will be accused. And for persecuting or massacres or for destroying the country, according to the [Myanmar Penal Code, Section] 122/1—it is about betraying the country. [Guilt for] that act requires the death penalty or life sentence, only two options. I would ask for the death penalty. It's clear. Death penalty.

Another former political prisoner, who spent a total of thirteen years as a political prisoner during two prison stays between 1976 and 2004, echoed these sentiments. In 2005, he began fearing he would be imprisoned again and did not see any hope in the SPDC leadership pursuing reconciliation, so he fled to Thailand. He believes that a transition will come only when the present leadership is out of office, and in a 2006 interview he emphasized the need for acknowledgment of past wrongs:

> For every country, if we want to get true reconciliation, we have to confess the past wrongfulness from every side, from both sides. . . . Some politicians can speak, they can make peace with their enemy by any means, forget the past. It's not as easy as just saying this.

These former political prisoners' views on dealing with the past include acknowledgment of past atrocities, accountability for torturers, and trials as well as rehabilitation programs and reparations for survivors of torture.

In contrast, villagers I interviewed from the Pa-O and Shan ethnic groups, who live in areas of northeast Burma, tend to have very different views on transitional justice. The rural Pa-O and Shan have been caught in one of the most volatile areas of Burma. Many of them are forced into roles in the armed conflict as combatants or with demands for material support, labor, and information. This collaboration with various sides of the armed conflict, amid blurry lines between willingness and coercion, has resulted in deadly infighting in the Pa-O and Shan populations. This complexity puts many Pa-O and Shan on the cusp of perpetrator and victim. Given the litany of human rights violations they also suffer, the Pa-O's and Shan's insights into transitional justice differ greatly from the political prisoners' views. In a 2005 interview, one Pa-O village leader, now living in Thailand, said:

> The worst violence we experienced was in 1978 and the four-cuts campaign.[16] Soldiers from all the factions came to the village—Burmese, Shan, Pa-O—it was like a nightmare all over southern Shan state. All the villages are gone. In a situation like that, who can you blame? I don't want to blame anyone. We just want to farm our land. . . . As for the victims, I think we have *noung thao wang* [in Pa-O—"victim mentality"]. Even though my brother was killed, we moved away because we don't want to be killed ourselves. The only thing we can do for the victims is a religious thing, offer some donations. The *noung thao wang* is for our own protection. It's the situation that is to blame, not any one person. If we stay, all will be killed, so it is better to leave. Blaming someone is not good. We had to move because of the situation. When water buffaloes are fighting, if you stay there you will be killed. But you don't blame the water buffaloes for fighting.

Like this village leader, most villagers I have interviewed consider accountability for past violations an impossible task that may not even be desirable, because so many people have some level of guilt. They also have had no exposure to a judicial system that functions independently and upholds basic rule-of-law standards. They say they just want the military to leave them alone.

These testimonies show a contrast in priorities, but they also demonstrate a common emphasis on the importance of security. The former political prisoners see criminal justice measures as an option only if political stability is already established. For the Pa-O headman, his community's physical security has been so tenuous for so long that it has become the only priority worth consideration. To echo Paul van Zyl's views discussed in this volume's introduction, these priorities may change over time if his community becomes confident of its sustained physical security. In addition, the attitudes toward priorities that emerged at transitional justice trainings during the scenarios activities, discussed in the above section, showed the heterogeneity of responses within demographic categories: people from within the same ethnic group, of the same gender, with similar experiences of violence would come down on different sides of whether an amnesty was acceptable. The trainings suggested hypothetical, simplified situations, and we can expect that when faced with the complex realities, attitudes toward justice will be layered and contextually variable.

To add further complexity to the matter, a 2001 interview with an elderly Shan villager demonstrates that the dichotomy between "educated political prisoners who want justice" and "illiterate Pa-O and Shan villagers who want peace" is too simple an analysis. The villager had had limited formal education and had never participated in any forum to learn legal and political concepts. In an interview, he explained that dealing with the past would require a judicial system that relied on evidence, cross-examination of witnesses, and the principle of innocent-until-proven-guilty. In short, he recognized and insisted on the rule of law. The elderly man was using religious terms and said he had come to this understanding from listening to monks at his local temple teach about Buddhism. His testimony disrupts the easy assumption, from the previous interviews, that with more education comes a stronger urge for justice. A great deal more research is needed to tease out the nuances and complexity of attitudes and values toward justice in Burma.

Conclusion

Transitional justice may become a core component of a democratic transition in Burma, whether sanctioned by a transitional government or not. With international advocacy focused on ending the mass atrocities being perpetrated in Burma, dealing with past human rights violations and guarding against impunity in the future are likely to be part of that agenda, and several questions need to be addressed from a place-based perspective.

Transitional justice as a field has matured to recognize that different measures are more effective in some settings than in others. Given the authoritarian nature of the regimes in Latin America, transitional justice measures tended to emphasize the need to uncover the truth that had been kept hidden by regimes, sometimes quite literally in mass graves or secret files, about their acts of violence. As many of the other chapters in this volume point out, an overemphasis on truth seeking in post-conflict settings, such as Sierra Leone and Burundi, may be counter to the wishes of the very people the transitional justice measures are designed to assist. Like the Pa-O headman I interviewed, sometimes the most that people caught between water buffaloes want is to steer clear of the wreckage. One of the ways Burma is unique is the dual nature of the conflict. It mimics Cold War–era Latin American authoritarian tactics with arrests and torture of political prisoners, killings of unarmed demonstrators, and an extensive spy network. With conflicts over land, natural resources, and cultural rights that have a distinctly ethnic component, Burma's conflict also bears similarities with Timor-Leste and the former Yugoslavia, where people with shifting roles in the conflict now find themselves neighbors once again.

What would "peace" look like in a Pa-O or Shan village with so many people on the cusp between victim and actor, and what are the implications of that question for transitional justice policies? An effective national transitional justice policy in Burma would have to take into account the complexity of a combined authoritarian and civil war conflict. These two "types" are hardly distinct from a place-based vantage point. The urban-based '88 Generation Students found that livelihood issues are top priorities among their survey participants. The areas of ethnic nationalities are also devastated by the structural violence that affects the populations' livelihoods, particularly in terms of food, land, education, and health. Can transitional justice measures help former political prisoners address the need for rehabilitation of torture victims and also address the desperate economic issues around which their activism is based?

Not only do current activities around human rights documentation contribute to present-day advocacy, but the collaborative nature of ND-Burma also lays the groundwork for a localized truth-seeking process that can grow out of the affected communities' own priorities. Research on attitudes and values toward justice provokes dialogue and encourages tolerance of varying views, and trainings on comparative case studies are motivating activists to raise further awareness in their communities and consider creative policy options that could be brought to the negotiating table.

Afterword

Elevating Transitional Local Justice or Crystallizing Global Governance?

Moses Chrispus Okello

Writing a postscript to a book whose moral arguments and ethical foundations one believes in is a tall order! What remains to be said when the practical dilemmas arising out of the book's subject matter have been so eloquently
and, in some chapters, dramatically illustrated? Perhaps the most that can be
done is to explore some of the same philosophical issues raised in the work
while attempting to further push the boundaries of the intellectual debate. Of
particular interest to practitioners of transitional justice are the ways in which
theory shapes and informs practice and how everyday situations are molded
by preexisting frameworks, sometimes to the detriment of intended benefi-
ciary communities.

As a starting point, it may be worthwhile to ask whether the elevation (or
indeed recognition) of local justice practices contributes toward making the
field of transitional justice truly universal. Why are ideas of "locality" increasingly becoming emphasized in transitional justice? How is "local" defined
and interpreted, and by whom? To what extent is it possible to question the
hierarchies of transitional justice without questioning the hierarchies of international justice? Like the book itself, these questions give rise to new ones
and pose dilemmas that cannot be easily resolved. This is as it should be: the
field of transitional justice remains fluid and it is within this fluidity that the
potential for genuine transformation of the international balance of power resides. For this reason it would have been particularly encouraging to see more
contributions from practitioners and academics based in countries themselves
affected by international legal processes into which they have historically had
little input. Such a lineup would have marked an important step forward in

recognizing the need for a global shift toward an understanding of transitional justice co-constructed by those whom it affects most.

It may also be worthwhile to deliberate on whether international justice (from which transitional justice draws some of its core values) has come of age, and by extension whether the boundaries of the transitional justice paradigm have been set. A central dilemma for many practitioners is whether the paradigms they are applying have in fact been sufficiently theorized and whether they are as all-encompassing as some proponents of international justice would have us believe. This question is central to almost all chapters in the book and can be linked to discourses around the universality of legal principles and the pitfalls of over-relying on the highly politicized language of human rights as an organizing framework.

Implicit in this book is the belief that positioning is everything and there is no such thing as an "unsituated" observer. While this postmodernist stance has been widely accepted within the social sciences, international legal frameworks and international justice practitioners lag behind. The prevailing assumption behind many of these mechanisms is that while individuals may indeed be shaped by their cultures and biases, the law itself is "objective," embodying principles that are universal and on which universal consensus has either been achieved or is in the process of developing. Yet the law has never been divorced from politics or culture, and international law in particular emerged in a context where large portions of humanity were entirely excluded from contributing, an exclusion that in some ways continues to the present day. To take international law's underlying philosophical assumptions for granted is to ignore its construction as a series of legal relationships between nation-states, representing at best a compromise between the particular jurisdictions involved in the original negotiations. Furthermore, not only are the specific laws arrived at a product of their historical context, but so also is the method of their production. This is the basic point made in the chapter by Pierre Hazan, in which he cites Michel Foucault in emphasizing that the methods by which truth is "manufactured" are themselves contingent on their historical context. International law's preoccupation with codification and universality in itself represents a view of the world that is culturally and temporally bounded. To the extent that transitional justice is tied to the structures of international law, it is also tied to the same genealogy that produced international law and is subject to the same pitfalls.

What Is Transitional Justice?

A second point that needs to be stressed (highlighted in the chapter by Lars Waldorf through a reference to "mass justice for mass atrocity" in Rwanda) is that transitional justice has not yet crystallized as a field. This book attempts to question some of the conclusions of transitional justice that are beginning to emerge as "truths"; to critically examine the practical implications, shortcomings, and applications of the accepted principles of transitional justice; and to challenge the universalist assumptions underlying transitional justice itself.

The vocabulary of transitional justice itself is limiting, as is the language of the law and of human rights generally. To really question the theoretical assumptions underlying transitional justice, it may be necessary not only to interrogate the effectiveness or provenance of its acknowledged components but to go outside of the particular view of the world that created them in the first place. If, as the editors claim, a fundamental shift needs to take place within the field of transitional justice, then a new language will have to be invented to reflect this broadened understanding. Simply pointing out that transitional justice ought to place more emphasis on the "local" does not in itself represent a shift in the underlying assumptions of the field—at most, it is a shift in emphasis. The editors thus criticize the ways in which locality has been conceptualized by and incorporated into transitional justice, distinguishing these from what they term "place-based" approaches. A shift to "place-based" forms of justice is not merely a matter of equity but offers a means of moving our conceptual frame beyond that of international law by allowing local critiques, priorities, and practices to show us alternative ways of conceptualizing justice and rights.

Universalism: Fact or Fiction?

One of the assumptions of transitional justice that should have been further questioned in the book, however, is the extent to which the existence of universal norms of justice is relevant to or necessary for transition. An examination of these norms could lead us into truly developing "new sets of possibilities" (in the words of the introduction).

Underlying transitional justice's preoccupation with universalism is an ideological framework that favors homogenizing jurisdictions and cultures in the guise of developing global governance mechanisms. While greater uniformity may be both useful and possible from an economic standpoint, it remains to be seen whether it is advisable in areas such as law and justice. An alternative would be to think of the law (and justice) as a set of interlocking relationships among communities, states, and individuals that need not be uniform in order to function well together. Reflected in the jurisprudence that emerged out of the European Convention for the Protection of Human Rights and Fundamental Freedoms is the concept of a "margin of appreciation," which underscores states' legitimate interest in retaining some flexibility in their laws and their application even as they subscribe to the broader norms enshrined in the convention. This leeway represents a recognition that all the state parties to the convention subscribe to similar underlying principles of justice and can be partly trusted to adapt these principles for domestic purposes. The one attempt to articulate a similar philosophy in the African context never really succeeded: it made African practices subservient to the African Charter on Human and Peoples' Rights, itself imposed through funding and nudging by "international" organizations. Yet despite the lack of a legal document outlining the broad principles of African justice, "traditional" justice mechanisms proliferate on the continent even in the absence of strong support by the international community, which tends to view their application with skepticism.

It would appear that where nonwestern countries are the subject of discussion, it is not enough for them merely to develop a broad set of legal principles that can be tailored to the needs of individual communities and cultures: those principles must also be in line with Euro-American ones, a point recounted in Lars Warldorf's chapter exploring the contradictions and problematic consequences of Rwanda's *gacaca* courts. Encouraging processes aimed at establishing truly "local" justice mechanisms would enrich international justice by contributing to international legal principles already emerging, including the International Criminal Court's (ICC) *complementarity* principle. Such a move would not only make the creation of new international law a *two-way mutually shared process* but would also ensure that the court becomes sincerely complementary.

The lack of confidence evidenced by nonwestern states in their hesitation to develop regional mechanisms is in part a product of the paternalistic attitude of "developed" states toward "developing" ones,[1] and, not surprisingly, provokes a knee-jerk negative reaction among many nonwesterners. Such an attitude finds reflection also in another underlying assumption of transitional justice, namely, that of historical progress and development. As pointed out by the editors of this book, transitional justice arises out of a liberal paradigm that emphasizes redress of past harms as a means of ensuring a future in which violence does not occur. The question that is raised, but that is not sufficiently addressed in the book's pages, however, pertains to the unintended consequences of assuming that we are all progressing toward the same destination. This theory is burdened with historical assumptions of racial superiority and current beliefs about some cultures being more developed than others. Underlying it again is the notion of universality, the belief that all states inevitably follow the same "developmental" route, and that legal principles derived from Euro-American law and embodied in various international instruments reflect the pinnacle of that development.

Universalism can be further problematized through an examination of the ways in which different kinds of supposedly universal rights are emphasized in different contexts by international justice bodies and actors. Thus, for instance, several western nations have stressed the need for reparations for Holocaust survivors and other victims of the Nazis. These same actors downplay the need for such reparations in other contexts—for example, in northern Uganda, a region that has been struggling to emerge from several decades of devastating conflict, and in which international agencies are unwilling to contribute to reparation schemes despite funding expensive ex-combatant reintegration projects and costly international prosecutions. In this context, the kinds of rights that are presented as non-negotiable are determined in part by the perceived legitimacy and potential largesse of international actors supporting them, mainly international nongovernmental organizations (INGOs) and donors. When applied to Africa, for example, civil and political rights are frequently prioritized by donors, with little understanding of how such prominence fails to address local realities. This is the part of the politics of reparations and victimhood that Kimberly Theidon movingly describes in her chapter. Most transitional justice processes have so far failed to come to terms with the ways in which civil and political abuses are tied up with the social and economic structures underlying oppressive systems and the perpetuation of economic inequality and marginalization. Because these transitional justice processes remain effectively blind to the consequences of the underlying socioeconomic structures, they are unable to conceptualize remedying the socioeconomic consequences of civil and political violations (for instance, through reparation schemes that encompass the restored right to access education, health, etc.). This double standard with regard to nonwestern

states[2] leads one to question whether claims of universalism are merely a facade for what amounts in practice to a differential application of the underlying principles.

Same Harms, Different Losses

Such an approach flies in the face of the African experience, which has taught
us that many victims of gross human rights violations stress the ways in which
a breach of their civil or political rights resulted in severe and long-term socioeconomic losses. For this reason, it may well be that a justice regime focused
on repairing such socioeconomic losses would speak more directly to victims'
sense of justice. This debate is reflected in part in the chapter by Weinstein et
al., in which the authors highlight the importance of listening to local voices
as one way of identifying community needs. Disregarding a grassroots call for
reparations, international bodies and actors frequently focus instead on punishing the offender, as evidenced by the massive investment in international
criminal tribunals and the ICC prosecutions, as contrasted with the minimal
funding designated for reparations. By interpreting socioeconomic rights as
falling within the purview of the state, and specifically of the state's developmental obligations, international actors ignore those rights' significance in
developing a model of justice that is responsive to community needs. The bigger point, in fact, is also that transitional justice practitioners need to come to
terms with the concept of "development,"[3] rather than use arguments drawn
from the field of development as a means of not addressing the structural causes
of violence.

Although the reason often offered for this discrepancy is that reparations
require a massive economic commitment, this does not explain why such ex-
penditure is not viewed as problematic when its beneficiaries are considered a
political threat. For example, World Bank–sponsored ex-combatant reintegration programs receive massive funding, in part because ex-combatants are
viewed as a potentially destabilizing political force, with a high conflict-carrying
capacity. To the extent that the victims of human rights abuses are powerless,
their calls for reparations rarely, if ever, receive priority. Rosalind Shaw ably
describes the potential fallout of such an approach when she speaks of the link
between accountability and the reintegration of ex-combatants and the false
dichotomy between victims and perpetrators in Sierra Leone.

The above debate can also be rephrased as a need to examine the language
of "rights" generally and to question its usefulness in particular circumstances.

In some cases it may be more useful to focus instead on the experience and perceptions of violence, and what remedies are considered most relevant by the communities in question. What may emerge from such an analysis is the need to de-link commonly accepted "rights" from their standard remedies. For example, while most civil and political rights remain significant in a non-western context, it is also possible (as per the discussion above) that the remedies that would be applied in a western context to counter their breach (for example, punishment of the perpetrator) are not appropriate in situations where a breach of a particular civil or political right comes with massive socioeconomic consequences for the victim. In such a context, an appropriate remedy may require careful sequencing of the need to restore the victims' socioeconomic well-being and the symbolic restoration of "justice" that comes from retributive justice models.

It may also be that violence in communities leads to harms that are not adequately captured by the language of "rights," but that still need to be addressed in order for the community to flourish. When considered from this perspective, it becomes clear that some critiques of international initiatives such as the International Criminal Court (ICC) (see Sverker Finnström's chapter for more on these criticisms and the nuances of the ICC's involvement in the conflict in northern Uganda) come not from a lack of understanding of the particular rights the ICC seeks to uphold, but rather from the belief that the remedies offered by the process will do little to actually alleviate the harm done or prevent it from recurring. Remedies focused on the symbolic restoration of dignity to the victim by seeing the perpetrator punished are simply less compelling in a context where the victims continue to suffer the socioeconomic harms initiated by the breach of a civil or political right.

A Note on Hierarchies

For the above shift to be possible, transitional justice language would undeniably have to move away from a hierarchical understanding of justice processes to one based upon place. In discussing the idea of place-oriented justice, the book makes this point very clearly. What remains unclear, however, is how successful such an endeavor can be unless the philosophical assumptions underlying international law as a whole are correspondingly challenged. Transitional justice exists in a global legal framework in which the definition of conflict itself is stratified: for instance, conflicts are ranked as either internal or international, with international ones being granted higher status under international law as reflected by their prominent position in instruments including the Geneva Conventions on the Laws of War, etc. In other words, the global rules of engagement are already stratified, and as long as the state is privileged in international legal definitions, transitional justice is inherently constrained to operate within a hierarchical context. Yet this international legal framework favoring the state is becoming increasingly obsolete in a world where serious conflicts are perpetrated by non-state forces engaging in what amounts to international conflict.

How might a place-based approach adequately address transitional justice realities in situations where armed conflict is internationalized? An example of such a situation is one in which the Lord's Resistance Army (LRA), the government of Uganda, and the Democratic Republic of the Congo's (DRC) and Sudanese armies recently found themselves engaged in; in this conflict, armies of the three states are pursuing the LRA, an armed group that has essentially transformed into rebels without borders and commits serious atrocities within the territories of three different countries. Another example is that of Sierra Leone, in which international mining syndicates were implicated in perpetuating the conflict. In that case, justice was pursued through a combination of national processes (the Truth and Reconciliation Commission), the internationally run Special Court, and, in regard to the foreign funders of conflict, civil lawsuits in the United States instituted under the Alien Torts Act. Since international borders represent different legal jurisdictions, a place-*bound* framework that divides justice simply along place lines would be unable to fully address the increasing complexities of these present-day conflicts. The book's place-*based* argument, however, is not that local justice mechanisms ought to be favored over other ones. Rather, attention to local experiences and priorities can provide different orientation points that help to reveal which kinds of processes provide the maximum benefit to victims and communities involved in a given conflict.

The Politics of Place

Another issue relevant to the concept of "place" will probably emerge in contexts where more than one transition is taking place concurrently. An example of this can be found in states that have never fully solidified, and in which the justice system itself may be in a state of flux. Differentiating local and foreign-imposed notions of justice is complicated in circumstances where the local formal justice system may itself be a colonial construction. In such a state, transitional justice is not merely a matter of restoring the society to where it was before conflict began, but reinventing aspects of it (including in the fashion described by Lars Waldorf in his chapter about Rwandan gacaca courts) in part through building legal infrastructure that speaks to the people's sense of justice and that either did not exist in the first place or was perverted through the process of colonization. A further complication may arise where the transitional justice process needs to occur without a corresponding "political transition" or regime change, such as in Uganda.

Finally, the concept of "place" needs to be considered also by examining the nexus between transitional justice mechanisms and forced migration. In places such as the Great Lakes region of Africa, transitions go hand-in-hand with forced migration, and forced migrants often find themselves caught up at the center of transitional justice issues (for instance, when dealing with property restitution). Similarly, processes that initiate transitions, such as peace negotiations, are frequently accompanied by massive population movements. This characteristic of "modern-day" transitional justice was also the grim trademark of the post-conflict transitions in West Africa, in particular Sierra Leone and Liberia, where returning refugees found themselves embroiled in property disputes, even as they tried to confront the root causes of their forced displacement.

Conclusion

The above debates are all ones that transitional justice practitioners find themselves negotiating on a daily basis in the absence of adequate theoretical frameworks with which to conceptualize these issues. We operate in a context where not only are the rules of intellectual engagement unclear, but they are also further complicated by on-the-ground realities, especially when working in states that themselves may enjoy different levels of democracy, may be heavily militarized, lack resources, and generally perceive any kind of transitional justice process as a threat to the existing regime.

As previously stated, the field of transitional justice is a relatively new one, and its boundaries have not yet been clearly defined. By highlighting some of the underlying issues, this book is a blessing to those who wish to challenge transitional justice's unspoken assumptions and push the envelope of what it is realistically possible to achieve with transitions. It is equally important, however, that when the definition of transitional justice does solidify, it is not unduly skewed toward a particular kind of understanding, especially that of academics and practitioners from regions of the world that traditionally see themselves as arbiters of justice and whose views are already over-represented in international law. This latter point is hinted at in the chapter by Pierre Hazan, who posits that "[t]ransitional justice stems from a paradigm of transition developed by a few American political scientists . . . in the mid-1980s." Contrary to the vision of transitional justice as a toolkit containing the predefined components conceived of as "pillars," should we not as practitioners be advocating instead for reflection on the subject of justice understood more broadly and ensure that diverse voices are able to join in the debate? Given the increased focus on localized mechanisms and their corresponding proliferation, the next decade is bound to generate much more debate in the field of transitional justice, especially if the ICC continues to apply its current modus operandi of intervening in situations of ongoing conflict. Some of the shortcomings in this book notwithstanding, this work is without a doubt an important first step toward this debate and represents a significant contribution to the field.

Notes

Chapter One

Our invited contributors originally included a balance of scholars and practitioners, several from outside North America and Europe. It speaks to some of the pressures to which both practitioners and scholars outside the North Atlantic are subject that only one was able to contribute to this volume.

Chapter Two

1. The banners of the South African Truth and Reconciliation Commission proclaimed that "Revealing Is Healing" (Hamber 2001).

2. Over the past fifteen years there has been an evolution in the broad expectations that surrounded the establishment of the ICTY and ICTJ (Byrne 2006:485–98). Byrne notes that "from the moment that the Security Council established the international criminal tribunals with the expectation that they would contribute to peace and national reconciliation, modesty was never a restraining force on the projected role these courts were supposed to play in the broader political order." (2006:486). However, this is not to say that these expectations have diminished. Lionel Beehner, in a Council of Foreign Relations Backgrounder (2007), bemoans the travesty of the Saddam Hussein trial and execution, which was "billed as an exercise in reconciliation." In promoting passage of the law that established the Extraordinary Chambers in the Courts of Cambodia (ECCC), the finance minister, Keat Chhon, argued "This is for memory and justice. In practice, we are strengthening peace, national agreement and national reconciliation, transforming and developing our country" (Etcheson 2006:14).

3. Other scholars have raised questions about the discrepancies that exist between the expectations for transitional justice mechanisms and their outcomes (Fletcher and Weinstein 2002; Fletcher and Weinstein with Rowen 2009; Leebaw 2008; Meernik 2005; Thoms, Ron, and Paris 2008).

4. Emphasis added.

5. Margaret Popkin notes that the December 1996 Guatemalan National Reconciliation Law allowed amnesty in certain cases (1996:173). In 2005, the Constitutional

Court ruled that the amnesty law did apply to massacres (Watts 2005). Thus impunity for some of the most egregious crimes persists.

6. Stover and Weinstein 2004; and International Center for Transitional Justice and U.C. Berkeley Human Rights Center 2004, 2005.

7. On August 27, 2006, the government of Uganda and the LRA signed an agreement to cease hostilities. As part of an overall peace settlement, President Museveni has indicated that he will offer a total amnesty to the LRA leadership.

8. A repeat survey of 2,875 respondents in northern Uganda in 2007 (U.C. Berkeley Human Rights Center, Payson Center for International Development, Tulane University and the International Center for Transitional Justice 2007) demonstrated that attitudes to justice and peace are influenced by peace processes, the frequency of violence, and perhaps an enhanced sense of security. Important changes had occurred. "In comparison to views expressed in 2005, the 2007 data also show that while most respondents favor accountability, there is some willingness to compromise for the sake of peace." When asked what should happen to the LRA leaders, up to 52 percent of respondents chose forgiveness, reconciliation, or reintegration for LRA leaders. Twenty-two percent of respondents wanted the LRA leaders to be tried and, if convicted, sent to prison. Seventy-eight percent said that the rank-and-file LRA should be forgiven, reintegrated, or reconciled with, while 17 percent mentioned that they should be tried and, if found guilty, punished. Forty-one percent of respondents favored "harder" options including trials and/or punishment, including imprisonment or death. In the 2005 survey, 66 percent of respondents favored trials, imprisonment, or death for LRA leaders, while 22 percent favored forgiveness, reconciliation, or reintegration. As in the earlier survey, only 3 percent listed justice as their top priority. There is a nexus of critical factors ranging from ignorance of judicial or other options to lack of trust in state institutions to cultural practices that influence how specific questions may be answered (Pham et al. 2007:36–37).

Chapter Three

1. This instrumental vision joins also that of Archbishop Desmond Tutu, chairman of the South African Truth and Reconciliation Commission, who said that there exist "tools new and old, foreign and domestic, but above all, practical and effective to design a reconciliation process appropriate to a particular set of circumstances" (Desmond Tutu in Bloomfield, Barnes, and Huyse [2003]).

2. The genocide in Rwanda took place a few months after a number of U.S. soldiers were killed in Somalia, reactivating the Vietnam syndrome.

3. Article 101 of the Durban Declaration and Program of Action (DDPA):

With a view to closing those dark chapters in history and as a means of reconciliation and healing, we invite the international community and its members to honour the memory of the victims of these tragedies. We further note that some have taken the initiative of regretting or expressing remorse or presenting apologies, and call on all those who have not yet contributed to restoring the dignity of the victims to find appropriate ways to do so and, to this end, appreciate those countries that have done so. (United Nations 2001)

4. Transitional justice, then, offers a glimpse of a way to move beyond the crime by paying debts contracted and proposes several methods of settlement that, according to the circumstances of each case, power relationships, and the interests of different actors, may be used separately or not and may be spread across time. These methods of settlement are the traditional tools of transitional justice (the international criminal tribunals, truth commissions, financial compensation, public expressions of repentance, opening of archives, and diverse procedures of commemoration).

5. Three defense lawyers were murdered, three judges left the five-member panel, and the original chief judge was replaced. In addition, important documents were not given to defense lawyers in advance, no written transcript was kept, and paperwork was lost. The defense was also prevented from cross-examining witnesses, and the judges made asides that prejudged Saddam Hussein.

6. It was not seen as relevant by the U.S. authorities that the LRA has as its distinctive feature the kidnapping of children, who then formed the main element of its forces. This was the first time that a movement composed mainly of abducted children was labeled a terrorist organization. In this context, it is also worth mentioning that the Ugandan army has been accused of committing war crimes and crimes against humanity.

7. On the campaign trail, candidate Bush told ABC News reporter Sam Donaldson, "I don't like genocide and I don't like ethnic cleansing, but I would not send our troops [to stop them]" (Power 2002).

8. On July 14, 2008, Luis Moreno-Ocampo, Prosecutor of the International Criminal Court (ICC), presented "evidence" showing that Sudanese President Omar Hassan Ahmad al-Bashir committed the crimes of genocide, crimes against humanity, and war crimes in Darfur. On March 4, 2009, the ICC judges issued a warrant for the arrest of the president of Sudan, for war crimes and crimes against humanity.

9. This is also the analysis of the UN expert for Afghanistan, who, in the face of this "systematic impunity," encouraged the Afghan government "to consider the full array of transitional justice strategies, including investigations and commissions of inquiry, criminal prosecutions, reparations, mechanisms of memorialization and education, non-criminal sanctions against responsible individuals such as limiting their participation in government and/or military service, and various aspects of broad institutional reform" (Bassiouni 2004). Without result, so far.

10. The United States has launched the Trans-Sahara Counter-Terrorism Initiative with a dozen countries in North Africa to stop terrorist networks from settling in the "Saharan corridor," where state power hardly exists.

11. The Commission's final report notes repeatedly that the ERC has been unable to clarify certain historical facts because of lack of cooperation by the police, army, gendarmerie, and security forces.

12. This marked the establishment of the Arbitration Commission, which also awarded reparations to five thousand former political prisoners at the time King Mohammed VI came into power.

Chapter Four

My thanks to Sameena Mulla, Ross Parsons, Rosalind Shaw, Colleen Crawford Cousins, Patti Henderson, and Lesley Green for their insightful readings. All errors are, of course, my own.

1. At the time of the Commission's hearings and of Zuma's trial, rape was defined as penile penetration of the vagina, thus defining victims as female and perpetrators as male. The Criminal Law (Sexual Offences and Related Matters) Amendment Act, finally passed in 2007 (ironically, on National Reconciliation Day), broadened the definition, and rape is now a statutory offense defined as sexual penetration without consent, irrespective of gender. The changed definitions have made it difficult to track patterns in rape reporting year on year (see SAPS 2009:3–4). For the six month period October 1, 2008–March 31, 2009, police records indicate a total of 71,500 "sexual offences" (including sex work), of which 27,750 are defined as rape and a further 3,199 as sexual assault (SAPS 2007:7–8).

2. The Commission did not take sufficient note that violence against women and children may increase during political transition (see Moffett 2006; Turshen and Twagiramariya 1998).

3. The definition of rape at the time meant that some sexualized violence is classified as "indecent assault" and is not included in the data on rape.

4. *Umalume* describes a mother's brother. In classificatory terms, he bears a special relationship to the children of his sisters, who are entitled to act toward him without the respect or reverence usually accorded men of a senior generation. A child may turn to him for assistance. The judge implies (Van der Merwe 2006:38) that as the appellant called other senior people in exile umalume, the term is merely one of generic respect, but I suggest that, particularly in such a fraught context as a political movement in exile, the term would continue to carry many of its historic cultural meanings as people sought to widen as far as possible the networks on which they could rely. Ironically, Khwezi's claims to the cultural significance of this relationship were widely denied, yet Zuma's culturalist claims received widespread valorization.

5. The cross-examination generated furious media discussion and great anger that the amendments to the Sexual Offences Bill, which would make one's prior sexual history inadmissible, had not yet been passed, despite having been in the offing for almost ten years.

6. Trauma literature refers to this as "secondary rape." Several testifiers described such experiences to me after the hearings.

7. The Stuart Commission (1984) investigated abuses in ANC camps and reported that men believed women were sex objects (p. 3) but does not explain how sexual offenders were dealt with. A confidential report submitted to the TRC (Report vol. 2:360) states that some ANC cadres found guilty of "major breaches of discipline"

were executed: five of these were men found guilty of murder and rape. The TRC offered evidence that women were sexually abused in the camps but made no finding regarding child abuse. Khwezi's case was apparently treated as an internal disciplinary matter by the ANC. The accused were judged by women and given light sentences. As a result of Khwezi's claims during the rape trial, the Democratic Alliance Women's Network (2006) called on the ANC's Women's League to investigate sexual violence in the ANC camps. There is clearly not yet "closure" on that period of the past, notwithstanding the work of two Commissions.

8. The legal system is now more sensitive in addressing sexual violence. Nevertheless, few lay charges, and when they do, successful prosecutions are uncommon. Yet, as the Supreme Court Reportable Case no. 350/2003, *The State versus Khehlani Mvamvu*, makes clear, there is still a tension between the premises of human rights and the judicial understandings of culture that seem to be deeply imbued with—and legitimate—a masculinist bias. In that case, in which a man was found guilty of multiple acts of rape of his customary law wife, a magistrate found that the defense's "conservative" Xhosa culture offered mitigating circumstances for reducing the mandatory fifteen-year sentence. When taken on appeal to the Supreme Court, the judges, two of whom were women, found that the man's "deep" rural upbringing and his lack of familiarity with modern institutions and understandings of marriage were sufficient circumstances to warrant a somewhat reduced term. The facts that the complainant grew up in the same area and that it is highly unlikely that the man's actions received sanction from a local community do not appear to have been factored into the court's decision.

9. Charges were dropped in April 2009, shortly before the general elections, won by the ANC with Zuma as its President.

10. Such patterning is not particular to South Africa. O'Barr's research (1982) in American courtrooms demonstrates that men are more likely to wield the kinds of direct talk admissible as evidence. Their habitual speech forms correspond more closely with the norms of legal language. Gender and social class shape testimonial reception. Where supporting evidence is available, this need not bear directly on legal decisions, but where matters of narrative interpretation are at stake, linguistic form matters, and the implications for social justice, recognition, and the endurance of trusting relationships are considerable.

11. As Khwezi noted, "this is essentially a patriarchal society. Men make the rules. They can break the rules. It is their interpretation, their understanding and definitions that carry the most weight" (Cavanagh and Mabele 2006). Patriarchy is seldom offered in explanations for violence. The Commission noted that "it is clear that patriarchy and the cult of masculinity has been embedded deeply in each of the various cultural streams: black, Boer, British. Its significance as a contributing factor should not be undermined" (Report 2004 vol. 7:291), but it goes no further. There is, to the best of my knowledge, no feminist assessment of the Commission's (limited) usage of "patriarchy" as an explanatory device.

12. As are racialized patterns of master–slave relations; see Feldman (2003).

13. See Taylor (1997) on gendered social patterns under the Argentine *junta*.

14. Most rapes described in the Commission's Report (1998) were committed by state representatives.

15. Derrida argues that justice is a relation of responsibility before the dead (cited in Sanders 2007:66). This renders Zanele Zinxgondo's request for an investigation still more poignant.

16. Ritual processes, for example, may be important in reintegrating people into destroyed communities, acknowledging experiences and reestablishing the norms, rules, and values through which social life can occur (Honwana 1999). However, we should not assume that the values they seek to restore or inculcate are intrinsically beneficial. If, as is widely held, rituals restore the status quo, then they are as likely to reinscribe old systems of power and discrimination as to afford new possibilities.

17. The Report's data are not disaggregated by age. We are not told whether the 140 cases of rape were reported by older or younger women.

18. Questions such as "How could a lesbian have male lovers?" "Why had she not taken steps to protect Zuma against HIV infection?" "How credible were her claims of multiple rape?" were posed, including by the presiding judge in his findings. The questions rest on a set of problematic assumptions about the fixedness of sexual identities, women's responsibilities as nurturers, a conscious and knowing self, rape as an exceptional event.

19. Early in the Commission's process, commentators in KwaZulu-Natal, at the time still wracked with internecine violence between the ANC and IFP, argued that the Commission was commencing its work too soon.

20. This is not uncommon. In Europe and America, it has been only since the 1980s that a complainant's history has become inadmissible (Sameena Mulla, pers. comm., September 28, 2006).

21. Among those with whom I worked, prison was considered polluting. On their release, many detainees underwent cleansing rituals. In most African traditions, purification rituals are an important part of all life-cycle rituals and are integral to traditional healing practices.

Chapter Five

I thank the United States Institute of Peace, the Weatherhead Center for International Affairs, and the Instituto de Estudio Peruanos for the funding that made this research possible. I thank the Wenner-Gren Foundation for supporting valuable writing time. For keen discussions on the themes I address in this article, I thank the wonderful group of researchers who participated in the workshop "Beyond the Toolkit: Rethinking the Paradigm of Transitional Justice," at the Bellagio Conference Center. I am especially grateful to my colleagues Rosalind Shaw, Lisa J. Laplante, Billie Jean Isbell, José Coronel Aguirre, Carlos Iván Degregori, Edith Del Pino, and Leonor Rivera Sullqa for many stimulating conversations. Finally, my deepest gratitude goes to the many Peruvians who have been so generous with their time and knowledge.

1. Diary entitled *Plumas y montañas: Suni puni,* written during 1985–87 by an anonymous Shining Path militant based in the highlands of Huanta, Ayacucho. Copy of diary on file with the author.

2. Within the polarized political climate of the Fujimori years, to suggest dialogue with members of SL was taboo. As Richardson argues, "There is a widespread view that to endeavor to understand or to explain terrorism is to sympathize with it. I reject this view. Indeed, it is a central tenet of this book that the best way to contain terrorism is to understand its appeal and to use this understanding to forge effective counterterrorist policies. The Peruvian government's campaign against the Shining Path is one example of how an effort to understand a terrorist movement can be much more effective at ending terrorism than an effort to squash it" (2006:xx). While Richardson is correct that careful intelligence gathering—in contrast to the indiscriminate use of violence—was what allowed the Peruvian government to capture Abimael Guzmán, the understanding of SL did not extend much beyond the appreciation for the "cult of personality" that made the decapitation strategy successful. However, there was scant effort to understand the motivations of lower-level militants, because talking with "terrorists" was seen—and continues to be seen—as an "apology for terrorism."

3. Decreto Supremo no. 065-2001-PCM (June 4, 2001). Available at: www.cverdad .org.pe/lacomision/nlabor/decsup01.php.

4. David Stoll was perhaps the first social scientist to invoke the idea of a civilian population caught "between two fires" or "between two armies," based upon his research in Guatemala (1993). For a critique of the *"entre dos fuegos"* model see Theidon 2004 and Oglesby 2007.

5. For an excellent discussion of the contradictory tensions in Peruvian human rights law and practice, see Laplante, forthcoming.

6. I will return to this again when considering the PIR and how the reparations program defined "victims" to exclude anyone who was a member of a "subversive group" at the time their rights were violated.

7. An "Aprista" is someone who belongs to the political party Alianza Popular Revolucionaria Americana (APRA).

8. I began working with these communities as one component of my research with the TRC's office in Ayacucho. I directed a project on community mental health, reparations, and the micropolitics of reconciliation practiced at the communal and intercommunal levels. For further discussion of these themes, see Theidon 2004, 2006a, and forthcoming.

9. I am frequently asked if no one "broke ranks" vis-à-vis these communal "memory projects." The answer, of course, is yes. In part, my research has been made possible by those alternative versions. However, those versions emerged slowly over time and, in several instances, from people who visited me late at night or at my home in Huamanga to ensure that no one in their community would see them.

10. See Theidon 2007a for a gendered analysis of the TRC, which includes a more detailed discussion of this focus group.

11. For an excellent discussion of the debates regarding the applicability of the "Clean Hands Doctrine" in Peru, see Guillerot and Magarell 2006 and Laplante, forthcoming. The "Clean Hands Doctrine" dictates that the wrongdoing of an injured party may limit his or her claim to reparations. However, as Laplante skillfully argues, this doctrine violates human rights principles and laws, having been developed for common law disputes seeking to balance blame in determining causation of injury of harm between equal parties, such as states. The tensions that arise when applying this doctrine to human rights violations are multiple: if only those with "clean hands" are legitimate subjects of human rights protection, then the stigma of past militancy—or even accusations to that effect—are sufficient to sully far more than an individual's hands.

12. People in a number of communities lamented the death of their animals, rhetorically asking me, "What possible guilt could an animal possibly have?"

13. Former president Alán García, *Correo*, August 14, 2003.

14. Congressperson Lourdes Flores Nano, *La República*, August 10, 2003.

15. Valentín Paniagua, *La República*, August 10, 2003. Mr. Paniagua was noting that he had created a truth commission, not a truth and reconciliation commission. It was his successor, Alejandro Toledo, who added reconciliation to the commission's name and mandate.

Chapter Six

1. Richards (2005b:136) makes a different argument for an expansion of ideas of justice. He suggests that the TRC and Special Court should have considered the circumstances of RUF bush camps as social environments that fostered the development of a millenarian world-view that, in turn, profoundly shaped the actions and dispositions of RUF combatants.

2. The TRC's Final Report (2005, vol. 3b, chap. 5) includes a chapter on urban youth and revolutionary youth culture but does not confront the exclusion faced by rural youth.

3. A pseudonym.

4. This does not mean that local practices of reintegration and redress form a "traditional" baseline with which "modern" and "universal" principles of justice engage: most parts of the world have experienced international interventions for decades. Rather, they represent practices for remaking lives in an environment that *includes* post-conflict interventions, rapid NGO-ization and UN-ization, and expanding discourses of rights and justice.

Chapter Seven

This article is based on anthropological fieldwork in Acholiland, the immediate war zone in the north of Uganda, conducted in recurrent phases from 1997 to 2007, and on material that partly appears in "Uprooting the Pumpkins," in Sverker Finnstrom, *Living with Bad Surroundings: War, History, and Everyday Moments in Northern Uganda*, pp. 197–232 (excerpts requested cover 219–32). Copyright, 2008, Duke University Press. All rights reserved. Used by permission of the publisher. An earlier version of this article was presented at the African Studies Association (ASAUK) biennial conference ("Debating Africa"), London, September 13–15, 2004, on the invitation of Tim Kelsall. I thank Rosalind Shaw, Adam Branch, and Mikael Kurkiala for comments and essential input. For encouragement in life, I thank Helena and Rut Edin. Research in Uganda was endorsed by the Uganda National Council for Science and Technology, and financed by the Research Department of the Swedish International Development Cooperation Agency.

Chapter Eight

1. This study was carried out with the assistance of Miparec (acronym for, translated, Ministry for Peace and Reconciliation), a Burundian NGO established in 1996 dedicated to promoting peace and reconciliation through nonviolent conflict resolution training, social rehabilitation, and economic reconstruction.

2. Most of the returned refugees at the time of the research fled during the latest crisis beginning in 1993; viewpoints of refugees from the events of 1972 may be underrepresented.

3. Vandeginste 2009 makes the fascinating points that whatever so-called transitional justice occurred in the past (a) reflected the balance of power in the country and (b) served as a means for the consolidation of power.

4. Reasons for this difference are discussed below.

5. The reader should be reminded here that throughout the country, Hutu and Tutsi live side by side, speak the same language, etc.

Chapter Nine

The author wishes to thank Rosalind Shaw for her incisive comments on an earlier version of this chapter. He owes an enormous intellectual and personal debt to Alison Des Forges, the historian and human rights activist.

1. Rwanda objected to the Tribunal's location in Tanzania, limited temporal jurisdiction, primacy over Rwandan national courts, exclusion of civil parties, and refusal to apply the death penalty. Rwanda's cooperation with the Tribunal has always been marked by distrust, partly due to the threat that the Tribunal might prosecute members of the current government for war crimes (see Peskin 2008: 186–231).

2. A few post-conflict states have used customary practices selectively and sparingly in conjunction with truth commissions (East Timor and Sierra Leone), while others have adopted a hands-off approach to those practices (Mozambique) (see, e.g., Huyse and Salter 2008).

3. By contrast, both criminal trials and truth commissions usually focus their efforts on high-level or representative perpetrators for reasons of symbolism, deterrence, and limited capacity. Some have critiqued the transitional justice paradigm's preference for targeting high-level state actors (see, e.g., Drumbl 2007:23–45; Stover and Weinstein 2004:335).

4. There is a highly politicized debate over the numbers of perpetrators and victims. Straus (2006:115–18) estimates 200,000 perpetrators, whereas an influential Rwandan senator recently put the number at two million (Remarks of Senator Antoine Mugesera, International Conference on the Tutsi Genocide and Reconstruction of Knowledge, Kigali, July 25, 2008 [author's notes]). While Human Rights Watch calculates that 500,000 perished during the genocide (Des Forges 1999:15–16), the government contends that at least a million died (Ministère de l'administration locale 2002:24). See Reyntjens 2004:178 n. 1.

5. The RPF's Anglophone Tutsi leaders, who grew up in exile in Uganda and Tanzania, have an uneasy relationship with the Francophone Tutsi survivors. In the late 1990s, Tutsi survivors publicly criticized the RPF, particularly over the reintegration of suspected génocidaires into the government, the failure to create a reparations fund, and the RPF's manner of commemorating the genocide. The RPF reacted in 2000 by accusing prominent Tutsi elites of corruption and plotting the return of the Tutsi king from exile. Some fled, others were arrested, and one was assassinated under mysterious circumstances. That same year, the RPF installed one of its central committee members as the president of IBUKA, the leading survivors' organization. See Human Rights Watch 2000a:10–11; International Crisis Group 2002:4; Reyntjens 2004:180; Rombouts 2004; Vidal 2001. For a fascinating personal account of how the Tutsi Speaker of Parliament was forced to flee Rwanda, see Sebarenzi 2009: 37–207.

6. Hutu and Tutsi are not easily classifiable as separate ethnicities, as both groups speak the same language, share the same culture, practice the same religion, live together, and often intermarry. There is a contentious debate over whether ethnic differences existed in precolonial Rwanda (Eltringham 2004:12–27; Newbury 1988; Pottier 2002:110–23).

7. The parliamentarian, Dr. Leonard Hitimana, was "disappeared" after being accused (Human Rights Watch 2003). As of December 2009, his fate remains unknown.

8. For more detailed descriptions of gacaca, see Avocats Sans Frontières 2005, 2008; PRI 2005; Waldorf 2006.

9. There has been little written about precolonial and colonial gacaca. The best descriptions are Karekezi 2001 and UN High Commissioner for Human Rights 1996, while Clark 2007 provides a helpful overview. Curiously, there appear to be no contemporaneous accounts of gacaca before the 1980s.

10. The number of judges was reduced with the 2004 amendments to the gacaca law.

11. Rwanda's administrative organization has changed several times since the genocide and is still being transformed. Gacaca was based on the former administrative division of the country into eleven provinces, 106 districts, 1,545 sectors, and 9,201 cells. At that time, a cell averaged 830 people, although there were considerable variations (Vandeginste 2003:252, n. 60).

12. Under the various gacaca laws (as well as the 1996 genocide law governing national court trials), persons are guilty of genocide if they committed various acts

(murder, manslaughter, assault, and sexual violence) during the genocide—without any showing of the special and specific genocidal intent to destroy the Tutsi qua Tutsi (as required under the 1948 Genocide Convention).

13. The inclusion of property offenses in the 1996 genocide law and the various gacaca laws was always legally problematic. Property crimes do not figure in the definition of genocide in either the 1948 Genocide Convention or the 1998 Rome Statute for the International Criminal Court.

14. Even as knowledgeable a Rwanda scholar as Longman (2006:209–13) incorrectly depicts gacaca as a mix of customary and modern law.

15. The initial election of inyangamugayo was not as democratic as it first appeared: local officials often nominated candidates in advance, and many of those candidates were already involved in local administration (PRI 2002b:34–35).

16. These include the local-level poverty reduction program (*ubudehe*) and the district performance contracts (*imihigo*).

17. This made it difficult for poorly educated gacaca judges "to follow and understand a procedure that evolves without end" (PRI 2008).

18. From July 2006 to September 2008, sector-level gacaca courts tried 443,467 murder and assault cases, while cell-level gacaca courts tried 609,144 cases involving property offenses (SNJG 2009).

19. This provision was subsequently added to the amended gacaca law of May 2008.

20. That made gacaca less participatory and more susceptible to corruption, while also reinforcing the power of state officials at the expense of gacaca judges and local communities (PRI 2006:2, 6–24).

21. Those NGOs, which once criticized the government for lengthy detentions without trial, suddenly found themselves in the awkward posture of protesting speedy trials.

22. Longman (2006:214) asserted that gacaca enjoys "immense popularity" based on attitudinal surveys he conducted *before* it began, while overlooking subsequent reports (including some by the government itself) documenting gacaca's unpopularity (see Karekezi, Nshimiyimana, and Mutamba 2004:82; LIPRODHOR 2002:9; PAPG 2003:5; PRI 2003a:27, 2004b:76, 80).

23. Quotes from gacaca proceedings and interviews were collected by my research assistants or me, except where otherwise noted. In order to protect my research assistants and our informants, none of those quotes has been attributed, and the gacaca location has not been specifically identified.

24. Gacaca became even more of a burden on ordinary Rwandans when trials started to be held two or three days a week in numerous communities as part of the process to speed it up.

25. In 2008, the Rwandan government put four soldiers on trial for the notorious massacre of the Rwandan archbishop, three bishops, and several other clergy in 1994. The trial ended with acquittals of two high-ranking officers and guilty pleas from two low-ranking soldiers.

26. This number later doubled to 612,000 (SNJG 2009).

27. Such mediation more closely resembled the neotraditional gacaca run by local officials before the genocide.

28. Approximately 10,000 Category 1 cases were transferred to gacaca courts (SNJG 2008b).

29. This was problematic on two counts. First, it meant rape could be punished more severely than intentional killing. Second, it retroactively applied a harsher penalty than existed at the time of the genocide, thereby violating the human rights covenants ratified by Rwanda.

30. She also stressed that "those [judges] who let out secrets will be put in prison for one to three years" (Conference on the Tutsi Genocide, Kigali, July 2008).

31. Anne Aghion's remarkable series of four documentary films captures pre-gacaca and gacaca proceedings in one community over a nine-year period (Aghion 2002, 2004, 2009a, 2009b).

32. There was a real basis to such fear: survivors and witnesses in some communities were intimidated and killed to prevent them giving evidence in gacaca (see Human Rights Watch 2007). IBUKA, the survivors' organization, told me that approximately thirty-one survivors and witnesses were killed from January 2007 to August 2008. A few gacaca judges I interviewed in mid-2008 also complained about harassment and intimidation.

33. There were even reports that some common criminal suspects confessed to genocide, calculating that they would be released earlier under gacaca than under the ordinary penal code.

34. For a discussion of witchcraft and poisonings in rural Rwanda before the genocide, see Taylor 1988.

35. Indeed, one of the most widely used human rights textbooks includes a case study of gacaca in its latest edition (Steiner, Alston, and Goodman 2008:1319–30).

36. In one of my research sites, survivors even briefly boycotted gacaca in 2002, after the man they regarded as the leader of the Interahamwe (the extremist Hutu militia) in the community was acquitted by a national (not gacaca) court. One survivor angrily asked, "Why should we try cattle thieves in gacaca if leaders of the genocide are released?" Eventually, top provincial officials (including the governor, police chief, prosecutor, military, and court president) had to be called in to quell the boycott. They held an open-air meeting with several hundred people, mostly survivors. The governor, a Tutsi returnee, reminded the survivors that they were not above the law and stated, "You cannot make a strike." The next day, gacaca resumed without incident (Northern Province, September 2002).

37. For a much more positive appraisal, see Clark 2009.

38. The government tried to make perpetrator confessions more meaningful to survivors by requiring public apologies with the 2004 amendments to gacaca.

39. These findings contest claims that "[m]any everyday Rwandans also believe that greater 'unity' is a likely outcome of this dialogue at gacaca" (Clark 2007:50).

40. Several researchers found the same phenomenon in the former Yugoslavia with respect to individual trials at the International Criminal Tribunal for the former Yugoslavia (see Stover and Weinstein 2004).

41. The high-end figure of one million suspects assumes that most of the more than one million gacaca cases involved different perpetrators. However, it is likely that some suspects had multiple cases against them (i.e., for different crimes committed in different localities).

42. Barbara Oomen argues that gacaca prompted donors to give more aid to the justice sector and that "it also deflected the international community's attention from all the real injustice that was taking place" (Oomen 2005:906).

43. Donor assistance to Rwanda is a complicated and contentious issue (see, e.g., Hayman 2007).

44. Ellen Lutz overlooks this distinction when she writes, "The gacaca process was created by Rwandans who looked to their own history and culture to find a culturally acceptable solution to an overwhelming problem" (Lutz 2006:335).

45. But see Arriaza and Roht-Arriaza, this volume, for alternative local truth-telling initiatives in "safe spaces" in Guatemalan communities.

Chapter Ten

Authors' names are in alphabetical order, authors contributed equally to this article. Special thanks to Domingo Hernández, Marcie Mersky and Kimberly Theidon for their thoughts on the subject, as well as to all our informants in Guatemala. Thanks as well to the Fulbright Commission, under whose auspices Laura Arriaza was a research fellow in Guatemala during 2008. A version of this chapter based on earlier field research appeared as (1) "Social Repair at the Local Level: The Case of Guatemala," in Keiran McAvoy and Lorna McGregor, *Transitional Justice from Below*, pp. 143–66 (London: Hart Publishing, 2008). Copyright, 2008, Hart Publishing. All rights reserved. Used by permission of Hart Publishing, and (2) "Social Reconstruction as a Local Process," in the *International Journal of Transitional Justice*, Vol. 2 (2), 2008, pp. 152–72. Authors' copyright, 2008.

1. Survivor from northern Quiché area of Guatemala, describing a local project to map out the conflict in his region. Interview, Madrid, Spain, February 2008.

2. In Guatemala, *ladino* refers to people who self-identify as non-Indian through their use of the Spanish language, non-use of traditional dress, and the like. A majority of the Guatemalan population belongs to indigenous groups descended from the pre-Columbian inhabitants of the region. Although these groups identify themselves largely based on their languages and places of origin (Ki'che, Q'eqchi, K'achiquel, Achí, etc.), in the last few years, they have begun to also self-identify as Maya, and that word will be used here to refer to the indigenous population as a whole.

3. This process is not unique to Guatemala; the same process of state building and creating refounding myths took place in South Africa through the South African Truth and Reconciliation Commission (Wilson 2001).

4. These include, but are not limited to, national court systems, truth commissions, infrastructure repairs, national education campaigns, etc.

5. See, for example, the work program of the Peruvian Commission for Truth and Reconciliation. Volume 4, chapter 1 of the Commission's Final Report is entitled "Violence in the Regions" and divides the country into several distinct regions with distinct histories of violence and repression (Commission for Truth and Reconciliation, 2003). The Moroccan Equity and Reconciliation Commission also paid special attention to regions that had been hard-hit by repression or had suffered because of proximity to repressive sites.

6. These efforts are sometimes referred to as "reconciliation." While we understand this to mean the complex process by which individuals, families, communities and polities come to terms with past atrocities, conflicts, and state repression, we are not convinced that the overtones of forgiveness and atonement implied by the term are necessarily applicable in every case. Like Fletcher and Weinstein (2002), we prefer the term *social reconstruction,* although we add that this implies a transformative element, not simply a return to an unjust status quo.

7. For example, in Guatemala the worst period of violations took place in the early 1980s, yet because of the drawn-out peace negotiations and funding issues, the Truth Commission did not begin work until over a decade later and presented its findings in 1998. A national reparations program emerged only in 2004.

8. This description is based on interviews with participants in the initiative from the Ixil region of Quiché Province in February and June/July 2008. Lieselotte Viaene's investigation in the area of Alta Verapaz notes a similar group working to construct local memory in twenty communities of that region (Viaene 2007).

9. Some communities are considering compiling their testimonies into a book, and many are working with the legal organization CALDH (Centro de Acción Legal de Derechos Humanos) to paint the picture of the conflict in the region in the 1980s in support of the genocide cases against former dictator Gen. Efraín Ríos Montt and others in the military high command. Still other communities are debating displaying their communal time-line braid in public venues.

10. In addition to the PNR, several Guatemalan communities have received reparations through judgments of the Inter-American Court of Human Rights.

11. A second cross was put up in the mountains of Alta Verapaz to commemorate another 400-plus massacre victims. See also Viaene 2007.

Chapter Eleven

1. As the editors note in their introduction, the concept of "transition" was originally formed in the context of states emerging from repression at the end of the Cold War, yet since then most cases have involved post-conflict rather than post-repression justice—and this should perhaps lead to more nuanced understandings of the concept.

2. Other measures can also be possible during the conflict. For example, Palestinian victims of violence by the Israeli army have been attempting to gain individual

compensation in Israeli courts, and in some sporadic cases have succeeded. This could also be seen as part of "transitional justice," but is beyond the remit of this paper.

3. We use the term "civil society" loosely to denote any unofficial or nongovernment activity, ranging from ad hoc voluntary engagement to established organizations with paid staff, whether or not they describe themselves as "civil society."

4. In her recommendations Hayner even adds that the more official a commission, the better; that is, a truth commission created through a law is better than one established by presidential decree, and so on.

5. Their Web site address is www.healingofmemories.co.za.

6. See also Laura Arriaza and Naomi Roht-Arriaza's chapter in this volume, on local truth-seeking initiatives in Guatemala.

7. See http://memo.ru/eng/about/whowe.htm (all Web sites were last accessed on December 7, 2009, unless indicated otherwise).

8. See HTR's Web site at www.healingthroughremembering.info/ and on the "private reflection" initiative at www.dayofreflection.com.

9. Another important example for unofficial truth-seeking initiatives is that of the commissions of inquiry established by the African National Congress (ANC) in 1992–93 to examine past abuses against alleged collaborators with the Apartheid regime. It is not included in the above list of examples, as, although not state-led, it was organized by a non-state actor, or national liberation movement, rather than by civil society as such. Finally, see Patrick Falvey's chapter in this volume, on local civil society truth-seeking initiatives in Burma.

10. This lack of self-definition may be common to similar "transitional justice from below" activities in other countries as well (McEvoy 2007).

11. In other areas of the world there has often been a regional learning process that helped facilitate the introduction of transitional justice concepts into new settings. Thus Latin American countries like Guatemala were able to rely on earlier experiences in Chile or Argentina, and the South African example helped introduce concepts to, for example, Sierra Leone. The lack of any precedent in the Middle East may have contributed to the lack of systematic awareness of these concepts among Palestinians and Israelis (the truth commission in Morocco seems too remote to affect this situation).

12. This exclusion is not meant to suggest that there is necessarily something normatively or politically wrong in such activities, but simply that they are beyond the framework of this particular chapter.

13. This is not meant as an exhaustive list.

14. For this and other details see the Web site www.combatantsforpeace.org/?lng =eng.

15. Lately the group has been complementing this method with public solidarity actions, for example, rebuilding Palestinian houses that were demolished by the Israeli authorities.

16. See their Web site at www.shovrimshtika.org/about_e.asp. See also Lavie (2004) for an interview with the group founder.

17. Notes from a public meeting of CFP, September 2006 and May 2007. This claim for special status has its critics. One veteran Israeli pacifist activist I spoke with felt that "by claiming a special role for combatants, they just reinforce the militaristic nature of Israeli society." Others have pointed to the distinctly masculine tone of the organization. While the group recognizes some of these shortcomings, they emphasize the tactical appeal of their identity as warriors. Responding to such critique, Alik Elkhanan told the audience in a meeting I attended: "None of you would have come here if we were mathematicians, same thing regarding the Palestinians. I was a soldier, not a very happy one and not very good—they would have sacked me if it was possible to sack a soldier—but when I introduce myself as a former combatant people listen to me." It should be added, though, that as this group becomes more and more involved in the anti-occupation activity in the Territories, together with other Israeli-Palestinian initiatives, it loses its "special status," and its members are seen like all "peaceniks" regardless of their personal histories.

18. See also their Web site at www.theparentscircle.com.

19. See more on their Web site: www.vispo.com/PRIME/.

20. For English translation see www.vispo.com/PRIME/leohn1.pdf.

21. See their Web site www.nakbainhebrew.org.

22. Quoted from the English version, www.nakbainhebrew.org/index.php?lang=english.

23. Another enabling factor may have been the (perhaps delayed) effects of the work of the Israeli historians known as the "New Historians." Since the late 1980s and early 1990s, a group of prominent historians, including Benny Morris, Avi Shlaim, and Tom Segev, among others, have produced "myth-breaking" studies of the history of Israel, in particular calling to attention abuses committed by Israel during the 1948 war and after, thus questioning the foundation of Israel's collective memory. The New Historians usually connected these historical insights to a radical pro-peace approach to contemporary affairs. These works provoked numerous high-profile debates in Israeli media and society and provided important groundwork for the current critical engagement with the past in the Israeli initiatives described here.

24. For example, the International Center for Transitional Justice, the leading organization in the field, details many transitional justice tactics in its introductory Web page (www.ictj.org/en/tj/) but does not include reform of textbooks or educational reform in general.

25. While it is clear that ministries of education on both sides would not adopt the new books as mandatory reading any time soon, the ambition of these projects is that the books will be used in some schools as additional or optional materials.

26. It might also be that the engagement with school textbooks represents a shift to a "long view" of the conflict: an understanding that full sustainable peace is not around the corner, and thus there is a need to pay attention to the next generation.

27. Talking about *two* narratives is of course simplistic: there are dozens of different narratives in both Israeli and Palestinian society, of people with different political,

social, or religious backgrounds. Nevertheless, the commonality of most narratives within each and in contrast to the other suffice to, for the sake of the argument, categorize them as *two* main narratives.

28. De Waal wrote this in the context of the effects of international funders on human rights NGOs in Africa.

29. This is not a critique of the type often targeted at funding institutions such as the World Bank, which are frequently accused of imposing agendas for countries in the South where these agendas had no indigenous resonance, but rather a more nuanced concern.

30. In any case, the number of activists is not necessarily crucial: many human rights NGOs with a very small number of staff members have important influence.

31. Usually, there is a brief "window of opportunity," right after a transition, to establish official mechanisms. Thus early work by civil society could be useful and helpful in quickly establishing them. In South Africa, work by civil society—conferences, consultations, papers—that took place before the 1994 elections was instrumental in facilitating the relatively quick decision to establish a TRC.

Chapter Twelve

1. A plethora of reports have been published about human rights violations in Burma. See reports by the Women's League of Burma (at www.womenofburma.org) and the Karen Human Rights Group (at www.khrg.org) as well as the United Nations Special Rapporteur on the situation of human rights in Myanmar (www.ohchr.org/english/countries/mm/index.htm), and various reports by Human Rights Watch and Amnesty International.

2. Because of these varying claims of autonomy and independence, and the long-standing resistance of some ethnic groups to being affiliated with the Burmese nation-state, I generally use the category "ethnic nationalities" for these groups, except when citing other researchers who use the term "ethnic minorities."

3. Some major ethnic nationalities were not represented at the conference, either because they were not invited (Mon) or because they boycotted (Karen).

4. As reported in the official government press, Saw Maung, the SLORC chairman, addressed the nation on the day of the coup, declaring, "I and all my colleagues, and all Tatmadawmen, most respectfully and honestly give our word to all rahans [Buddhist monks], laity and the people that we do not wish to cling to State power for long." For a thorough review of the events of 1988, see Lintner 1990.

5. Some armed insurgent groups continue to fight the SPDC, especially in Karen, Karenni, and Shan States. Human rights violations in these areas are the most severe in the country.

6. Smith quotes a Rangoon diplomat after the elections: "The army leaders are paralysed by fear—fear of the revenge of the people. It's the Nuremberg syndrome which held up political reform in Argentina and Chile for so long." Throughout ten years of working on this issue, the author has consistently faced this question from Burmese colleagues and Burma observers.

7. Daw Aung San Suu Kyi has also spoken generally about "tempered justice" in several interviews (see Houtman 1999 and Stewart 1997).

8. Daw Aung San Suu Kyi has been under house arrest from July 1989 to July 1995, September 2000 to May 2002, and May 2003 to the present.

9. ND-Burma is comprised of twelve organizations, including women's and youth groups from the Arakan, Kachin, Lahu, and Palaung ethnic groups; community-based human rights organizations working in Mon, Karen, Karenni, and Shan states; organizations of former political prisoners and human rights educators; and an environmental/human rights organization.

10. Martus is a free, open-source software available from the Benetech Initiative at www.martus.org.

11. On January 12, 2007, the Security Council voted on a resolution brought forward by the United States calling for an end to attacks on civilians in eastern Burma and to strengthen the mandate of the UN Secretary-General to facilitate a democratic transition in Burma. Nine members voted for the resolution, but China and Russia both vetoed it, South Africa voted against it, and Indonesia abstained. However, a 2006 Security Council vote keeps the situation in Burma on its permanent agenda.

12. "The crackdown" here refers to the use of deadly force against the monks and other demonstrators. During the five weeks of demonstrations before September 26, many people were beaten, and most '88 Generation Students leaders were detained.

13. For more information on measures developed by NGOs that resemble truth commissions but are not official government commissions, see Bickford 2007, Arriaza and Roht-Arriaza (this volume), and Dudai and Cohen (this volume).

14. These assertions are, admittedly, broad generalizations. I base these views on occasional interaction and discussions with Burmese political leaders who claim (with varying justification) to represent one constituency or another. Among organizations engaged in human rights and transitional justice work, as well as with transitional justice training participants, there is a recognition that many opposition political leaders, for reasons of political expediency and ambition, hold a pro–blanket amnesty view.

15. Beginning in 2002, to date HREIB has conducted over thirty transitional justice trainings with a variety of organizations, including journalists, political activists, former political prisoners, women's and youth groups, frontline combatants in conflict zones, and activists in urban centers of Burma.

16. The Tatmadaw's four-cuts campaign aims to cut off food, funds, intelligence, and recruits to opposition armed forces.

Afterword

1. I write "in part" for two reasons. First, because Central American and Latin American states have nevertheless helped develop the American Commission and Court. Second, because a further reason why Africa, Asia, and the Middle East have

such weak regional systems is that so many states in those regions do not want checks on their human rights abuses.

2. As well as to Bosnia, with its Muslim majority, and to minorities within western states (slavery and indigenous rights in the United States, for example).

3. For an example of such engagement, see the special issue on development in the *International Journal of Transitional Justice* (vol. 2, no. 3 [December 2008]).

Bibliography

'88 Generation Students. 2008. The findings in the Open Heart letter campaign in January 2007. Available at: www.burmalibrary.org/notice.php.

Adam, Heribert, and Kogila Moodley. 2005. *Seeking Mandela: Peacemaking Between Israelis and Palestinians.* Philadelphia: Temple University Press.

Adwan, Sami, and Dan Bar-On. 2004. Shared history project: A PRIME example of peace-building under fire. *International Journal of Politics, Culture and Society* 17:513–21.

Afghan Independent Human Rights Commission (AIHRC). 2005. A call for justice: A national consultation on past human rights violations in Afghanistan. Available at: www.aihrc.org.af/Rep_29_Eng/rep29_1_05call4justice.pdf.

African Commission on Human and People's Rights, Dakar Declaration, September 11, 1999. Available at: www.chr.up.ac.za/hr_docs/african/docs/achpr/achpr2.doc.

African Rights. January 2003. Gacaca justice: A shared responsibility.

Agamben, Giorgio. 1998. *Homo Sacer: Sovereign Power and Bare Life.* Stanford, CA: Stanford University Press.

Agha, Hussein, and Robert Malley. August 9, 2001. Camp David: The tragedy of errors. *New York Review of Books* 48, no. 13.

Aghion, Anne (dir.). 2002. *Gacaca, Living Together Again in Rwanda* [documentary film].

———. 2004. *In Rwanda We Say . . . The Family That Does Not Speak Dies* [documentary film].

———. 2009a. *My Neighbor My Killer* [documentary film].

———. 2009b. *The Notebooks of Memory* [documentary film].

Akec, John. 2006. Northern Uganda has lived on a knife's edge for too long. Accessed July 2, 2006, at http://johnakecsouthsudan.blogspot.com/.

Akhavan, Payam. 2005. The Lord's Resistance Army case: Uganda's submission of the first state referral to the International Criminal Court. *American Journal of International Law* 99:403–20.

Aldana, Raquel. 2006. A victim-centered reflection on truth commissions and prosecutions as a response to mass atrocities. *Journal of Human Rights* 5:107–26.

Allen, Tim. 1988–1989. Violence and moral knowledge: Observing social trauma in Sudan and Uganda. *Cambridge Anthropology* 132:45–66.

——. 2005. War and justice in northern Uganda: An assessment of the International Criminal Court's intervention. London: London School of Economics/Crisis States Research Centre. PDF version accessed March 15, 2005, at www.crisis-states.com.

——. 2006. *Trial Justice: The International Criminal Court and the Lord's Resistance Army.* London: Zed Books.

——. 2007. The International Criminal Court and the invention of traditional justice in northern Uganda. *Politique Africaine* 107:147–66.

——. 2008. Ritual (ab)use? The problem with traditional justice in northern Uganda. In *Courting Conflict? Justice, Peace and the ICC in Africa,* ed. Nicholas Waddell and Phil Clark, pp. 47–54. London: Royal African Society.

Altsean-Burma (Alternative Asean Network on Burma). October 5, 1999. Transcript: Part 2 of Aung San Suu Kyi interview.

America WOLA. October 16, 2003. Available at: www.wola.org/central_america/guatemala/testimony_chrc_oct03.htm.

Amnesty International. 1992. *Uganda: The Failure to Safeguard Human Rights.* London: Amnesty International.

——. 2002. *Rwanda: Gacaca: A Question of Justice.* London: Amnesty International.

Anonymous. June 24, 2006. Out of Africa, into The Hague. *Economist.*

Appadurai, Arjun. 1988. Putting hierarchy in its place. *Cultural Anthropology* 3:36–49.

Apuuli, Kasaija Phillip. 2006. The ICC arrest warrants for the Lord's Resistance Army leaders and peace prospects for northern Uganda. *Journal of International Criminal Justice* 41:179–87.

Arbour, Louise. October 25, 2006. Economic and social justice for societies in transition. Annual Lecture on Transitional Justice, New York University School of Law.

Archibald, Steven, and Paul Richards. 2002. Converts to human rights? Popular debate about war and justice in rural central Sierra Leone. *Africa: Journal of the International African Institute* 72:339–67.

Arnott, David. 2004. Burma/Myanmar: How to read the generals' "roadmap." Burma Online Library. Available at: www.ibiblio.org/obl/docs/how10.htm.

Arthur, Paige. 2009. How "transitions" shaped human rights: A conceptual history of transitional justice. *Human Rights Quarterly* 31:321–67.

Arusha Peace and Reconciliation Agreement for Burundi. August 28, 2000. Available at: www.usip.org/library/pa/burundi/pa_burundi_08282000_toc.html.

Aspen Institute Papers. November 4–6, 1988. State crimes: Punishment or pardon. Aspen Institute, Papers and Reports of the Conference, Wye Center, Maryland.

Avocats Sans Frontières. 2005. Monitoring des Juridictions Gacaca, Phase de Jugement, Rapport Analytique, Mars–Septembre 2005. Available at: www.asf.be/publications/publications_rwanda_monitoring_gacaca_mars-sept2005_FR.pdf.

——. February 2008. Monitoring of the Gacaca Courts, Judgment Phase, Analytical Report No. 3, October 2000 –April 2007. Available at: www.asf.be/publications/publication_rwanda_Rapport_analytiqueIII_FR.pdf.

Back, Rachel. 2006. A meeting of the dispossessed and the possessors: The Miar-Yaad Initiative. Paper presented in Memory, Narrative and Forgiveness conference, University of Cape Town, November 2006.

Backer, David. 2003. Civil society and transitional justice: Possibilities, patterns and prospects. *Journal of Human Rights* 2(3):297–313.

Badie, Bertrand. 2002. *La diplomatie des droits de l'homme.* Paris: Fayard.

Baines, Erin K. 2007. The haunting of Alice: Local approaches to justice and reconciliation in northern Uganda. *International Journal of Transitional Justice* 1:91–114.

Ballengee, Morris. 1999. The critical role of non-governmental organizations in transitional justice: A case study of Guatemala. *UCLA Journal of International Law and Foreign Affairs* 42:477–510.

Barkan, Eleazer. 2000. *The Guilt of Nations: Restitution and Negotiating Historical Injustices.* New York: W. W. Norton.

Bass, Gary. 2000. *Stay the Hand of Vengeance: The Politics of War Crimes Tribunals.* Princeton, NJ: Princeton University Press.

Bassiouni, Cherif. 2002. *Post-Conflict Justice.* New York: Transnational Publishers.

———. 2004. September 21 Report of the Independent Expert of the Commission on Human Rights on the Situation of Human Rights in Afghanistan, UN General Assembly, A/59/370.

Beehner, Lionel. January 5, 2007. Impediments to national reconciliation in Iraq. Council on Foreign Relations. Available at: www.cfr.org/publication/12347.

Behrend, Heike. 1999. *Alice Lakwena and the Holy Spirits: War in Northern Uganda, 1985–97.* Oxford: James Currey.

Bell, Christine. 2000. *Peace Agreements and Human Rights.* Oxford: Oxford University Press.

———. 2003. Dealing with the past in Northern Ireland. *Fordham Law Review* 26:1095–1118.

Bell, Christine, and Joanna Keenan. 2004. Human rights nongovernmental organizations and the problem of transition. *Human Rights Quarterly* 262:330–74.

Besheer, Margaret. March 11, 2006. Milosevic death a blow to victims and tribunal. *Voice of America News.* Available at: www.voanews.com/english/2006-03-11-voa24.cfm.

Bhargava, Rajeev. 2000. Restoring decency to barbaric societies. In *Truth v. Justice: The Morality of Truth Commissions,* ed. Robert I. Rotberg and Denis Thompson, pp. 45–67. Princeton, NJ: Princeton University Press.

Bickford, Louis. 1999. The archival imperative: Human rights and historical memory in Latin America's Southern cone. *Human Rights Quarterly* 21:1097–122.

———. 2007. Unofficial truth projects. *Human Rights Quarterly* 294:994–1035.

Biggar, Nigel. 2003. *Burying the Past: Making Peace and Doing Justice After Civil Conflict.* Washington, DC: Georgetown University Press.

Bloomfield, David, Teresa Barnes, and Luc Huyse. 2003. *Reconciliation After Violent Conflict: A Handbook.* Stockholm: Institute for Democracy and Electoral Assistance.

Boraine, Alex, Janet Levy, and Ronel Scheffer (eds.). 1994. *Dealing with the Past: Truth and Reconciliation in South Africa*. Cape Town: IDASA.

Borer, Tristan Anne. 2003. A taxonomy of victims and perpetrators: Human rights and reconciliation in South Africa. *Human Rights Quarterly* 25:1088–116.

Borneman, John. 2002. Reconciliation after ethnic cleansing: Listening, retribution, affiliation. *Public Culture* 14:281–304.

Bourdieu, Pierre. 1990. *The Logic of Practice*. Stanford, CA: Stanford University Press.

Brahm, Eric. October 6–8, 2004. Getting to the bottom of truth: Evaluating the contribution of truth commissions to post-conflict societies. Presentation to the Wisconsin Institute for Peace and Conflict Studies 20th Annual Conference, Challenges and Paths to Justice, Marquette University, Milwaukee, WI.

Branch, Adam. 2005. Neither peace nor justice: Political violence and the peasantry in northern Uganda, 1986–1998. *African Studies Quarterly: The Online Journal for African Studies*. 82:1–31.

———. 2007. Uganda's civil war and the politics of ICC intervention. *Ethics and International Affairs* 212:179–98.

Brett, E. A. 1995. Neutralising the use of force in Uganda: The role of the military in politics. *Journal of Modern African Studies* 331:129–52.

Brinkley, Douglas. 1997. Democratic enlargement: The Clinton doctrine. *Foreign Policy* 106:110–27.

Brooks, Rosa Ehrenreich. 2003. The new imperialism: Violence, norms, and the "rule of law." *Michigan Law Review* 101:2275–340, pin cite 2336.

Brown, Wendy. 1995. *States of Injury*. Princeton, NJ: Princeton University Press.

Bruckner, Pascal. 2006. *La tyrannie de la penitence*. Paris: Grasset.

Burnet, Jennie E. 2008. The injustice of local justice: Truth, reconciliation, and revenge in Rwanda. *Genocide Studies and Prevention* 3:173–93.

Bush, George W. September 20, 2001. Address to a Joint Session of Congress and the American People, United States Capitol, Washington, DC, Office of Press Secretary.

Byrne, Rosemary. 2006. Promises of peace and reconciliation: Previewing the legacy of the International Criminal Tribunal for Rwanda. *European Review* 144:485–98.

Cabrera, María Luisa. 2006. *Violencia e impunidad en comunidades mayas de Guatemala: La massacre de Xamán desde una perspectiva psicosocial*. Guatemala: ECAP.

Cairns, Ed, and Michael Roe. 2005. *The Role of Memory in Ethnic Conflict*. London: Macmillan.

Callahan, Mary. 2003. *Making Enemies: War and State Building in Burma*. Ithaca, NY: Cornell University Press.

Campbell, Kirsten. 2001. The trauma of justice. Presented at the Human Frailty: Rights, Ethics and the Search for Global Justice conference, University of West England.

Carmack, Robert (ed.). 1988. *Harvest of Violence: The Mayan Indians and the Guatemalan Crisis*. Norman: University of Oklahoma Press.

Carothers, Thomas. 2002. The end of the transition paradigm. *Journal of Democracy* 13:1–21.

Cavanagh, Dawn, and Prudence Mabele. May 10, 2006. Article based on an interview with Khwezi. Available at: www.mask.org.za/article.php?cat=southafrica&id =1066. Also in *City Press*, March 14, 2006, p. 4.

Center for Excellence in Disaster Management and Humanitarian Assistance. 2008. Cyclone Nargis update. Available at: www.coe-dmha.org/myanmar.htm.

Chanock, Martin. 1985. *Law, Custom and Social Order: The Colonial Experience in Malawi and Zambia*. Cambridge: Cambridge University Press.

Chaumont, Jean-Michel. 2002. *La Concurrence des victimes*. Paris: La Découverte.

Chayes, Antonia, and Martha L. Minow (eds.). 2003. *Imagine Coexistence: Restoring Humanity After Violent Ethnic Conflict*. San Francisco: Jossey-Bass.

Chesterman, Simon. 2002. Justice under International Administration: Kosovo, East Timor, and Afghanistan, International Peace Academy Special Report, New York.

Clark, Phil. 2007. Hybridity, holism, and "traditional" justice: The case of the gacaca courts in post-genocide Rwanda. *George Washington University International Law Review* 39, no. 4.

———. 2008. Law, politics and pragmatism: The ICC and case selection in the Democratic Republic of Congo and Uganda. In *Courting Conflict? Justice, Peace and the ICC in Africa*, ed. Nicholas Waddell and Phil Clark, pp. 37–46. London: Royal African Society.

———. 2009. The rules (and politics) of engagement: The *gacaca* courts and post-genocide justice, healing and reconciliation in Rwanda. In *After Genocide: Transitional Justice, Post-Conflict Reconstruction and Reconciliation in Rwanda and Beyond*, ed. Phil Clark and Zachary D. Kaufman, pp. 297–319. London: Hurst.

Clarke, Kamari Maxime. 2007. Global justice, local controversies: The International Criminal Court and the sovereignty of victims. In *Paths to International Justice: Social and Legal Perspectives*, ed. Marie-Bénédicte Dembour and Tobias Kelly, pp. 134–60. Cambridge: Cambridge University Press.

Cobban, Helena. 2006. International courts. *Foreign Policy* 153:22–28.

———. 2007. *Amnesty After Atrocity? Healing Nations After Genocide and War Crimes*. Boulder, CO: Paradigm.

Cockayne, James. 2005. The fraying shoestring: Rethinking hybrid war crimes tribunals. *Fordham International Law Journal* 28:616–80.

Cohen, David. 2006. Indifference and accountability: The United Nations and the politics of international justice in East Timor, East-West Center Special Report no. 9, Honolulu.

Cohen, Hillel. 2007. *The Rise and Fall of Arab Jerusalem, 1967–2007* [in Hebrew]. Jerusalem: Jerusalem Institute for Israel Studies.

Cohen, Stanley. 2001. *States of Denial: Knowing About Atrocities and Suffering*. Cambridge, UK: Polity Press.

Cole, Elizabeth. 2007. Transitional justice and the reform of history education. *International Journal of Transitional Justice* 1:115–37.

Colloquium of Prosecutors of International Criminal Tribunals. November 2004. Report of proceedings on "the challenges of international justice."

Colonomos, Ariel. 2005. *La morale dans les relations internationales*. Paris: Odile Jacob.

Comisión de Esclarecimiento Histórico. 1999. *Memoria del Silencio/Memory of Silence*, vol. 3. Guatemala. Available in Spanish at: http://shr.aaas.org/guatemala/ceh/mds/spanish. Summary and recommendations available in English at: http://shr.aaas.org/guatemala/ceh/report/english/conc2.html.

Commission for Reception, Truth and Reconciliation in East Timor. CAVR. 2006. *Chega!* [Enough!]: Final Report, Part 7.2, at 248, 264–93. Available at: www.ictj.org/en/news/features/846.html.

Commission for Truth and Reconciliation. 2003. Final Report, Lima, Peru. Available at: www.cverdad.org.pe/ingles/pagina01.php.

Coulter, Chris. 2006. Being a bush wife: Women's lives through war and peace in Northern Sierra Leone. PhD diss., Department of Anthropology, University of Uppsala, Sweden.

———. 2009. *Bush Wives and Girl Soldiers: Women's Lives Through War and Peace in Sierra Leone*. Ithaca, NY: Cornell University Press.

Cowan, Jane K., Marie-Bénédicte Dembour, and Richard A. Wilson (eds.). 2001. *Culture and Rights: Anthropological Perspectives*. Cambridge: Cambridge University Press.

Crepeau, Pierre, and Simon Bizimana. 1979. *Proverbes du Rwanda*. Tervuren, Belgium: Musée Royal de l'Afrique Centrale.

Crumley, Carole. 2002. Exploring venues of social memory. In *Social Memory and History: Anthropological Approaches*, ed. Jacob Climo and Maria Cattell, pp. 39–52. Walnut Creek, CA: Altamira Press.

Dajani, Mohammed, and Baskin Gershon. 2006. Israeli-Palestinian joint activities: Problematic endeavour, but necessary challenge. In *Bridging the Divide: Peacebuilding in the Israeli–Palestinian Conflict*, ed. Edy Kaufmann and Walid Salem, pp. 87–109. London: Lynne Rienner.

Daley, Patricia. 2006. Ethnicity and political violence in Africa: The challenge to the Burundi state. *Political Geography* 25:657–79.

Das, Veena. 1996. Language and body: Transactions in the construction of pain. *Daedelus* 125:67–92.

———. 2000. The act of witnessing: Violence, poisonous knowledge, and subjectivity. In *Violence and Subjectivity*, ed. Veena Das, Arthur Kleinman, Mamphela Ramphele, and Pamela Reynolds, pp. 205–25. Berkeley: University of California Press.

———. 2007. *Life and Words: Violence and the Descent into the Ordinary*. Berkeley: University of California Press.

Das, Veena, and Arthur Kleinman. Introduction. 2000. In *Violence and Subjectivity,* ed. Veena Das, Arthur Kleinman, Mamphela Ramphele, and Pamela Reynolds, pp. 1–18. Berkeley: University of California Press.

DDR and Stability in Africa. 2007. Final report: Second International Conference on Disarmament, Demobilization, Reintegration, and Stablity in Africa, Kinshasa. Available at: www.un.org/africa/osaa/reports/DDR%20report%20Kinshasa_final October%2024%202006.pdf.

Degregori, Carlos Iván. 1990. *Qué difícil es ser Dios: ideologya y violencia en Sendero Luminoso.* Lima: El Zorro de Abajo.

Degregori, Carlos Iván, José Coronel, Ponciano del Pino, and Orin Starn. 1996. *Las rondas campesinas y la derrota de Sendero Luminoso.* Lima: Instituto de Estudios Peruanos.

Del Pino, Ponciano. 1998. Family, culture, and revolution: Everday life with Sendero Luminoso. In *Shining and Other Paths: War and Society in Peru, 1980–1995,* ed. Steve J. Stern. Durham, NC: Duke University Press.

Del Pino, Ponciano, and Kimberly Theidon. 2000. El Chino ya murió, Ayacucho lo mató: Crónica de una muerte no anunciada. *Ideele: Revista del Instituto de Defensa Legal* (127):49–53.

Democratic Alliance Women's Network. 2006. Letter to the ANC Women's League. Copy in author's possession.

Derrida, Jacques. 1999. Le siècle et le pardon. *Le Monde des débats* 9:10–17.

Des Forges, Alison. 1999. *"Leave None to Tell the Story": Genocide in Rwanda.* New York: Human Rights Watch.

De Waal, Alex. 2003. Human rights organizations and the political imagination: How the West and Africa have diverged. *Journal of Human Rights* 24:475–94.

Dexter, Tracy, and Philippe Ntahombaye. 2005. *The Role of Informal Justice Systems in Fostering the Rule of Law in Post-Conflict Situations: The Case of Burundi.* Geneva: Henry Dunant Centre for Humanitarian Dialogue.

Diaz, Catalina. 2007. Colombia's Bid for Justice and Peace draft. Workshop 5—Lessons from Negotiated Justice Options in South Africa and Colombia. Available at: www.humansecuritygateway.com/showRecord.php?RecordId=23299.

Dill, Kathleen. 2005. International human rights and local justice in Guatemala: The Rio Negro Pakoxom and Agua Fría Trials. *Cultural Dynamics* 17:323–50.

Drexler, Elizabeth. 2009. Addressing the legacies of mass violence and genocide in East Timor and Indonesia. In *Genocide: Truth, Memory, and Representation,* ed. Alexander Laban Hinton, pp. 219–47. Durham, NC: Duke University Press.

Drumbl, Mark. 2007. *Atrocity, Punishment and International Law.* Cambridge: Cambridge University Press.

Dudai, Ron. 2007a. A model for dealing with the past in the Israeli-Palestinian context. *International Journal of Transitional Justice* 12:249–67.

———. 2007b. Does any of this matter? Transitional justice and the Israeli–Palestinian conflict. In *Crime, Social Control and Human Rights: Essays in Honour of Stan-*

ley Cohen, ed. Christine Chinkin, David Downes, Conor Gearty, and Paul Rock, pp. 329–42. Cullompton, UK: Willan.

Duthie, Roger. 2005. Transitional justice and social reintegration. Paper prepared for the Stockholm Initiative on Disarmament, Demobilisation, Reintegration (SIDDR). Available at: www.sweden.gov.se/content/1/c6/06/54/02/7545e870.pdf.

Elsea, Jennifer. September 3, 2005. U.S. policy regarding the International Criminal Court. *Congressional Research Service*. Washington, DC.

Elster, Jon. 2004. *Closing the Books: Transitional Justice in Historical Perspective*. New York: Cambridge University Press.

Eltringham, Nigel. 2004. *Accounting for Horror: Post-Genocide Debate in Rwanda*. London: Pluto Press.

Eltringham, Nigel, and Saskia Van Hoyweghen. 2001. Power and identity in post-genocide Rwanda. In *Politics of Identity and Economics of Conflict in the Great Lakes Region*, ed. Ruddy Doom and Jan Gorus, pp. 215–42. Brussels: VUB Press.

Englund, Harri. 2006. *Prisoners of Freedom: Human Rights and the African Poor*. Berkeley: University of California Press.

Etcheson, Craig. April 18, 2006. A fair and public trial: A political history of the extraordinary chambers. *Justice Initiative*. Available at: www.krtrial.info/showarticle.php?language=english&action=showarticle&art_id=935&needback=1.

Evans-Pritchard, E. E. 1940. *The Nuer: A Description of the Modes of Livelihood and Political Institutions of a Nilotic People*. Oxford: Clarendon Press.

Faltas, Sami. 2005. DDR without camps. Topical chapter for the conversion survey (BICC). Available at: www.sweden.gov.se/content/1/c6/06/54/02/5d16fcf2.pdf.

Faulder, Dominic. July 13, 1990. We will play fair (interview). *Asiaweek*.

Feitlowitz, Marguerite. 1999. *A Lexicon of Terror: Argentina and the Legacies of Torture*. Oxford: Oxford University Press.

Feldman, Allen. 1991. *Formations of Violence*. Chicago: University of Chicago Press.

———. 2003. Strange fruit: The South African Truth Commission and the demonic economies of violence. In *Beyond Rationalism: Rethinking Magic, Witchcraft and Sorcery*, ed. Bruce Kapferer, pp. 234–65. Oxford: Berghahn Books.

Ferme, Mariane. 2001. *The Underneath of Things: Violence, History, and the Everyday in Sierra Leone*. Berkeley: University of California Press.

Fernandez, James W. 1965. Symbolic consensus in a Fang reformative cult. *American Anthropologist* 674:902–29.

Fernandez Meijide, Graciela, et. al. 1992. The role of historical inquiry in creating accountability for human rights abuses. *Boston College Third World Law Journal* 12:269–306.

Fink, Christina. 2000. An overview of Burma's ethnic politics. *Cultural Survival Quarterly* 24(3).

———. 2001. *Living Silence: Burma Under Military Rule*. London: Zed Books.

Finlayson, Ruth. 1984. The changing nature of *isiHlonipho sabafazi*. *African Studies* 43:3137–46.

Finnström, Sverker. 2006. Wars of the past and war in the present: The Lord's Resistance Movement/Army in Uganda. *Africa* 762:200–20.

———. 2008a. An African hell of colonial imagination? The Lord's Resistance Army/Movement in Uganda: Another story. *Politique Africaine* 112:119–39.

———. 2008b. *Living with Bad Surroundings: War, History, and Everyday Moments in Northern Uganda*. Durham, NC: Duke University Press.

———. 2009. Fear of the midnight knock: State sovereignty and internal enemies in Uganda. *Crisis of the State: War and Social Upheaval*, ed. Bruce Kapferer and Bjorn Bertelsen, pp. 124–42. Oxford: Berghahn Books.

Fletcher, Laurel. 2005. From indifference to engagement: Bystanders and international criminal justice. *Michigan Journal of International Law* 26:1014–51.

Fletcher, Laurel, and Harvey M. Weinstein. 2002. Violence and social repair: Rethinking the contribution of justice to reconciliation. *Human Rights Quarterly* 243:573–639.

———. 2004. A world unto itself? The application of international justice in the former Yugoslavia. In *My Neighbor, My Enemy: Justice and Community in the Aftermath of Mass Atrocity*, ed. Eric Stover and Harvey M. Weinstein, pp. 29–48. Cambridge: Cambridge University Press.

Fletcher, Laurel, and Harvey M. Weinstein with Jamie Rowen. 2009. Context, timing, and the dynamics of transitional justice: A historical perspective. *Human Rights Quarterly* 29:163–220.

Foucault, Michel. 2001. La vérité et les formes juridiques. In *Dits et écrits tome 1:1954–1975*. Paris: Gallimard.

Freedman, Sarah Warshauer, Déo Kambanda, Beth Lewis Samuelson, Innocent Mugisha, Immaculée Mukashema, Evode Mukama, Jean Mutabaruka, Harvey M. Weinstein, and Timothy Longman. 2004. Confronting the past in Rwandan schools. In *My Neighbor, My Enemy: Justice and Community in the Aftermath of Mass Atrocity*, ed. Eric Stover and Harvey Weinstein, pp. 249–65. Cambridge: Cambridge University Press.

Freeman, Mark. 2005. Transitional justice in Morocco: A progress report. New York: ICTJ.

———. 2006. *Truth Commissions and Procedural Justice*. Oxford: Oxford University Press.

Front Line Defenders. 2005. *Front Line Rwanda: Disappearances, Arrests, Threats, Intimidation and Co-option of Human Rights Defenders, 2001–2004*. Dublin. Available at: www.frontlinedefenders.org/ar/files/en/FrontLineRwandaReport .pdf.

Garapon, Antoine. 2002. *Des crimes qu'on ne peut ni punir ni pardonner: Pour une justice internationale*. Paris: Odile Jacob.

Gates, Scott. 2002. Recruitment and allegiance: The microfoundations of rebellion. *Journal of Conflict Resolution* 46:111–30.

Gersony, Robert. 1997. The anguish of northern Uganda: Results of a field-based assessment of the civil conflict in northern Uganda. Report submitted to United States Embassy, Kampala, and USAID, Kampala.

Gibney, Mark, Rhoda E. Howard-Hassmann, Jean-Marc Coicaud, and Niklaus Steiner (eds.). 2008. *The Age of Apology*. Philadelphia: University of Pennsylvania Press.

Gingyera-Pinycwa, A.G.G. 1992. *Northern Uganda in National Politics*. Kampala: Fountain.

Girling, Frank Knowles. 1960. *The Acholi of Uganda*. London: Her Majesty's Stationery Office.

Goldblatt, Beth, and Sheila Meintjes. 1997. *Gender and the Truth and Reconciliation Commission: A Submission to the Truth and Reconciliation Commission*. Johannesburg: Centre for Applied Legal Studies.

Goldmann, Matthias. 2006. Does peace follow justice or vice versa? Plans for postconflict justice in Burundi. *Fletcher Forum of World Affairs* 30:137–52.

Goodale, Mark. 2006a. Ethical theory as social practice. *American Anthropologist* 108:25–37.

———. 2006b. Introduction to anthropology and human rights in a new key. *American Anthropologist* 108:1–8.

Gration, Jonathan S. 2006. Maghreb roundtable series. Center for Strategic and International Studies, Washington, DC.

Gready, Paul. 2003. Introduction. In *Political Transition: Politics and Cultures*, ed. Paul Gready. London: Pluto Press.

———. Forthcoming. *Aftermaths: Truth, Justice and Reconciliation in Post-Apartheid South Africa*.

Griffin, Susan. 1982. *Made from This Earth*. London: Women's Press.

Guillerot, Julie, and Lisa Magarell. 2006. *Reparación en la transición peruana: Memorias de un proceso inacabado*. Lima: APRODEH.

Gupta, Akhil, and James Ferguson. 1997a. Beyond "culture": Space, identity, and the politics of difference. In *Culture, Power, Place: Explorations in Critical Anthropology*, ed. Akhil Gupta and James Ferguson, pp. 33–51. Durham, NC: Duke University Press.

———. 1997b. Culture, power, place: Ethnography at the end of an era. In *Culture, Power, Place: Explorations in Critical Anthropology*, ed. Akhil Gupta and James Ferguson, pp. 1–29. Durham, NC: Duke University Press.

Hagborg, Lars. 2001. Silence: Disputes on the ground and in the mind among the Iraqw in Karatu district, Tanzania. PhD diss., Uppsala University, Uppsala, Sweden.

Halbwachs, Maurice. 1980. *The Collective Memory*. New York: Harper and Row; 1950, original publication in French.

Hale, Charles R. (ed.). 2008. *Engaging Contradictions: Theory, Politics, and Methods of Activist Scholarship*. Berkeley: University of California Press.

Hamber, Brandon. 2001. Does the truth heal? A psychological perspective on political strategies for dealing with the legacy of political violence. In *Burying the Past:*

Making Peace and Doing Justice After Civil Conflict, ed. Nigel Biggar, pp. 131–48. Washington, DC: Georgetown University Press.

Harlacher, Thomas, Francis Xavier Okot, Caroline Aloyo Obonyo, Mychelle Balthazard, and Ronald Atkinson. 2006. Traditional ways of coping in Acholi: Cultural provisions for reconciliation and healing from war. Kampala, Uganda: Caritas Gulu Archdiocese.

Hassner, Pierre. 2002. The United States: The empire of force or the force of empire. *EU/ISS Chaillot Papers,* no. 54.

Hassner, Pierre, and Justin Vaïsse. 2003. *Washington et le monde: Dilemmes d'une superpuissance.* Paris: CERI/Autrement.

Hayman, Rachel. 2007. Milking the cow: Negotiating ownership of aid and policy in Rwanda. Global Economic Governance Working Paper 2007/26. Oxford: University College. Available at: www.globaleconomicgovernance.org/wp-content/uploads/hayman_rwanda_2007-261.pdf.

Hayner, Priscilla B. 2001. *Unspeakable Truths: Confronting State Terror and Atrocity.* London: Routledge.

Hazan, Pierre. 2006. Morocco betting on a Truth and Reconciliation Commission. United States Institute of Peace, Washington, DC, Special Report no. 165.

———. 2007. *Juger la guerre, juger l'histoire: Du bon usage des commissions vérité et de la justice internationale.* Paris: Presses Universitaires de France.

Heiberg, Marianne, Brendan O'Leary, and John Tirman. 2007. *Terror, Insurgency, and the State: Ending Protracted Conflicts.* Philadelphia: University of Pennsylvania Press.

Henkin, Alice. 1995. State crimes: Punishment or pardon (conference report). In *Transitional Justice: How Emerging Democracies Reckon with Former Regimes,* ed. Neil Kritz, vols. I–III, pp. 184–216. Washington, DC: United States Institute of Peace Press.

Hermann, Tamar. 2006. Civil society and NGOs building peace in Israel. In *Bridging the Divide: Peacebuilding in the Israeli-Palestinian Conflict,* ed. Edy Kaufmann and Walid Salem, pp. 39–58. London: Lynne Rienner.

Hoffman, Daniel. 2005. Violent events as narrative blocs: The disarmament at Bo, Sierra Leone. *Anthropological Quarterly* 78:329–54.

Hoffmann, Stanley. 2004. Clash of globalizations. *Foreign Affairs* 81:104–26.

———. 2005. American exceptionalism: The new version. In *American Exceptionalism and Human Rights,* ed. Michael Ignatieff, pp. 225–40. Princeton, NJ: Princeton University Press.

Hohe, Tanja, and Rod Nixon. 2003. Reconciling justice: Traditional law and state judiciary in East Timor. Report prepared for the United States Institute of Peace. Available at: www.grc-exchange.org/g_themes/ssaj_workshop0303.html.

Hollander, Nancy Caro. 2001. *Love in a Time of Hate: Liberation Psychology in Latin America.* New York: Other Press.

Honwana, Alcinda. 1999. Negotiating post-war identities: Child soldiers in Mozambique and Angola. *CODESRIA Bulletin* 1–2:4–13.

Houtman, Gustaaf. 1999. *Mental Culture in Burmese Crisis Politics: Aung San Suu Kyi and the National League for Democracy.* Study of Languages and Cultures of Asia and Africa Monograph Series no. 33. Tokyo: Tokyo University of Foreign Studies, Institute for the Study of Languages and Cultures of Asia and Africa.

Hovil, Lucy, and Joanna R. Quinn. 2005. Peace first, justice later: Traditional justice in northern Uganda. *Refugee Law Project Working Paper Series,* July 8. Working Paper no. 17.

Human Rights Watch. April 1, 2000. Rwanda: The search for security and human rights abuses. New York. Available at: www.hrw.org/en/reports/2000/04/01/rwanda-search-security-and-human-rights-abuses.

———. May 19, 2000. Sierra Leone: Expedited international criminal tribunal urged. New York. Available at: www.hrw.org/press/2000/05/sl-ltr0519.htm.

———. May 8, 2003. Preparing for elections: Tightening control in the name of unity. New York. Available at: www.hrw.org/legacy/backgrounder/africa/rwanda0503-bck.htm.

———. July 14, 2003. Abducted and abused: Renewed conflict in northern Uganda. PDF version, New York. Available at: www.hrw.org/reports/2003/uganda0703/.

———. May 2005. Concerns regarding torture and other cruel, inhuman or degrading treatment or punishment in Uganda. New York. Available at: www.hrw.org/legacy/backgrounder/africa/uganda0505/.

———. November 2005. Morocco's truth commission: Honoring past victims during an uncertain present, vol. 17, no. 11. New York. Available at: www.hrw.org/reports/2005/morocco1105/index.htm.

———. November 19, 2006. Judging Dujail: The first trial before the Iraqi High Tribunal. New York. Available at: www.hrw.org/en/reports/2006/11/19/judging-dujail.

———. January 2007. Killings in eastern Rwanda. New York. Available at: www.hrw.org/backgrounder/africa/rwanda0107/.

———. April 30, 2008. Vote to nowhere: The May 2008 Constitutional Referendum in Burma. New York. Available at: www.hrw.org/en/node/62239/section/1.

———. July 24, 2008. Law and reality: Progress in judicial reform in Rwanda. New York. Available at: www.hrw.org/en/node/62097/section/1.

Humphreys, Macartan, and Jeremy M. Weinstein. 2004. What the fighters say: A survey of ex-combatants in Sierra Leone June–August 2003. Interim report. Available at: www.columbia.edu/~mh2245/SL.htm.

Hutchinson, Sharon Elaine. 1996. *Nuer Dilemmas: Coping with Money, War, and the State.* Berkeley: University of California Press.

Huyse, Luc, and Mark Salter (eds.). 2008. *Traditional Justice and Reconciliation after Violent Conflict: Learning from African Experiences.* Stockholm: International IDEA. Available at: www.idea.int/publications/traditional_justice/index.cfm.

Ignatieff, Michael. 1996. Articles of Faith. *Index on Censorship* 5:110–22.

———. 2005. Introduction. In *American Exceptionalism and Human Rights*, ed. Michael Ignatieff. Princeton, NJ: Princeton University Press.

Ingelaere, Bert. 2007. Does the truth pass across the fire without burning? Transitional justice and its discontents in Rwanda's gacaca courts. Discussion paper, Institute of Development Policy and Management, University of Antwerp.

———. 2008. The Gacaca Courts in Rwanda. In *Traditional Justice and Reconciliation After Violent Conflict: Learning from African Experiences*, ed. Luc Huyse and Mark Salter, pp. 25–59. Stockholm: International IDEA.

Instance Equité et Réconciliation. 2005. Synthèse du rapport final (résumé), Rabat, Morocco: IER. Available at: www.ier.ma/article.php3?id_article=1496.

Instituto de Defensa Legal (IDL). 1995. *Informe de la Comisión de Juristas Internacionales sobre la administración de justicia en el Perú.*

International Center for Transitional Justice. 2004. *Truth Commissions and NGOs: The Essential Relationship.* New York: ICTJ.

———. 2008a. Mission statement. Available at: www.ictj.org/en/about/mission/.

———. 2008b. DDR and transitional justice. Available at: www.ictj.org/en/research/projects/ddr/index.html.

International Center for Transitional Justice and U.C. Berkeley Human Rights Center. 2004. Iraqi voices: Attitudes toward transitional justice and social reconstruction. Available at: www.ictj.org/images/content/1/0/108.pdf.

———. 2005. Forgotten voices: A population-based survey on attitudes about peace and justice in northern Uganda. Available at: www.ictj.org/en/news/press/release/262.html.

International Crisis Group. 2002. *Rwanda at the End of the Transition: A Necessary Political Liberalization.* Brussels: International Crisis Group.

Internews. 2005. *Justice in Rwanda 27.* Available at: www.internews.org.rw/video.htm (follow Newsreel 27 hyperlink).

Jackson, Michael. 2004. *In Sierra Leone.* Durham, NC: Duke University Press.

———. 2005. Storytelling events, violence, and the appearance of the past. *Anthropological Quarterly* 78:355–75.

Jamal, Amal. 2001. Mutual recognition, reconciliation and conflict transformation [in Hebrew]. *Israeli Sociology* 32:313–41.

James, Wendy. 1988. *The Listening Ebony: Moral Knowledge, Religion and Power Among the Uduk of Sudan.* Oxford: Clarendon Press.

Jelin, Elizabeth. 1994. The politics of memory: The human rights movements and the construction of democracy in Argentina. *Latin American Perspectives* 21:38–58.

———. 2002. *Los trabajos de la memoria.* Madrid: Siglo XXI.

———. 2003. *State Repression and the Labors of Memory,* trans. Judy Rein and Marcial Godoy-Anativia. Minneapolis: University of Minnesota Press.

Jewett, Aubrey, and Marc Turetzky. 1998. Stability and change in President Clinton's foreign policy beliefs, 1993–1996. *Presidential Studies Quarterly* 28.

Judicial System Monitoring Programme (JSMP). 2004. Unfulfilled expectations: Community views on CAVR's community reconciliation process. Available at: www .jsmp.minihub.org/new/otherreports.htm.

Kadende-Kaiser, Rose M., and Paul J. Kaiser. 1997. Modern folklore, identity, and political change in Burundi. *African Studies Review* 40:29–54.

Kagame, Paul. April 21, 2004. Speech by His Excellency Paul Kagame, President of the Republic of Rwanda, at the Woodrow Wilson International Center for Scholars.

———. April 22, 2004. Speech by His Excellency President Paul Kagame at the University of Washington.

———. September 19, 2005. The challenges of human rights in Rwanda after the 1994 genocide. Speech by His Excellency Paul Kagame, President of the Republic of Rwanda at the University of Connecticut.

Kagan, Robert. 2002. Power and weakness: Why the United States and Europe see the world differently. *Policy Review* (113):3–28.

Kahn, Paul W. 2003. The International Criminal Court: Why the United States is so opposed. *Crimes of War Project, The Magazine.* Available at: www.crimesofwar .org/icc_magazine/icc-kahn.html.

Kalyvas, Stathis N. 2006. *The Logic of Violence in Civil War.* New York: Cambridge University Press.

Karekezi, Urusaro Alice. 2001. Juridictions *Gacaca*: Lutte contre l'impunitie et promotion de la reconciliation nationale. *Cahiers du Centre de Gestion des Conflits* 3:9–96.

Karekezi, Urusaro Alice, Alphonse Nshimiyimana, and Beth Mutamba. 2004. Localizing justice: *Gacaca* courts in post-genocide Rwanda. In *My Neighbor, My Enemy: Justice and Community in the Aftermath of Mass Atrocity*, ed. Eric Stover and Harvey M. Weinstein, pp. 69–84. Cambridge: Cambridge University Press.

Katzenstein, Peter (ed.). 1996. *The Culture of National Security: Norms and Identity in World Politics.* New York: Columbia University Press.

Kaufman, Stuart J. 2006. Escaping the symbolic politics trap: Reconciliation initiatives and conflict resolution in ethnic wars. *Journal of Peace Research* 43:201–18.

Kelsall, Tim. 2005. Truth, lies, ritual: Preliminary reflections on the Truth and Reconciliation Commission in Sierra Leone. *Human Rights Quarterly* 27:361–91.

———. 2006. Politics, anti-politics, international justice: Language and power in the Special Court for Sierra Leone. *Review of International Studies* 32:587–602.

Kessel, Ineke van, and Barbara Oomen. 1997. One chief, one vote: The revival of traditional authorities in post-apartheid South Africa. *African Affairs* 96:561–85.

Khatib, Ghassan. September 4, 2005. Narratives revisited: Mind the gap. *Bitterlemons* 35.

Khwezi. March 14, 2006. Interview with Dawn Cavanagh and Prudence Mabele, 1 in 9, reported in *City Press*, p. 4.

Knight, Mark, and Alpaslan Özerdem. 2004. Guns, camps and cash: Disarmament, demobilization and reinsertion of former combatants in transitions from war to peace. *Journal of Peace Research* 41:499–516.

Koch, Klaus Friedrich, Soraya Altorki, Andrew Arno, and Letitia Hickson. 1977. Ritual reconciliation and the obviation of grievances: A comparative study in the ethnography of law. *Ethnology* 163:269–83.

Kostas, Stephen. 2006. Making the Determination of Genocide in Darfur. In *Genocide in Darfur: Investigating the Atrocities in the Sudan*, ed. Samuel Totten and Eric Markusen, pp. 111–26. London: Routledge

Kramer, Tom. September 2009. Burma's cease-fires at risk. Transnational Institute. Available at: www.tni.org/briefing/burmas-cease-fires-risk.

Kritz, Neil (ed.). 1995. *Transitional Justice: How Emerging Democracies Reckon with Former Regimes*, vols. 1–3. Washington, DC: United States Institute of Peace Press.

Krog, Antjie. 1998. *Country of My Skull: Guilt, Sorrow, and the Limits of Forgiveness in the New South Africa*. Johannesburg: Random House

Kunene, Daniel P. 1958. Notes on *hlonepha* among the Southern Sotho. *African Studies* 173:159–67.

Laely, Thomas. 1997. Peasants, local communities, and central power in Burundi. *Journal of Modern African Studies* 35:717–44

Lame, Danielle de. 2005. *A Hill Among a Thousand: Transformations and Ruptures in Rural Rwanda*. Madison: University of Wisconsin Press.

Laplante, Lisa J. 2003. El impacto de las audiencias publicas en los participantes. Final Report of the Truth and Reconcilation Commission. Lima: CVR. Available at: www.cverdad.org.pe/apublicas/audiencias/impacto.php.

———. 2004. Bringing effective remedies home: The inter-American human rights system, reparations and the duty of prevention. *Netherlands Human Rights Quarterly* 22:347–88.

———. 2006. Heeding Peru's lesson: Paying reparations to detainees of anti-terrorism laws. *Human Rights Commentary* 88:88–98.

———. March 7, 2006. Cloud of fear: Peru's anti-terror lesson. *Open Democracy*. Available at: www.opendemocracy.net/conflictinstitutions_government/peru_fear_3329.jsp.

———. 2007a. Entwined paths to justice: The inter-American human rights system and the Peruvian truth commission. In *Paths to International Justice: Social and Legal Perspectives*, ed. Marie-Bénédicte Dembour and Tobias Kelly. Cambridge: Cambridge University Press.

———. 2007b. The law of remedies and the clean hands doctrine: Exclusionary reparation policies in Peru's political transition. *American University International Law Review* 23:51–90.

———. 2007c. The Peruvian truth commission's historical memory project: Empowering truth tellers to confront truth deniers. *Journal of Human Rights* 6:433–52.

Laplante, Lisa J., and Kimberly Theidon. 2007. Truth with consequences: The politics of reparations in post-truth commission Peru. *Human Rights Quarterly* 291:228–50.

Lavie, Aviv. June 17, 2004. Hebron Diaries. *Haaretz*.

Leahy, Elizabeth. 2007. *The Shape of Things to Come: Why Age Structure Matters to a Safer, More Equitable World.* Washington, DC: Population Action International.

Leebaw, Bronwyn A. 2008. The irreconcilable goals of transitional justice. *Human Rights Quarterly* 301:95–118.

Lefranc, Sandrine. 2002. *Politiques du pardon.* Paris: PUF.

Lemarchand, René. 1996. *Burundi: Ethnic Conflict and Genocide.* New York: Woodrow Wilson Center and Cambridge: Cambridge University Press.

Leopold, Mark. 2005. Why are we cursed? Writing history and making peace in northwest Uganda. *Journal of the Royal Anthropological Institute* 11:211–29.

Levi, Primo. 1995. *Survival in Auschwitz.* New York: Touchstone.

Lintner, Bertil. 1990. *Outrage: Burma's Struggle for Democracy.* Bangkok: White Lotus.

———. January 25, 2007. Myanmar's '88 Generation comes of age. *Asia Times.*

LIPRODHOR. December 2002. Rescapés et droit humains: Problèmes actuels des rescapés huit ans après le génocide.

———. July 2003. Juridictions Gacaca: Potentialités et lacunes révélées par les débuts.

———. December 2005. Situation des droits de la personne au Rwanda: Rapport 2003–2004.

Liu Institute for Global Issues, Gulu District NGO Forum, and Ker Kwaro Acholi. 2005. *Roco Wat I Acoli: Restoring Relationships in Acholi-land: Traditional Approaches to Justice and Reintegration.* PDF version accessed at www.ligi .ubc.ca/.

Liyong, Taban lo. 1970. *Eating Chiefs.* London: Heinemann Educational Books.

Longman, Timothy. 2006. Justice at the grassroots? Gacaca trials in Rwanda. In *Transitional Justice in the Twenty-First Century: Beyond Truth Versus Justice,* ed. Naomi Roht-Arriaza and Javier Mariezcurrena, pp. 206–28. Cambridge: Cambridge University Press.

Longman, Timothy, and Alison des Forges. 2004. Legal responses to genocide in Rwanda. In *My Neighbor, My Enemy: Justice and Community in the Aftermath of Mass Atrocity,* ed. Eric Stover and Harvey M. Weinstein, pp. 49–68. Cambridge: Cambridge University Press.

Longman, Timothy, and Theoneste Rutagengwa. 2004. Memory, identity and community in Rwanda. In *My Neighbor, My Enemy: Justice and Community in the Aftermath of Mass Atrocity,* ed. Eric Stover and Harvey M. Weinstein, pp. 162–82. Cambridge: Cambridge University Press.

Lundy, Patricia, and Mark McGovern. 2005. A critical evaluation of the role of community-based truth-telling processes of post-conflict transition: A case study of the Ardoyne Community Project. Unpublished manuscript.

Lutz, Ellen. 2006. Transitional justice: Lessons learned and the road ahead. In *Transitional Justice in the Twenty-First Century: Beyond Truth Versus Justice*, ed. Naomi Roht-Arriaza and Javier Mariezcurrena, pp. 325–41. Cambridge: Cambridge University Press.

Malkki, Liisa. 1995. *Purity and Exile: Violence, Memory and National Cosmology among Hutu Refugees in Tanzania*. Chicago: University of Chicago Press.

Mamdani, Mahmood. 2001. *When Victims Become Killers: Colonialism, Nativism and the Genocide in Rwanda*. Princeton, NJ: Princeton University Press.

Manrique, Nelson. 1989. La década de la violencia. *Márgenes* 56:137–82.

Manz, Beatriz. 2004. *Paradise in Ashes: A Guatemalan Journey of Courage, Terror, and Hope*. Berkeley: University of California Press.

Maru, Vivek. 2006. The challenges of African legal dualism: An experiment in Sierra Leone. Available at: www.timapforjustice.org/news/.

Maughan, Karyn, Jeremy Gordin, and Gill Gifford. March 14, 2006. *Cape Argus*, p. 1.

Mbeki, Thabo. August 10, 2006. Women's Day speech, August 9. *Cape Times*, p. 1.

McAdams, Doug, Sidney Tarrow, and Charles Tilly. 1996. To map contentious politics. *Mobilization* 1:17–34.

McEvoy, Kieran. 2007. Beyond legalism: Towards a thicker understanding of transitional justice. *Journal of Law and Society* 34:411–40.

McEvoy, Kieran, and Lorna McGregor. 2008. Transitional justice from below: An agenda for research, policy and praxis. In *Transitional Justice from Below: Grassroots Activism and the Struggle for Change*, ed. Kieran McEvoy and Lorna McGregor. Oxford: Hart

McEvoy, Kieran, Harry Mika, and Kirsten McConnachie. Forthcoming. *Reconstructing Transitional Justice: Transforming Cultures of Violence "from Below."* Cambridge: Cambridge University Press.

McKay, Susan, and Dyan Mazurana. 2004. *Where Are the Girls? Girls in Fighting Forces in Northern Uganda, Sierra Leone, and Mozambique: Their Lives During and After War*. Montreal: International Centre for Human Rights and Democratic Development.

Meek, Sarah, and Mark Malan. 2004. Identifying lessons from DDR experiences in Africa. Section 1. Trends in peacekeeping in Africa. Workshop Report, ISS Monograph no. 106, Institute for Security Studies, Pretoria, South Africa. Available at: www.iss.co.za/pubs/Monographs/No106/Sec1.pdf.

Meernik, James. 2005. Justice and peace? How the international criminal tribunal affects societal peace in Bosnia. *Journal of Peace Research* 42:271–89.

Mégret, Frédéric. 2001. Three dangers for the International Criminal Court. *Finnish Yearbook of International Law* 12:193–247.

Menkhaus, Ken. 2000. Traditional conflict management in contemporary African crises: Theory and praxis from the Somali experience. In *Traditional Cures for Modern Conflicts: African Conflict Medicine*, ed. I. William Zartman, pp. 183–99. Boulder, CO: Lynne Rienner.

Merry, Sally Engle. 1995. Sorting out popular justice. In *The Possibility of Popular Justice: A Case Study of Community Mediation in the United States*, ed. Sally Engle Merry and Neal Milner, pp. 31ff. Ann Arbor: University of Michigan Press.

———. 2006. *Human Rights and Gender Violence: Translating International Law into Local Justice*. Chicago: University of Chicago Press.

Minow, Martha. 1998. *Between Vengeance and Forgiveness: Facing History After Genocide and Mass Violence*. Boston: Beacon Press.

Min Zin. May 4, 2008. Burma needs people power. *Bangkok Post*.

Moffett, Helen. 2006. "These women, they force us to rape them": Rape as narrative of social control in post-apartheid South Africa. *Journal of Southern African Studies* 321:129–44.

Moore, Sally Falk. 1986. *Social Facts and Fabrications: Customary Law on Kilimanjaro*. Cambridge: Cambridge University Press.

———. 1992. Treating law as knowledge: Telling colonial officers what to say to Africans about running their own native courts. *Law and Society Review* 26:11–46.

Morgenthau, Hans. 1951. *In Defense of the National Interest: A Critical Examination of American Foreign Policy*. New York: Knopf.

Moughrabi, Fouad. 2001. The politics of Palestinian textbooks. *Journal of Palestine Studies* 31:5–19.

Mtintso, Thenjiwe. August 2006. Now is the time, our age of hope: Paying tribute to the heroic women of 1956. *Umrabulo* 26. ANC. Available at: www.anc.org.za.

Mubirigi, D. March 2007. Rapport entre gouvernement—administration Parquets, Cours et Tribunaux. Bujumbura, Consultancy report for SCN.

Mulla, Sameena. December 2005. Durations of tragedy and projections for care: Time and emplotment within sexual assault interventions. Unpublished paper, American Anthropological Association, Special Session on Women and Time.

Murra, John. 1975. *Formaciones económicas y políticas en el mundo andino*. Lima: Instituto de Estudios Peruanos.

Mutibwa, Phares Mukasa. 1992. *Uganda Since Independence: A Story of Unfulfilled Hopes*. London: Hurst.

Myanmar Penal Code, Section 122/1, Punishment of High Treason.

Nader, Laura. 1990. *Harmony Ideology: Justice and Control in a Zapotec Mountain Village*. Stanford, CA: Stanford University Press

Naniwe-Kaburahe, Assumpta. 2009. The Institution of Bashingantahe in Burundi. In *Traditional Justice and Reconciliation After Violent Conflict: Learning from African Experiences*, ed. Luc Huyse and Marc Salter, pp. 149–79. Stockholm, International Institute for Democracy and Electoral Assistance. Available at: www.idea.int/publications/traditional_justice/upload/tj_fr_6.pdf.

National Committee for Disarmament, Demobilization and Reintegration, Government of Sierra Leone. February 3, 2004. Executive Secretariat Report. Available at: www.daco-sl.org/encyclopedia/8_lib/8_3/NCDDR_ExecSecretary_report.pdf.

National League for Democracy. 1995. The observations of the National League for Democracy on the National Convention press statement, November 22. Available at: www.burmalibrary.org/reg.burma/archives/199511/msg00175 .html.

———. May 14, 2004. Statement. Available at: http://burmalibrary.org/docs/NLDsmt .14-May-2004.htm.

National Unity and Reconciliation Commission. March 2008. Social Cohesion in Rwanda: An Opinion Survey 2005–2007. Kigali.

Ndangiza, Fatuma. June 18, 2008. The impact of Gacaca and TIG on the challenges of unity and reconciliation: 14 years after the genocide. Power Point presentation.

Ndikumasabo, Méthode, and Stef Vandeginste. 2007. Mécanismes de justice et de réconciliation en perspective au Burundi. In L'Afrique des Grands Lacs Annuaire 2006–2007, ed. Filip Reyntjens. Paris: L'Harmattan.

Neier, Aryeh. 1999. Rethinking truth, justice, and guilt after Bosnia and Rwanda. In Human Rights in Political Transitions: Gettysburg to Bosnia, ed. Carla Hesse and Robert Post. New York: Zone Books.

Nevins, Joseph. 2005. A Not-So-Distant Horror: Mass Violence in East Timor. Ithaca, NY: Cornell University Press.

Newbury, Catherine. 1988. The Cohesion of Oppression: Clientship and Ethnicity in Rwanda, 1860–1960. New York: Columbia University Press.

Ngoga, Martin. 2009. The institutionalisation of impunity: A judicial perspective on the Rwandan genocide. In After Genocide: Transitional Justice, Post-Conflict Reconstruction and Reconciliation in Rwanda and Beyond, ed. Philip Clark and Zachary Kaufman, pp. 321–32. London: Hurst.

Ni Aolain, Fionnuala, and Colm Campbell. 2005. The paradox of transition in conflicted democracies. Human Rights Quarterly 27:172–213.

Nichols, Hans. January 5, 2005. Truth challenges justice in Freetown. Washington Times. Available at: www.globalpolicy.org/intljustice/tribunals/sierra/2005/ 0105freetown.htm.

Niebuhr, Reinhold. 2001. Moral Man and Immoral Society: A Study of Ethics and Politics. Louisville, KY: Westminster John Knox Press. Originally published 1987.

Nordstrom, Carolyn. 1997. A Different Kind of War Story. Philadelphia: University of Pennsylvania Press.

Nye, Joseph. 2004. Soft Power: The Means to Success in World Politics. New York: PublicAffairs.

OAG. 2007. Analyse critique du fonctionnement de la justice de proximité au Burundi. Bujumbura: Observatoire de l'Action Gouvernementale.

O'Barr, William. 1982. Linguistic Evidence: Language, Power and Strategy in the Courtroom. San Diego: Academic Press.

Obote-Odora, Alex. 2005. Impunity in northern Uganda since 1986. Unpublished manuscript.

O'Donnell, Guillermo, and Philippe C. Schmitter. 1986. *Transitions from Authoritarian Rule: Tentative Conclusions About Uncertain Democracies.* Baltimore: John Hopkins University Press.

Office of the Prosecutor of the International Criminal Court. 2003. Paper on some policy issues before the Office of the Prosecutor. Available at: www2.icc-cpi.int/NR/rdonlyres/1FA7C4C6-DE5F-42B7-8B25-60AA962ED8B6/143594/030905_Policy_Paper.pdf.

O'Leary, Brendan, and John McGarry. 1993. *The Politics of Ethnic Conflict Regulation: Case Studies of Protracted Ethnic Conflicts.* London: Routledge.

Olsen, Lester. 1997. On the margins of rhetoric: Audre Lorde transforming silence into language and action. *Quarterly Journal of Speech* 83:49–70.

Olsen, Tillie. 1980. *Silences.* London: Virago Press.

OneinNine.org.za. 2006. Available at: www.oneinnine.org.

Oomen, Barbara. 2005. Donor-driven justice and its discontents: The case of Rwanda. *Development and Change* 365:887–910.

Otunnu, Olara A. July/August 2006. The secret genocide. *Foreign Policy,* pp. 44–46.

Overdulve, Cornelis M. 1997. Fonction de la langue et de la communication au Rwanda. *Nouvelle Revue de Science Missionaire* 53:271–83.

Oywa, Rosalba. 1995. Uganda. In *Arms to Fight, Arms to Protect: Women Speak Out about Conflict,* ed. Olivia Bennett, Jo Bexley and Kitty Warnock. London: Panos.

Pain, Dennis. 1997. *The Bending of the Spears: Producing Consensus for Peace and Development in Northern Uganda.* London: International Alert.

PAPG. 2003. Rapport de synthèse de l'état d'avancement des travaux des juridictions gacaca au cours des mois de mars–juin 2003. Kigali: PAPG

———. 2004. Les cas d'insécurité des temoins et des rescapés du genocide dans les juridictions gacaca. Kigali: PAPG

Parkin, David. 1985. Introduction. In *The Anthropology of Evil,* ed. David Parkin, pp. 1–25. Oxford: Basil Blackwell.

Payne, Leigh A. 2008. *Unsettling Accounts: Neither Truth nor Reconciliation in Confessions of State Violence.* Durham, NC: Duke University Press.

P'Bitek, Okot. 1986. *Artist, the Ruler: Essays on Art, Culture, and Values.* Nairobi: Heinemann Kenya.

PCAS (Policy Co-ordination and Advisory Services), Social Sector. 2006. A Nation in the Making: A Discussion Document on Macro-social Trends in South Africa. Office of the Presidency. Available at: www.info.gov.za/otherdocs/2006/socioreport.pdf.

Peacock, Susan, and Adriana Beltran, 2003. Hidden powers in post-conflict Guatemala. Washington, DC: WOLA. Available at: http://cgrs.uchastings.edu/pdfs/HiddenPowersFull.pdf.

Penal Reform International. January 2002. Interim report on research on Gacaca jurisdictions and its preparation (July–December 2001). Available at: www.penalreform.org/resources/rep-ga1-2002-preparations-en.pdf.

———. April–June 2002. Report III. Available at: www.penalreform.org/resources/rep-2002-gacaca3PilotPhase-en.pdf.

———. January 2003. Research on Gacaca (Report IV): The guilty plea procedure, cornerstone of the Rwandan justice. Available at: www.penalreform.org/resources/rep-ga4-2003-guilty-plea-en.pdf.

———. September 2003. Research on the Gacaca (Report V). Available at: www.penalreform.org/resources/rep-2003-gacaca5CellPreparations-en.pdf.

———. 2004. Report on Monitoring and Research on the Gacaca. The righteous: Between oblivion and reconciliation? Example of the province of Kibuye. London: Kigali. Available at: www.penalreform.org/resources/rep-2004-gacacaKibuye3-en.pdf.

———. May 2004. Research Report on the Gacaca (Report VI): From camp to hill, the reintegration of released prisoners. Available at: www.penalreform.org/resources/rep-ga6-2004-released-prisoners-en.pdf.

———. December 2005. Rapport de synthese de monitoring et de recherché sur la gacaca: Phase pilote janvier 2002–decembre 2004. Available at : www.penalreform.org/resources/rep-ga7-2005-pilot-phase-fr.pdf.

———. June 2006. Information-Gathering During the National Phase. London. Available at: www.penalreform.org/resources/rep-ga8-2006-info-gathering-en.pdf.

———. July 2007. Le jugement des infractions contre les biens Commises pendant le génocide: Le contraste entre la théorie de la réparation et la réalité socio-économique du Rwanda. London: Penal Reform International. Available at: www.penalreform.org/resources/rep-ga10-2007-offences-against-property-fr.pdf.

———. June 2008. Le témoignage et la preuve devant gacaca. (Draft).

Peralta, Ruiz, V. 2000. Sendero Luminoso y la prensa, 1980–1994. La violencia política peruana y su representación en los medios. Cuzco [Peru] Lima, Perú: Centro de Estudios Regionales Andinos "Bartolomé de las Casas" Casa de Estudios del Socialismo.

Peskin, Victor A. 2008. *International Justice in Rwanda and the Balkans: Virtual Trials and the Struggle for State Cooperation*. Cambridge: Cambridge University Press.

Peters, Krijn. 2007. Reintegration support for young ex-combatants: A right or a privilege? *International Migration* 45:35–59.

Peters, Krijn, and Paul Richards. 1998. Why we fight: Voices of youth combatants in Sierra Leone. *Africa* 68:183–210.

Pham, Phuong, Patrick Vinck, Eric Stover, Andrew Moss, Marieke Wierda, and Richard Bailey. 2007. When the war ends: A population-based survey on attitudes about peace, justice and social reconstruction in northern Uganda. U.C. Berkeley Human Rights Center, Payson Center for International Development, Tulane University, and the International Center for Transitional Justice.

Pham, Phuong, Harvey M. Weinstein, and Timothy Longman. 2004. Trauma and PTSD symptoms in Rwanda: Implications for attitudes toward justice and reconciliation. *JAMA* 2925:602–12.

Pido, J. P. Odoch. 2000. Personhood and art: Social change and commentary among the Acholi. In *African Philosophy as Cultural Inquiry*, ed. Ivan Karp and D. A. Masolo, pp. 105–35. Bloomington: Indiana University Press.

Pigou, Piers. 2003. Crying without tears: In pursuit of justice and reconciliation in Timor-Leste. International Center for Transitional Justice report. Available at: www.ictj.org/en/news/pubs/index.html.

Pirouet, M. Louise. 1991. Human rights issues in Museveni's Uganda. In *Changing Uganda: The Dilemmas of Structural Adjustment and Revolutionary Change*, ed. Hölger Bernt Hansen and Michael Twaddle, pp. 197–209. London, Kampala, Athens and Nairobi: James Currey/Fountain Press/Ohio University Press/Heinemann Kenya.

Podeh, Elie. 2002. *The Arab-Israeli Conflict in Israeli History Textbooks, 1948–2000*. New York: Bergin and Garvey.

Pogrund, Benjamin, and Salem Walid. 2005. *Shared Histories: A Palestinian-Israeli Dialogue*. Walnut Creek, CA: Left Coast Press.

Popkin, Margaret. 1996. Guatamala's national reconciliation law: Combating impunity or continuing it? *Revista IIDH* 24:173. Available at: www.juridicas.unam.mx/publica/librev/rev/iidh/cont/24/dtr/dtr7.pdf.

Posner, Eric A., and Adrian Vermeule. 2004. Transitional justice as ordinary justice. *Harvard Law Review* 117:761.

Post-Conflict Reintegration Initiative for Development and Empowerment (PRIDE). 2002. Ex-combatant views of the Truth and Reconciliation Commission and the Special Court in Sierra Leone. Available at: www.ictj.org/images/content/0/9/090.pdf.

Pottier, Johan. 2002. *Re-imagining Rwanda: Conflict, Survival and Disinformation in the Late Twentieth Century*. Cambridge: Cambridge University Press.

Power, Samantha. 2002. Genocide and America. *New York Review of Books*, p. 494.

Prensa Libre. May 29, 2008. Condenan a 5 por massacre en Río Negro, p. A1.

Pretoria Protocol on Political, Defence, and Security Power Sharing in Burundi. October 8, 2003. Available at: www.usip.org/library/pa/burundi/burundi_1008 2003.html.

Quandt, William. 2005. Israeli-Palestinian peace talks: From Oslo to Camp David II. In *How Israelis and Palestinians Negotiate: A Cross-Cultural Analysis of the Oslo Peace Process*, ed. Tamara Cofman Wittes, pp. 13–38. Washington, DC: United States Institute of Peace.

Quinn, Joanna. 2004. Constraints: The un-doing of the Ugandan truth commission. *Human Rights Quarterly* 262:401–27.

Ranger, Terence. 1994. The invention of tradition revisited. In *Inventions and Boundaries: Historical and Anthropological Approaches to the Study of Ethnicity and Nationalism*, ed. Preben Kaarsholm and Jan Hultin. Roskilde University, Occasional paper no. 11.

RCN. 2006. Pour une Justice Légitimée. BURUNDI Programme triennal 2006–2008. Bujumbura: Reseau de Citoyens/Citizens Network.

Refugee Law Project (RLP). 2005a. Peace first, justice later: Traditional justice in northern Uganda. Working Paper no. 17. Kampala: The Refugee Law Project. Available at: www.refugeelawproject.org.

———. 2005b. Whose justice? Perceptions of Uganda's Amnesty Act 2000: The potential for conflict resolution and long-term reconciliation. Working Paper no. 15. Kampala: The Refugee Law Project. Available at: www.refugeelawproject.org.

REMHI (Recovery of Historical Memory Project). 1998. *Guatemala Nunca Más*. Guatemala City: Office of Human Rights of the Archbishop.

Reno, William. 1995. *Corruption and State Politics in Sierra Leone*. Cambridge: Cambridge University Press.

Report of the Truth and Reconciliation Commission of South Africa. 1998 and 2004. Vols. 1–5 (1998) and Vols. 6–7 (2004). Cape Town: Juta Press.

Republic of Rwanda. January 1999. Les Tribunaux d'Arbitage dans les process du genocide perpetre au Rwanda a partir du 1 octobre 1990 jusqu'au 31 decembre 1994. Kigali.

———. July 1999. Gacaca tribunals vested with jurisdiction over genocide crimes against humanity and other violations of human rights which took place in Rwanda from 1st October 1990 to 31st December 1994. Kigali.

Republic of Uganda. 2000. *The Amnesty Act, 2000*. Kampala: Republic of Uganda.

Rettig, Max. 2008. Gacaca: Truth, justice, and reconciliation in Rwanda. *African Studies Review* 51:25–50.

Reynolds, Pamela. 2005. *Imfobe*: Self-knowledge and the reach for ethics among former, younger, anti-apartheid activists. *Anthropology Southern Africa* 28:62–72.

Reyntjens, Filip. 1990. La gacaca ou la justice du *gazon* au Rwanda. *Politique Africaine* 40:31–41.

———. 1995. Burundi: Breaking the cycle of violence. London: Minority Rights Group International.

———. 2000. Burundi: Prospects for peace. London: Minority Rights Group International.

———. 2004. Rwanda, ten years on: From genocide to dictatorship. *African Affairs* 103:177–210.

———. 2009. Rwanda: A fake report on fake elections. Available at: hungryoftruth.blogspot.com/2009/01/rwanda-fake-report-on-fake-elections.html.

Reyntjens, Filip, and Stef Vandeginste. 2005. Rwanda: An atypical transition. In *Roads to Reconciliation*, ed. Elin Skaar, Siri Gloppen, and Astri Suhrke, pp. 101–28. Lanham, MD: Lexington Books.

Richards, Paul. 1996. *Fighting for the Rain Forest: War, Youth, and Resources in Sierra Leone*. Oxford: James Currey.

———. 2005a. To fight or to farm? Agrarian dimensions of the Mano River conflicts (Liberia and Sierra Leone). *African Affairs* 104:571–90

———. 2005b. Green Book millenarians? The Sierra Leone war within the perspective of an anthropology of religion. In *Religion and African Civil Wars*, ed. Niels Kastfelt. London: Hurst and Company.

Richards, Paul, Steven Archibald, Khadija Bah, and James Vincent. 2003. Where have all the young people gone? Transitioning ex-combatants towards community reconstruction after the war in Sierra Leone. Unpublished report submitted to the National Commission for Disarmament, Demobilization and Reintegration NCDDR, Government of Sierra Leone.

Richardson, Louise. 2006. *What Terrorists Want: Understanding the Enemy, Containing the Threat*. New York: Random House.

Ricoeur, Paul. 2000. *The Just*. Chicago: University of Chicago Press.

Rigby, Andrew. 2001. *Justice and Reconciliation: After the Violence*. Boulder, CO: Lynn Rienner.

Robben, Antonius. 2007. *Political Violence and Trauma in Argentina*. Philadelphia: University of Pennsylvania Press.

Roht-Arriaza, Naomi. 2004. Reparations decisions and dilemmas. *Hastings International and Comparative Law Review* 27:157–219.

———. 2008. Making the state do justice: Transnational prosecutions and international support for criminal investigations in post-armed conflict Guatemala. *Chicago Journal of International Law* 9:79.

Rombouts, Heidy. 2004. Victim organisations and the politics of reparation: A case study on Rwanda. Ph.D. diss., University of Antwerp.

Roper, Steven D., and Lilian A. Barria. 2005. Assessing the record of justice: A comparison of mixed international tribunals versus domestic mechanisms for human rights enforcement. *Journal of Human Rights* 4:521–36.

Rose, Laurel L. 1992. *The Politics of Harmony: Land Dispute Strategies in Swaziland*. Cambridge: Cambridge University Press.

———. 1995. *Justice at the Local Level: Findings and Recommendations for Future Actions*. Kigali: USAID.

———. 2002. Women's strategies for customary land access in Swaziland and Malawi: A comparative study. *Africa Today* 49:123–49.

Roskilde University. 2006. Rape crisis. International Development Studies Occasional Paper no. 11. Accessed September 8, 2006 at: www.rapecrisis.org.za.

Ross, Fiona C. 2001. Speech and silence: Womens' testimony in the first five weeks of public hearings of the South African Truth and Reconciliation Commission. In *Remaking a World: Violence, Social Suffering and Recovery*, ed. Arthur Kleinman, Veena Das, Margaret Lock, Mamphela Ramphele, and Pamela Reynolds. Berkeley: University of California Press.

———. 2003a. *Bearing Witness: Women and the Truth and Reconciliation Commission in South Africa*. London: Pluto Press

———. 2003b. On having voice and being heard: Some after-effects of testifying before the South African Truth and Reconciliation Commission. *Anthropological Theory* 3:325–42.

———. 2005. Women and the politics of identity: Voices in the South African Truth and Reconciliation Commission. In *Violence and Belonging: The Quest for*

Identity in Post-Colonial Africa, ed. Vigdis Broch-Due, pp. 214–35. London: Routledge.

Ross, Fiona C., and Pamela Reynolds. 2004. Voices not heard: Small histories and the work of repair. In *To Repair the Irreparable: Reparation and Reconstruction in South Africa,* ed. Eric Doxtader and Charles Villa-Vicencio, pp. 106–14. Cape Town: David Philip.

Rotberg, Robert. 2006. Building legitimacy through narrative. In *Israeli and Palestinian Narratives of Conflict: History's Double Helix,* ed. Robert I. Rotberg, pp. 1–18. Bloomington: Indiana University Press.

Rotberg, Robert I., and Dennis Thompson (eds.). 2000. *Truth v. Justice: The Morality of Truth Commissions.* Princeton, NJ: Princeton University Press.

Rouhana, Nadim. 2006. Zionism's encounter with the Palestinians: The dynamics of force, fear, and extremism. In *Israeli and Palestinian Narratives of Conflict: History's Double Helix,* ed. Robert I. Rotberg, pp. 115–41. Bloomington: Indiana University Press.

Sampson, Steven. 2003. From reconciliation to coexistence. *Public Culture* 151:181–86.

Sanders, Mark. 2007. *Ambiguities of Witnessing.* Stanford, CA: Stanford University Press.

Sanford, Victoria. 2003. *Buried Secrets: Truth and Human Rights in Guatemala.* New York: Palgrave Macmillan.

SAPS (South African Police Services). 2005. Rape in the RSA. Crime information Analysis Centre. Accessed September 1, 2006 at www.saps.gov.za/statistics/reports/crimestats/2005/_pdf/crimes/rape.pdf#search=%22SAPS%20rape%22.

Sarkin, Jeremy. 2001. The tension between justice and reconciliation in Rwanda: Politics, human rights, due process and the role of the *Gacaca* courts dealing with the genocide. *Journal of African Law* 42:143.

Sarkin, Jeremy, and Erin Daly. 2004. Too many questions, too few answers: Reconciliation in transitional societies. *Columbia Human Rights Law Review* 35:101–68.

Savir, Uri. 1998. *The Process: 1,100 Days That Changed the Middle East.* New York: Random House.

Schabas, William A. 2003. The relationship between truth commissions and international courts: The case of Sierra Leone. *Human Rights Quarterly* 25:1035–66.

———. 2005. The Rwandan courts in quest of accountability: Genocide trials and *Gacaca* courts. *Journal of International Criminal Justice* 3:879–95.

———. 2007. *An Introduction to the International Criminal Court.* Cambridge: Cambridge University Press.

Schweiger, Romana. 2006. Late justice for Burundi. *International and Comparative Law Quarterly* 55:653–71.

Scott, James C. 1985. *Weapons of the Weak: Everyday Forms of Peasant Resistance.* New Haven, CT: Yale University Press.

———. 1992. *Domination and the Arts of Resistance: Hidden Transcripts.* New Haven, CT: Yale University Press.

Sebarenzi, Joseph. 2009. *God Sleeps in Rwanda: A Journey of Transformation.* New York: Atria Books.

Sein Beida. July 4, 1996. Politics is dead. *Kyemon* [Burmese government daily].

Service National des Juridictions Gacaca (SNJG). 2004. Les problemes constates dans le fonctionnement des juridictions *Gacaca* qui ont termine leur 7eme reunion.

———. June 10, 2005. Etat d'avancement du processus *Gacaca.* PowerPoint presentation.

———. 2006. Report on data collection in *Gacaca* courts. Kigali.

———. 2008. Situation des procès de la première catégorie au 30/08/2008.

———. June 18, 2008. Le processus des juridictions *Gacaca* au Rwanda. Power Point presentation.

———. 2009. Jugements du 15/07/2006 au 30/09/2008 pour la 2ème et la 3ème catégorie.

Shaw, Rosalind. 2000. *Tok af, lef af:* A political economy of Temne techniques of secrecy and self. In *African Philosophy as Cultural Inquiry,* ed. Ivan Karp and D. A. Masolo, pp. 25–49. Bloomington: Indiana University Press.

———. 2005. Rethinking truth and reconciliation commissions: Lessons from Sierra Leone. Special Report 130. Washington, DC: United States Institute of Peace.

———. 2007. Memory frictions: Localizing truth and reconciliation in Sierra Leone. *International Journal of Transitional Justice* 1:183–207.

Shifman, Pamela, Nozizwe Madlala-Routledge, and Viv Smith. 1997. Women in Parliament caucus for action to end violence. *Agenda* 36:23–26.

Shukla, Kavita, and Sarah Martin. January 3, 2009. Refugees international, northern Uganda: Political process must be bolstered to bring peace to the region. *InterAction.* Available at: www.interaction.org/newswire/detail.php?id=5579.

Sibomana, André. 1999. *Hope for Rwanda: Conversations with Laure Guilbert and Hervé Deguine,* trans. Carina Tertsakian. London: Pluto Press.

Sieder, Rachel. 2001. War, peace, and memory politics in Central America. In *The Politics of Memory: Transitional Justice in Democratizing Societies,* ed. Alexandra Barahona de Brito, Carmen González-Enríquez, and Paloma Aguilar, pp. 161–90. New York: Oxford University Press.

Sierra Leone Working Group on Truth and Reconciliation. 2006. Searching for truth and reconciliation in Sierra Leone: An initial study of the performance and impact of the truth and reconciliation commission. Freetown: Sierra Leone Working Group on Truth and Reconciliation.

Sierra Leone's Truth and Reconciliation Commission Act. 2000. Part III.6.1. Available at: https://www.usip.org/library/tc/doc/charters/tc_sierra_leone_02102000.html.

SLORC Declaration No. 11/92. April 24, 1992. Convening of the National Convention.

SLORC Order No. 13/92. October 1992. Formation of the Convening Commission for the National Convention.

Smith, Martin. 1999. *Burma: Insurgency and the Politics of Ethnicity.* Updated edition. Bangkok: White Lotus.

Snyder, Jack, and Leslie Vinjamuri. 2003–4. Trials and errors: Principle and pragmatism in strategies of international justice. *International Security* 283:5–44.

Sommers, Marc. 1997a. Review of *Purity and Exile: Violence, Memory, and National Cosmology Among Hutu Refugees in Tanzania*, by Liisa Malkki. *American Anthropologist* 99:217–18.

———. 2007b. West Africa's youth employment challenge: The case of Guinea, Liberia, Sierra Leone, and Côte d'Ivoire. United Nations Industrial Development Organization (UNIDO).

Soyinka, Wole. 1999. *The Burden of Memory, the Muse of Forgiveness*. Oxford: Oxford University Press.

Starn, Orin. 1995. To revolt against the revolution: War and resistance in Peru's Andes. *Cultural Anthropology* 10(4):547–80.

State versus Khehlane Mvamvu. 2006. Supreme Court of Appeal, Reportable Case no. 350/2003. Accessed February 2006 at: www.doj.gov.za.

Statistics South Africa. 2000. *Quantitative Findings on Rape in South Africa*. Pretoria: StatsSA.

Steiner, Henry J., Philip Alston, and Ryan Goodman (eds.). 2008. *International Human Rights in Context: Law, Politics, Morals*. Oxford: Oxford University Press.

Stern, Steve (ed.). 1998. *Shining and Other Paths: War and Society in Peru, 1980–1995*. Durham, NC: Duke University Press.

Stevens, Joanna. 1999. *Traditional and Informal Justice Systems in Africa, South Asia, and the Caribbean*. London: Penal Reform International.

Stewart, Whitney. 1997. *Aung San Suu Kyi: Fearless Voice of Burma*. Minneapolis: Lerner.

Stockholm Initiative on Disarmament, Demobilization, Reintegration (SIDDR). 2005. Final Report. Ministry for Foreign Affairs, Sweden. Available at: www.sweden.gov.se/content/1/c6/06/54/07/b4da3116.pdf.

Stoll, David. 1993. *Between Two Armies in the Ixil Towns of Guatemala*. New York: Columbia University Press.

Stover, Eric. 2005. *The Witnesses: War Crimes and the Promise of Justice in The Hague*. Philadelphia: University of Pennsylvania Press.

Stover, Eric, Hanny Megally, and Hania Mufti. 2006. Bremer's "Gordian knot": Transitional Justice and the US Occupation of Iraq. In *Transitional Justice in the Twenty-First Century: Beyond Truth Versus Justice*, ed. Naomi Roht-Arriaza and Javier Mariezcurrena, pp. 229–54. Cambridge: Cambridge University Press.

Stover, Eric, and Rachel Shigekane. 2004. Exhumation of mass graves: Balancing legal and humanitarian needs. In *My Neighbor, My Enemy: Justice and Community in the Aftermath of Mass Atrocity*, ed. Eric Stover and Harvey M. Weinstein, pp. 85–103. Cambridge: Cambridge University Press.

Stover, Eric, and Harvey M. Weinstein (eds.). 2004. *My Neighbor, My Enemy: Justice and Community in the Aftermath of Mass Atrocity*. Cambridge: Cambridge University Press.

Straus, Scott. 2006. *The Order of Genocide: Race, Power, and War in Rwanda*. Ithaca, NY: Cornell University Press.

Straus, Scott, and Robert Lyons. 2006. *Intimate Enemy: Images and Voices of the Rwandan Genocide*. New York: Zone Books.

Stuart Commission. 1984. *Commission of Inquiry into Recent Developments in the People's Republic of Angola*. Lusaka: ANC. Accessed September 1, 2006 at: www .anctoday.org.za.

Sunder Rajan, Rajeswari. 1993. *Real and Imagined Women: Gender, Power and Postcolonialism*. London: Routledge.

Tamari, Salim. 2006. Kissing cousins: A cautionary note on people-to-people projects. *Palestine-Israel Journal of Politics, Economics and Culture* 131:16–19.

Tavuchis, Nicholas. 1991. *Mea Culpa: A Sociology of Apology and Reconciliation*. Stanford, CA: Stanford University Press.

Taylor, Christopher. 1988. *Milk, Honey, and Money: Changing Concepts in Rwandan Healing*. Washington, DC: Smithsonian Institution Press.

Taylor, Diana. 1997. *Disappearing Acts: Spectacles of Gender and Nationalism in Argentina's "Dirty War."* Durham, NC: Duke University Press.

Teitel, Ruti G. 2000. *Transitional Justice*. New York: Oxford University Press.

———. 2003. Transitional justice genealogy. *Harvard Human Rights Journal* 16:69–94.

———. 2008. Transitional justice globalized. *International Journal of Transitional Justice* 2:1–4.

Tertsakian, Carina. 2008. *Le Château: The Lives of Prisoners in Rwanda*. London: Arves Books.

Tharckabaw, David. 2000. Speech presented at the Building Civil Society in Asia: Challenges and Prospects for Resolving Ethnic Conflict: The Cases of Indonesia, Burma and Philippines conference. Asian Social Issues Program.

Theidon, Kimberly. 2000. How we learned to kill our brother: Memory, morality, and reconciliation in Peru. In *Buletin de L'Institut Français des Études Andines* 29:539–54.

———. 2003a. Secuelas de la violencia: Violencia política y salud mental en Ayacucho. *Un paso hacia la verdad: Memoria de la CVR Ayacucho*. Comisión de la Verdad y Reconciliación Región Sur Centro, Ayacucho, Perú.

———. 2003b. La micropolítica de la reconciliación: Practicando la justicia en comunidades rurales Ayacuchanas. *Revista Allpanchis*, special issue on *Justicia Comunitaria en los Andes* 60:113–42.

———. September 2003. Entre prójimos: Violencia y reconciliación en el Perú. *Ideele: Revista del Instituto de Defensa Legal* (157):91–96.

———. 2004. *Entre Prójimos: El conflicto armado interno y la política de la reconciliación en el Perú*. Lima: Instituto de Estudios Peruanos.

———. 2006a. Intimate enemies: Towards a social psychology of reconciliation. In *The Psychology of Resolving Global Conflict*, ed. Mari Fitzduff and Chris E. Stout. Westport, CT: Praeger.

—— 2006b. Justice in transition: The micropolitics of reconciliation in postwar Peru. *Journal of Conflict Resolution* 50:433–57.

—— 2007a. Gender in transition: Common sense, women and war. *Journal of Human Rights* 64:653–78.

——. 2007b. Transitional subjects: The disarmament, demobilization and reintegration of former combatants in Colombia. *International Journal of Transitional Justice* 1:66–90.

——. 2009. *Intimate Enemies: Violence and Reconciliation in Peru*. Stanford, CA: Stanford University Press.

Thoms, Oskar N. T., James Ron, and Roland Paris. 2008. The effects of transitional justice mechanisms: A summary of empirical research findings and implications for analysts and practitioners. Ottawa: Center for International Policy studies, University of Ottawa working paper.

Totten, Samuel, and Eric Markusen (eds.). 2006. *Genocide in Darfur: Investigating the Atrocities in the Sudan*. London: Routledge.

Trouillot, Michel-Rolph. 1995. *Silencing the Past*. Boston: Beacon Press.

Trouwborst, A. A. 1962. Le Berundi. In *Les anciens royaumes de la zone interlacustre méridionale Rwanda, Burundi, Buha*. Tervuren: Musée Royal de l'Afrique Centrale.

Truth and Reconciliation Commission, Sierra Leone. 2005. Final Report. Available at: www.trcsierraleone.org/drwebsite/publish/index.shtml.

Tsing, Anna Lowenhaupt. 2004. *Friction: An Ethnography of Global Connection*. Princeton, NJ: Princeton University Press

Tully, L. Danielle. 2003. Human rights compliance and the *Gacaca* jurisdictions in Rwanda. *Boston College International and Comparative Law Review* 26:385–414.

Turshen, Meredith, and Clotilde Twagiramariya (eds.). 1998. *What Women Do in Wartime: Gender and Conflict in Africa*. London: Zed Books.

Tutu, Desmond. 1996. Foreword. In *To Remember and to Heal: Theological and Psychological Perspectives on Truth and Reconciliation*, ed. H. Ruseell Botman and R. Petersen. Cape Town: Human and Rousseau.

U.C. Berkeley Human Rights Center, U.C. Berkeley School of Law International Human Rights Law Clinic, and University of Sarajevo Centre for Human Rights. 1999. Justice, accountability and social reconstruction: An interview study of Bosnian judges and prosecutors. *Berkeley Journal of International Law* 18:133.

UN Commission on Human Rights. February 25, 2000. Report on the situation of human rights in Rwanda. UN Document E/CN.4/2000/41.

UN High Commissioner for Human Rights. 1996. Gacaca: *Le Droit Coutumier au Rwanda*.

UN Human Rights Committee. 2009. Concluding observations of the Human Rights Committee. Rwanda.

United Nations. 2001. Report of the World Conference Against Racism, Racial Discrimination, Xenophobia and Related Intolerance. Durban, South Africa.

———. 2004a. Report of the Secretary-General on the rule of law and transitional justice in conflict and post-conflict societies. UN Doc. S/2004/616.

———. 2004b. Report by the Special Rapporteur on the Situation of Human Rights in Myanmar. UN Doc. E/CN.4/2004/33

———. 2005. Resolution of 10 November 2005 adopting by consensus/without a vote the basic principles and guidelines on the right to a remedy and reparation for victims of gross violations of international human rights law and serious violations of international humanitarian law. U.N. Doc. A/C.3/60/L.24.

———. March 11, 2005. Report of the assessment mission on the establishment of an international judicial commission of inquiry for Burundi. UN Security Council, Doc. S/2005/158.

———. December 7, 2007. Report by the Special Rapporteur on the situation of human rights in Myanmar. UN Document A/HRC/6/14.

UN Office of the High Representative for Least Developed Countries, Landlocked Developing Countries and Small Island Developing States and U.N. Development Program. 2006. Governance for the future: Democracy and development in the least developed countries. New York.

Utas, Mats. 2005a. Building a future? The reintegration and remarginalization of youth in Liberia. In *No Peace, No War: An Anthropology of Contemporary Armed Conflicts*, ed. Paul Richards, pp. 137–54. Oxford: James Currey.

———. 2005b. Victimcy, girlfriending, soldiering: Tactic agency in a young woman's social navigation of the Liberian war zone. *Anthropological Quarterly* 78:403–30.

Uvin, Peter. 2001. The introduction of a modernized *gacaca* for judging suspects of participation in the genocide and the massacres of 1994 in Rwanda. Available at: http://fletcher.tufts.edu/faculty/uvin/pdfs/reports/Boutmans.pdf.

———. 2008. *Life After Violence: A People's Story of Burundi*. London: Zed Books.

Vandeginste, Stef. 1998. A *Truth and Reconciliation Approach to the Genocide and Crimes Against Humanity in Rwanda*. Antwerp: Center for the Study of the Great Lakes Region of Africa, May 1998.

———. 2003. Victims of genocide, crimes against humanity, and war crimes in Rwanda: The legal and institutional framework of their right to reparation. In *Politics and the Past*, ed. John Torpey, pp. 249–76. London: Rowman & Littlefield Publishers.

———. June 25–27, 2007. Transitional justice for Burundi: A long and winding road. Paper delivered at Nuremberg International Conference Building a Future on Peace and Justice.

———. 2009. Law as a source and instrument of transitional justice in Burundi. PhD diss., University of Antwerp.

Van der Merwe, Willem. 2006. Judgment, *State versus Jacob Gedleyihlekisa Zuma*. Case: S v Zuma 2006 (7) BCLR 790 (W). Case No. JPV 2005/0325.

Vargas Llosa, Mario et al. 1983. Informe de la Comisión Investigadora sobre los sucesos de Uchuraccay. Mimeograph.

Vera, Yvonne. 1996. *Under the Tongue*. Harare: Baobab Books and Cape Town: David Philip.

Viaene, Lieselotte. 2007. Justicia transicional y contexto cultural en Guatemala: Voces Qeqchies sobre el programa nacional de resarcimiento. In *La Vida no tiene precio: Acciones y omisiones de resarcimiento en Guatemala*, pp. 133–71. Guatemala City: PNR.

Vidal, Claudine. 2001. Les commemorations du genocide au Rwanda. *Les Temps odernes* 56(613):1–46.

Waldorf, Lars. 2006. Mass justice for mass atrocity: Rethinking local justice as transitional justice. *Temple Law Review* 79:1–88.

———. 2009a. Revisiting *Hotel Rwanda*: Genocide ideology, reconciliation, and rescuers. *Journal of Genocide Research* 11:105–25.

———. 2009b. Goats and graves: Reparations in Rwanda's community courts. In *Reparations for Victims of Genocide, Crimes Against Humanity and War Crimes*, ed. Carla Ferstman, Mariana Goetz, and Alan Stephens, pp. 515–39. Leiden: Martinus Nijhoff.

Walsh, Declan. June 12, 2006. UN report accuses Afghan MPs of torture and massacres. *Guardian*. Available at: www.guardian.co.uk/afghanistan/story/0,1795546,00.html.

Washington Office on Latin America (WOLA). September 26, 2006. Illegal armed groups: A threat to the administration of justice and rule of law. Available at: www.wola.org/index.php?option=com_content&task=viewp&id=421&Itemid=2.

Watts, Simon. February 5, 2005. Guatemala halts war crimes trial. *BBC News*. Available at: http://news.bbc.co.uk/2/hi/americas/4238417.stm.

Wedeen, Lisa. 1999. *Ambiguities of Domination: Politics, Rhetoric, and Symbols in Contemporary Syria*. Chicago: University of Chicago Press.

Weilenmann, Markus. 2005. *Rapport d'evaluation du programme triennal "Pour une égale protection devant la loi."* Bujumbura: RCN.

Weschler, Lawrence. 1990. *A Miracle, a Universe: Settling Accounts with Torture*. Chicago: University of Chicago Press.

White, Hayden. 1987. *The Content of the Form: Narrative Discourse and Historical Representation*. Baltimore: Johns Hopkins University Press.

White House. 1996. A national security strategy of engagement and enlargement. Washington, DC.

Wierzynska, Aneta. 2004. Consolidating democracy through transitional justice: Rwanda's Gacaca courts. *New York University Law Review* 79:1934–69.

Wilson, Richard A. 1997. *Human Rights, Culture and Context: Anthropological Perspectives*. London: Pluto Press.

———. 1998. The politics of remembering and forgetting in Guatemala. In *Guatemala After the Peace Accords*, ed. Rachel Sieder, pp. 181–95. London: Institute of Latin American Studies, University of London.

———. 1999. *Maya Resurgence in Guatemala: Q'Eqchi' Experiences*. Norman: University of Oklahoma Press.

————. 2001. *The Politics of Truth and Reconciliation in South Africa: Legitimizing the Post-Apartheid State*. Cambridge: Cambridge University Press.

Working People's' Daily. July 1990. Vol. 4, no. 7. In the Burma Press Summary 1987–1996 created and edited by Hugh MacDougall, Counsellor at the U.S. Embassy in Rangoon, pp. 198–84. Available at: www.ibiblio.com/obl/docs3/BPS90-07.pdf.

Zartman, I. William (ed.). 2000. *Traditional Cures for Modern Conflicts: African Conflict Medicine*. Boulder, CO: Lynne Rienner.

Zaw Oo and Win Min. 2007. *Assessing Burma's Ceasefire Accords*. Washington, DC: East-West Center.

Zeghal, Malika. 2005. *Les islamistes marocains: Le défi à la monarchie*. Paris: La Découverte.

Zeldin, Theodore. 1998. *An Intimate History of Humanity*. London: Vintage Books.

Zur, Judith. 1998. *Violent Memories: Mayan War Widows in Guatemala*. Boulder, CO: Westview Press.

Zyl, Paul van. November 2, 2006. Personal communication.

Index

Stanford Studies in Human Rights brings together established and emerging voices from the interdisciplinary field of human rights studies. The series publishes work from a range of perspectives, including ethnographic studies of human rights in practice, critical reflections on the idea of human rights, new proposals for a more effective international human rights system, and historical accounts of the rise of human rights as a globalized moral discourse.